Minority Rules

BODY,

COMMODITY,

TEXT

Studies of Objectifying Practice

A series edited

by Arjun Appadurai,

Jean Comaroff, and

Judith Farquhar

Minority Rules

The Miao and the Feminine

in China's Cultural Politics

Louisa Schein

Duke University Press

Durham & London

2000

© 2000 Duke University Press

All rights reserved

Printed in the United States of America on acid-free paper ∞

Designed by C. H. Westmoreland

Typeset in Dante by Tseng Information Systems, Inc.

Library of Congress Cataloging-in-Publication Data appear on the last printed page of this book.

Portions of the following chapters have been previously published: chapters 4 and 5, in *Modern China* 23, no. 1 (1997): 69–98; chapter 9, in *Cultural Anthropology* 14, no. 3 (1999): 361–395.

To

my parents

Mary and Ed

and to

Ernie, Sophia, and

Little 'Nesto

Contents

Illustrations

Preface and Acknowledgments

This book is about *minʒu*—the official Chinese term for ethnic groups. It is also about modernity, and about how both *minʒu* and modernity figure in the cultural politics of post-Mao China. But the project comes from very different roots. It owes its inception to the Hmong who have come to the United States as refugees from Laos. I first became acquainted with the Hmong in 1979 as an undergraduate in Providence, Rhode Island, where I became intensely engaged with their immediate realities—with teaching English to women, with learning Hmong, with developing a handicrafts cooperative, and with documenting their experiences in a film on their migration to the United States. Hmong visions, however, extended out of the present into the past and future, and they pushed me to look beyond the struggles of resettlement. One of their chief concerns was loss—of cherished family members, of their land, and of their ancient culture. They saw this cultural loss, unlike those of family and land, not just as a consequence of the history of intervention in the Vietnam War by the United States, which employed Hmong as secret anticommunist guerrillas in Laos, rendering them political refugees upon U.S. withdrawal. Cultural erosion was remembered as commencing centuries earlier with Hmong migrating southward across and out of China. In Hmong American popular memory, their ancestors fled with almost nothing, preserving only fragments of the lore that had been theirs. It was out of this conviction that Hmong in the United States told me over and over: "If you really want to understand our people, you should go to China, to our homeland."

In 1982, upon finishing college, I received a fellowship to trace the path that ancestors of the Hmong in the United States had charted. My plan was to visit Hmong communities in France, in the Thai refugee camps, in rural Thailand, and in China. Through a comparative approach, I hoped to uncover the cultural substrate that Hmong assured me was there, uniting them even in their dispersal. For four months I lived in Hmong communities in France and Thailand, learning the language and deepening my familiarity with customs that those in the diaspora saw as imperiled with extinction. Then, in the spring of 1982, I arrived in Beijing heady with anticipation about finally finding Hmong roots. I was the first Western scholar since normalization to have been granted permission to do long-term research in residence at the Central Nationalities Institute. I had learned a great deal of Hmong language, and I had brought slides and artifacts. I used the term "Miao" to denote the official state category under which I expected to find Hmong heritage intact.

A few days after my arrival, the Institute's Foreign Affairs Office arranged for my first meeting with some "Miao" on campus. When they arrived at my room, I was initially disconcerted by the difference between their costumes and those I was familiar with from Southeast Asia, but I rushed to greet them in Hmong. Their faces were blank. They greeted me in their language and I could not make out a word they were saying. Through a Chinese translator, we laboriously began to list cultural traits and found almost no points of convergence. I became increasingly disoriented, and my "research" was beset with a multitude of questions. Were these people really Hmong? If so, why did their culture seem completely different from that of the Hmong outside China? If they were not Hmong, why were they being presented as representatives of the "Miao," the ethnonym I understood to be the Chinese equivalent of Hmong? And, given that according to the Hmong abroad it was a derogatory name, why were they being called Miao anyway?

I spent seven months in 1982 trying to answer those questions. Miao areas were not open to foreign travel at the time, so I worked out of Nationalities Institutes in Beijing, Sichuan, Yunnan, and Hubei (Guizhou province was completely closed). What I surmised was that, while not coterminous with the Hmong, the Miao were in a certain sense an ethnic group, but one widely scattered and unified by neither a shared culture nor a universally intelligible language. What constituted the Miao as an ethnic group was their official classification based on historical and linguistic analysis *and* their contemporary acceptance of this common category. Highly mediated by the history of Maoism and post-Mao marketization, Miao characteristics were a far cry from the timeless "traits" my Hmong American friends and I had assumed would be definitive. But this did not mean that ethnicity was less than a potent part of cultural life in China. Nor did it mean that even within China certain traits were not naturalized as essential features of Miao cultural identity. It was my desire to understand the way in which politics molds discrete and stable social categories out of heterogeneity that brought me to anthropology.

I made four subsequent trips to China—in 1985, 1986, 1988, and 1993—and visited about thirty villages of different Miao subgroups in Guizhou, Yunnan, and Hunan provinces. Altogether the research totaled more than two years, including a year of fieldwork in the large Miao community of Xijiang in the mountains of Southeast Guizhou as well as considerable time in urban centers such as Beijing and Guiyang. The dialects of Miao language vary widely by region, and many are mutually unintelligible. Hence, I relied on Chinese (Mandarin and variations of southwestern dialects) as my chief field language, except in Xijiang where I acquired a knowledge of the local Miao subdialect and mixed it with my more extensive Chinese vocabulary. The majority of Miao I encountered spoke a considerable amount of Chinese, and when they did not, I used local Miao-Chinese translators. I rarely spoke in English, except in 1982 when I had very little knowledge of Chinese. The translations that appear in the text are in the *hanyu pinyin* romanization of standard Chinese. Translations from Chinese into English, unless otherwise noted, are mine. Names of persons in the text are changed, except in instances where individuals expressly intended that I should write about them using their real names.

Those people beyond China's borders who refer to themselves as Hmong are adamant that that be the only ethnonym by which they are called. They have been successful in virtually abolishing the use of the Miao term (and related appellations such as Meo) in the West and to some extent in Southeast Asia. Most Hmong I have known outside China intensely desire that the Hmong term also be adopted for their coethnics within China. However, the people I have known who now call themselves Miao in China do not share this desire. Nor do the majority of people who classify themselves as Miao refer to themselves as Hmong in their own language. Rather, they employ a number of related ethnonyms, only one of which is Hmong. As detailed in coming chapters, the Chinese context has seen a different politicization of names than that which has taken place in the West. Meanwhile, since the time of my first China trip in 1982, a considerable number of Hmong American elites have garnered the resources and citizenship to travel to China themselves. They report that Hmong citizens of China living along the Southeast Asia border also challenge the Miao term in favor of their own self-appellation. In consideration of this disjunction, I use Hmong, and never Miao, for those outside China out of respect for their preference. Out of regard for those within China who have adopted the term that was once projected onto them by outsiders, I follow their convention of referring to themselves as Miao. This awkward compromise is not intended as a dismissal of Hmong American stances, but as a recognition that these divergent assumptions of ethnonyms are consequences of political histories whose specificities will become apparent in the body of this work.

I owe my deepest debt of gratitude to the Miao in China and to the Hmong outside China's borders who have shared their lives and knowledges with me in so many ways. From Providence, Rhode Island, to California's Central Valley, from chill Minnesota to the heat of Thai refugee camps, and from institutes in Beijing to the mountains of Southeast Guizhou, they have made their homes mine, pressing liquor to my lips in welcome, naming me in their dialects (Ad Nax in Hmu, Maiv Liag in Hmong), and teaching me in innumerable ways about their concerns and struggles. I especially thank key teachers and sponsors in China who took a chance on me in the early years of China's cautious opening and made my research possible: the Central Nationalities Institute, the Guizhou Nationalities Institute, the Southwest Nationalities Institute in Chengdu, the Yunnan Nationalities Institute, the South Central Nationalities Institute, Song Shuhua, An Yifu, the late Zhang Zhengdong, Li Tinggui, and Yang Renjing. Many were made responsible for me in other modalities; among them Hong Fang, Yang Tongying, Li Jun, Li Hui, Li Chao, and Wurlig Bao deserve special mention, although there were many, many more who helped, including, in alphabetical order: A Sang, Cao Cuiyun, Chen Qiguang, Feng Xianyi, Guo Jing, Ji Ling, Jia Guohua, Jin Ou, Lan Ke, Li Bingze, Li Jinping, Li Renshan, Long Jiangang, Luo Xiuying, Ma Shulan, Pan Xinxiong, Wang Xiuying, Yang Bing, Yang Ge, Yang Qiming, Zhang Xiao, and Zhou Liang, as well as others too numerous to list fully here. In France and later in the United States, Yang Dao has been a consistent resource, as have other Hmong Americans, including KaYing Yang, Yuepheng Xiong, and Tzerxa Cherta Lee. In most cases it is not individuals who are to be thanked, but the entire, and sometimes extended, families of the people listed here, who took me in and assumed responsibility for my welfare. To the residents of Xijiang, my *di er guxiang,* who transformed it into the best of all the places I lived in China, I owe my sanity during the tribulations of fieldwork. These persons and institutions may not wholly agree with the arguments made here, but their contributions have nonetheless assisted in multiple ways in bringing the project to fruition.

For research support during the years from 1982 through 1993, I am grateful to many organizations. My 1982 project was supported by a Samuel T. Arnold (Watson) Fellowship from Brown University. Shorter trips in 1985 and 1986 were made possible by grants from the Department of Anthropology Lowie Fund, the Institute of East Asian Studies, and the Humanities Institute, all at the University of California, Berkeley. My 1988 fieldwork was funded by the Committee on Scholarly Communication with the People's Republic of China and the Fulbright-Hays Doctoral Dissertation Research Abroad Program. Partial support for dissertation writeup was provided by a Soroptimist International Founder Region Fellowship and a Phi Beta Kappa Association Scholarship. My 1993 fieldwork was assisted by the Rutgers University Research Council. I also would like to note with gratitude that many organizations and individuals in China bore a portion of my expenses through opening their doors and reducing my living costs with a generosity that far exceeded obligation.

My intellectual debts in conceiving, executing, and refining this work are considerable and encompass mentors for my Ph.D. dissertation at Berkeley as well as colleagues and students at Rutgers and beyond. Aihwa Ong's incisive guidance as dissertation committee chair challenged and promoted my academic praxis, and her challenging intellectual presence continues to inspire me. Jack Potter's moral passion for the Chinese people and for engaged anthropology was an important model for me, and Fred Wakeman's boundless interest, insight, scholarly breadth, and good humor enriched both the project and my enthusiasm for it. Other members of the Berkeley Anthropology faculty that guided me included Gerald Berreman, Stanley Brandes, Elizabeth Colson, George Devos, Alan Dundes, and Nelson Graburn. Among those who generously took it upon themselves to mentor me from outside

Berkeley were Ann Anagnost, Tani Barlow, Gail Kligman, and Brackette Williams. I also would like to note several friends and mentors who lent advice and inspiration in my earliest years of becoming an anthropologist: my undergraduate adviser Bob Jay, the late Wolfram Eberhard, the late Morton Fried, Ann Waltner, Kamaruddin Said, and especially the late Mark Saroyan.

Numerous people have contributed to strengthening the manuscript through incisive readings. Early on, Jenny Beer and Marcy Darnovsky, the members of my dissertation writing group, gave me their limitless patience and indispensable critical commentary. Drafts of the entire book were carefully critiqued by Vincanne Adams, Susan Brownell, Edgar Rivera Colon, Michael Moffatt, Ed Schein, the members of the Rutgers/Princeton China reading group — Yu Chun-fang, Dorothy Ko, Sue Naquin, Ruth Rogaski, and Buzzy Teiser — and two anonymous reviewers for Duke University Press. Others closely read chapters or critiqued ideas in the manuscript: Lila Abu-Lughod, Karen Barad, Elaine Chang, Nina Cornyetz, Debra Curtis, Harriet Davidson, Elin Diamond, Judy Farquhar, Leela Fernandes, Jim Hevia, Laurel Kendall, Andrew Kipnis, Ralph Litzinger, Marc Manganaro, Tim Oakes, Bruce Robbins, Cynthia Saltzman, Caridad Souza, Ted Swedenburg, Nick Tapp, and Zhang Xudong. The Center for the Critical Analysis of Contemporary Culture and the Institute for Research on Women, both at Rutgers, provided fellowships and collegial engagement in a key year of writing. I am indebted to the fellows of each institute for their close questioning of the chapters that they read. Mary Murrell at Princeton University Press was a valued interlocutor during the time we worked together. I, of course, am solely responsible for the final result.

It is difficult to convey the significance of the role of Ken Wissoker, my editor, in the making of this book. From his believing in it long before I did, to his patience in meticulously advising every stage of the process, and, more important, to the sustaining force of his larger vision on intellectual projects such as mine, his impact is immeasurable. Katie Courtland, Pam Morrison, Bob Mirandon, and others at Duke University Press also gave invaluable support. Kaidi Zhan and others at the Berkeley Center for Chinese Studies provided translation assistance. Nat Clymer consulted on the illustrations. Mike Siegel at Rutgers Geography made the map. Dolores Spinola offered all manner of clerical support. John Wiggins did impeccable work on the index.

Dr. Kate Gaioni, Joe Mancuso, and Bob Davis at the Rutgers Health Center may not know just how indispensable they were, for they kept my fingers moving when keyboard stress threatened to stall writing. Chen Wenjin, Danielle Marganoff, Margie Rothblatt, and the Gaurs did pinch-hitting with childcare.

The members of my family deserve special tribute. My two grandmothers, Hilde and Lyla, stayed throughout most of this process and imparted their strength as they took their leave, each at the age of ninety-three, during the writing of this book. Ever enthusiastic, Hilde — who once began an intellectual project for me to finish — would collect relevant publications for me, while Lyla traveled to China at the age of eighty-three, visiting Beijing two days before Tiananmen in 1989. All my in-laws, but especially Bebe and Ernie, were tireless in their support and helped out with grandchildren during my geographic and work-induced absences. My parents, Mary and Ed, who contributed to the project from the moment they began nurturing my intellect at a very young age, buoyed me with their enthusiasm and even ventured to visit me in Xijiang during my fieldwork. Ed also did a painstaking reading of every chapter of the manuscript. Sophia and Ernesto, my ebullient children, good-humoredly assisted me in giving birth to this book while they were living through their own infancies — from nursing at the keyboard, to playing (not so) quietly beside a cyborg mother plugged into a computer terminal, to reordering manuscript pages for me. Their constant warmth brightened the darkest moments of writer's angst. Finally, this project, from the moment it commenced, could not have come off were it not for the unreserved support and devotion of Ernie Renda. It would take pages to list his contributions, to say nothing of his sacrifices, but all of the childcare, computer work, China sojourns, and cheering-up calls from long distances cannot begin to compare to his ever-sunny outlook, the nurturing quality of his affection, the generosity of his love — and inexhaustible quantities of humor.

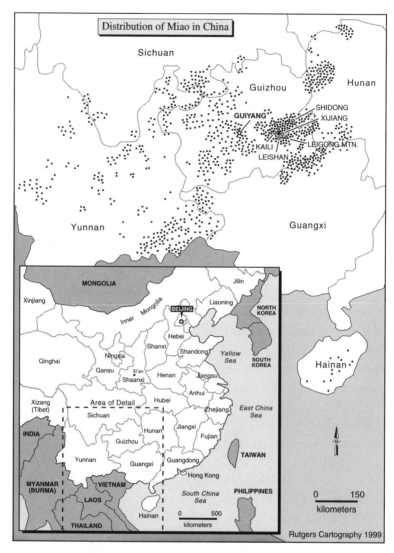

Distribution of Miao in China. Distribution of officially recognized Miao communities in southwest China, showing the Xijiang field site and other key places in the text.

1

Introduction

In one area, I visited every family. On leaving, I put needle and thread
into my hostess' hand, and she would invariably rush to find a piece of
embroidery and ask us to take it to Chairman Mao, "for he loves our
embroidery." At one enjoyable gathering, Miao women surrounded our
girl comrades who were singing and playing, and tied pieces of embroidery on them, practically covering them. These are the women's dearest
tokens, usually given only to their lovers. . . .
— Fei Hsiao-t'ung, Account of the Central Greeting Delegation, 1951

When I first read this vignette, penned by China's premier anthropologist[1] after he visited the Miao minority in Guizhou province on behalf
of the Communist Party, it took some time for me to understand why I
was so captivated by it. As I have pondered its import, I have come to see
that it condenses, in a few sentences, many of the themes of this book.
It was written at the moment of the inception of *minzu,* the official units
that came to designate non-Han peoples and granted them their social
existence. How, I wondered, did the encounter play out? Had Communist Party cadres actually given needles and thread to Miao women? And
had the women routinely offered up their embroidered handiwork in
return, believing it would be put into Chairman Mao's admiring hands?
Did Mao Zedong cherish Miao handicraft, and what was the nature
of his pleasure in it? Can the offering of needle and thread be seen as
an interpellating call toward which Miao women turned by presenting
their quintessential cultural selves? How can we understand this highly
gendered interchange in which Miao peasant women lavished their embroidered attentions on China's highest leader, substituting him for their
lovers? And what of the assailing of the female cadres with handworked
gifts: was it Miao women solicitously enjoining the Communist dele-

gates to go native? What is the rhetorical effect of a Han Chinese expert telling this story of almost cloyingly affectionate gifting at the historical juncture of Communist Liberation?

Minority Rules is about cultural politics in a complex, multiethnic state. It is about the production of discourses — of ethnicity, of gender, and of modernity — and the maneuverings of people within and around these axes of difference. Through an ethnographic account, I show the ways that culture matters in the establishment and maintenance of hierarchized orders that entail forms of exclusion and minoritization. The very presence of exclusions and margins generated a complex field of practice in which variously situated cultural actors negotiated their positionings. In the process, the social order, with its intricate structures of inequality, was not only reproduced, but also sometimes destabilized.

This book is about China as much as it is about the Miao minority people upon whom the ethnography is focused. It spans the 1980s and 1990s, when China embarked on a program of social reforms that can be called postsocialist. As China poised itself to take a new role in the global economy, it transformed its internal social and economic life with sharp ramifications even for those who were little involved with its burgeoning transnationality. The intersection of ethnic and gender politics was a site where the less-reported effects of post-Maoism were being energetically worked out. A society organized around notions of modernity and backwardness, of openness, connectedness, and remoteness, was being elaborated, and there were high material stakes. One way that exclusions from new prosperities and modernities were ratified was through the conjoining in discourse and practice of the ethnic with the feminine, the interior, and the agricultural.

The period of my fieldwork was the 1980s and early 1990s when the so-called new prosperities and modernities were to have emerged like a huge watershed after Maoism. But the processes that I chart have deeper histories in the socialist era (1949 to 1979), in the first half of the twentieth century, and even much earlier. Continuities were drawn upon and sustained in the cultural production of the post-Mao period. It is crucial, with the reworking of cold war scholarship entailed by the postsocialist transition, that China's recent cultural politics be understood with reference to a longer history than that of the era shaped by Communist leadership.

In the West, China is still largely thought of as homogeneous, a singular, ancient, and continuous civilization. Indeed, this characterization has been a leitmotif in Western representations of China's difference. My account undermines this image by suggesting that China's identity has had to be continually crafted out of heterogeneity and that cultural others have played a variety of parts in this productive endeavor. Furthermore, the Chinese people have been pictured as homogeneous in their relation to power. Images of oriental despotism and Maoist totalitarianism have predominated, even into the post-Mao era, fueling a vision of undifferentiated masses in a uniform dyadic relation with a political center. I question this paradigm, not by offering straightforward accounts of resistance, but by presenting cross-cutting instances of power that only sometimes coincide with official structures. An understanding of domination and hierarchy in China must go well beyond a critique of the state and must venture into the murky and shifting currents of popular practice.

Even as I propound heterogeneity to counter stereotypes of China's uniformity, I also interrogate the foundations of just this difference. Much of the heterogeneity that one encounters on the ground and that constitutes the basis of hierarchy is itself produced. This is not to negate difference, or to say that it is not there. Rather, it is to focus attention on the mechanisms by which the limitless raw material of heterogeneity comes to be socially marked, or politically charged, creating the conditions for the stabilization of particular differences—of ethnicity, gender, class, status—in the constitution of the social order. Instead of asking how the mass cultures of either capitalism or socialism create sameness, my emphasis is on the modes by which such systems also foster and organize distinctions.

An Elusive Object

The people that were placed in the Miao category after 1949 were counted as members of China's fifth-largest minority group. This aggregate has significant numbers—7.39 million in 1990[2]—measurable political recognition, and high visibility in popular culture. But who are these Miao who appear as a fixed entity in public representation? Attempts to secure them with objective markers are frustrating at best. Scattered over more than seven provinces, with densest concentrations in Guizhou, Yunnan, and Hunan, the so-called Miao are speakers of several mutually unintelligible dialects and have little contact between regions (see map facing page 1). Primarily agriculturalists, they grow either wet or dry rice, maize, potatoes, buckwheat, or other grains, depending on the region they inhabit. Some of them have long settled in riverine valleys, while others are seminomadic, using swidden farming on mountain slopes.

Beyond China's borders, they have migrated into Vietnam, Laos, Thailand, and Burma (now Myanmar).[3] There, they refer to themselves as Hmong, one of the many ethnonyms in use among the Miao in China. During the Vietnam War, highland Hmong were recruited by the U.S. Central Intelligence Agency to wage a secret anticommunist war in Laos. As a consequence, many became refugees upon U.S. withdrawal from Indochina in 1975. Thus began a global diaspora that has scattered Hmong to the United States, France, Australia, Canada, French Guyana, and other Western countries. Dispersal, for most, has meant the end of subsistence farming and entry into a new form of minoritization structured by wage labor and social welfare.

From this sketch, it should be clear that who the Miao are has been contingent on their location within particular states. In this spirit, this book does not presume to present the Miao separate from their relational positioning within the Chinese polity. But while I deliver no pristine, independent Miao, I take very seriously Miao efforts to define themselves, both in their unity and in their contrast from other ethnic groups within and beyond China. While attributing significant agency to Miao persons, my account avoids presenting "the Miao" as a unitary agent. To the extent that the Miao appear as unitary, it is as a social category produced and reified in the myriad operations of the cultural arena. Consequently, I tack back and forth between Miao practices and the larger contexts that both inform them and naturalize their putative difference, from categorical definitions of the Miao to contrastive definitions of the Chinese, from the dominant fascination with quaint local customs to the Miao commitment to a vigorous modernity.

The Global and the Remote: Geopolitics and National Economics

The Miao and many other minorities—the peasants and herders of China's "interior"—have been conventionally known for their "remoteness." Portrayed as isolated in inaccessible and forbidding territory, they have been seen as culturally incompatible with and marginal to the pulse of life not only in China's metropolitan hubs, but even in its fertile and productive valley agriculture. As Ralph Litzinger (1994) has pointed out, the notion of the remote (*pianpi*) has a double significance in the Chinese imagination. On the one hand, it signifies geographic distance and the romance of a pristine landscape enshrouded in mystical beauty, but, on the other hand, it is a moral construction of the stigmatized margin, a "site of lack, of uncivilized vulgarity, a land of economic and social malaise, of dispossessed people living in deep poverty, scratching out a living in the most infertile of China's hill country" (1994:206). These attributes, I would add, are figured as the feminine counterparts to forward-moving, dynamic centers that are gendered masculine.

Deep into the history of the Chinese imperium, the territory of the southwest has been a ground of political struggle and competition for resources. Over the course of the Ming Dynasty (1368–1644), an influx of migrants (Lee 1982) doubled the population of the region, increasing its heterogeneity. Inhabited by a multitude of different ethnic groups — some of whom were settlers from more northerly locations that were experiencing land pressure — the region always contained a variegated mix of cultures, languages, and forms of rule. Hence, remoteness may be an apt characterization for the topography of the terrain, for its historical isolation from traffic and trade, and for what appears to be the cultural insularity of its inhabitants, but this definition obscures the way in which the Miao and their regions have for centuries been implicated in China's relations with the outside — in China's global positioning. Both territorial and discursive elements have shaped this process.

The southwest was the frontier, an unevenly governed area that marked the outer reaches of empire, a place where borders, taxes, and subjection were regularly contested. While the Qing dynasty (1644–1911) was to double the lands under imperial rule, the southwest, having already been secured as provinces, was undergoing what Millward (1996) calls a frontier process, a conflictual internal colonization (Spencer 1940) peppered by resistance.[4] In the transition from the Han-ruled Ming dynasty to the Manchu-ruled Qing in the mid-seventeenth century, for instance, it had been a stronghold and a battleground. Meanwhile, foreign trade and defense gave the territory particular strategic importance. Tributary missions from Laos and Burma traversed Yunnan, trade in tea and silk with Southeast Asia flourished, and occasionally the region served as a base for military campaigns into Burma and Tibet (Naquin and Rawski 1987:199). In the nineteenth and early twentieth centuries, minority areas in the south were also implicated in Chinese struggles with the British and French based in Southeast Asia (Moseley 1973:25–26).

The region's mineral resources were crucial in garnering the state's attention. In the eighteenth century the need to keep pace with rising imports of silver from abroad intensified the exploitation of copper mines. Under Qing government sponsorship, copper mining increased tenfold, and from 1700 until 1850 the region's copper output accounted for a full one-fifth of the world's production. Meanwhile, the mining boom attracted more migrants, swelling the area's population fourfold during the same 150 years. Migrants from the north and east developed a metropolitan culture that remained far removed from that of the rural agriculturalists, many of whom were non-Han (Naquin and Rawski 1987:199–202).

The other key product that linked Miao to larger systems was opium. Opium was not widely used among the Miao, and it plays no central cultural or ritual role. However, it was used for some medicinal purposes. Miao cultivation of the opium poppy, by contrast, for three related reasons became widespread in China during the late nineteenth and early twentieth centuries. Once the British had introduced Indian opium as a trade item to the Chinese populace, demand for an indigenously produced variety steadily rose with increased addiction and, especially, in response to Chinese efforts to curtail British imports. Chinese attempts to ban domestic production only encouraged its cultivation in the mountainous minority regions least subject to policing. Finally, Miao swiddeners found the crop uniquely suitable to a mobile existence in which interruptions in agriculture required a portable trade item that could be exchanged for cash to purchase rice and other essentials.[5]

Non-Han had been governed since the Yuan dynasty under what was called the *tusi* system (Jenks 1994:30–41; *Miaozu Jianshi* 1985:73–105; Sutton n.d.). A variant of the ancient technique of "using barbarians to rule barbarians" (*yiyi zhiyi*), this system, essentially, was one of indirect rule in which natives were recruited to serve in hereditary, rank-ordered offices and to extract taxes and tribute from those whom they governed.

During the Qing, regulations concerning *tusi* succession to office and mandatory schooling of *tusi* in Chinese ritual and culture were made more stringent. Later, under the Yongzheng reign (1723–1735), the policy of *gaitu guiliu* (replacing native chieftains with regular officials) was implemented with the ultimate aim of eliminating native rule altogether. The move sparked a series of rebellions, especially one among the Miao in the 1720s.

The extent to which Miao had submitted to bureaucratic control was indexed by a widely circulated pejorative taxonomy of "raw" (*sheng*) and "cooked" (*shu*). *Shu* Miao referred to those who lived closer to Han settlements in sedentary communities where they were under some kind of governance, paid taxes, did corvee labor, and manifested a modicum of Chinese cultural influence. The *sheng* Miao were by definition unruled, paid no taxes or service, and lived in terrain that, from the Han point of view, was more rugged and isolated.[6] As late as the 1940s, German ethnologist Inez deBeauclair (1960) noted *"sheng"* Miao in the vicinity of Leigong Mountain in Southeast Guizhou, the region where I was to do fieldwork four decades later.[7]

To take *sheng* and *shu* as two distinct modes of contact, however, is to oversimplify the social reality in which all manner of dealings, accommodations, resistances, and conflicts characterized Miao-Han relations. In the early nineteenth century, for instance, a famous Hunan scholar wrote derogating the Miao for their acephalous social organization. Although his narrative purports to describe the savagery and unruliness of the *sheng* Miao, at the same time it gives testimony to Miao relations with the Chinese and their impact on Miao society:

> The raw Miao are all separated into settlements . . . the terrain interlocks like the teeth of a dog. There are tribes, but no chiefs. They ordinarily do not value human life. In a stockade, a dozen or even several dozen fathers and sons, elder and younger brothers, vie for supremacy. If someone is able to speak to the officials in Chinese, then everyone in the stockade stands in awe of him and selects him as head of the stockade. (in Jenks 1994:34)

What this book argues for the late twentieth century, this passage suggests for much earlier—that Miao prestige systems were hardly autonomous from those that surrounded them (Tapp 1989:177). Nonetheless, the eighteenth and nineteenth centuries saw vigorous cultural produc-

1. Miao women transplanting rice in the Miao albums. Bare feet reveal
large toes, and a man and a woman leer immodestly at one another.

tion of images of the Miao as intransigent cultural others, curiosities to be exoticized and, in times of strife, to be reckoned with. The so-called "Miao albums" are the best known example of the genre of representation that framed the Miao in idioms of strangeness and uncivility. Created between the mid-eighteenth and the mid-twentieth centuries, the albums consisted of paintings cataloguing varieties of Miao and other peoples by ascribed group names, sometimes with descriptive text in classical Chinese. According to Hostetler (1995), these descriptions were part of a Qing dynasty effort to better secure control over non-Han peoples through the compilation of "scientific knowledge" about them. Yet what was produced were stereotyped caricatures, "visual tropes," that reduced each group to an emblematic feature such as hunting, courting, or fighting (Hostetler 1995:44). On the whole, they stressed two irregularities from the Chinese perspective: the absence of an extended community or lineage, and the presence of gender role reversal and sexual transgression (Diamond 1995:103). The result was a portrayal of wildness, couched in the format of cultural miscellany.[8]

That gender and sexual mores would have come in for especially heavy representation is not surprising, given the volatile sexual politics of the period. Since the vast majority of in-migrants to the southwest were male, local women (including the non-Han) must have triggered tremendous ambivalence, appearing as the most likely potential sexual and marital partners and also as tabooed objects with whom no intimate intercourse could be tolerated. The southern woman had long captured the imagination of northern Chinese migrants and travelers, as chronicled by Schafer (1967) for Tang times (618–907). Sexually enticing, imaged in verse as one whose "rose-tinted dress clings tightly [and who] laughs confidently by the river bank, and beckons to the stranger come from afar" (Schafer 1967:84), she also connoted such threats to male supremacy as matrilineal descent and female shamanistic skills. As ethnic boundaries hardened over the nineteenth and twentieth centuries, the vilification of southern gender norms intensified, making desire for the non-Han woman even more transgressive. That desire, however, was never extinguished; indeed, it may have been fostered by the presence of taboos, since the post-Mao liberalization saw a proliferation of sex tourism in Yunnan where Han travelers sought after ethnicized sexual adventures.

During the twentieth century the province of Guizhou many times became a key site in military and economic maneuvers that affected the Miao. The Long March (1934-35), in which soldiers of the Red Army relocated from bases in the eastern province of Jiangxi to Yan'an in the northwestern province of Shaanxi, followed a route that passed directly through Miao areas of Guizhou. As recalled by a Jiangxi peasant who joined the March: "The Miao people were frightened by the Red Army, ran from their huts and hid in the mist of the mountains. To them an army meant robbery, rape, murder, the burning of houses, the theft of rice and millet" (Salisbury 1985:106).[9] The experiences of passing through the Miao and other minority areas was to shape the minority policies of Mao and other party leaders; in their struggle for power in the 1930s and 1940s, instances of conflict and antagonism were acute enough that it became imperative for the Communists to disseminate the proposal of the right for minorities to secede in order to ameliorate the minorities' distrust. Some Miao were sufficiently impressed to join the Red Army and participate in the March.[10]

After Liberation in 1949, wave after wave of policies issued from the Maoist state, overhauling the countryside not only through the reorganization of production (land reform and collectivization) but also through fiscal and political decisions. As detailed later, the southwest region was targeted as an interior site for military buildup, and its mineral reserves were extracted at an ever greater pace in the national interest. Under the cultural and economic liberalizations of the Dengist reform period, Miao culture itself became treated as a resource capable of riveting the gaze of exoticist tourists from abroad and from inside China.

On Culture, Structure, and Practice

The Miao, then, over centuries of different relations to the state, and despite their purported remoteness, have been linked in various ways through the practices of the central administration and by merchant capitalists and entrepreneurs to global economics and politics. Their resource-rich regions went from being part of the unsubdued frontier, to being strategic areas for defense buildup, to being fostered as bastions of tradition attractive to foreign spending. Over the history of Miao encounters with the Chinese imperium, a representational order was put in place that articulated with the economic relations of colonization and internal colonialism. The Miao went from being savage and insurgent to being backward and culturally exotic, never quite fitting with the pace and standards of the nation, but always somehow signifying its limits, its margins, its feminized other (Bhabha 1994).[11]

In some ways, what the post-Mao period has wrought is a renewal and intensification of the cultural practices that constitute marginality. I argue that this is happening because the correspondence between different structural arrangements that position the Miao in relation to China has been under contest. Powerful forces, both material and discursive, both Chinese and transnational, press the Miao and the province of Guizhou to continue to serve as resources in a configuration characterized by extraction. Yet the years of Maoist and post-Mao redistributive philosophy, however uneven in implementation, have forced a contradiction. How can the Miao and other Guizhou peasants be exploited producers in a system that has pledged commitment to more egalitarian relations of production and of cultural difference? The frenetic cultural work documented in this book takes place precisely at this site of contradiction.

The following chapters, therefore, center on cultural practices, insisting that these practices are not epiphenomenal to livelihood, to material production, or to power relations. Cultural practices do significant work in constituting the social order. Culture — or, in this case, minority culture or Miao culture — is what Lancaster has described as "not simply a form of 'consciousness,' not 'ideology' in the classical understanding of the concept, but a field of productive relations" (1992:19).[12] The difference implied in the notion of Miao essence yields a system of asymmetrical relations that shape the lives not only of Miao but of all people in China. It is a system of differences — of relative wealth, of social stature, of political power — that Maoist philosophy was hostile to in principle. And yet, so many of the specific policies designed to eradicate these disparities only reinstated them. In the post-Mao era the tolerance of widening gaps in wealth and social power has been transmuted into a triumphal celebration of the market and of the very differences that the market generates and commodifies.

The meanings of culture in this book are strategically heterodox, disturbing the fragile boundary between anthropology and cultural studies. Multiple senses of culture have been in play in and beyond Western anthropology for more than a century. It becomes almost futile to attempt to circumscribe them, for, in many ways, the possibilities generated at their intersections propel the writing of this ethnography. Nonetheless, at this point I want to disaggregate three of these usages to bring them into relief in relation to one another.[13]

Totality The first sense of culture is the one conventionally thought of as the purview of anthropology. In this usage, culture is a totality, as epitomized by Tylor's famed definition: "Culture or Civilization, taken in its wide ethnographic sense, is that complex whole which includes knowledge, belief, art, morals, law, custom, and any other capabilities and habits acquired by man as a member of society" (1871:1). In this version — especially later with the work of Franz Boas — such interrelated parts not only were thought to cohere in holistic fashion, but also to distinguish groups from each other.[14] The sense of particularity and distinction came to be critical; culture, in the anthropological genealogy, became multiple cultures, "the constituting medium of different thought-worlds" (Stocking 1987:19). The concept came to stand as a diacritic of difference between social entities, one hailed as a marked improvement on the more biologically based notion of race. This version of culture is often used interchangeably with ethnicity to carve up the world into discrete peoples marked by putatively distinct social organization, language, customs, productive techniques, etc.[15] Accordingly, the Miao would be identified by a set of taxonomic features as exemplified, for example, by the Human Relations Area Files, which organize data on language, location, settlement patterns, housing, economy, productive activities, descent, marriage, family, religion, and sociopolitical organization to produce distinctive ethnographic profiles (Lebar et al. 1964:64–72).[16]

However, as many critics have observed and as Abu-Lughod (1991:154) has forcefully argued, this kind of carving up has many liabilities, most notably its attribution to the cultures in question of the regular features of homogeneity, coherence, and timelessness. What was the norm over the history of anthropology was that anthropologists from the West, through their privilege of traveling to and conducting studies of non-Western peoples, froze them into social hierarchies in which their differences became the index of their inferiority vis-à-vis a Euro-American world with a progressive history that had supposedly left non-Westerners in stasis. Change and internal heterogeneity become virtually inconceivable when such non-Western cultural traits are conceived as evenly distributed across all members of each group in question and as shaping consciousness in almost deterministic fashion. What Abu-Lughod advocates as a corrective is that anthropologists write "against culture," favoring instead a narrative style about individuals' lives that reveals their relation to particular cultural tropes but also makes their humanity visible in tactical ways that defy readings of them as inalienably other (1993:25–42).

Abu-Lughod's move is salutary. However, what this book proposes is not to write *against* culture, but away from culture as static, timeless, and bounded, and toward it as produced, contingent, and deployable. Culture in this sense is thought of as cultural production, marked by the fixing of traits and the manufacturing of traditions to support and/or subvert power relations.

Discourse, Hegemony My second sense of culture focuses on the domain of powered discourse. This version refuses the idea that culture evenly saturates certain populations; instead, it emphasizes the association of culture with dominant or elite sectors.[17] It is preceded by an elite sense associated with the nineteenth-century English poet and critic Matthew Arnold, who defined culture as "a pursuit of our total perfection by means of getting to know, on all the matters which most concern us, the best which has been thought and said in the world" (1994 [1869]:5). But my emphasis is more on power relations than on the marking off of elite status per se. Culture here becomes endemic to the mechanisms of social domination, separable from but supplemental to political-economic relations. Some strands of this version are shaped by a marxian binary between economic base and political-juridical-ideological superstructure, aiming to complicate the way in which the two are related. In the Gramscian version (1971), the interests of the dominant classes, or, indeed, the whole system of domination itself, is naturalized through the workings of "hegemony" such that dominant interests permeate all classes without appearing to be imposed. The institutions of civil society — churches, schools, etc. — together with the state are complicit in renewing and defending the ongoing hegemonic order. "Educative pressure [is] applied to single individuals so as to obtain their consent and their collaboration, turning necessity and coercion into 'freedom' " (Gramsci 1971:242). A prevailing hegemony, then, wins subordinate consent through naturalizing the former as com̃ ͏ ͏ sense; in Raymond Williams's words, "the whole lived social process is practically organized by specific and dominant meanings and values" (1977:109). In the Foucauldian version (1979b, 1980a, 1980b), usually connoted with the shorthand "discourse" or "power/knowledge," authoritative statements and knowledges are produced by professionals and governing elites. These "orders of things" organize and constrain social experience, creating particular kinds of subjectivity and social-political subjection. Contrary to the purely linguistic sense of "discourse," these are scenarios in which culture is always materialized in the institutional structures that comprise social life.

When contemporary China is interpreted through these theoretical framings, the inquiry into domination often gives rise to an exclusive focus on the state (about which I later will say much more). The Miao and other minorities, for instance, are seen to be created as ethnic groups by state discourses and classification techniques. Because the state recognizes them in a certain way, they come to live their identities around this dominant definition of them and of their roles within the Chinese nation. These are powerful insights that begin to address the liabilities posed by Abu-Lughod in assuming that any a priori naturalness inheres in distinct cultural groups or essences. But a fuller understanding of the way in which culture, politics, and social life intersect to produce dominant-subordinate orders requires engagement with a third sense of culture.

Mass Culture and Consumption   Also seeking to analyze modes of social domination, other theorists have pursued an analysis of popular or mass culture. Although most of these theories were developed with advanced capitalism as the object of critique, they have much to offer to the study of Chinese contexts. The broad dissemination of culture to revolutionize the masses was a hallmark of the Maoist period; more recently, this technique has confronted other forms of popular culture — such as global broadcasting — that force issues of ideological control vs. more grassroots cultural expression.[18] It was the commercial massification of popular culture that troubled critics who are identified with the school of Western Marxism and with what is known as the Frankfurt School. European Marxist intellectuals, confounded by the failure of the working classes to come to power under either Stalinism or Western capitalism, developed a theory of cultural mediation that challenged the orthodox deterministic relation between the economic base and the cultural superstructure. They developed a vision of the ideological workings of capitalism in which social and cultural institutions and processes created a mass of "one-dimensional" (Marcuse 1964) workers perfectly tailored to the needs of capital. Horkheimer and Adorno's (1944) watershed analysis of the "culture industry" argued that the separation of an elite corps of profit-seeking producers of mass media from the masses themselves was a critical element in securing subjection.

These mass-culture theorists worked with a notion of cultural production that was closely linked to technology and commodification. They mourned the diminishing autonomy of "art" and its replacement by an increasingly uniform and mass-produced culture for sale. In what Benjamin called the "age of mechanical reproduction" (1969), the manufacture of cultural products suffered a stultifying standardization, as did the consciousness of every member of society. "Culture now impresses the same stamp on everything," lamented Horkheimer and Adorno (1944:120). They sketched a sinister "culture monopoly" that performed a double service to capitalism: it programmed people as docile laborers, and, through the creation of particular consumption desires, it primed them to be compulsive purchasers of the commodities that they themselves had produced. This was a quintessentially top-down formulation in which consumers of mass culture led scripted lives, wanting nothing other than to exercise their choice to be the same through their frenetic consumption of identical commodities.

Later theorists of consumption, however, have attempted in various ways to restore a measure of agency within a massified cultural arena. One moderate example of this approach is found in Bourdieu's *Distinction* (1984). Much earlier, Max Weber (1946) had identified the process by which status groups in a society mark their boundaries through their consumption styles rather than, as with economic classes, through their relation to production. Thorstein Veblen (1899/1953) had tagged "conspicuous consumption" as the hallmark of a leisure class emulated by all others. Focusing on the bourgeois notion of taste, Bourdieu insisted on a dynamic link between consumption and the delineation of economic classes in France: "Taste classifies, and it classifies the classifier" (1984:6).

While Bourdieu's analysis presented consumption as a mechanism of class reproduction, Michel de Certeau (1984) argued that consumption was a form of subordinate production, one that creatively and tactically resisted the homogenizing character of centralized dominant culture. This suggests an alternate sense for cultural production. Here, the myriad ways in which people make use of received cultural products presents a measure of possibility, not only for autonomy, but also for subversion of the dominant order. Such interpretations have been extended and nuanced in the field of "reception studies," in which increasing weight is placed on the production of meanings through the activities of consuming culture.[19] The sense of the cultural is effectively expanded beyond the products churned out by the turning gears of mass production to include the myriad modalities in which these products are circulated, appropriated, and made to signify in social life. This emphasis on creativity—what Willis (1990) called "symbolic creativity" because of its communicative dimension—has been the theme of a number of expositions of the rich productivity of youth and ethnic cultures.[20]

A focus on reception or consumption is a significant corrective to perspectives that allow only for the passivity of the less powerful. This perspective also has shifted our gaze from readings of the products of dominant culture as transparent texts from which social effects can be inferred.[21] However, I want to push beyond a framework that bifurcates social actors into producers and consumers and assumes that culture originates in the hands of an elite few. One of the things that this book strives to document is that within China even those as marginal as the Miao are producing culture in ways that are consequential to the social order. This is not to say that Miao necessarily produce oppositional culture, or that their position of subordination entails that the culture which they produce will be somehow different or resistant. Rather, critical to understanding social process in post-Mao China is the idea that neither the state nor a handful of cultural elites can be conceived as monopolizing the cultural-discursive domain.

What, then, comprises the cultural "domain"? Broadly inclusive, my focus is on those cultural practices that contribute to highlighting difference. Aspects of village life, from rituals to social mores to costume embroidery, are classed as cultural practice, as are, for example, contemporary choices in fashion and media consumption. Likewise, commodification endeavors, from tourist performances to the mass production of handicrafts, are also part of culture. The crafting of images of others — in lore, art, journalism, scholarship, and popular media — is yet another form of cultural production. So are such consumption practices as spectatorship, tourism, and the purchasing of ethnic objects. My usage encompasses both senses of "the popular" — the massified sense that refers to those cultural products which are widely circulated and consumed, as well as the oppositional sense that refers to those activities which are autonomous from state, official, or mass culture. Throughout, I maintain that it is critical to eschew the making of distinctions between a kind of unreflective everyday cultural life and a self-conscious representation of culture; the boundaries between these modalities are blurry at best and are based on a spurious dichotomy between the authentic and the manufactured (Adams 1996a).

The Work of Cultural Production

My notion of cultural production retains the three senses of culture in tension. One strategy of seeing culture as always in production is that it obviates notions of culture as straightforwardly inertial; instead, even when culture apparently stays the same, it needs to be produced again and again, and the roles it plays in the social order may be significantly changed. What comes to constitute culture as "time-honored tradition," for instance, is shaped and incited by discourse, by the kinds of discourse that define differences and ethnicities; these ongoing definitions and characterizations include official/academic forms of knowledge as well as the realm of popular and widely circulating representations. In China, images are found of minority exoticism, Western modernity, and the imagined futures for Chinese modernity. But these are not representations that appear outside Miao worlds and are simply beamed in through television and loudspeakers; Miao throughout China also are producing such representations either by engaging with cultural producers in the industry or by becoming representers themselves. They also are enmeshed in struggles based on these representations and the norms of prestige implied by them. Miao social lives are replete with moments in which status positioning vis-à-vis other Miao and/or the dominant culture is negotiated. In the post-Mao era, what is at stake in these struggles are not only status and prestige, but also their convertibility to a more economically defined class positioning. Increased social maneuverability under reform, as we shall see, has made it eminently possible to parlay cultural capital into material wealth, or conversely to use accumulated wealth to improve social status.[22]

In many ways, this ongoing dynamic between what Western social scientists have called "class" and "status" is at the heart of much of the cultural production documented in this book. Interpreters of China have long struggled with the notion of class and its applicability to either historical or contemporary periods.[23] Some scholars have argued that class is simply not a useful concept to describe Chinese stratification because little evidence can be found that class has been a socially significant category of difference or identification (except of course during Maoism). In a volume on worker identities in East Asia, for instance, Elizabeth Perry proposed countervailing axes of identification as more salient for workers in East Asia: "educational aspirations, family pressures, gender roles, state directives, native-place origins, and clientelist networks have proven every bit as decisive as class consciousness in shaping the behavior . . . of East Asian workers. . . . [W]orkers in this part of the globe appear to have been more consumed with the politics of 'place' — a quest for social and cultural status entailing a desire to elude, rather than to embrace the ranks of the proletariat" (Perry 1996:3). This characterization is compelling, for it troubles any mechanistic application of unitary class concepts in comparing social systems. However, it is ultimately a static culturalist argument that assumes a continuity in East Asian subjectivities that appear ever organized around specific kinds of identifications. China's history of social transformation particularly defies any such facile characterization. Indeed, Kuhn (1984) argues that even deep into the Chinese past the concept of social hierarchy was more akin to steps on a scale or rungs on a ladder, combining several axes of social differentiation, including occupational status (according to the fourfold scheme: scholars, agriculturalists, artisans, merchants), rulership versus subordination, and level of bureaucratic achievement in the system of scholar-officials. Moreover, the bifurcations of rural/urban and manual labor/mental labor carried considerable weight. Although many of these categories were tinged by heredity, one could change one's designation through a shift in occupation, bureaucratic attainment, marriage, or migration.

The Maoist system further complicated the schema, for it rested in part on a more marxian-derived definition of class imported through

Japan, creating in practice what best can be thought of as a composite concept that melded older Chinese definitions with Mao's Marxism. It is most critical to consider the system of "class-statuses" (*jieji chengfen*) put into place in the 1950s, for, as Billeter (1985) so lucidly points out, this was a moment when Chinese leaders instituted just such a composite, distributing prestige in new ways in the name of economic redistribution and the correcting of older class wrongs. Through its implementation over several decades, the class-status classification, in turn, "organized a new system of inequalities" (Billeter 1985:130) through the awarding of material and symbolic benefits based on fixed and morally freighted designations.[24]

It was this amalgamated system that conditioned much of the maneuvering of the post-Mao era. Mao had built in a thereotical rationale for such maneuvering, adjusting marxian class theory to allow more subjective factors to play a role: "of course, individuals had to be judged according to their class status, but their subjective attitude (*sixiang*) toward the socialist regime and their individual behaviour (*biaoxian*) also had to be taken into account" (Billeter 1985:133). Upward mobility within the new system that ranked people by class attributions could be achieved through appropriate behavior and attitude. This upward mobility, reanchored in materialist pursuits but closely tied to durable prestige systems, was just what so many players in the post-Mao era were up to. The concept of *biaoxian* is key, for it carries the performative senses of display, expression, or rehearsal, which, as we shall see, became so fundamental to quests for social mobility.

Theoretically, then, to say that class — as defined by relation to the means of production, by income levels, or by identification with a certain class sector — is a distinct and parallel stratification system to that of status — as defined by a cultural system of honor and prestige, by control of symbolic capital, or by consumption patterns — occludes precisely that relationality between the two systems that drives so much of the social process. When Miao struggled for the prestige of their cultural attributions, it was not only a matter of ethnic dignity; it also was about their resisting consignment to economic marginality under the sign of "backwardness" or "tradition." When they performed modernity, it was not simply out of hunger for the trappings of global culture; it was, at the same time, about attaining the forms of affluence that "modernity" had come to connote. In this book, therefore, I use such terms as class, status, prestige, hierarchy, and rank strategically to point to the entanglements between them.

How, then, do we regard these stratifications so as to be mindful not only of their permeability but their durability as well? The notion of cultural *work* is critical, for it implies that the *reproduction* of asymmetrical relations or structures is also contingent on ongoing practices. Paul Willis described this relationship: "cultural and subjective processes, and actions which flow from them, . . . actually produce and reproduce what we think of as aspects of structure. It is only by passing through this moment that determinations are made effective in the social world at all" (1977:120–21). At the same time, transformations, or at least momentary subversions, of structural relations are potentially generated through these same processes. As Hall has put it, "the structure of determinations in any situation—can also be understood, from another point of view, as simply the result of previous practices. Structure is what previously structured practices have produced as a result" (1985:95).

Hall is critiquing a more unilaterally determinist reading of marxian social theory in favor of Marx's well-known axiom that he rehearses: "we make history, but on the basis of anterior conditions which are not of our making" (1985:95). This history-making activity is by no means openended and unconstrained; indeed, it is powerfully shaped so that most often it eventually reproduces existing orders. As Farquhar and Hevia have put it: any " 'space' in which an always potentially contradictory subjectivity can be sustained" is considered in tension with "collectively produced constraints on the thinkable and the knowable characteristic of a historical period or a cultural locale" (1993:514).

From the position that structures do not persist without the ongoing activity of social agents, it is yet another step to suggest that structures, or normative orders, do not exist without the many moments in which they are reiterated by social actors. This is the step taken by performance theorists, and it has come to mark a divide between the often antagonistic camps of structuralism and poststructuralism. My project here is not to align myself with one or the other camp, but to demonstrate that fragments from both powerfully illuminate the ethnographic material at hand. As discussed in chapter 9, performance theory suggests that the reiterating, or "citing," of social norms actually brings those norms into being with such a degree of social force that they constrain and even coerce everyday practice. It is not that an a priori social order demands that its drones slavishly repeat its substantiality, but rather that these myriad moments of reiteration are what give the prevailing order its authority, its aura of inevitability. Performativity is not a voluntaristic argument about an open-ended constitution of the social order in which all manner of things are possible on a daily basis. Very little appears possible when the prevailing order confronts social actors with such authority that it seems the natural order of things.[25]

The mechanisms compelling social actors to perform a multitude of reiterations, then, include the formation of subjectivities that are molded by authoritative orders. Here, the Althusserian process of interpellation and the Foucauldian process of subjectivation come into play. Through these mechanisms, people come to recognize themselves, to experience selfhood, on the terms that have defined them, that have positioned them. An important dualism always exists in this process. In Foucault's felicitous phrasing: "There are two meanings of the word *subject:* subject to someone else by control and dependence, and tied to his own identity by a conscience or self-knowledge" (1983:212).[26] In the course of acquiring a social existence, one simultaneously becomes subordinated to the very social power that has the capacity to initiate one's subjecthood (Butler 1997:2). But just as people are dependent on power for social existence, so is power dependent on people for its renewal. "The reiteration of power not only temporalizes the conditions of subordination but shows these conditions to be, not static structures, but temporalized—active and productive" (Butler 1997:16).[27] In this vein, just as notions of static structure give way to productive activity, so too do unitary identities. Making the case that identities are constituted within, not outside, representation, Hall enjoins us to understand identities as contingent, "produced in specific historical and institutional sites within specific discursive formations and practices, by specific enunciative strategies. Moreover, they emerge within the play of specific modalities of power, and thus are more the product of the marking of difference and exclusion, than they are the sign of an identical, naturally-constituted unity" (1996a:4).[28] This continual activity— which is ever full of the potential to simultaneously reinstate and transform both social orders and identities—is the ethnographic substance of this book.

Modernity and Nationalism as Cultural Productions

Many chapters in this book chart the co-production of modernity and nationalism during the emergence from Maoism. For China, the 1980s marked a decade of reversals and innovations, tumultuous, promising, and threatening. Economic reforms entailed decollectivization in agriculture and the relaxing of state controls in urban productive sectors. These changes gave rise to entrepreneurial experimentation, a renewed emphasis on profit and prosperity, and growing disparities of wealth. The door was thrown open to foreign trade, tourism, and cultural exchange. While Asian neighbors such as Japan and Hong Kong were significant, much of the popular imagining about the world beyond China's formerly sealed borders focused on the emblematic riches and modernity of the West. In an attempt to imbibe what was perceived as the source of Westerners' "freedom" and relative wealth, more and more Chinese studied, scrutinized, and emulated all things Euro-American. An almost obsessive gaze was turned toward the "culture" of the Occident, both in terms of contemporary lifeways and mores (from dishwashers to divorce) and in terms of a high cultural canon taken to encompass such disparate elements as the Bible and Picasso. Programs to study Western culture were instituted in schools; English language instruction proliferated; translations of Western works and Western media products were ravenously devoured. An abundance of commodity images glutted China's mass media, glamorizing the world of consumption beyond the border.[29]

Not only through texts and representations was the West encountered, however. Business dealings in import-export and joint venture transactions brought a flood of foreigners with designs on the cheapest labor around and on the world's biggest market — tremendously attractive conditions for flexible accumulations (Harvey 1989). A growing exchange of scholars, students, and teachers intensified academic contact. In addition, international tourism rapidly grew — up to 31.7 million tourists in 1988 from a meager 5.7 million in 1980 (National Tourism Administration 1990).

The influence of these images and encounters dovetailed with the prevailing state discourses of modernization (*xiandaihua*) and civilization (*wenming*) that were deployed as China's leaders tried to distance themselves from the chaos of the Cultural Revolution. These normative discourses that came to structure subjectivities and generate social positionings had the effect of ranking China, in the eyes of its inhabitants, as humiliatingly backward (*luohou*) on a scale of progress held to be universal. The result was the discomfiting sense, particularly for China's urban elite, that to the extent that the figure of the Western other loomed large, inspiring awe and envy, the Chinese self, rejected as stagnant and retrograde, was rendered void. Some responded to this sense of inferiority by a virtually wholesale renunciation of things Chinese and an enthusiastic embrace of things Western. Others, disturbed by the acceptance of inferior status implicit in this type of mimicry, mounted an intense inquiry into Chinese cultural identity, seeking to salvage its unique and meritorious qualities. The so-called "culture fever" (*wenhua re*) that swept Chinese cities in the mid-1980s was largely propelled by these two paradoxical quests (China Daily 11/26/86:4; Wang He 1986; Wang Jing 1996; Xudong Zhang 1997).

Contemporary social theorizing of modernity has struggled in multiple modalities to exorcise the ghosts of earlier formulations of the modern. Nuanced as efforts may have been to characterize a radically unprecedented complex of social-economic organization, sensibility, and spatial interconnectedness, such portraits of modernity are still often haunted by older evolutionary and stage theories of transition to the paradigmatic Euro-American norm. Anthropologists and postcolonial critics in particular have repeatedly interrogated whether discussions of modernity in the West echo Morgan-Engels progress narratives and/or Rostowian (1960) modernization theory. The question has become no less urgent for having begun to be entertained: What are the implications of paradigmatic sketches of modernity for analyzing the lives of those who are seen, in one way or another, to fall outside it?

This problematic was very much at play in the China of the 1980s and 1990s as the architects of new nationalist forms of identity struggled over the symbolics of modernity. Unsatisfied with their diminished standing and fearful of engulfment by a Western-defined modernity, they quested for a locus of resilient Chinese identity. Theorists of nationalist cultural production have long noted the creation out of heterogeneity of national or subnational groups, which are then portrayed as unitary. Both Anderson's notion of imagined communities (1983) and Hobsbawm and Ranger's notion of invented traditions (1983) characterized this process as tremendously productive. Whereas Anderson foregrounded the rise of print capitalism and the ensuing consolidation of linguistic communities in the development of nationalism, Hobsbawm and Ranger emphasized the invocation of a fabricated past in the manufacture of group cohesion. Solidary political collectivities were premised not only on their own putative homogeneity, but also on their presumed contrast with other parallel entities.[30] For Tölölyan (1991), the elision or containment of internal difference was the precondition for crystallizing the external national boundary. At the same time, as theorists of gender and nationalism have pointed out, certain forms of difference have remained crucially constitutive of the nation. Even as a masculine figure appears as the national agent marching toward the future in a world of comparably modern nations, conservation of the sense of nationhood has tended to rely on a figure of woman as the guardian of traditional values and mores, the locus of national essence. This representation of the national as premised on unity-in-difference, as a complementarity between masculinized progress and feminized heritage, has appeared with remarkable regularity in nationalisms worldwide.[31]

In post-Mao China's nationalist construction, internal difference was managed in disparate ways. Some cultural producers consolidated the center, valorizing aspects of Confucianism as constituting the "spirit at the core of China's traditional culture" (Wang He 1986). But many found the "core" bankrupt, and they began to situate "uncontaminated" Chinese culture in the social/geographic periphery of the Chinese polity. The domains of the peasant, the folk, and the *non-Han* minorities came to be regarded by many as the sites where "traditional culture" was preserved untainted. In this vision, the figure of the minority, usually feminine, came to be included in what was considered to constitute the authentically Chinese, appropriated to serve as contrastive with the figure of the West. A modernity that drew on a feminized folk Chineseness for its distinction, but simultaneously defined itself by its progressive motion away from timeless fixities, was crafted with ardor.

The modernizing fever that both referenced and othered Miao was also the social milieu in which post-Mao subjectivities were being formed. Even as their social existence relied on being ethnics, Miao were beckoned by norms of progress to shake off their purported backwardness. In this cultural ambience, Miao too played their part in constructing a Chinese modernity through performative disavowals of the very tradition by which they had come to be recognized. Viewed from an ethnographic vantage point, it is clear that the meaning of modernity was being actively manufactured in the frenzied clamor of post-Mao cultural politics.³² In their everyday struggles, people not only positioned themselves vis-à-vis a particular modernity, but they also strove to reposition themselves, sometimes through deploying the very codes of the modern that had framed them as its others. My approach in this study, then, is to take modernity as a structure of feeling—what Rofel called an "ideological trope" (1992:96)—that is repeatedly instantiated by myriad performative acts that are elaborated and codified in the course of various moments of sociality.

Ethnography All Over

The stories that make up this ethnography position Miao within the productive arena in which China's national identity was being molded in relation to discourses of modernity. These stories could not have been told only on the basis of long-term research in a single locality. In a certain sense, the larger narratives to be presented here concern the gaps between localities and between peoples, the ways in which relational positionings were negotiated and places came to bear social significance. This became increasingly clear to me as I moved between spaces and sites, stretching my method to respond to the conditions of research in the post-Mao era.

The project began in 1982 when, pursuing the urgings of Hmong refugees in the United States, I went to China as the first Western researcher to take up long-term residence at the Central Nationalities Institute in Beijing. I was housed in a dormitory room in a building reserved for foreigners that I shared with Japanese businessmen enrolled in a Chinese language course. The Institute arranged meetings with scholars and experts, some Miao and some Han, who came to my room to brief me on Miao history, culture, and language. Access to the building was closely controlled by the Foreign Affairs Office on the first floor, and I was to have no meetings without the presence of my *peitong*— or companion — a young English teacher from Inner Mongolia who had been assigned to accompany me everywhere and to keep the authorities posted on my activities. After several months of formal research in Beijing, I traveled on my own to other universities. I was hosted in similar fashion at the Southwest Nationalities Institute in Chengdu, Sichuan, and the Yunnan

Nationalities Institute in Kunming, Yunnan. Over the next decade I was to return to China in 1985, 1986, 1988, and 1993.

Although most reports of the early days of China's opening to foreign research emphasize aspects of authoritarian control and tightfisted xenophobia, for many of my hosts it was an acute concern for my safety and well-being while in their charge that accounted for many of the restrictions and the extent of supervision under which I was placed. As a white Western woman who had undertaken to live in a part of China notorious for being rugged and remote with people known for their "backwardness," I constituted a striking anomaly and an object of considerable fascination. My identification with the Miao transgressed conventional social categories and prompted efforts to recuperate them. This effort was manifested in a clamor of commentary on and imaging of me that revealed much about Miao and Chinese conceptions of the social order. Off-handed comments, official statements, and media portrayals all struggled to position me, and in so doing, to crystallize otherwise unsettled identities—of gender, class, and nationality.

As I have written elsewhere,[33] conventions for hosting were inseparable from considerations of status; indeed, they were instances in which status was expressed and elaborated. In my case, especially in the early years, my status was complicated and subject to repositioning by my hosts. In one sense, I was received as the distinguished white American scholar, requiring certain levels of comfort, protection, and deference. The bestowing of comforts and protections also affirmed my gendered status as a female less suited to hardship. But at the same time, my gender cross-cut my high status, as did my age (I was in my twenties and thirties), and university rank (student). The early willingness of institutes, authorities, and scholars to receive me was in part a consequence of the fact that to do so was not a high-stakes venture, especially at the beginning. I did not fit in the category of a journalist whose writing would be widely disseminated, nor was I a senior scholar who might shape the field of Western sinology.

The research that I did in universities and in cities might be dismissed by conventional anthropological standards as the antithesis of fieldwork, as secondary or "armchair" anthropology. By such definitions, I had not yet reached a site—defined as a rural, face-to-face community—in which I would conduct participant observation. Yet the scholars' briefings, the museums and exhibitions I visited, the performances and fes-

2. Offering embroidery for the perusal of the foreign ethnographer. Community of Gaopo, 1993.

3. The community of Xijiang.

tivals I attended, the postcards and trinkets I perused in hotel gift shops during my urban sojourns were more than context, more than supplementary data. They were fragments of discourse, representations in textual, aural, and visual genres, that played a part in constituting both who the Miao were as well as the multiethnic social order in which they were located. They were an integral part of the kind of multi-sited fieldwork that Marcus has described as moving "out from single sites and local situations of conventional ethnographic research designs to examine the circulation of cultural meanings, objects, and identities" (1995:96). What had begun as frustrating restrictions on field access gradually impressed themselves on me as inextricable elements of just what I was doing. The project ceased to be about bounding and defining the Miao, turning instead to a more systemic understanding of the production of difference. Shopping, incidental conversations on trains and buses, the stares and queries my fieldworker mode elicited—these kinds of things became vital components of what I have called "itinerant ethnography" (Schein 1998a, 1998b).

Eventually, after two additional highly mobile trips across Miao terrain, I did settle in for long-term residence in an agricultural locality. I requested the well-known Miao market community of Xijiang in Southeast Guizhou province (Qiandongnan) precisely because it was less bounded than the smaller mountain villages that were the norm. Xijiang is a huge settlement of more than 5,000 people that sprawls up the steep slopes of a river ravine and is divided by clans into contiguous sectors of the community. From Xijiang (see frontispiece map) it takes almost two hours—riding a creaky, overcrowded bus on a dusty, unpaved road that sometimes becomes impassable because of land slides after rain—to reach the small city of Kaili. To travel to the provincial capital of Guiyang, which most Xijiang locals never do, requires a full day or more, depending on the timing of public transportation. Long sedentary, Xijiang residents farm paddy rice on mountain terraces and, until recently, exploited the game, timber, herbs, and other resources in the uninhabited forests of Leigong Mountain, the tallest peak in the region. Some 99.5 percent of Xijiang's population is identified as Miao.[34] In Chinese ethnological practice, Xijiang has been canonized as a site of quintessential Miao culture. Meanwhile, it serves as a social hub, with its periodic market and its main street dotted with tiny shops. It houses an administrative seat that now governs and taxes seventy outlying villages, and it is where, during the commune period, peasants came to turn in their grain. It is heavily traveled by marketgoers and touristed by urban exoticists.

For the year that I lived in Xijiang, the legendary Miao remote became my center. Making it home, I traveled out to the county seat, the prefecture seat, the provincial capital of Guizhou, and to Beijing and other metropolises. Following the well-worn paths of the market circuit, I undertook what Tsing (1993:65) has called "walking fieldwork" in which I "negotiated multiple arrivals and departures" (1993:66) among the outlying villages that made of Xijiang a cultural, administrative, and economic hub. Everywhere, whether in Beijing, the Leishan county town, or the countryside, I was the recipient of Miao hospitality, the cup of liquor pressed to my mouth with two outstretched hands. Much of my account here derives from my "immersion" in Xijiang's quotidian affairs, but just as much emerges from my mobile sense of Xijiang's social-spatial positioning. Such practices of hosting and guesting are critical in relating localities to each other, both within Miao circuits and between villages and urban centers.

One question that sinologists often ask is how a tiny town like Xijiang, or a minority group like the Miao, can tell us anything about China. One possible answer would be to protest that neither the group nor the site was what my research was about. But this would overstate my protest, for neither are the Miao or Xijiang simply vehicles for a more macro account. I present Miao and local specificities as irrevocably meshed with Beijing, with transnational culture, with regimes of representation, less because of a voluntarily selected academic strategy and more because of what attentive fieldwork demanded of my account. Multi-sited ethnography "arises in response to empirical changes in the world and therefore to transformed locations of cultural production" (Marcus 1995:97).

Responding to the turf policing that anthropology has been engaging in with regard to cultural studies methods, Gupta and Ferguson suggest: "Genres seem destined to continue to blur. Yet instead of assuming that truly anthropological truths are only revealed in 'the field,' and attempting to seal off the borders of anthropology from the incursions of cultural studies and other disciplines, it might be a far healthier response to rethink 'the field' of anthropology by reconsidering what our commitment to fieldwork entails" (1997:38). One thing that this book enacts is precisely this genre-blurring, a demonstration that engaging cultural texts and media products and representations, their production, distribution, and social effects—far from being a contamination of the field's authenticity—is an inalienable part of the field. Likewise, if identities are produced in representation, then anthropological research needs to work out techniques for coming to terms with the textual-discursive as integral to the social matrix in which fieldwork gets conducted. Much work still needs to be done in elaborating methods for recasting the field along these lines.

Outline of Chapters

Earlier, I offered a historical overview of ethnic politics in China, of the structural relationships between Han and non-Han and between the center and frontier regions, as well as of some of the material exchanges and inequalities that characterized these relationships. In chapter 2, questions of "Who are the Miao?" and "What is their history?" are entertained by interrogating each question. Divergent versions of Miao origins—both geographic and "ethnic" (in terms of the Miao term as ethnonym)—reveal the identity politics of their producers. Chapter 3 concerns Maoist and post-Mao state policy toward minorities and their regions, charting the constitution of a multiethnic polity out of the turbulent frontier relations that characterized former eras. This examination entails an account of the changing political economy of the southwest; I argue that by the 1980s a certain routinization had taken place in such a way that "Miao" emerged as a legitimate and unitary category of ethnic agency that came to supersede the plurality out of which it had been assembled.

Chapter 4 shifts the emphasis from state discourses to those generated out of a broader nationalism. It charts the growing Chinese fascination over the course of the twentieth century with non-Han ethnic cultures as both repositories of identity-bestowing tradition and of exotic backwardness against which to define civilization. This account engages theories of representation—particularly Edward Said's *Orientalism* (1978)—proposing a related regime, that of "internal orientalism," in which feminized minorities within the Chinese state became oppositional objects in a colonizing process. I document this process ethnographically at sites of social interaction where it was possible to see the intersecting roles of urban elites and minority villagers, particularly women. Chapter 5 makes a more general statement about how culture and domination should be conceived in post-Mao China. Exceeding the state as locus of discursive and imagistic control, the messages revealed in state-produced culture are seen to coincide with those of a broader sector, suggesting a form of domination that flows from the common concerns of Chinese elites—whether state or nonstate, whether Han or minority—with civilization, national identity, prosperity, and modernization.

The chapters in Part II expand the argument that Miao were not only objects of representation, but were themselves cultural producers. For the Miao cultural agents discussed in chapter 6, the marketizing climate of the 1980s and 1990s was seen not as a corruption of culture, but as a sensible way to preserve and celebrate it through commodification. For decades, certain Miao cultural producers had been processing culture for mass consumption in the service of Maoist publicity aims. Some striking disjunctions arose, as performers who had spent decades professionalizing their performance styles found themselves competing for marketability with entrepreneurs who responded better to the desire, especially on the part of foreign tourists, for a rawer simulation of authenticity. Meanwhile, nostalgia also saturated Miao self-knowledge in the upheavals of the 1980s, and a passion for cultural revival and canonization informed the activities of certain Miao agents at every level. Chapter 7 describes modes of cultural recovery in which Miao were engaged as they emerged from the suppressions of the Cultural Revolution.

In the course of struggling to be recognized as modern, minority cultural players also disavowed backwardness, displacing it onto yet another other who became framed as the subaltern. Strategies of disavowal are the subject of chapter 8, in which we see not only the production of "authentic" or "traditional" culture, but also the enactment of difference by which some assert their modernity over others. Chapter 9 reveals that, in a myriad of venues, Miao are seen to enact a "modern" positionality through such practices as reflexivity, social posturing, spectatorship, and performance. Rather than appearing as a globally recognizable standard to which peoples and nations fail or succeed to "measure up," modernity becomes itself a site of cultural contest as Miao eschew their feminized positionality of being objects of consumption and instead assume the masculinist gaze of the privileged nostalgic, the modern *minzu*.

In many ways the writing of this book has been guided by what Stuart Hall has called theoretical "struggle," or "wrestling with the angels" (1992:280). Writing about the Miao and China, I have felt compelled to both engage and detach from certain canons: specifically, the ways that anthropologists have seen ethnicity, the ways that Asianists have seen China, and the ways that social theorists have seen power. These frameworks have confronted me with canonic force precisely because my understanding of my material was at once so profoundly affected by their visions and yet so unsettlingly discontinuous with them. Taking seriously Hall's position that "the only theory worth having is that which you have to fight off" (1992:280), the conclusion highlights the specific sites where wrestling has taken place.

Part I

Nation/
Representation

2

Of Origins and Ethnonyms

Contested Histories, Productive Ethnologies

Oh, heaven, this land is not so good as that former land of ours. In that
country of ours, the birds never stopped singing, and the weather was
always warm. During the whole year there was fruit.
—Origin legend of the Sichuan Miao, collected by Graham

Many of them were probably blond and blue-eyed. Such Hmong are still
to be found, though they are few in number. They are testimony to the
Hmong's Caucasian ancestry, and to an original homeland in southern
Russia or on the Iranian plateau.
—Conjecture of U.S. academic Keith Quincy

The Miao come from the "Jiuli" of the Huangdi period and the San Miao
of the Yao Shun period. The "Jiuli" are a tribe that lived in the middle
and lower reaches of the Yellow River basin five thousand years ago.
After being defeated in a conflict with the Huangdi tribe, they retreated
to the middle and lower Yangzi River and formed the "San Miao" tribe.
—Miao scholar Long Boya in *Guizhou Shaoshu Minzu*

This chapter is about the problems that arise when the question is asked,
"Who are the Miao?" And it is about what gets generated when many
different parties attempt answers over time. Historiography, ethnology,
and minority policy purport to fill out the content of the Miao category
and also to position the Miao in relation to other groups as well as to a
larger polity. Situated at the nexus of power and knowledge, these discourses have the aura of authority and the effect of definitively identifying, framing, and stabilizing what constitutes "Miao-ness." Unlike what

is considered to be "authentic" culture—which is regarded as legitimate only if produced by the ethnic group in question—these discourses are seen as highly legitimate, perhaps even more reliable, when produced by non-Miao. Miao *self*-definitions are thickly intertwined with dominant representations; hence, this account replicates Miao and non-Miao renditions in their ambiguous entanglements.

Of Origins and Ethnonyms: Dissent in Miao Historiography

Most attempts to flesh out "Who are the Miao?" are highly politicized. And it is common that these attempts begin with the genealogical question, "Where did they come from?" Like other ethnohistorical writing, the myriad responses I will analyze here are invariably interested accounts that position the Miao in relation to dominant history and/or to the "historian" creating the account. They are tales of earliest time, which locate the Miao in terms of territory and in terms of the majority group with which they contrast. These discourses of origins are fundamentally about legitimacy, about priority, and about ownership (Williams 1991, 1989:436). They reflect what Lowenthal (1985:55) calls a "cult of origins" upon which claims to power, prestige, and property can be based. These claims are negotiated through the manufacture of Miao history, and they reflect the aims not only of the Miao and their neighbors, but also of the authors of those histories.

By emphasizing the interested character of origins discourse, I do not mean to dismiss the claims as false or fabricated. Rather, the immense productivity inherent in claims to origins is precisely about the inaccessibility of a unitary "true" origin in Miao ethnohistory. In the absence of a single, definitive version, what is most relevant here is the contemporary effects of certain origin claims, the social process of their production, circulation, and reception. Following Ivy, I suggest the futility of questing for the actual origin event isolated in retrospect from its discursive production: "The event never simply exists as such, but produces its effects after the fact, in a repetition that becomes its own spectral origin" (1995:22). The social life that emerges in the practices of repetition is what Jensen, describing the transnational and transhistorical "manufacture" of Confucianism by European Jesuits and Chinese intellectuals, calls "a dialectic of works and lives, or . . . a dialogue between texts and interpretive communities" (1997:24).[1] As Litzinger (1995) has argued for the Yao making of history in the People's Republic, engaging in such dialogues, whether figuratively or literally, can generate new forms of identification for those practicing history or the recovery of tradition.

The next sections present three elements of Miao historiography often considered crucial to their ancient identification: their ethnonym, their relationships to other groups, and their original territory and migrations. In the second part of the chapter, I read ethnological accounts, unpacking the manner in which certain features have secured a Miao cultural profile.

The "Miao" Term

Of central concern to those involved in tracing and placing Miao origins is the problem of the ethnonym. Since the Miao, in the absence of their own writing system, did not keep historical records themselves, the quest for beginnings, which spans several millennia, relies on legend and Chinese documentary evidence. Reconstructions have hinged on the appearance of the term "Miao" in a variety of records to lend continuity to the history of the ethnic group. The impulse has usually been to trace an unbroken line to the deepest past of this contemporary ethnic formation and to crystallize an alteric relationship with what accounts usually refer to as the "Chinese," the "Han," or their antecedents under different names. This is a tricky undertaking: in the periods of antiquity in question, even the so-called Chinese were a congeries of groups-in-formation, and centuries of interruptions occurred in the use of the Miao term.

In whatever hands, the Miao ethnohistorical project has repeatedly invoked the textual authority of Chinese classics such as the *Zhanguo Ce* (Plots of Warring States) and the *Shi Ji* (Records of the Grand Historian) where scholars have found reference to a group variously called Miao (苗), Miaomin (苗民), Youmiao (有苗) or San Miao (三苗). This group is regularly mentioned in contexts of military conflict, where it figures as a key player in early imperial Chinese history. Ruey Yih-fu, a Taiwanese ethnologist and expert on the Miao who published extensively from the 1940s through the 1960s and who attempted a comprehensive evaluation of the documentary evidence, cited a passage in the *Shujing* (Book of Documents) in which the "four criminals" (*si ʒui*), among whom were the San Miao, were banished early in the third century B.C.E. by the legendary Emperor Shun to the region of Sanwei, later identified as present-day Gansu province. Then, according to the *Shujing,* the San Miao joined forces with seven other "tribes" to assist the first king of the Zhou dynasty (1122? B.C.E.–221 C.E.) in bringing down the Shang dynasty (16th–11th centuries B.C.E.) by subjugating their last king. Other brief mentions, as chronicled by Ruey, occur into Qin times (221 B.C.E.–207 C.E.), but attempts to confirm these as early references to the contemporary Miao have been confounded by the disappearance of the Miao term for several centuries thereafter; it did not reemerge until its occasional mention in the Tang and Song dynasties (618–1279). Ruey notes (1962:146) that the term does not recur in official dynastic histories until the Yuan (1271–1368) and Ming (1368–1644) dynasties. Ironically, at this point, beginning in the Ming and continuing into the Qing (1644–1911) periods, the issue is further complicated by the fact that "Miao" then came to have a much broader referentiality, encompassing a wide array of non-Han ethnic groups in southern China.

Identity with the San Miao of old imparts a legendary stature to the present-day Miao, positioning them as important players during the formative period of the Han people. This identification also bestows the dignity of great antiquity and a firm standing in the documentary record. Most authors on Miao history have accepted this interpretation, and in writing about it they have reproduced its authoritativeness (see Bernatzik 1947:15–20; Bliatout 1982:2; Chen 1987:658; Geddes 1970:1; Gu 1980; Mottin 1980:16–17; Pan 1989:6; Quincy 1988:30–51).

The official *Brief History of the Miao* (*Miaozu Jianshi*) is one of a collection of authoritative histories of officially designated minorities produced in the People's Republic. Begun in 1958 under the sponsorship of the central government, the compilation project was interrupted in 1963 and not resumed until 1979. The result was a 350-page book, the collective product of sixteen principal authors — Miao and non-Miao — published by the Guizhou Nationalities Press in 1985. Divided into chapters on different historical periods and social evolutionary stages, the book was part of a major series that described its mission in this way: "In order to stimulate a sense of pride among the people of each nationality toward their own history, to develop a patriotic spirit, to move forward in strengthening unity among the nationalities, and advance together toward the construction of socialist modernization, we decided to officially publish the set 'The Minority Nationalities of China Collection'" (Miaozu Jianshi 1985:1).

The *Brief History*'s first chapter opens with a discussion of the "San Miao," their territory, and their early conflicts with tribes of the Yellow Emperor; they are described as "numerous and powerful" (*ren duo shi da*) and as "abundant in strength" (*shili xiong hou*) (1985:1). The book assembles textual references and other scholarly works to support the argument that the Miao lineage can be traced to the "San Miao." But, according to some of these scholars in 1982 interviews with me, whether these "San Miao" can be confirmed as the "true" Miao ancestors was still a subject of research and dissent in mainland academic circles. More recent publications on Miao history have continued to debate the meaning of the "San Miao" phrase itself as well as its relation to present-day Miao (He 1991; Lu 1987 [1934]; Ma 1988; Zhang 1989).[2]

Conjecture over the "Miao" term has also combined with speculation as to the semantics of the character itself. Ambiguity in the signifier has provided fertile ground for strategic claims regarding the signified. Composed of the "grass" radical (艹) over a "field," (田) the character (苗) has been interpreted in a variety of ways. Eickstedt (in Wiens 1954:72-73) thought this combination of components meant that the Miao were not originally rice farmers of the moist valleys but rather nomads of the mountain steppe, thus identifying them with the topography of the grasslands and therefore with the Gansu "San Miao." However, Wiens (1954:73) points out that a more common definition (from the authoritative *Cihai* dictionary) is simply that of "rice-plant shoot." Weins's view is echoed by Enwall (1992:26), who gives "young plant" (as does a 1980 Beijing dictionary) for the most common contemporary usage of "Miao." According to a legend from Graham's Sichuan Miao informants, the term—which Graham renders as "sons of the soil"—derives from the time when the Chinese, having usurped lands originally belonging to the Miao people, relied on the Miao to cultivate rice for them as tenant farmers (Graham 1978:31). "Sons of the soil," based on its meaning of those who do farming, has in turn been regularly elaborated by Western authors (Crisler 1937:47; Jamieson 1923:380; MacGowan 1869-70:124) to mean "indigenous" or "aboriginal" people, honoring them with chronological priority over the Chinese.

Further etymological speculation has proliferated in a variety of sources. One theory, which ties the early Miao to a location, identifies the term as a reference to a name of an ancient place, presumably that in which the Miao originally resided, north of the Yellow River in Henan (Wiens 1954:73, Mottin 1980:3). Another, which recurs widely, links the Miao to cats in various ways. In interviews in Beijing in 1982, I was told that, as a consequence of "Great Han Chauvinism" (*Da Han Zhuyi*) in the Song Dynasty, a component meaning "claws" was added to the original character for Miao, thus transforming the meaning to "cat." Some have suggested that such a designation was prompted by a Han sense that the Miao language was similar to the mewing of cats or that the Miao were as nimble as cats in climbing mountains (see Bernatzik 1970:7–8). Enwall suggests that a derogatory connotation has persisted in Southeast Asia because of the mispronunciation of the Thai term "Meo," which when spoken in a different tone does refer to cats (1992:26). Hmong refugees from Laos also regularly gave me the "cat's meow" explanation as the reason that they reject the Meo ethnonym.

Those concerned over derogatory connotations have gone a step further to flatly assert that "Miao" itself means "barbarian." Beyond a sense of contempt that may have been *attached* to the term because it designated cultural others or foreigners (Bernatzik 1970:8; Tapp 1986:9), the assertion also has been made that the semantic content of "Miao" itself carries that meaning. This viewpoint is promulgated by the Hmong intellectual Yang Dao, now in the United States, in his account of millennia of aggression on the part of the Han Chinese against the peaceful Hmong people. He states: "These invaders gave to the Hmong the appelation [*sic*] 'Miao,' which later became 'Meo' and which means 'barbarian'" (1982:6).

Such debates over meaning have been dismissed by those who suggest that "Miao," along with other ethnonyms such as "Man" and "Mao," may have been attempts in ancient Chinese to approximate the peoples' self-appellation. This interpretation is based on the similarities of the sounds of these words with those claimed as ethnonyms by contemporary Miao, such as Hmong, Hmu, etc. As one mainland scholar concludes: "When Han scholars used these characters [i.e., Miao, Mao, Man] to refer to the Miao, this author believes it was a phonetic transcription of Miao self-appellations and used only the sound not the meaning" (Yang Tongru 1989:68). This analysis has the potential effect of defusing an escalating contentiousness about the use of these terms and the significance of such choices.

Relations to Other Groups

The issue of positioning vis-à-vis other groups that appear in the documentary sources has been another site of maneuver. Some conjecture that the Miao are identical with two other groups, the Jiuli and the Taotie, an assertion that would fill out the story of their earliest times by allowing additional textual inferences and an even longer legacy. But it would give those in search of a history only the perspective of their erstwhile adversaries who described the Jiuli and the Taotie as people of "hereditary wickedness," "with profuse hair," "with wings under their armpits," "greedy, licentious and unreasonable," with customs divergent from those of the "Chinese" who defied and were eventually suppressed by the legendary rulers Yao, Shun, and Yu (quotes in Ruey 1967:50–51). The ugly portraits painted by their opponents notwithstanding, such claims of longer lineage in their ancestry continue to be compelling to Miao historians. The official *Brief History* asserts an "intimate relation" (*miqiede guanxi*) between the Miao and the Jiuli "tribal federation" (*buluo lianmeng*), which, under the mythical leader Chiyou, "opened the land" and "developed the productive forces," becoming a powerful eastern tribe before being defeated by another tribal federation from the upper reaches of the Yellow River under the Yellow Emperor, another legendary hero (*Miaozu Jianshi* 1985:1). This rendition exalts Miao bravery under assault, and it echoes the "deeply moving" Miao sagas about Chiyou "describing the successes of the Chinese and the cruel defeats of the Miao" recorded by the missionary W. H. Hudspeth in the early part of the twentieth century (1931:224).[3]

Despite the position of other contemporary mainland scholars who have been adamant that the Miao-Jiuli identity is untenable based on geographic and temporal disparities in the records (Wu 1982, Zhang 1984), the legend of Chiyou is very much alive. In the summer of 1998, I received an invitation to a conference to be held in Hebei province, cosponsored by the Guizhou Miao Studies Association. Titled the "Symposium on the Culture of Three Chinese Foresbears [*sic*]—Emperor Yan, Huang and Chi & Economy and Trade Cooperation," the English attachment to the invitation, directed at Hmong coethnics overseas, promised: "Because Emperor Chi You is ancestor of our Hmong people, the government will hold a memorial ceremony for Emperor Chi You during the conference. There will also have [sic] some traditional cultural activities during this meeting."

Two critical issues are at stake in these discourses on beginnings. The first concerns how the emerging Miao are situated with regard to the ancestors of the Han, theories of which invariably bespeak current concerns. Accounts based on documentary evidence, such as those regarding the Jiuli, usually proceed from the establishment of the Miao and Han ancestors as independent groups engaged in a struggle in which the Miao predecessors are the vanquished, accounting for their dispersal and southward migration. This version has the contemporary effect of asserting Miao legitimacy as an autonomous entity and of exonerating them from responsibility for their present state of putative "backwardness."

Other versions reproduce Miao oral historical legends that emphasize their temporal precedence over what eventually came to be their Han oppressors by asserting that "the Miao were in China before the Chinese" (Mottin 1980:16; also Schotter 1908-9:409). Or, "Wherever the Chinese are now in the north and east, the Miao were there before them" (Clarke 1907:252). The missionary Hudspeth suggests that they are "possibly the oldest of the *pre-Chinese* races" (1922:702, emphasis added). Crisler, also a missionary, claims that an early nomadic "Han race . . . found the Miao in possession of the fairest of the farming lands and upland pastures" in north and central China; furthermore: "in sealed caves and in ancient graves in the basin of the Hwang Ho [Yellow River] and north of the Yangtze, are found artifacts bearing silent yet indisputable witness to the former occupancy of those parts of China by races other than those now dwelling there" (Crisler 1937:47). These claims reveal their missionary authors' sympathy with the Miao of their conversion designs, depicting the Miao as primordial inhabitants of lands unfairly usurped, as victims worthy of advocacy. By contrast, a contemporary mainland Han scholar, Weng Dujian, writing on the general history of the nationalities, keeps every group in its distinct place, asserting in passing that the Jiuli and the San Miao, far from competing with the Han ancestors for central lands, could be classed instead under the rubric of the southerners called "Man" (1984:1).

Another approach, characterized by claims of a genealogical "intimate relationship" between the Miao and the Han, is reflected in linguistic analyses that argue for the closeness of, for example, the grammars of the Miao and ancient Han languages (Zhang and Cao 1984). A variant of the intimacy thesis is widely found in Miao legend and posits an elemental kinship bond between the ancestors of the Miao and the Han (Eberhard 1982:82). Legends of this sort portray the groups as descendants of two siblings, or as bonded affinally, usually though not always (see below) through the marriage of a Miao daughter to a Chinese emperor. Stories of sibling relationship differ as to whether the Miao or the Han was the elder brother, but in either case birth order operates as a metaphor for the struggle over status positions (Tapp 1989:159–66). In the 1920s, Graham (1978:27) recorded a tale in Sichuan which held that the eldest brother was originally Miao, but that the two brothers forgot their common ancestry and quarreled over the rights to worship at their ancestors' graves. Later, the Han became more powerful and numerous, thus consigning the Miao to the role of younger, weaker brother. A story collected in 1956 by the Miao scholar Li Tinggui told of Han and Miao brothers who came to a great river as they traveled southward. The Miao carried the Han across; on his head was the Han book, while the Miao book was in his mouth. When the river became deep, he ate his own book, thus explaining why the Miao use their minds to remember history while the Han use written inscription (personal communication, 1982).[4] Both tales call the inferior status of Miao (based on political/numerical weakness or illiteracy) into question by restoring to them a mythic era when their position was at least equal to that of the Han.[5]

Han stories of relationship with the Miao bespeak a kind of guarded respect for their ancient other. Kinkley suggests that Han historians, chiefly of the Ming and Qing periods, "fascinated by the resistant and resilient Miao, have reconstructed them as worthy foes . . . by conferring on them an ancient genealogy" and by linking "the fate of their two 'races' according to various forms of primordial enmity or sibling rivalry" (1987:11).[6] Indeed, in an account of Guizhou's Miao-Man peoples, the Qing scholar-official Luo Raodian (1793–1854) wrote that the legendary Emperor Yan (or Shen Nong) married a daughter of the Miao-Man region; he stated: "Of old, Kweichow was ever a state of [good] reputation and [high] civilization; therefore, its chief became connected by marriage with the imperial family" (in Lin 1940:270).

That marriage with the Han was a means to high station is further demonstrated in a Miao story collected by Graham; in it a Miao "emperor"[7] remarks upon his marriage to a Chinese woman: "'Now we have gotten a Chinese bride like a good official. This Chinese girl has come to make a good breed' (to help create a fine breed of people)" (1978:29–30). A more subversive treatment of intermarriage (and marriage resistance) can be found in the Miao legend of the "Ribbon Maiden," in which a Miao young woman, desired by the emperor for her beauty and her skill in embroidery, uses her wile and that same needlework craft to evade a forced concubinage. The emperor thrice promises her release on the condition of her creating a living being (a rooster, a partridge, then a dragon) out of embroidery, and each time she uses her own blood to endow with life a creature that attacks and eventually destroys the emperor (Shi 1985:16–21). The scenario of being desired by, but rejecting and ultimately overthrowing, the embodiment of Han power elevates the otherwise denigrated Miao to a status of superiority earned by their own merit. Interestingly, the lore about Miao craft as a vehicle for access to power resurfaced when Chinese anthropologist Fei Hsiao-t'ung paid a friendship visit to the Miao in 1951. As retold in the beginning of this book, embroidery was tenderly remembered by this Han member of the Central Greeting Delegation as an instrument of deference, a vehicle by which Miao women conveyed their adoration for their beloved leader.

Geographic Origins

Closely linked to the issue of the Miao-Han relationship in earliest times is the third issue critical to discussions about beginnings — that of place or geographic origins. Theories range widely and, again, are implicated in the politics of Miao spatial/temporal priority or its negation. From the perspective of their present population centers in Hunan, Yunnan, and particularly Guizhou, Miao ancestors are said in discrepant versions to have migrated from the north, the south, the east, the west, or China's center.

The North Savina, a French missionary who did extensive historical studies of the Miao early in the twentieth century, locates their source at perhaps the farthest remove (*"a l'antipode"*) from their current settlements. He subscribed to a theory of Mesopotamian origins prompted by Miao legends of travel through "a land of snow and ice" "behind the back of China," which he interpreted to be Siberia and Mongolia (1914:115–19).[8] In the summary of Savina's writings presented by Jean Mottin, another Christian missionary, the desire propelling these origination legends becomes more transparent:

> It is true the Miao have a rather fair skin, nearly white. Their hair easily becomes reddish to the point that certain adults, but above all the children, are light complexioned. Equally, listening to their legends, one is forced to admit their surprising similitude with the Babylonian narratives concerning the creation of the world. These people too speak not only of a unique God, but of the creation of the world, the creation of the first man, the creation of an original couple, of the first sin, of a deluge, of a "tower of Babel," of the confusion of tongues and the hope of the coming of a savior. (1980:15)

The thesis of northern origins, then, reaches far beyond Mongolia to a place of alternate civilization, hardening — even in racial terms — Miao difference from Chinese and in some cases intimating Miao putative ancestral affinity with Europeans. It lays the foundation for Miao to be receptive targets of Christianization. This version has been both widely reiterated (deBeauclair 1970:10; Mottin 1980:15) and categorically refuted (Ruey 1962:143).

Another related legend, one frequently encountered in the United States and widespread among Hmong presently in or from Southeast Asia, elaborates on the idea of Mongolian roots, citing as proof the phonetic similarity between the ethnonym "Hmong" and the phoneme "Mong-" in Mongolia. Assuming a north-south migratory trajectory for China's earliest peoples — which is also the most recent experience in Miao collective memory — the argument for Mongolian origins would, again, serve to put Miao spatially "before" the Han originating in the Yellow River basin.

The discursive force of this longing for priority reveals itself in the experiences of Yang Kaiyi, a Miao from China who traveled to Hmong communities in the United States and reported: "when I was in the States, every person I met, no matter man or women [sic], would ask me, 'Are Hmong Mongolians?' It was more interesting when someone told me directly, 'Hmong are Mongolians from the Republic of Mongolia,' and then added, 'We want to conduct a study in Mongolia'" (1996:54). Contesting the theory in a Hmong American journal, Yang unpacks the reasons that Hmong in the West may have this conception, offering, among other explanations, the conjecture that Mongolians in the southwest during the Yuan—or Mongol—dynasty (1271-1368) infiltrated the Miao; in addition, lore about particular Mongolian parents and grandparents was eventually transmuted into a general impression of ancestry. Here, the positioning of different groups of Miao/Hmong from within and beyond China can be charted in terms of their respective locatedness vis-à-vis their origins, with those at the farthest reaches from the putative homeland also being the ones who are reaching farthest back into the space before memory.

The South In sharp contrast to the frigid climes of the legends that Savina collected are those told by the Miao of Sichuan, among whom Graham worked as a missionary. They lamented their departure from warmer regions where they were not assaulted by cold. Their nostalgia, in Graham's opinion, was for the Guangdong region whence the Sichuan Miao claimed to have come. A confirmation of such southern origins was undertaken by Beijing linguist Cao Cuiyun's study of Miao language. She found that the presence and absence of certain terms in the Miao lexicon pointed convincingly to the conclusion that they could not have originated farther north than their present distribution.[9] In this vein, others have conjectured that Indo-China was the earliest Miao territory, classing the Miao as members of the Mon-Khmer language group (cf. Davies 1909:338-43; Graham 1937:19). Recent etymological research by U.S. linguist Martha Ratliff on words that indicate environmental context also points strongly to the conclusion that "no linguistic evidence has been discovered to date to suggest that the HmM [i.e., Miao] people have lived in any place other than southern China" (n.d.:3).

The East The Miao epic poem from southeast Guizhou, "The Westward Upriver Migration," or "Scaling Mountains and Fording Streams" (Tian 1981:88), states unequivocally: "Our fathers and mothers originally lived in the East" (Ma 1983:297). A theory of eastern origins is also reflected in the belief, reported by the missionary Clarke (1904:195-98), by Johnston (1908:276), and by Jamieson (1923:378), on the part of the Hei (Black) Miao as well as the "Chungchia" (Zhongjia, now Bouyei) people, that they came from Jiangxi province. In the 1940s, German ethnologist Inez deBeauclair (1970:62), who was based at Guizhou University, encountered similar lore in southeast Guizhou and cited a story from the Miao of Sichuan about the conquest of Miao-inhabited Jiangxi by the militarily superior Chinese (Graham 1954:28). I also found claims of Jiangxi origins among the southeast Guizhou Miao with whom I spoke in 1988, but even more strident assertions to this effect were made by the ethnic Han villagers scattered throughout this densely Miao region. Betts (1900–1901:85–86), another missionary, traced the Han villagers' accounts to a specific forced migration during the reign of the Hong Wu emperor of the Ming dynasty, in which incoming Han from Jiangnan (including Jiangxi) intermarried with local Tujia (a Shan people of the Tai language group), thus creating what was called the "Zhong-jia" or "Second Race." Mickey (1944:57) found lore of Jiangxi and the Pearl River as sites of origin given by Miao in south central Guizhou as well. That the question of earliest origins is closely linked to the configuring of the Miao-Han relationship is suggested by these Miao claims in which, despite being in a location in which they might be classified as the "first" or indigenous people, they emphasized instead an origin site identical with that of their present Han neighbors.

The West   Another set of theories—those that position the Miao as coming from the west—can be divided into two versions, both of which ultimately locate the Miao as deriving from elsewhere before their settlement in the west. Many accounts to this effect are spinoffs from the passage in the *Shujing* in which the "San Miao" were banished to present-day Gansu, whence they made their way east as far as Hunan or even the Dongting lake area. Eickstedt (in Wiens 1954:72–73) sees the west as the cradle of Miao culture and finds traces of the life of the mountain steppe deeply imprinted on their contemporary culture. But in a 1948 historical work, Jiang Yingliang (in Wiens 1954:73–80) saw the Miao as deriving from present-day Shanxi, migrating to Sichuan and eastern Tibet, coming into conflict with the ancestors of the Qiang people, and then from Zhou times to the third century C.E. migrating eastward along the Yangzi to become the ancestors of the Chu.

The Center   The *Brief History of the Miao* (1985) positions the ancestors of the Miao and of the Han adjacent to each other in the region of

China's heartland. The Miao ancestors, the book contends, occupied the middle and lower reaches of the Yangzi River as well as the lower (more easterly) reaches of the Yellow River, while the Han ancestors expanded out from the upper reaches of the Yellow River, eventually defeating their eastern neighbors. A related account, told to me by historians of the Miao at the Central Nationalities Institute in 1982, portrays these rival "clans" as well-matched adversaries who fought long and hard; ultimately the Han ancestors under the legendary Yellow Emperor were victorious only by virtue of a trick. This kind of "egalitarian historiography" that eschews favoring any particular group and instead places them on a par spatially, temporally, and in terms of merit coincides with contemporary framings of the Chinese social order in which all ethnic groups are to occupy comparable legal and status positions. Accounts that have situated Miao origins in the Yellow River and Yangzi River territories are not limited, however, to recent Chinese writings (Yang 1993:xiii). Lebar (1964:63) cites sources that have them moving northward from the Yangzi toward the Yellow River basin in pre-Han times.

An Interest in History

Although the disjunctive origin theories summarized here would appear to be irreconcilable, a history that sequences them as phases in a gradual Miao dispersal has been proffered by Li Tinggui, a prominent Miao scholar and key author of the *Brief History*. When Li traveled to the United States in 1992, he answered refugee Hmong questions about their origins in a short speech on migrations. The account is one of diaspora, presenting a continuous ethnic group scattered across China and later the world by the vicissitudes of a 5,000-year history.[10]

Li claimed in an unequivocal assertion of priority that the Yellow River basin was first inhabited around 3000 B.C.E. by the Jiuli tribe, members of which he designates as ancestors of the Miao. This group was attacked by the nomadic Huangdi tribe that came from the west. After the Jiuli's defeat, members of the tribe fled to the middle and lower Yangzi River basin where they established the San Miao state together with southerners already living there. Then, around the twenty-first century B.C.E., the Huangdi tribe, which had continued as aggressors to the south, defeated the San Miao, causing them to scatter widely. Some San Miao went to present-day Qinghai and Mongolia, thus accounting for legends

of northern and western origins. Some went to what is now Hunan, Hubei, Jiangxi, and Anhui, thus accounting for claims of eastern origins.
This dispersal, Li suggested, explains the disparate subgroups among
the present-day Miao. After that time, Miao continually migrated south-
westward, with a major move into Southeast Asia following defeats in
rebellions of the eighteenth and nineteenth centuries. Beginning in 1975,
what Li calls their fourth major migration gave Miao/Hmong a global
presence as they were resettled as refugees in many Western countries
after the war in Vietnam and Laos.

Each of the five versions of the origin site recounted here can be linked,
if tenuously, to the contexts of historical recovery in which they were
produced. The impulse to articulate a clear alteric positioning between
Miao and what eventually came to be called the Han drives many of
these projects and can be understood as an artifact of twentieth-century
interethnic relations within and beyond China proper. In most cases, the
strategy on the part of scholars and other commentators was to tease
apart the complex stories of ethnic entanglements and transformations,
isolating a single thread as the Miao line and a different one as that of
the Han.

Taken together, the voices and versions presented here confound assessments of authority or validity. They cannot be straightforwardly
grouped into "camps" or "schools," but they emerge in their discontinuity as emblematic of the conflictual artifice that is historical production. I intermingle the positions of Miao, Han, and Western scholars to
show that these do not represent unified and distinct positionings. Particular historical spins cannot be consistently read off of fixed subject
positions such as "Han scholar," "Miao elite," "missionary," or "Hmong
émigré." Of course, identifiable politics inform these subject positions,
but, at the same time, they are in ongoing formulation, and the generation of historical accounts is part of that process. It is not surprising,
then, that the global diaspora eventually precipitated a recognition of
Miao/Hmong disunity over time and space, giving rise to an effort to
braid disparate origins back together, adding the dispersal out of Asia
into one intertwined narrative. We turn now to how cultural rather than
historical disunity has been handled in discursive production.

Nutshell Ethnology

By and large, the Miao and/or Hmong have been "known" in the West only in partial, capsulized form. In the early 1980s they inspired outpourings of aid and anticommunist sympathy when they were reported to be targets of "yellow rain" genocide undertaken by the Vietnamese in Laos.[11] The magazine *National Geographic* has showcased them a number of times during recent decades in features or in articles cataloguing ethnic groups in the China/Southeast Asia region (Garrett 1974; Moore 1951:464; Sherman 1988; White 1971:323; Williams 1935:518; Wong 1984). Marked by turbans and swaying pleated skirts, they have provided ornamental backdrop for adventure movies about mercenary armies and MIA rescues in Southeast Asia such as *Air America* (1990) and *Uncommon Valor* (1983). They received occasional mention—as opium traffickers and as China's victimized "barbarians"—in anthropologist Eric Wolf's compendium, *Europe and the People Without History* (1982:30, 53, 343), which aimed to decenter Europe and restore agency to those outside the grand European narrative. In Jared Diamond's ecological biohistory *Guns, Germs, and Steel* (1997:322–33), they make a cameo appearance as foils for the story of China's spatio-political unification. At the time of writing, both American medicine and American medical anthropology were buzzing with the impact of a journalist's book about the death of an epileptic Hmong girl in California at the hands of "the collision of [healing] cultures" (Fadiman 1997). Perhaps most striking was an event at London's Westminster Abbey in 1998, when it unveiled a refurbished exterior displaying ten new statues chosen to represent Christian martyrs of the twentieth century. Among them—representing all of Asia—was a Miao, Wang Zhiming, who had been killed during China's Cultural Revolution (personal communication, Alison Lewis, June 1999). Meanwhile, the colorful Hmong handicrafts have infiltrated, in tones muted for the bourgeois Western consumer, the living rooms of folk art lovers in metropolitan centers around the globe.

Likewise within China. Long branded as intransigent rebels, the Miao have loomed as figures of threat on China's ethnic frontier. Their resistance to Han domination has been woven with great regularity into the historiography of Han/non-Han encounters (Chen 1987:658). Accounts were regularly tinged with a fascinated exoticism. For centuries, the Miao, particularly Miao women, have been feared for their mastery of the so-called *gu* poison, which is said to inflict death from a distance with excruciating slowness (Clarke 1911:63; Diamond 1988; Eberhard 1982:83; Feng and Shryock 1935; Mickey 1947:61). In the seventeenth and eighteenth centuries, the Miao were canonized in the so-called "Miao albums," which purported to catalogue the array of different Miao "tribes" through the medium of paintings accompanied by cryptic notes on curiosities of custom.[12] During the Cultural Revolution, Miao were featured in a revolutionary opera about their liberation that played in major cities.[13] The designs of their much-acclaimed handiwork have made appearances in dominant culture through such various channels as its presentation as tribute to the Imperial Court (Mottin 1980:29–30) and, especially in the last decade, its increasingly standardized production for a growing market of urban Chinese consumers (Wang Yongyao 1989; Eitzen 1988:92–93). As of 1988, a rendition of a Miao "flying song" (*feige*) had even been worked into the musical soundtrack that entertains tourists over a PA system at the Great Wall outside Beijing, and an ornately headdressed Miao girl graced the face of the half-yuan bill.

These are the proverbial snapshots, the distilled images that give their receivers a sense that they know a little more about the world's cultural diversity. They are not troubled by complexities, by the Miao distribution over seven provinces in China and four countries in Southeast Asia, their division into subgroups with dialects and subdialects and costume styles too numerous to count.[14] By contrast much of the "ethnology" written about the Miao has undertaken to classify and organize this diversity. To do so, however, requires identifying and, in the process, fixing cultural units. In the following pages, I delve into how the cultural content of the Miao category has been variously filled, both by those who generalize about the whole group and by those who work with its tremendous internal variation. As in earlier sections, I emphasize a plurality of representational processes, examining the production of a cultural entity — the Miao — as a cacophonous process that extends well beyond conventional ethnography. My focus is on what is more appropriately termed "ethnology" and includes China's *minzuxue*, Western studies, missionary writings, accounts by Chinese and Western travelers and sojourners among the Miao, as well as general stereotyping practices.[15]

General Overviews Several sources both Chinese and Western, have produced thumbnail sketches of the Miao and Hmong, sometimes as entries in compendia of comparable attributes for parallel groups (Chen 1987:658; Diamond 1995:92–99; Donnelly 1994:19–47; Eberhard 1982: 82–86; Jenks 1994:29–36; Lebar 1964:63–81; Lewis 1984:100–133; Tapp 1986:11–18, 1989:16–21; Zhongguo Shaoshu Minzu 1981:444–57). The following account condenses their chief features, momentarily stabilizing an ethnic profile. Western sources include consideration of the Hmong of Southeast Asia. All writings map their distribution chiefly in Hunan, Guizhou, Yunnan, Guangxi, and Sichuan as well as in Vietnam, Laos, and Thailand. More recently, of course, their numbers in Western countries have swelled with the refugee diaspora.[16]

The tonal and monosyllabic Miao language, studies report, is fragmented into dialects (Strecker 1987), but overall it probably can be classified together with the so-called Yao (Mien) language as a branch of the Sino-Tibetan language group. Historically, no written form of the language exists, but missionaries and Chinese linguists have developed several scripts over the course of the twentieth century. All dialects are extremely complex phonologically (Matisoff 1983; Smalley, Vang, and Yang 1990:40–52) with a range of six to eight tones.

Miao everywhere, and by all reports, were agriculturalists, often tenants, and rarely landlords, except in Southeast Guizhou where they were more prosperous and more class-differentiated. They typically lived in small villages averaging ten to twenty households on mountain slopes remote from centers of Han settlement. In some places, village orientations were determined by geomancy, or *"feng shui."* Their houses were constructed of wood, stone, or mud brick, depending on location. Using either swidden or paddy methods, they grew a variety of grains, including wet and dry rice, maize, buckwheat, millet, barley, gaoliang, and wheat. Their diet was supplemented with the cultivation of potatoes, vegetables, beans, and rape (for oil), with eggs and tofu, with hunting, and with domestic chicken, fish, pork, and occasionally beef. Opium, tobacco, and liquor also were produced, and different regions boasted other trade products such as tung oil, lacquer, herbal medicines, wool, and, most importantly, timber. They manufactured their own clothes with homegrown cotton, hemp, indigo, and other natural dyes and with techniques of weaving, dyeing, embroidery, and batik.

Miao society was predominantly patrilineal and generally organized in terms of exogamous village/lineage units. A patronymic system was widespread with surnames, of which there were no more than ten or twenty in use, borrowed from the Chinese. These surname groups constituted clanlike structures, which for purposes of mutual aid and large-scale rituals occasionally superseded the otherwise local village and patrilineal political organization. In some areas neolocal and/or matrilocal residence was found, but patrilocal residence was the most common. Premarital sex and courtship were characteristic among the Miao in most places, and arranged marriage was primarily according to the right of priority of a girl's maternal uncle to marry her to his son. Courtship took place at markets and festivals in which a special site sometimes was found for mingling, dancing, or antiphonal singing. Bride-price and sometimes dowry were provided by parents, once they approved their children's choices of partners. In some places, delayed transfer marriage[17] was practiced, and divorce was acceptable, especially before the first child. Polygyny was uncommon, but not unknown. Inheritance was patrilineal, except for heirloom clothing and silver jewelry, which passed through the matriline.

Women, who never bound their feet, participated in most productive activities except plowing and hunting. They typically had a greater share in the family duties since they tended vegetable gardens, were often the ones who carried water, and did most of the household chores such as preparing food and washing clothes. Men did crafts such as silversmithing, woodworking, and basketry; women wove and decorated clothing. Childcare was shared. As a rule, men had higher status and more extensive roles in ritual activities, although elderly women were often honored in ritual, and women could become ritual experts such as shamans.

Miao religious practices comprised animistic, ancestor worship, and shamanistic elements. Animal sacrifice and other forms of propitiation were key parts of all these practices. For ceremonies and exorcisms, and sometimes depending on the nature of the occasion, ritual experts and shamans could be male or female, and they were skilled in incantations, animal sacrifice, and the manipulation of various objects. They were engaged for a variety of healing purposes as well as for life-cycle rituals. Other sorcerers, particularly women, operated surreptitiously in the practice of so-called *gu* witchcraft in which they controlled others through harm or the threat of harm inflicted by poisons gleaned from insects. In addition to these belief systems, a considerable (but never tallied) number of Miao had converted to Christianity beginning in the nineteenth century.

Festivals were abundant and differed widely by region, although the New Year was commonly of central importance. Everywhere the Miao *lusheng* or bamboo reed pipe organ was a key musical instrument along with drums, different horns and flutes, a kind of jew's harp, and a long tubular instrument called the *mantong*. Blowing through leaves also was widespread. Multiple genres of song were accompanied by numerous conventions for their social usages. Other activities at festivals included processional dancing, bullfights, horse races, cock and other bird fights, mountain climbing, ball tossing, and dragon boat races.

Clothing, perhaps the most noted aspect of Miao culture, was tremendously varied. The number of distinct costume styles, which have long been thought to be identical with distinct subgroups, is frequently estimated at fifty to one hundred. Subgroup names applied by observers often reflected features of dress such as Short Skirt Miao, Cowrie Shell Miao, or Pointed Headdress Miao. Five overarching categories simply designated salient costume colors: Black Miao, White Miao, Red Miao, Blue/Green Miao, and Flowery Miao. Costumes were made of cotton, hemp, wool, and some silk; they were dyed a variety of colors with an indigo blue-black being especially common. Other widespread features were the pleated skirt of varying lengths as well as leggings and aprons worn by the women, rich embroidery in geometric and representational patterns, painstakingly detailed batik work, silver ornamentation both on the costume and for jewelry and headdress, and elaborate techniques of styling and supplementing the hair with cloth, wood, and metal accessories. In many areas, men as well as women wore decorated clothing; the dress of young children and corpses received particular attention.

Debating Cultural Tropes

The above compendium presents certain "cultural traits" as definitive elements of Miao identity. Variations on the ground are rendered, in turn, as deviations from a norm. The struggle for a stable cultural definition has been repeatedly ruptured over time by voices of contestation that suggest rival versions and interpretations of what does and does not characterize the Miao. In the following subsections, I show how several of the prevailing stereotypes of the Miao and Hmong mask much more complex situations and debates.

Migrant Mountain Dwellers What does it mean to say of a group that they are "highlanders"? Do they live in the mountains by cultural propensity or because they are compelled to for political or ecological reasons? This problem has produced constant contention in representations of the Miao. The French missionary Jean Mottin wrote: "seek among the highest and most inaccessible mountains and there you will find them, for it is there they find themselves at home" (1980:10). The China anthropologist Morton Fried cites a source in which the Miao said of themselves: "As fish are to water and birds are to air, so the Miao are to the mountains" (1952:408).

Unequivocal assertions such as this one render the highland attribution immutable. But they still allow many possible explanations for the association between the Miao and the mountains. Several such explanations have been advanced, including the natural defenses that the mountains offer (Jenks 1994:34), and Miao genetic maladaptation to the disease-ridden lowlands (Bernatzik 1970:42). Savina (1923:174) was offered a number of explanations when he asked Miao for their own reasons; they suggested health issues, agricultural customs, a desire for ethnic endogamy, and a desire to keep a physical and cultural distance from lowlanders (also D'Orleans 1894:160). The Hmong scholar Yang Dao accepts several of these theories, concluding that defensibility, cool climate, and availability of land all attracted the Hmong ancestors to mountain locations (1993:xiv).

A version of far less voluntary highland settlement paints the Miao as victims of force and usurpation at the hands of the Han (Wiens 1954:73). "The poor Miao have been constantly pushed out of the little plots in the valleys . . . [and] are making their last stand in the mountain fastness, and a poor, beggarly lot they are," lamented a Western traveler in 1917 (Fritz 1981:37). The mountains to which they were driven, reported another Westerner at the turn of the twentieth century, were so precipitous that the Miao had had to "perform marvelous feats in the art of agriculture and irrigation" (Betts 1900–1901:87). A Miao folk tale also gave a variant of this position, recounting the Miao move to the mountains as the forced consequence of the legendary Jade Emperor (Yu Huang Da Di) orchestrating a flood to avert the potential power gained by a Miao man marrying a dragon's daughter (Xu 1985:204-5). Indeed, when an investigation team visited Miao villages in Yunnan in the 1950s, villagers told government representatives that they had lived in the flatlands before and that the Han had driven them to the mountains where they had experienced great hardship; their request was to be allocated land in the flatlands where they had formerly lived (Yunnan 1986:51). Fei Hsiao-t'ung encountered similar accounts among the Miao of Guizhou (1951:292).

The mountain-dwelling attribute also has been commonly coupled with the description of the Miao as "nomads" (Hudspeth 1922:703), or as "seminomadic," as reflected, for instance, in the title of the ethnography by cultural ecologist W. R. Geddes, *Migrants of the Mountains* (1976). Two types of migration are invoked here: large-scale diaspora and small-scale movement for shifting cultivation. Often at issue in these representations is the question of whether Miao movement is a matter of lifestyle or of exigency. Ma Xueliang, a prominent Han expert on the Miao, cites his translation of the phrase "Go to the West to seek a good life" in Miao historical legends as the basis for asserting that such movement was not prompted by class conflict or war (1983:6-7). Likewise, the use of swidden cultivation as an intractable productive mode has been given by many observers as the reason that the Miao, especially in more southwesterly locations, have continually changed their residence in response to soil exhaustion (Grandstaff 1979:70; Lewis 1984:120; Yang 1993:48; personal interviews in Beijing 1982). In contrast, others have argued that swidden agriculture, given land sufficient for adequate fallow periods, only periodically requires villages to pick up stakes and relocate, thus warranting the prefix "semi" before nomadic (Cooper 1984:1; Lee 1981:130). Still others point out that many Miao settlements are virtually permanent, as was my field site, Xijiang, relying on river valleys or elaborate mountain terraces for wet rice cultivation (deBeauclair 1970:82; Mickey 1947). That no one form of agriculture is definitive for the entire group is further suggested by Tapp's claim that Han officials historically classified the Miao as *sheng* (wild, raw) if they lived at higher elevations and practiced shifting cultivation and as *shu* (tame, cooked) if they were permanently settled in the lowlands and paid taxes

(1986:10). This claim is consistent with Thierry's assertion that for the Han sedentarization was the equivalent of civilization (1989:78).

Opium In Southeast Asia the Hmong have been dubbed the "opium people," a ubiquitous association not without its heavy stigma. Numerous Western articles and books link the group with opium (Bo 1975; Geddes 1970, 1976; Grandstaff 1979; Larteguy 1979; Tapp 1986). By contrast, opium goes virtually unmentioned in discussions of the Miao in Chinese sources. The disagreement occurs around whether they grew the plant for trade as well as around whether they used opium. Is the opium poppy an intrinsic element of Miao economy or culture? And, if so, how recent a phenomenon is it?

In China, earlier in the century, some observers felt that reluctant Miao had been forced to grow opium for sale by their Han landlords (Kemp 1921:166), while others categorically denied that it was grown or used by Miao at all (Mesny 1905:148-49). Clarke (1904:204) reported that they grew it but used it much less than the Han (also Pollard 1921:238 on Nosu). During the late Qing period and into the twentieth century, opium unquestionably was cultivated in Guizhou, even though the climate and soil apparently produced an inferior plant (Hosie 1890:25). After 1949, and to some extent before then (Mickey 1947:5), stringent government efforts succeeded in eradicating the opium poppy from the Chinese landscape, leaving only small pockets in border areas where it still may have been illegally produced (Geddes 1976:206). I saw no sign of it during my travels in Guizhou and Yunnan (1982-93).

Some observers who have written from a Southeast Asian perspective have defended the Hmong dependence on opium cultivation as economically mandated. They present it as an efficient and ecologically irreplaceable cash crop on which the Hmong in the face of increasing land scarcity have had no choice but to rely (Geddes 1976; Tapp 1989; Yang 1993:63). In addition to raising it for income, Lemoine (1972:91), Tapp (1986:22), and Yang (1993:65) documented its uses primarily for medicinal purposes, and Cooper (1984:xix) and Westermeyer (1982:129-31) found significant numbers of addicts. Clearly, situations of external demand, not the least of which were the Opium Wars in China (Grandstaff 1979:72) and the opium trafficking that supported the CIA's secret war in Laos during the Vietnam War (Bo 1975:75; Feingold 1970:339) had a great deal to do with the extent of Miao/Hmong involvement with the drug. The ebbs and flows of their relationship with opium—both its cultivation and its use—defy attempts to meld it with cultural identity in any static way.

Rebellious by Character Many sketches have been made of what might be described a Miao "national character," pointing to collections of personal traits and emotional dispositions attributed to the group as a whole. In their many characterizations by Westerners, the Miao have been painted as "passionate, easily offended, suspicious, revengeful, brave, and indifferent to hunger and cold" (Edkins 1870:74), as "friendly and hospitable" (Betts 1900–1901:104), as "a very lovable people, quick to recognize right and wrong, kind and gentle in their association with one another, buoyant and joyous, and at times industrious almost beyond belief" (Crisler 1937:51-52), as "much given to litigation" (Clarke 1907:258), and as "warlike, frank, lawless, primitive, openhearted, opposed to trading and city life" (Kemp 1921:177). Miao self-description and recent mainstream Chinese portrayals have emphasized other attributes, equally as reified. In one rendition, they are considered to have common psychological qualities (*gongtong xinli suzhi*) such as being "warmhearted and forthright" (*reqing haoshuang*), "loving and pursuing freedom" (*re'ai he zhuiqiu ziyou*), having a strong "pioneer spirit and the ability to live on their own" (*kaituo jingshen yu ziwo shengcun nengli*) (Yang 1989:19). Fei Hsiao-t'ung praised their willingness to labor, calling them "*qinlao de Miaozu*" (the hardworking Miao) (1988:31) as well as "*ke ai de*" (likable, lovely) (1988:36).

All attributions of peaceful warmheartedness have done little to counterbalance one of the characterizations most frequently attached to the Miao—that of their intrinsically rebellious and warlike nature. The most large-scale and well-documented "Miao rebellions" in modern history were in 1735–40, 1795–1806, and 1854–72, but many other incidents have been read overwhelmingly as stemming from ethnic conflict. Mesny, accompanying a Han general in a Guizhou stronghold against the so-called "Miaozi" in 1905, sensationalizes hills "black with the enemy" (1905:247) and the intense Miao desire for scalps to "take home as proof of their prowess" (1905:88). The Miao entry in a 1980s mainland *Dictionary of Ethnic Groups* mentions the resistance of the western Hunan Miao to the "oppression of the Guomindang reactionaries" in a 1936–38 uprising (Chen 1987:658). The romantic image of a long history of resistance to outside domination has been simultaneously attractive for Miao self-representation as ethnically viable (Liu 1988:160–65), for Westerners concerned with political issues of ethnic autonomy, and for a Chinese Communist history that valorizes peasant uprisings in a meta-narrative of class struggle (Litzinger 1995; Wang 1979:179).

Meanwhile, countervailing representations dissociate the Miao and rebelliousness, stressing their peace-loving character. In my conversations with Miao scholar Li Tinggui he repeatedly protested that one of the Miao "psychological qualities" is a deep love of peace (re'ai heping). Similarly, the U.S.-based Hmong scholar Yang Dao describes his people as "generally peaceable but with a wild, proud spirit of independence" (1993:xiii). Westerners, too, have troped them as "peace-loving" (Gamewell 1919:807) when they were not reproducing the Miao reputation for being "bellicose" warriors (Davies 1909:371; Gourdon 1931:92).

Another counter to the stereotype of Miao rebelliousness can be found in revisionist historiography that interprets the so-called Miao uprisings over the centuries as less ethnically defined than their name would suggest. This is the implicit if not explicit message of mainland accounts that reframe an array of historical conflicts in terms of class struggle (Li and Huang 1982). Consistent with minority policy of the Maoist era, these accounts present historically continuous peoples acting in concert against class oppression over the long process of their social evolution toward modernity. In a related vein, American historian Robert Jenks (1994), who examined sources concerning the protracted "Miao Rebellion" of 1854–72, finds evidence of solidarity among Han, Miao, and other minorities whose experience of land expropriation, excessive taxation, and other forms of socioeconomic oppression led them to oppose the government: "grievances, which are a normal part of life, often act indirectly on the incidence of social conflict by enhancing the solidarity and potential for mobilization of different social formations" (1994:168). Jenks's argument was that the rebels in the uprisings were by no means limited to the Miao, that even Han participated when prompted by poverty. Furthermore, he asserts, Qing authorities, well aware of the multiethnic character of the conflicts, still labeled them as "Miao" in official historiography so that "the stigma of having rebelled and caused vast destruction and misery was attached squarely to the Miao and not the Han" (1994:4). Here, once again, the malleability of the content of the Miao category is foregrounded.[18]

From *Gu* to Goods: Troping Miao Women

Although the attributes of the purportedly homogeneous Miao have had the appearance of timelessness, they have undergone considerable changes, along with the vicissitudes of Miao relations to different neighbors, observers, and rulers. The figure of the Miao woman, always subject to forms of scrutinizing gaze, is a revealing index of these transformations. In earlier centuries, Miao women, in the eyes of the Han and other dominant groups, had been the focus of a widely denigrated gender transgression, according to which barbarism was contrasted with Chinese civilization. Their unbound feet and scanty dress represented a kind of bodily excess, which, coupled with courtship mores of permissible premarital sexual play, signified an unconstrained and perhaps too seductive sexuality. Unbound feet also indicated a blurriness in the gender division of labor, with women engaging in hunting and agriculture alongside men. Too much license for young women to court their own marriage partners also meant a deviation from the strictures of arranged marriage by which the social fabric was to be kept intact.

Miao women were especially feared by the Chinese for their ability to manipulate, bring sickness, and cause death to people through the famed *gu* poison. In one of the best-known methods, crafty Miao women put venomous insects in a jar, stored it in the dark, and removed it to find a single insect that had eaten all the others whose body could then be ground into a lethal poison. It was used for purposes revolving around sexuality—seduction, revenge for infidelity, control of sexual partners—and Han harbored ample lore about the dangers of Miao women using it on them. Anthropologist Norma Diamond (1988), who reviewed evidence that *gu* was actually traceable to the Han, suggests that such lore was prompted by a need to enforce ethnic boundaries in light of the scandalous sexual and gender mores of the Miao and the fear that intermarriage or sexual relations with their women would mean irrevocable contamination. In an insightful analysis, Diamond (1988) addressed the problem of the danger surrounding minority sexuality and marriage practices through an examination of Han allegations of Miao women's use of magic poison. Diamond suggests that the power attributed to Miao women to cause illness and even death through *gu* poison sorcery was a projection of the fear held by Han Chinese of the perceived strength and relative freedom in Miao women's gender roles. This strength and relative freedom profoundly threatened the Confucian moral order, which already saw Han women as dangerous because of their liminal status as those who moved, through marriage, between competitive or hostile lineages (Potter 1990: 252–54). The threat implied by outside women marrying in was compounded by the fact that during the Ming and Qing dynasties large numbers of male migrants and demobilized soldiers who had been sent to suppress Miao rebellions had settled in the southwest provinces. In the absence of Han women, they depended on the Miao and other non-Han for marriage partners, making the maintenance of a "safe" distance impossible (see Sutton n.d.). A few stories of poison potency constructed by the Han in this context continue today. They are a kind of mythmaking generated by attempts to resolve a highly contradictory relationship in which the "other" woman's attractiveness and sexual availability also constitute her danger.

The *gu* fear has diminished in contemporary times (although some Miao villagers I spoke with still affirmed the potency of *gu*), yielding to other more pacified imagings. Now, Miao women are celebrated most often for the beauty rather than the impropriety of their clothing (cf. Lam 1985; Ma 1981; Reilly 1987; Zhao 1985). As we will see, the ornately costumed Miao woman has become a widely circulated symbol of ethnic otherness, now rendered in a consumable, unthreatening, and even desirable form. This more celebratory spin began under Maoism as a vehicle for presenting unity in difference through the image of a diversely costumed throng of nationalities smiling as they marched toward socialism. As the pleasures of consuming ethnic color have intersected with the logics of the market, especially under the 1980s economic liberalization policies, an assortment of actors have worked vigorously to commodify the handicrafts produced by Miao and other minority women for sale to domestic consumers and international tourists (cf. Schein 1985; Wang Yongyao 1989). This commodification and a burgeoning quantity of publishing on ethnic costume (cf. Guizhou Nationalities Affairs 1987; Liu 1981; Lu 1981; Ma 1986; Rossi 1986, 1987, 1988; Shanghai Museum 1999; Yang 1982) have augmented the visibility of the Miao woman as "colorful," not only in dress, but also in custom. As will be seen in chapter 3, the effects of this kind of celebration also act in subtle ways to crystallize who the Miao are and how they are to be related to the dominant society.

Fashioning Essence: What Markers Matter?

So far in this chapter I have made two points. First, external definitions of who the Miao are, despite their manifold contradictions, have a considerable authority in the ongoing process of identity formation. Second, the Miao because of historical circumstances and cultural-political ambience, have embraced some of these definitions in a dialogic accommodation with the modes by which they were typified. The defining of the Miao is not reducible to a form of knowledge/power in which external agents script and draw the boundaries of Miao identity for them. Studies of representations of the Miao from the Qing period and earlier (Hostetler 1995; Diamond 1995) are necessarily constrained by the limits of historical documentary evidence to emphasize the imposition of authoritative versions onto social existence. But ethnography is positioned both to come to terms with the edifice of discursive authority and to entertain the imperfect and always incomplete project of subject-making. Recent studies (Cheung 1996; Gladney 1991; Harrell 1995b; Litzinger 2000; Rudelson 1997) have been able to chart more carefully the roles that minority elites themselves play in crafting authoritative discourse. What emerges is a complex field in which Miao and non-Miao, within China and beyond, orchestrate versions of an entity called the Miao amid contradictory views and diversity on the ground.

In this section I sketch some of the main characteristics that Miao people considered to be the markers of their ethnic identity in the 1980s and 1990s. This picture is necessarily partial, focusing on what the Miao whom I encountered thought were their defining attributes; hence, it privileges Southeast Guizhou and the subgroup of Miao that call themselves Hmu. While not necessarily unique to the Miao, such features were taken by many of them to be constitutive elements of their ethnic self-definition. As components of ethnic identity, they were characteristically tagged as *"women minzu xiguan"* (our ethnic customs) or *"women minzu chuantong"* (our ethnic traditions), revealing the imprint of their typifications during the Maoist and post-Mao years. Yet they only partially coincided with the tropes by which dominant representations typed them.

Lusheng Many Miao considered the bamboo reed pipe instrument called the *lusheng* to be the symbol of their people. Although it varied greatly in its form, size, and conventions for use, its symbolic importance was central. The *lusheng* carries an aura of venerability and sacredness, and its use was strictly regulated by customary law. In some places it was played only by men, and in others women played it as well. Its uses varied, ranging from courtship to funerals, from festival celebrations to summoning soldiers to war. In many places its music was accompanied by specific forms of dance, usually sedately processional, but sometimes acrobatic. Those initiated into the instrument's secrets were said to be able to understand a special language contained in its music.[19] So potent was its cultural and communicative function that *lusheng* use was suppressed in many historical periods, including the Guomindang era and the Cultural Revolution. One expert player told me that the *lusheng* was revered to such an extent that if one fell while holding it, one should break the fall by risking one's body to keep the instrument intact.

Conventions of Sociality Miao villagers especially, and Miao urbanites as well, felt that the etiquette surrounding socializing, guesting, hosting, and feasting was of critical importance in who they were. These conventions, particularly visible on such ritual occasions as weddings and funerals, also applied to almost any occasion in which participants beyond the immediate household gathered to dine. Hospitality and food etiquette, of course, have been seen as crucial cultural elements for most of China's ethnic groups, including the Han. It was the particular forms of Miao sociality that they considered to be definitive. Among these were highly codified norms of reciprocity, offering food with bare hands and drink with two hands, improvised singing back and forth between hosts and guests, and copious amounts of drinking.

Drinking Almost all of the Miao villagers whom I knew (with the exception of those who had been Christianized) emphasized the canonically prescribed consumption of alcohol as an immutable Miao trait. Most commonly imbibed were *baijiu,* which was home-brewed or factory-produced grain liquor with a high alcohol content. People also

4. *"Jiaobei."* Exchanging drinks at a wedding.

purchased beer and fruity, carbonated alcoholic sodas for special occasions. Offering home-brews was the most honorable; a common inducement to drink was the hosts' proclamation that what was being offered was *"wo jia mijiu"* (my homemade rice wine). Etiquette dictated that a host's responsibility was to urge guests to drink as much as possible; drunkenness, for such social occasions, was without stigma, even if inebriation reached the point of vomiting or loss of consciousness. Men and women drank equal amounts, with a slight lessening of obligation for pregnant women. It was not uncommon for women to drink together, independent of men. Women's copious use of alcohol, I was told with prideful bravado, was a key distinguishing feature of the Miao.

In Xijiang, intricate conventions governed alcohol use, and a breach of protocol was a serious social offense. Drinking alone, whether by oneself or in the presence of others, was particularly frowned on, for drinking was associated with offering or exchange. Several forms were favored such as a cross-offering called *jiaobei,* in which two people held cups of liquor to each others' lips and then drank simultaneously. Commonly, the presentation of a drink was preceded by a song of welcome or gratitude on the part of hosts or guests. The songs were characteristically self-effacing and suffused with warm emotion for the recipient, thus making it virtually mandatory that the drink be taken in good humor. A ubiquitous technique for increasing the recipient's intake was a double offering in quick succession justified by the phrase "it takes two legs to walk." It was acceptable for a guest to withdraw from a wine-soaked feast, but only by certain prescribed forms of subterfuge such as feigning total drunkenness or claiming to go to the outhouse and failing to return to the table. Stating that one declined to drink any more was tantamount to rupturing the good feeling established between guest and host.

Song In addition to drinking songs (*jiuge*), Miao in Southeast Guizhou had several forms of song that they considered crucial aspects of their cultural lore. Chief among these were *feige* (flying songs), which were improvised and used for communication and to ameliorate boredom when peasants were working in the mountains. Songs would be cast across valleys from mountain peak to mountain peak as individuals entered into sung dialogues. Although I almost never observed such singing in practice, many Miao whom I met insisted that *feige* was a musical form central to their identity. Likewise for the *duige* (dialogue songs) used for courtship on festival occasions. This form of antiphonal singing, which could take place only after nightfall, entailed groups of boys facing groups of girls and exchanging verses filled with longing, intimate suggestion, and natural imagery. They were regarded as key vehicles for the eventual selection of marriage partners.

Costume Ethnic dress was everywhere of primary importance for Miao identity. Although costume styles differed widely and were critical in signifying distinctions between subgroups, the degree of skill and some of the techniques used were uniformly treasured by all Miao. Chief among these were the use of tremendously detailed, minute, and varied embroidery stitches to adorn costumes of men, children, and especially women. Costumes for special occasions were cherished, painstakingly stored, and passed down from generation to generation. Silver ornaments were likewise considered a hallmark of Miao costume, and they have been the way in which families stored their wealth and passed it on to younger generations. Distinctive styles of grooming hair (often determined by age grades and marital status) were cited, and a great deal of energy went into choices about public appearances.

Many other Miao features could be catalogued, such as their language, their legends and stories, their customary law, specific features of their rituals, their reverence for ancestors, trees, stones, bridges, and mountains, etc. But none had the public symbolic force of the features I have described. One task in the following chapters will be to explore the cultural politics that accounted for the emergence of such specific hallmarks of Miao identity.

Making the Nation, Fixing the *Minzu*

The effort to stabilize the Miao as an historically continuous and culturally homogeneous entity is a project that has its own history. Two twentieth-century movements have pushed it to prominence as the salient mode for apprehending ethnic diversity. Within China, the effort on the part of the People's Republic to make its populace not only governable, but also representable in self-governing, meant that it was imperative to isolate distinct units in a manageable quantity with which the state could transact affairs. These national imperatives departed from the frontier sensibility that prevailed, even as the Qing imperium gained closer and closer control of non-Han territories, a sensibility that had given rise to the "Miao albums" form of classification and generated a seemingly unlimited profusion of splinter groups and costume styles, of myriad and disjunctive customs. Whereas the modern nation-state was about the inclusion and even-handed administration of predictable and quantifiable parallel units, what it had superseded was a notion of empire in which dominion was always being negotiated at the ragged and unruly fringe.[20]

Even as the People's Republic was systematizing its peoples, Western anthropology saw the rise of systematized aggregation projects such as the Human Relations Area Files, established in 1949, in which fragments of disparate data were collated to provide a more comprehensive picture of the world's cultures.[21] Working outside China, with firsthand knowledge of the Hmong in Southeast Asia who were much more internally homogeneous, Western scholars struggled to produce a unity and a genealogy for this otherwise ungraspable collection of peoples. Both within and beyond China, Miao and Hmong had active roles in these projects, and their sense of ethnic fixity was shaped by the minoritization processes inherent in the system of cleanly demarcated multiethnic states that was replacing more colonial types of relationship. The suturing of official discourses of identity to particular ethnic subjects, however, remains an unfinished project. The nuances by which the Miao category gets embedded in contemporary social life remain to be explored.

3

Making *Minzu*

The State, the Category, and the Work

The Soviet Government of China recognizes the right of self-determination of the national minorities in China, their right to complete separation from China, and to the formation of an independent state for
each national minority. All Mongolians, Tibetans, Miao, Yao, Koreans,
and others living on the territory of China shall enjoy the full right to
self-determination.
— Constitution of the Soviet Republic, Jiangxi, November 1931

Each national autonomous area is an inseparable part of the People's
Republic of China. . . . The People's Republic of China will become
a big fraternal and cooperative family composed of all its nationalities
(*minzu*).
— Common Program of the Chinese People's Political Consultative
Conference, Beijing, September 1949

Miaozu is one of China's largest minority nationalities. Over several
thousand years, they have had a long history, a wide dispersal, a rich
and colorful culture, and a rebellious nature that is strong and world-
renowned.
— *Miaozu Jianshi* (*Brief History of the Miao*)

The Maoist period beginning in 1949 instituted a homogeneous national
system that spread to the very limits of the hard boundary that now defined the territory of China. It was the end point of a process — begun in
the geopolitics of the nineteenth century — of creating a national space

out of a dynastic one. As Benedict Anderson describes this distinction: "In the modern conception, state sovereignty is fully, flatly, and evenly operative over each square centimetre of a legally demarcated territory. But in the older imagining, where states were defined by centres, borders were porous and indistinct, and sovereignties faded imperceptibly into one another" (1983:19). No longer offering secession as a mode of (dis)engagement with the Chinese central state — as the above brief quotations reveal — Maoism instead strove to create state subjects out of the diverse peoples who had been unevenly governed for centuries.

What does it mean to create state subjects? The process was more complicated than the exaction of submission by a coercive state. For one thing, there were distinct ways of being folded into the state; the non-Han were to interact on the basis of their ethnic difference. They were slotted into discrete categories equipped with specific sets of rights and forms of representation. When instated, official categories sometimes clashed with peoples' experiences of their ethnic identity. But the story of this chapter is how these categories, through the articulation of state and non-Han peoples' practices, became significant dimensions of ethnic agency.

Population figures reveal in numerical terms the import of the Miao category, for they increase dramatically in the half-century since 1949. Whereas, in 1965, 2.68 million Miao were counted, by 1978 there were 3.92 million, a number that jumped dramatically with the comprehensive census of 1982, when 5.02 million identified as Miao. Most striking, however, was what ensued in the post-Mao era, for by the next comprehensive census only eight years later, the people identifying themselves as Miao had increased half again to 7.4 million. The expanded number, even allowing for lenient implementation of birth planning policies, can be explained only as a wave of reclassification in which persons previously identified as Han converted to Miao status, a trend that obtained for many minority categories (see Table of Populations). What kind of history, policy, and practice accounts for the remarkable swelling of minority population figures within the categories of identification offered by the state? My contention in this chapter is that we need to think in terms of a lengthy process in which state designations became irrevocably entangled with non-Han subjectivities.

Table of the Populations of Chinese Nationalities in the 1980s

Nationality	1982 Census (Population)	1990 Census (Population)	Growth Rate (%)
Total	1,008,175,288	1,133,682,501	12.45
Han	940,880,121	1,042,482,187	10.80
Mongolian	3,416,881	4,806,849	40.68
Hui	7,227,022	8,602,978	19.04
Tibetan	3,874,035	4,593,330	18.57
Uygur	5,962,814	7,214,431	20.99
Miao	5,036,377	7,398,035	46.89
Yi	5,457,251	6,572,173	20.43
Zhuang	13,388,118	15,489,630	15.70
Bouyei	2,122,389	2,545,059	19.91
Korean	1,766,439	1,920,597	8.73
Manchu	4,304,160	9,821,180	128.18
Dong	1,426,335	2,514,014	76.26
Yao	1,403,664	2,134,013	52.03
Bai	1,132,010	1,594,827	40.88
Tujia	2,834,732	5,704,223	101.23
Hani	1,059,404	1,253,952	18.36
Kazak	908,414	1,111,718	22.38
Dai	840,590	1,025,128	21.95
Li	818,255	1,110,900	35.76
Lisu	480,960	574,856	19.52
Va	298,591	351,974	17.88
She	368,832	630,378	70.91
Gaoshan	1,549	2,909	87.80
Lahu	304,174	411,476	35.28
Shui	286,487	345,993	20.77
Dongxiang	279,397	373,872	33.81
Naxi	245,154	278,009	13.40
Jingpo	93,008	119,209	28.17
Kirgiz	113,999	141,549	24.17
Tu	159,426	191,624	20.20
Daur	94,014	121,357	29.08
Mulam	90,426	159,328	76.20
Qiang	102,768	198,252	92.91

Table of the Populations of Chinese Nationalities in the 1980s (*cont.*)

Nationality	1982 Census (Population)	1990 Census (Population)	Growth Rate (%)
Bulang	58,476	82,280	40.71
Salar	69,102	87,697	26.91
Maonan	38,135	71,968	88.72
Gelo	53,802	437,997	714.09
Xibe	83,629	172,847	106.68
Achang	20,441	27,708	35.55
Pumi	24,237	29,657	22.36
Tajik	26,503	33,538	26.54
Nu	23,166	27,123	17.08
Uzbek	12,453	14,502	16.45
Russian	2,935	13,504	360.10
Ewenki	19,343	26,315	36.04
Deang	12,295	15,462	25.76
Bonan	9,027	12,212	35.28
Yugur	10,569	12,297	16.35
Jing	11,995	18,915	57.69
Tatar	4,127	4,873	18.08
Drung	4,682	5,816	24.22
Oroqen	4,132	6,965	68.56
Hezhen	1,476	4,245	187.60
Moinba	6,248	7,475	19.64
Lhoba	2,065	2,312	11.96
Jinuo	11,974	18,021	50.50
Other unidentified nationalities	881,838	749,341	
Foreigners of Chinese citizenship	4,842	3,421	

Source: *Beijing Review* 33 (52) (December 24–30, 1990):34.

Subject Formation in a Differentiated Nation Space

The Maoist period pursued a firm-handed sociopolitical incorporation of the non-Han that departed significantly from earlier eras. In the first half of the twentieth century, especially during the Republican period (1911–49), the edges of the nation had been continued to be thought of as borderlands (*bianjiang*), vast territories—60 percent of China by Deal's (1979:33) account—in which non-Chinese were insufficiently subdued. Because of the political and infrastructural limitations on policy implementation, however, "minorities affairs, like most other aspects of government, were left to the provinces to handle as they saw fit" (Dreyer 1976:15–16). Despite this ongoing independence of border provinces from central control (cf. Moseley 1973:31), the program was one of assimilation to dominant Han culture, of concerted efforts to make Chinese out of as many of the non-Han as possible through practices of cultural suppression and sinification. Republican leader Sun Yat-sen prescribed: "We must facilitate the dying out of all names of individual peoples inhabiting China, i.e. Manchus, Tibetans, etc. . . . unit[ing] them in a single cultural and political whole" (in Dreyer 1976:16). Place-names in non-Han areas were given new Chinese versions, and people were encouraged to adopt Han surnames (Deal 1979:34). Miao women had their topknots cut off and their pleated skirts shredded by Republican troops; Ge women in Guizhou recalled having their red headdresses removed and fastened to dog's heads (Cheung 1996:70). Meanwhile, the opening of roads to minority areas brought cholera and more aggressive tax collection (Dreyer 1976:32). Han immigration to and appropriation of minority lands were supported by the government.

The assimilationist effort underwent a marked shift in the People's Republic era. The country was to be unified, but not—as in the Republican era—in terms of a movement toward an ever more singular Chineseness. Now the right to secession, promised in the 1931 Constitution before the communists had come to power, had become practically unthinkable. Instead, the state that Chinese Communist leaders envisioned was *multinational*, made up of an agglomeration of culturally distinct and politically legitimate units. Unity was to be effected through the reorganization of production and the standardization of social policy, not through the suppression of cultural difference. Although there were extended periods in which cultural difference was in fact suppressed, the overarching vision was one of creating solidarity out of protected forms of diversity. And this goal meant the establishment of certain permissible forms of difference, together with the occlusion of all other sorts of unruly heterogeneity.

Chapter 2 explored how historiography and ethnology, both broadly construed, produced representations that fixed Miao identity in terms of cultural content and relations to others. Taken together, such representations, in their contradictory multiplicity, had the effect of troubling any homogeneous Miao identity by exposing its fragmented and contested nature. This chapter also describes the production of Miao identity, but it differs in that it explores a much more unitary discursive practice in which the Miao and China's other ethnic groups were framed and organized by the classificatory theories and policies of the post-1949 Chinese government. Here, we are dealing with a far more clear-cut (though not monolithic) agency and a progressively more unified content. It was a process in which the production of a distinct form of multinational nationalism resulted in the shaping of ethnicity in favor of legitimately recognized formats. These formats, and their effects on the subjectivity of those they defined, can be thought of as a kind of interpellation.[1] We can think of this process as one in which the terms of social existence became set in such a way that to figure within the Chinese polity meant to assume the ethnic form that the state had designated, not to exceed or resist it. This process is not repressive but productive, one that calls — or in Althusser's words, "hails" — selves into being. Butler points to the link between hailing and subjection: "Social categories signify subordination and existence at once. . . . Subjection exploits the desire for existence, where existence is always conferred from elsewhere; it marks a primary vulnerability to the Other in order to be" (1997:20–21).

What the People's Republic put in place, in a political form unprecedented for China, was a seamless and saturated social field of the nation. This system produced a subjection marked by duality; not a simple subordination to central rule, but a formation of new kinds of subjectivity that inhered in one's insertion into a social order of national multiethnicity. Here, literary critic Homi Bhabha's formulation of nation-making resonates: "The scraps, patches and dregs of daily life must be repeatedly turned into the signs of a coherent national culture, while the very act of the narrative performance interpellates a growing circle of national subjects" (1994:145).

I begin by sketching PRC economic policy toward the minority regions of the southwest, followed by a history of official minority policy in conjunction with an account of how minorities were imaged in different periods. I then turn to a more subjective focus, describing one career that illustrates the state-designated practice of nationalities work (*minzu gongzuo*), and finally discuss some of the effects of policy on minorities' self-identification. These sections offer a sense of the scope of the theory-policy-discursive field in which Miao subjects pursued cultural production—the subject of Part II.

Resources and Capital: The Southwest, Guizhou, and the Miao in State Economic Designs

David Goodman (1983), a Chinese politics specialist, has described the early years of the People's Republic as a period of "internal colonization." Markedly different from the uneven and contentious governance of the frontier in Qing and Republican times, the center made an unprecedented effort toward normalization and incorporation." [2] At the outset, policy was gradualist, allowing for regionally specific strategies of development. What Guizhou presented was a poverty-ridden land, with a history of violent conflict with government authorities, inhabited at the time of liberation by 60 percent non-Han peoples (Moser 1985:96). Land reform—the seizure of land from landlords and its more equitable redistribution among farming households—was implemented in minority areas but it was begun only in 1955 and proceeded at a slower pace than in other parts of the southwest. In Guizhou, industrialization was delayed while the province was aided in increasing food production; by 1954–55 it not only had attained self-sufficiency in grain, but had even begun to export it to other provinces (Goodman 1983:116). At almost all levels the appointed leaders were indigenous.

In 1957 the "internal colonization" of Guizhou took a more stringent turn as a new approach calling for more uniform development was adopted after the Third Plenum of the Eighth Central Committee of the Communist Party. Now Guizhou was to industrialize at a rate comparable to other provinces. The central government began making sizable

5. Plowing rice terraces on Xijiang's hillside.

investments in the province to build up its mineral extraction infrastructure, especially to supply iron ore and coal to the already industrialized metropolis of Chongqing in Sichuan. This program of rapid industrialization was closely linked with a defense policy referred to as the "Third Line" (*San Xian*) that was established in 1964 and continued through the 1970s. A spatially designated region in the interior was to constitute China's Third Line of defense after the vulnerable eastern seaboard (the First Line) and an intermediate buffer belt (the Second Line) (Kirkby and Cannon 1989:8). Railroads were laboriously built over the precipitous mountains to connect Sichuan, Guizhou, and Yunnan provinces while the government allocated tremendous resources to the buildup of key sectors such as the nuclear industry, metallurgy, aerospace and aviation, electronics, chemical engineering, and machine-building (Kirkby and Cannon 1989:9–10). In this initiative, Sichuan and Guizhou were the two most important provinces.[3] Meanwhile, Miao and other peasants residing amid these grandiose projects continued to scratch out grain from steep terraces or mountain slopes, most of them living on the edge of hunger in roadless villages without electricity. The wage work offered by the growth of industry was negligible to them. Although the scale of defense industrialization involved a work force of 16 million and occupied as much as one-third of the total state payroll in the mid-1960s, a pittance of that income went to locals. Instead, most of the labor force was imported from other parts of the country (Oakes 1998:109-10).

The state's designs on Guizhou as a site for military-industrial buildup, then, despite the intensive investment of central funds, were of dubious benefit to Miao and other minority peasants concentrated in the region. Indeed, some have argued that it only impoverished them further, the province having been transformed into a giant extractive industry built on the exploitation of resources and peasants in order to accumulate mineral wealth (coal, iron ore, aluminum, manganese, phosphorous, iron, sulfur, and gold) and to bolster an expanding national defense apparatus (Goodman 1983; Oakes 1999). While in effect in the 1960s and 1970s, the *San Xian* project put a massive 200 billion yuan into 29,000 state enterprises across the region (Kirkby and Cannon 1989:9). Agriculture was left to stagnate: grain production decreased, and Guizhou became increasingly dependent on central financial assistance. State sector investments throughout the Maoist periods strongly favored industry to the neglect of agriculture, but whereas the years from 1950 to 1957 had seen 80 percent of funds directed toward heavy and light industry, the *San Xian* period of 1958 to 1978 tilted the balance much further in favor of industry. Only 580 million yuan were invested in agriculture over those years compared to 8,571 million yuan for industrial projects, a ratio of 15:1 (Oakes 1998:113).

Returning to Goodman's (1983) analysis, the post-1957 Maoist period was one in which Guizhou's integration with the Chinese state was consolidated in the structural form of internal colonialism. Relations of economic dependency became ossified, and the province's economy was increasingly organized around a single productive endeavor—that of the extraction of mineral resources for the nation's industry. Leadership of the province had come to be dominated by party officials appointed from outside, and few if any minorities were in positions of top leadership. In this internal periphery, marginal to the development schemes that organized the national economic scene, peasants and workers were to labor ceaselessly, while the state compensated them with fewer and fewer social services and forms of aid.

The reform era inaugurated by Deng Xiaoping in 1978 saw still other configurations of Miao territory. Decollectivization of agricultural and industrial production meant a return to household farming for Miao peasants under what was called the "responsibility" system. This was a welcome change, which increased grain outputs, but it was not without consequences. As the national economy raced toward integration with the global capitalist system, inflation soared and Miao peasants, facing an ever-widening gap between their meager cash flow and the fast-paced big-money privatized national economy, were left to their own devices for making do. The nationwide call to advance China's modernization by getting rich through private ventures was unattainable for the vast majority of Miao peasants: they lacked the resources for start-up, their regions were relatively isolated from transport making export difficult if not impossible, and the land was only amenable to a handful of cash crops such as fruit, tea, or tobacco. The Special Economic Zones established along the coast courted foreign investors with tax breaks, reduction of red tape and other incentives, leaving other areas to vie for foreign funds at a sharp disadvantage (Phillips and Yeh 1989). By 1987 the disparities were striking as evidenced in figures for foreign investments in China: the coastal sector accounted for 92 percent of the total, while the western region accounted for only 2.6 percent and Guizhou for only .22 percent (Yang 1990:248).[4]

Meanwhile, the province itself, limping along under the withdrawal of central funds and questing after glitzy joint ventures with foreign firms, made matters worse for Miao peasants. In the decade from 1984 through 1994, the central state's contribution to Guizhou's total budget had already dropped from 47 percent to 30 percent. But the 1990s saw an even more precipitous decline in forms of state assistance to the province. Whereas in 1992 only 48 percent of fixed capital investments had to be financed by the province rather than Beijing, that number had increased to 70 percent by 1995 (Oakes 1999:43). The province transferred the burden to county governments, which, in turn, struggling to meet their remittance quotas to the province, withheld salaries and invented new fees and surcharges to exact from rural households.

Over the course of the post-Mao period, then, the central government increasingly abandoned less affluent peasants as well as redistributive policies in general. The overwhelmingly dominant discourse of modernization scripted economic policies based on competition and market logics, which especially in the absence of anything like a level playing field, insured that the Miao would be consigned to exacerbated poverty and to the stigma of backwardness. In the 1990s, two of Guizhou's most profitable products—liquor and tobacco—were subjected to increasingly heavy taxes, more and more of the revenues from which were hoarded by the central government rather than going to the provincial government. In a feeble effort to compensate rural regions for their multiple forms of disadvantage under reform policies, the state in 1980 established a Fund to Aid the Development of Underdeveloped Regions. The effects were minimal, however, since only 0.38 of the central state budget went to the fund from 1980 through 1986, and this money was spread over 60 percent of China's counties (Ferdinand 1989:46). Moreover, in an attempt to encourage "people in poor areas to form 'economic entities, service organizations and enterprises' so that they will be able to 'shake off poverty' and have a stable income later on" (Yang 1990:243), the funds were disbursed in the form of low-interest loans for the start-up of small businesses rather than the traditional relief money that had been directed at alleviating the conditions of poverty in these regions (Yang 1990:243). For Miao peasants, this availability of funds meant that a handful of the most prosperous among them were able to enrich themselves further through small ventures, while the majority lost their access to even the trickle of aid for which they had been eligible earlier.[5]

At the same time, despite Guizhou's economic peripheralization at the hands of domestic fiscal policy, the province was drawn into more direct engagement with the global economy. As Deng's encouragement of joint venture development continued to founder on the constraints of Guizhou's material and infrastructural limitations, the province, with the advent of the open door, was in a sense "discovered" as rich in yet another precious resource — cultural traditions and quaint rural lifestyles that might be exploited for tourist demand. A plethora of high-profile projects followed this "discovery"; these were geared not only to a speedy garnering of revenues but to an overhauling of the province in cultural terms more conducive to "modernization." As geographer Tim Oakes describes it: "Tourism was to be the principal vehicle by which potential investors and consumers were brought to Guizhou. It would also serve as a primary means by which the countryside could cast off its 'traditional thinking' and adopt a 'commercial conscience' in order to solve its impending subsistence crisis" (1999:46).

Results were mixed. The sprawling tourist industry entailed an explosion in state — and, later, private — agencies and personnel, all angling to siphon profits away from the local level. Despite reinforcing the pat-

6. *Minzu* hospitality at the Nationalities Guest House.

tern of extraction that had characterized the foregoing decades, however, the advent of ethnic tourism in Guizhou profoundly transformed Guizhou's links with the world. Numbers of both foreign and domestic tourists skyrocketed in the earlier years. International arrivals to Guizhou increased annually at a rate of 30.4 percent between 1980 and 1990; whereas in 1980, only 1,694 foreigners visited Guizhou, in 1993 the number was 102,483 (Oakes 1995a:247–48). Domestic numbers were similarly striking: 2 million Guizhou visitors in 1984 compared to 14 million in 1992 (Oakes 1995a:255).

Tourism development was a key moment of ethnic interpellation. Suddenly, as custodians of fast-disappearing traditions that were craved in transnational circuits, the Miao and other rural groups were remade into resources rather than liabilities. They came to be conceived as the critical hinge that would allow Guizhou to court foreign attentions that it had never received before.[6] In the eyes of its advocates, the strategy of marketing culture was touted as a means through which Guizhou would seek its modernization, and pursue the national fever for *"Zou Xiang Shijie"* ("Marching Toward the World").

Policies and Imagings: A Periodization

By the time that the tourist industry exploded in the 1980s, China's cultural diversity had been organized in terms of fifty-six legitimate groups, which, in exchange for their social recognition, now acted as ethnic agents in relation to the state. How did these groups come to obtain their particular social existence? What constitutes the set of officially recognized nationalities in China today is the historical outcome of government policy during the last four decades. Three major stages can be identified in the development of nationality cultural policy, which roughly paralleled the major political and economic trends since 1949. At first glance, the state's concern for minorities may appear disjunctive with its extractive economic policies. What ties the two together is the effort of nationalization, of rational incorporation into the polity.

1949–1957 In an account by China's premier anthropologist Fei Hsiao-t'ung (Fei Xiaotong), the potential solidarity among the peoples of China had, for a century before 1949, been impeded by class interests among minority and Han elites and by imperialist aggression from the West and Japan. He quotes a retrospective poem by Chairman Mao:

> Long was the night and dawn came slow to the Crimson Land
> For a century demons and monsters danced in sinister band
> And the union of five hundred million people was not at hand
> (in Fei 1981:22).

The communist victory was to change all that. As Fei retells it: "After protracted and dauntless struggles, the people of China's many nationalities finally overthrew the three big mountains weighing on their backs — imperialism, feudalism and bureaucrat-capitalism — and the revolution was crowned with success. Since then our unitary multi-national state has been united into a fraternal cooperative family" (Fei 1981:22–23). Upon Liberation, the work of making the Chinese polity function as a fraternity lay before the victors.

According to Fei, the adoption of the term *minzu* carried a particular political freight. Commonly translated as "nationalities," it was not used in the Western sense, which implies identification with a bounded territory and a certain state. Although it still harbored some of the connotations of uniform citizenship within a state, its more salient meaning came to be that of the culturally distinct, officially recognized peoples within that state (Harrell 1996:276-78). And it was meant to designate *all* ethnic groups, including the Han,[7] an assertion that all were to be considered of equal status regardless of their numbers or levels of historical development (Fei 1980:97). This usage differed from that of the Soviet Union, where differential designations such as "nation," "nationality," and "ethnic group" corresponded to different rights, privileges, and degrees of administrative autonomy. At least for the time being, China was not to be a culturally homogeneous nation-state, but rather a "unitary, multi-national state" as defined by the constitution: "There should be unity and fraternal love among the nationalities and they should help and learn from each other" (Leung 1981–82:76). Although critics have stressed that gradual assimilation was always seen by Chinese theorists as both a desirable and an inevitable outcome of the historical process (Connor 1984; Deal 1979; Dreyer 1976; Heberer 1989; Moseley 1966; Thierry 1989), it was seen as a distant eventuality with little bearing on the management of China's pronounced diversity at that time. Instead, the vision was one of discrete ethnic units arranged horizontally in relation to each other and to the Han majority, free of any system of ranking but for their isomorphic subordination to the central state. Such submission, of course, had become key, since the right to secession was no longer promised.

After the October founding of the People's Republic, the new government set about to implement policies of regional autonomy and to allocate seats for minority representation in county, provincial, and national government. To establish exactly which ethnic units were to do business with the state, a formal self-registration process was carried out in which ethnic groups were asked to identify themselves. The result was the registration of more than 400 different groups, all claiming status as separate nationalities; the province of Yunnan accounted for more than 260 of these (Fei 1981:64). The government faced a dilemma: "For how could a People's Congress allocate its seats to deputies from different nationalities without knowing what nationalities there were? And how could the nation effect regional autonomy for the nationalities without a clear idea of their geographical distribution?" (Fei 1981:60). From the administrative point of view, such a plethora of groups was not considered expedient, constituting an impediment to the process of allocating rights to autonomy and representation. Furthermore, ethnologists did not consider this degree of plurality to be ethnographically accurate, but rather a consequence of such processes as historical splintering, migration, and political antagonism. A decision was made to override subjective identifications in favor of political exigencies and expert determinations.

From 1953 until 1957 a large-scale survey and research project was implemented with the aim of definitively identifying China's nationalities. At this point, specialists in linguistic and ethnological methods, in a classic knowledge/power alliance, took on a crucial role in organizing ethnicity, making the formerly undifferentiated mass of alien peoples within China's boundaries intelligible to the state in a new way. Beginning in 1951, nationalities institutes had been established to train minority cadres to work in official posts in minority regions; now these institutes geared up for serious applied research as well (Guldin 1994:101). The leading ethnologist Lin Yaohua recalls: "they always started by getting to the bottom of the actual conditions prevailing in those nationality areas and striving to attain at least a preliminary understanding of such things as the stage of development of the society and the economy, class situation, and relations among the various nationalities, so as to provide [the relevant authorities] with the necessary data and basis for ethnic guidelines and the formulation of a concrete nationalities policy" (1988:39). Among the specialists recruited were people of rural backgrounds — both Han and minority, men and women [8] — who were trained in research methods and then sent back to their original region for fieldwork. In a directive criticizing Han chauvinism in 1953, Mao had prescribed: "Delegations led by comrades who are familiar with our nationality policy and full of sympathy for our minority nationality compatriots still suffering from discrimination should be sent to visit the areas where there are minority nationalities, make a serious effort at investigation and study and help Party and government organizations in the localities discover and solve problems. The visits should not be those of 'looking at flowers on horseback'" (Mao 1977:87).

Following the call, researchers "went down" to minority villages and lived with peasants for months, even years, in order to learn the local languages, collect folklore, and ultimately to decide who was who. To determine which groups were "genuinely" deserving of official recognition, the government inaugurated a program called "*minzu shi-bie*" (distinguishing nationalities) (Chao 1986:17-20; Fei 1981:60-77; Gu

1984:102-4; Guldin 1994:105-8; Harrell 1995b:81-84, 1996:274-79; Mc-Khann 1995). *Minzu* workers equipped themselves with an adapted version of Stalin's 1913 identification criteria for nations that specified "an historically evolved, stable community of language, territory, economic life, and psychological make-up manifested in a community of culture" (Stalin 1975 [1913]:22). In China, because of such factors as geographic dispersal, shifting contacts during migrations, and linguistic change, many peoples lacked stable communities tied to specific territories. No longer unified by language and economic life, they also manifested great degrees of cultural discontinuity and, needless to say, were without a common sense of belonging. Researchers turned to historical and linguistic methods to determine—more genealogically—which groups might actually merit nationality status.

In my interviews with some of these specialists, many of whom are still employed as researchers and instructors in universities, they characterized these years as a heyday of cultural pluralism, a time when minority cultures were carefully researched, documented, and, in the process, also celebrated on their own terms.[9] Their studies were tremendously detailed and included data on agriculture and land tenure patterns, significant sidelines and handicrafts, costumes and material culture, history and legends, kinship and social organization, marriage practices, ritual and festival activities, funeral practices, customary law, taboos, as well as the progress of land reform.[10] Some 268 extensive reports were assembled on specific villages and compiled in Beijing for comparative purposes (Wong 1979:89); many were republished in the 1980s in recognition of their ethnological and historical value (cf. Guizhou 1986, 1987; Yunnan 1986).

In the course of research, another classification was taking place, one that claimed a social scientific rather than a practical significance. This was the categorization, or de facto ranking, of ethnic groups according to a schema adapted from Morgan by way of Engels (Ou 1984; Wang and Chen 1984:1). Research was to type ethnic groups in terms of five successive modes of production (primitive, slave, feudal, capitalist, and socialist) in which it was assumed that the Han at the time of Land Reform (1949-1951) occupied late feudalism, whereas most minorities occupied earlier stages (Harrell 1991:3). Stage classification was carried out dispassionately and scientistically as if no evaluation was being made of the respective stages (cf. Song 1984:40-41). Nonetheless, two implicit value systems were at work. On the one hand, minorities were denigrated as less civilized because of their classification in earlier stages. On the other hand, they were valorized for their purported innocence of the negative aspects of feudalism. "Except for a few individual landlords, most Miaos owning spare land continue to work . . . ," Fei Hsiao-t'ung exclaimed in an assessment of the Miao social order. "Economically, the Miaos have entered feudalism, although under the oppression of Han political power, it was very difficult for a landlord class to evolve among the Miaos. Internally, Miao feudal influence is very weak" (1951:294). He went on to laud Miao exceptions to feudal social forms, saying that "feudal society despised labor, but the Miaos loved labor," and "free marriage is still preserved among the Miaos owing to the weakness of feudalism" (1951:294).[11]

The result of the *minzu shibie* classification process was that, of the more than 400 groups that had originally registered, (1) some were considered to be actual members of the Han majority, (2) some were recognized as discrete nationalities, and (3) some were identified as subgroups of those nationalities. By 1956, the original set of self-identified groups was collapsed into fifty-one officially recognized minority nationalities (Liscak 1993:13). These included the Mongolians and Tibetans, several Islamic groups including Uyghur and Hui, Koreans, Russians, the Mans or Manchus, the Dai or Thai, and about thirty different highland and lowland groups in the southwest, including the Miao, Yao, Yi, and Zhuang. The Tujia, Pumi, Menba, and Luoba were then reconsidered and were added in subsequent years (Lin 1988:37). The Jinuo people of Yunnan province were given official nationality status only in 1979 (Zhi 1980).

In the classification process, Miao was maintained as a broad category that encompassed multiple subgroups. Doing away with old designations, researchers settled on linguistic distinctions for designating these groupings. They held that the Miao language was a single language that was, together with Yao, a branch of the Sino-Tibetan language group. Although Miao speakers who had been geographically isolated from each other often found their dialects mutually unintelligible, linguistics experts calculated that 40 percent of the lexical and phonetic elements were common to all dialects.[12]

Dialect groups in turn became the exclusive basis on which legitimate reference to subgroups could be made. Three main divisions were designated. The Xiangxi or Eastern dialect, which was relatively unified, was spoken in Hunan and northeastern Guizhou by those who had formerly been classed as the Red Miao. The Qiandong or Central dialect, also relatively unified, was spoken in southeast Guizhou and into Guangxi by those who had formerly been called the Black Miao. The Chuanqiandian or Western dialect, which was far more complicated, was spoken from central Guizhou west through Yunnan and Sichuan and included those who had formerly been called the White, the Blue/Green, and the Flowery Miao. The language of the Flowery Miao was considered to be a major subdialect called Diandongbei (Northeast Yunnan) dialect. In addition, the other subdialects (*ci fangyan*) recognized as making up the Western dialect group were: the Guiyang, Huishui, Mashan, Luopohe, and Chonganjiang (Wang Fushi 1985:3). Miao linguists included a seventh subdialect within Chuanqiandian, the Qiandong.[13] Within these major dialect groups, further distinctions in colloquial speech (*tuyu*) were acknowledged but not standardized (Wang Fushi 1985:3). At least thirteen self-appellations used by members of the Miao category, some of which were clearly cognates, were recorded (Wang 1985:1–2; Purnell 1972:2).[14]

Once the three major dialects and the one major subdialect had been established, subsequent initiatives entrenched them as the standard. During surveys conducted in 1955 (Fu 1957), a single village was designated to represent (*daibiao*) each of the four dialects (see Zhongyang 1985). Then written scripts, based on speech in the original "representative" site, were developed and taught to locals. Scripts, once in place, furthered the routinization of those particular forms as unitary.[15] But the speech situation on the ground remained extremely complicated. In Xijiang, for instance, two mutually intelligible variants of local speech were used, neither of which exactly matched the "standard" (*biaozhun*) Qiandong dialect. Even within the co-residential community, people referred to themselves with two different ethnonyms: Hmu and Ghanao (my romanization). Three decades later, standardization had barely affected local language usage.

The classification process, though its accuracy was vigorously defended by those who were closely involved with it, resulted in a considerable amount of disjunction between peoples' experiences of ethnic difference on the ground and the formal categories into which they were being fitted. In Yunnan in the 1970s the twenty-one officially recognized *minzu* themselves claimed 130 ethnic names, while they had 157 ethnic names given to them by neighboring groups (Liscak 1993:13). Two distinct trajectories emerged: (1) the strident appeals for reclassification, which continue today, and, conversely, (2) the routinization of state categories such that they became part of the habitus of Chinese life.

1958–1976 The second period in the history of nationality cultural policy since 1949 was characterized by a greater emphasis on cultural uniformity. It began in 1957 with the Anti-Rightist Campaign and the Great Leap Forward and ran through the Cultural Revolution to the late 1970s. In his 1957 speech "On the Correct Handling of Contradictions Among the People," Mao Zedong had characterized national contradictions as "non-antagonistic (*fei duikangxing maodun*)," which meant that ethnic differences were now cast as ideological problems that could be resolved through a subjective "desire for unity." He stated that "neither Great-Han chauvinism nor local nationalism can do any good to unity among the nationalities, and they should both be overcome as contradictions among the people" (Mao 1977 [1957]:406).

Mao's statements signaled an end to minorities' special treatment. In keeping with the nationwide movement toward leveling difference, unity among the nationalities was to be achieved through cultural homogenization and parallel participation in economic development. Recall that this period also was one in which the southwest was briskly industrialized and developed for mineral extraction and Third Line defense. Formerly permissible national sentiments were now reevaluated as divisive tools of elite exploitation, concealing commonality in class interests by fostering invidious national loyalties (Liu 1966:11). This formulation took the former legitimacy out of ethnicity. Now given a negative spin as "local nationalisms"—impediments to the unity of the people—ethnic sentiments were effectively deauthorized, subsumed within a moral order that sought socialist transformation by casting out differences through a process of criticism and struggle. Beginning in this period and throughout the Cultural Revolution, cultural uniqueness was disarmed by making it no longer a valid basis for claims to particular treatment.

In keeping with changes in the political climate, ethnological research and bilingual education programs in minority areas were terminated as of 1958. In 1966, nationalities institutes also were closed down. A wide range of activities seen as representative of old ways were suppressed, especially those identified with religion or superstition. In interviews that I conducted, nationalities specialists recalled being sent to the countryside to labor or being assigned to teach Chinese or Marxism-Leninism. At the same time, the number of indigenous cadres appointed to work in minority areas, which had been rising steadily — from 10,000 in 1949 to 500,000 in 1963 — stagnated since the institutes that had trained new personnel each year no longer operated (Connor 1984:290).

The images of minorities that emerged in this period melded surface features of minority cultures with various socialist agendas. They emphasized production, material well-being, progress, and revolution — concerns that were, of course, shared by the Han majority. Whereas, for instance, a 1956 book on Guizhou batik (Guizhou 1956) had contained painstaking details of the patterns in actual minority costumes, with captions specifying the precise area in which they were collected (thus emphasizing local particularity), a book on the costumes for four "fraternal minorities" (*xiongdi minzu*) from 1976 featured black-and-white line drawings of Miao, Bouyei, Dong, and Hui in which the figures only sometimes appeared in ethnic costume (Guizhou 1976). In addition to singing and dancing, these ethnic prototypes were shown engaged in activities such as painting a poster for "Politics Night School," throwing a hand grenade, or dispensing medicine (see fig. 7). The overall effect was of a leveling of difference to be effected by the engagement of everyone in the common activities of developing a socialist country.

At the same time, minority song and dance forms, recalling the early Yan'an tradition of using folk music to convey socialist messages, were likewise harnessed.[16] A 1965 picture book, *A Hundred Flowers Bloom* (Yeh 1965), for example, showed minority performers in purportedly "amateur" performances at a Beijing festival. The song titles included "We Have Electric Lights Now" (Owenk), "How I Want to See Chairman Mao" (Uyghur), "Delivering Public Grain by Mule Carts" (Hui), and "The Party and the People are Inseparable" (Molao) (ethnonyms transcribed as they appeared in the text). Meanwhile, in the Miao countryside, culture was being thoroughly reshaped; local customs — from the crafting of the *lusheng* instrument to the practice of shamanistic healing — were vigorously condemned as retrograde holdovers from less progressive times. Throughout these two decades and until the late

7. *Minzu* women of the Cultural Revolution. Left: two young women crush medicinal herbs at the East Wind commune. Caption reads: "Miao young women's clothing (Zhijin Region)." Right: assuming martial postures. Caption reads: "Miao women's clothing (Southeast Guizhou Region)."

1970s, a common Chinese socialist culture was to gradually supersede local cultures.

1980s–1990s The third period, characterized by a cultural liberalization paralleling that which was taking place in China at large, had its inception in the late 1970s after the demise of the Cultural Revolution. In keeping with the reversals that marked the renunciation of the Cultural Revolution, minority cultures, rather than being suppressed or forced into the mainstream, were perhaps more than ever before fostered and promoted — with the market never far from the scene. The proclaimed promotion of difference was all too consonant with a revised economic vision that tolerated the growth of economic disparities in the uneven rush to modernize.

In 1979 the government proclaimed its renewed commitment to "developing" minority spoken and written languages. It stated that in 1978 more than 30 million textbooks had been published in such minority languages as Korean, Mongolian, Uygur [sic], Kazak, and Tibetan and that this was the largest number since the beginning of the Cultural Revolution in 1966 (FBIS 3/15/79:E10). Bilingual education was reinstituted in certain areas, which in turn prompted a publishing boom. I collected ten regionally published children's school texts in five different Miao scripts, and undoubtedly many more existed. Local newsletters began to be published using various Miao scripts that had been developed in the 1950s. For Christian areas, a Bible was printed in Kunming in a Miao script that had been developed by a missionary at the turn of the twentieth century. A pledge also was made to dub many more films in minority language (FBIS 3/15/79:E10). These moves had a dual significance: they promoted plurality, while making state messages more communicable to isolated folk through their own now-standardized languages.

At the same time, large-scale research on nationalities was resuscitated, including linguistic surveys, folklore collection, and some ethnographic studies. Scholars cultivated a renewed interest in long-term fieldwork while adopting newfangled Western methods.[17] An explosion in publishing accompanied these efforts, and compilations of minority folklore and literature, new journals on ethnology, translations from foreign source materials, and republished materials from earlier decades of research flourished. At the same time, a spate of introductory publications were issued in foreign languages, proclaiming the diversity and cultural tolerance that were to make up China (cf. *China Reconstructs* 1984; Jin 1981; Ma 1989, 1985; Mai 1987; Xin 1987; Yin 1977; Zheng 1981; Zhong 1983, 1984).

Perhaps the most visible aspect of the revival spirit, after the proliferating commodities that ornamented shops everywhere with colorful ethnic objects, was the flourishing of all manner of reworked or invented ethnic festivals. In villages, many local festivals took on a spectacle function and were clogged with tourists. Minorities who had strong presences in urban centers put on single-nationality celebrations in honor of important ethnic occasions. In addition, the government sponsored all manner of multinational festivals. These events usually took the form of song and dance festivals or sports meets. They had a decidedly sanitized recreational quality and brought different nationalities together to parade their particular skills in formats usually structured by competition. Guizhou province, for instance, boasted a series of "Minority Youth Vocal Music Competitions" (Guizhou Nianjian 1988:284).

8. A Miao festival at the Central Nationalities Institute, Beijing, 1982. Professional dancers enact a courtship ritual in which the young woman signals her affection by tying an embroidered band on her suitor's *lusheng*. Miao soldiers and literati look on.

A larger-scale example was the Third National Art Festival of China held in February 1992 in the city of Kunming in which the "various nationalities showed off their unique cultures and customs" and at the same time had an opportunity to "learn from one another, to make friends and to unite with each other" (Cao 1992:11–12).

Ultimately, the dissemination of images of valorized/derogated difference may have had more to do with the state's representation of itself — both to the people it aimed to govern, and to the outside world with which it hoped to establish a dialogue — than it did with the "others" it ostensibly portrayed. Since official policy stressed a horizontal relationship among the nationalities, each of which was formally recognized as having equal status in the Chinese polity, it fell to the cultural domain to stage this revamped relationship. Some of the most vivid examples were the media-saturated parades of colorfully dressed minorities in national events such as the 1990 Asian games in Beijing (Gladney 1991) or in the inaugural ceremonies for the People's Congress (cf. *South China Morning Post,* March 17, 1993). In the reform period, the relegitimation of cultural difference also took on a new valence as a metaphor for economic pluralism. As we will see, subtle rankings nonetheless persisted as the modernization drive generated new representational space for a masculinized Han figure in the vanguard.[18] Here, however, I turn away from the representational domain toward an account of an actual Han man whose life rode the waves of all these political shifts.

Peopling the *Minzu* Industry

It is clear that throughout the Maoist and post-Mao periods the state's approach to minorities was closely tied to the exigencies of socialist development and rational governance. Implementing minority policies in itself became a major bureaucratic undertaking that involved thousands of workers. The work was referred to as *minzu gongzuo* (nationalities work), and it became a significant form of employment in branches such as the Nationalities Affairs Commission (Minzu Weiyuanhui), the Nationalities Research Institutes (Minzu Yanjiusuo), and the collegelike Nationalities Institutes (Minzu Xueyuan)—all with presences in Beijing as well as in the capitals of provinces with significant minority populations. For many women and men, Han and minority, who were brought into the structure in the early research years as fieldworkers for the *minzu shibie* project, nationalities work became a lifelong career. They pursued it with ardor and a conviction that they were contributing to bettering the lot of those whom they studied and administered.

When I began meeting with him in 1988, Zhang Zhengdong was a distinguished, silver-haired, sixty-nine-year-old man who described his life as having been devoted to *minzu gongzuo*.[19] His story illustrates the kind of trajectories that careers in nationalities work entailed. Zhang's personal commitment began in the turbulence of the Republican period and the war with Japan (1931–45), well before communist rule. Born in Henan in 1919, he had been a child of Han privilege and cultivated status, educated in elite centers in Henan, Beijing, and Shanghai. His father had been a doctor and a Presbyterian; perhaps because of the political danger during so many of the Maoist years, Zhang told me only that he had attended church and some Christian schools when growing up. He did not identify himself as Christian.

In 1938, as a young man of nineteen, Zhang had his first experience of the lands of the non-Han frontier. Fleeing the Sino-Japanese conflict in the east, he traveled overland to Kunming, capital of Yunnan province, for his college studies. Like the Red Army on the Long March, he passed through rugged and impoverished areas inhabited by peoples who spoke no Chinese and followed unrecognizable customs. At that moment he made the decision to devote his life to *minzu gongzuo*. His vision was to learn more about these peoples while working to ameliorate their cultural and material deprivations. From then on, he would make his life in the southwest.

Zhang enrolled in the study of sociology at the Southwest Union University in Kunming, a school that had been jointly established by Beijing University, Qinghua University, and Nankai University as a college-in-exile from the ravages of the war with Japan. During the late 1930s and early 1940s it was one of the most prestigious educational institutions in China, graced by some of the country's leading intellectuals who, like Zhang, had migrated west. Upon graduation in 1942, he took his first job, which was as a director of the Tribesmen's Service Station in Yunnan where he worked providing development aid and conducting social surveys. This fusing of research with development projects was an approach adopted throughout both the Republican and the socialist periods. Social knowledge was always to be linked to applied programs. What counted as social knowledge, however, was open-ended; enthusiastic intellectuals from the east, dazzled by the cultural and topographical curiosities they encountered in their southwestern exile, produced copious accounts of whatever they saw, fervently recording everything that struck them as novel. One of Zhang's first publications, "Deqin Travelogue" (*Deqin Xingji* 1942), was serialized over four issues in a Yunnan journal called *Frontier Culture (Bianjiang Wenhua)*. It recounted his trip from Lijiang to Deqin county in western Yunnan and sights along the Jinsha and Lancang Rivers. From 1944 until 1946, he contributed as deputy general editor and author to the "Draft Gazetteer of Weixi County," coauthored the "Survey Report on Lisu Social History," and wrote survey reports for Zhongdian, Weixi, Deqin, Gongshan, Fugong, and Yongsheng counties; in 1986 two of these were republished in Chengdu as part of the cultural recovery project of the 1980s. He recalled that from 1941 until 1949 he published more than twenty different pieces, but he lamented: "From the 1931 Japanese invasion of China to the 1976 end of the Cultural Revolution, the greater part of my time was spent in social turmoil, so some of my publications have been lost."

In 1946, Zhang worked as a principal and a teacher, first in a middle school and then in a teacher's vocational school in Lijiang. In 1948 he had an opportunity to pass on some of his practically acquired knowledge by becoming an instructor in cultural anthropology at Yunnan University. This appointment came to an abrupt end when, after the Communist victory, he was sent to a Revolutionary college in 1950. For the next seven years he was to return to middle school teaching—history, geography, and Chinese—in Kunming. Along with the shifts in policy in 1957 came his transfer by the government to the Guizhou Nationalities Institute, where he taught the most privileged of the province's minority students at the college level. He participated in writing and editing the first draft of the *Brief History of the Yi* (*Yizu Jianshi*) in 1959, but that year also saw the closing of the college along with the more general termination of special programs for minorities, including the *Brief History* project. Zhang was transferred to the Guizhou Nationalities Research Institute for twenty years. In the early years he worked on a major project culling the Guizhou materials from the *Da Qing Li Chao Shi Lu* (a collection of texts translated as the Qing Veritable Records) and editing them for a 1964 publication of 761,000 characters. After that, his account of his publications and of his *minzu gongzuo* falls silent for over a decade. In the era of the Cultural Revolution, projects expressly related to minority and ethnological concerns were suppressed and Zhang labored as a janitor.

The national cultural climate again shifted on Mao's death in 1976 and the inauguration of reform policies in 1978. Suddenly, minority research was once again in demand, and Zhang contributed to *Guizhou's Minority Nationalities* (*Guizhou Shaoshu Minzu*), a volume that covered the Miao, Bouyei, Dong, Yi, Shui, Hui, Gelao, Zhuang, and Yao and was published in 1980. He was reassigned to college teaching in 1979, and he assumed a position in the politics department and, later, the history department (1982–84) of the Guizhou Nationalities Institute, where he taught ethnology, demography, and sociology. Having devoted more than four decades to teaching whatever the authorities needed him for, broadening his specialties to include history, anthropology, ethnology, demography, geography, and Chinese language, he returned in 1988 to the field of his original training. In keeping with the revival of social sciences that had gained legitimacy across China by the late 1980s, he was invited to prepare and establish a sociology department at the Nationalities Institute. His publishing in the 1980s took a turn toward demographics. Among other work, he edited and contributed to the Guizhou volume of a series called *China's Population* (*Zhongguo Renkou — Guizhou Fence* 1988).

Tall, gaunt, and wrinkled when I knew him in 1988, Zhang was at a point in his career when many Chinese intellectuals would have been thinking about retirement, withdrawing from active professional pursuits. But Zhang's devotion extended beyond the demands of his institution and had spanned the ideological aims of many political moments. As a full professor in 1988, he still taught classes and advised advanced students. At the same time, he held official posts in eight off-campus organizations: the Guizhou Committee of the China Democratic League, the Guizhou Nationalities Research Society, the Guizhou Sociology Society, the Guizhou Miao Studies Research Association, the Guizhou Demography Association, the Guizhou Birth Planning Association, the Guizhou Women's Studies Association, and the Guizhou Elderly Studies Association.

Unlike many intellectuals who exploited the relaxed constraints on mobility of the reform era, Zhang did not attempt to move back to the Henan of his youth or the Yunnan of his early adulthood. There he might have had a more comfortable life and reunited with people from his formative past. He did travel extensively for conferences, but he had decided to make his life in Guizhou, a place where he felt his concern for social betterment could best be pursued. In the concrete faculty apartment buildings at the Nationalities Institute he, together in an apartment with his wife and his grown son, lived in two bedrooms, a small living room, kitchen, and water closet. His tremendous luxury was a tiny space off the living room, sealed off only by a curtain, a study filled with books and a desk where I invariably found him, pen poised, still working on one of his many ongoing projects. When cataracts interfered with his vision, he made sure that someone read to him so that he could keep up with scholarship. For Zhang, *minzu gongzuo* had become a lifetime vocation.

From Category to Identity

In the half-century of the People's Republic, *minzu gongzuo* had effects that stretched far beyond the lives of those directly engaged in it. In its initial coinage, *minzu gongzuo* had a more ideological sense. According to

Moseley (1966:7-8), the term originally referred to the project of securing the solidarity of different nationalities after their territories had been militarily subdued, and it proceeded according to the tenets of Marxist-Leninist theory on the national question. It remained to later decades for the term to become normalized as a form of work that involved development projects, social research, and other more technocratic dimensions. Stevan Harrell offers a kind of intermediate definition of the work as "creating autonomous regions, implementing educational and developmental plans, bringing leaders of the peripheral peoples into the Party-state apparatus that carries out the center's project—in general fulfilling the promise that all *minzu,* equal legally and morally, would march together on the road to historical progress, that is, to socialism" (1995a:24).

Understanding the effects of *minzu gongzuo,* I think, entails considering the inseparability of ideology and practice. Over the decades in which *minzu gongzuo* was undertaken, its logics, its discursive certainties, grew in legitimacy because of the way they were cited again and again in publications and in policy decisions. What began as state ideology was transformed through the myriad practices of thousands of nationalities workers into what I have called a habitus. Notions such as historical stages of social development, the emblematic cultural essences of the discrete groups, and the official ethnonyms that designated those groups became naturalized—became the limits to the imagining of cultural diversity.

For the minorities that were recognized in the streamlining process of *minzu shibie,* we can think in terms of a process of state interpellation. Yet that is only a starting point, for the ensuing decades saw a consequent structuring of subjectivity and agentive engagement with the categories that had been instituted. Stuart Hall (1995:65) has described identity as

the meeting point . . . between, on the one hand, the ideological discourses which attempt to interpellate or speak us as social subjects, and, on the other, the psychological or psychical processes which produce us as subjects which can be spoken. . . . You only discover who you are because of the identities you are required to take on, into which you are interpellated: but you must take up those positionalities, however temporarily, in order to act at all. Identities are, as it were, the forms in which we are obliged to act, while always knowing that they are representations which can never be adequate to the subject processes that are temporarily invested in them.

It is useful to think of *minzu* categories as positionalities, for much of the maneuvering that has taken place within and around them has to do precisely with social and political locations. As we will see, charting the many acts around *minzu* identities reveals that contestation and assumption were of a piece; both processes indicate the agentive character of identity production.[20] What was also produced along the way could be called minoritization, a more hegemonic sense of the enclosed multinational Chinese polity as the arena of positional tactics.

For the Miao, the classification process of the 1950s marked a decisive turn toward the use of the umbrella term "Miao" to embrace all subgroups. Former appellations such as "Flowery" (*Hua*) Miao or "White" (*Bai*) Miao, while still retained in some of the survey reports of that period (cf. Yunnan 1986:7), were thereupon dismissed as imposed by non-Miao and in some cases as carrying derogatory connotations rejected by the Miao themselves (*Miaozu Jianshi* 1985:6).[21] By contrast, Hmong in the West in recent decades have consistently rejected the Miao term itself as derogatory. The *Brief History of the Miao* (1985) explained the adoption of the general Miao name as legitimate for several reasons: (1) it has had a long history, (2) it is known to all, and (3) it is commonly accepted by the Miao people. Hence, the *Brief History* states: "after liberation, according to the *Miao peoples' own wishes,* the ethnic name was unified as Miaozu" (*Miaozu Jianshi* 1985:6, emphasis added).

When, after the Cultural Revolution, pride in ethnicity was reinstated and more than ever before officially sanctioned, the advantages of assuming minority status were manifold. First, minorities were generally exempt from the one-child and even two-child birth planning policies.[22] Second, minorities had superior educational opportunities in the form of special minority schools, state subsidies for primary and secondary education, and preferential admissions policies for higher education in Han institutions. Third, if they met certain conditions, minorities were entitled to autonomous government and, regardless of how tiny their numbers, to representation in the central government. Fourth, cultural activities and religious practices were not only less restricted than those of the Han, but also in some cases were promoted and even granted subsidies. Economic advantages also included the privilege of autonomous areas to retain more taxes for local spending, rather than remitting these funds to the central government (Gladney 1990:69), and special allocations of funds through the Nationalities Affairs Commission for local development in minority areas. Thus, the state, through an array of policies and practices, had strengthened categories of legitimate difference to which vast numbers of Chinese citizens desired to lay claim.

The renewed valorization of minority identity was resoundingly reflected in the population statistics of the 1990 census (see Table of Populations). In 1982 the population of China's fifty-five minority nationalities had totaled 67 million. Individual groups' numbers ranged from the Zhuang with 13.4 million to the Lhoba with only 1,066 persons, yet both groups were granted equal entitlement to central representation. In 1990, according to the national census, the total minority population had increased from the 67 million of 1982 to 91.2 million, and their proportion in relation to the Han had increased from 6.7 percent in 1982 to 8.04 percent in 1990 (*Beijing Review,* November 12–18, 1990:22, December 24–30, 1990:34).

Several developments are striking in the population figures for the largest nationalities. The Man, or Manchu, who in 1982 had ranked as China's sixth-largest minority, moved in 1990 to the position of second-largest minority after the Zhuang, the Manchu numbers having more than doubled, from 4.3 million in 1982 to 9.8 million in 1990. The Miao moved up from the fifth-largest to the fourth-largest group, with the Hui in third place. Miao population now totaled 7,398,035 and had increased by more than 46 percent. Even taking into account natural growth and the fact that exemptions from birth planning would enable the minority populations to increase at a faster rate, the kind of increases reflected here and their proportion relative to the majority suggest a dramatic movement of individuals newly acknowledging or demanding status as minorities. In Hunan, where the greatest movement toward reclassification as Miao took place, the number more than doubled in eight years from 761,754 in 1982 (*Minzu Yanjiu* 1984:75) to 1,557,073 in 1990 (National Population Census Office 1991:18). Another form of reclassification that was under way involved regions and the allocation of autonomy. In many places, new designations of autonomous units were made in response to ethnic groups' asserting that they possessed the requisite population density. These newly recognized aggregations of minorities were in large part a cumulative consequence of individuals —

sometimes in the hundreds of thousands — who had formerly identified themselves as Han now converting to minority status.

Desirability of minority categorizations notwithstanding, in the post-Mao period there also has been a renewed recognition in popular consciousness of the distinctions between subgroups. Whereas in 1982, Chinese colleagues and contacts had been adamant that the people I was researching were simply "the Miao," by 1985 many were asking me which *subgroup* I was specializing in, referring explicitly to the older form of classification that marked Miao groups by their distinctive costume features, i.e., "White Miao," "Black Miao," "Flowery Miao," etc.[23] Colleagues increasingly judged my work unscientific if I was unclear about subgroup distinctions.

Ethnic classification, then, was revived as a ground of contention during reform. In keeping with the heightened attention to diversity in the 1980s, ethnic identifications were reconsidered, and some reclassifications were made. As mentioned, the Jinuo had received official status as an independent nationality only in 1979. This independent status was based on their differences from neighboring groups, despite the fact that any independent historical origins remained undocumented (Zhi 1980:55). Subgroups of several existing nationalities, such as the Pingwu Tibetans, the Deng, and the Kucong, also requested such recognition and were under consideration (Fei 1980:102). In the 1990s the Kemu, the Baimadi, and the Xiaerba were pressing claims for independent status (Guldin 1994:108). In the flux of these movements, some provinces that had large numbers of minority groups had already recognized new nationalities, the status of which was still being deliberated by the Central Nationalities Affairs Commission.

Consistent with this spirit, formerly amalgamated groups were splintering. In these situations, members of the splinter group and their neighbors both appropriated dominant linguistic forms and manipulated them. The Ge (formerly Gedou) people of southeast Guizhou, who were still officially considered part of the Miao but whose identity had long been in question (Fei 1952:62), adopted such a tactical linguistic approach in their quest for official recognition. Local Ge authorized their independent status by appropriating the state suffix *"-zu"* (denoting nationality) to replace the former *"-jia"* (family, people). Their struggle continued into the 1990s, even taking the form of a popular movement to withhold grain tax from the state to achieve recognition (Cheung

1996). At the same time, certain Miao elites rejected the Ge attempt at separation, claiming that it was motivated only by a historical antagonism between subgroups, not by an actual ethnic difference.

The post-Mao period, even as it witnessed heightened questioning of the ethnic categories that had prevailed in previous decades, at the same time contributed in several ways to the overall routinization of existing categories. Whether the impulse was toward splintering or toward amalgamation, categories such as "Miao" became increasingly hegemonic as a consequence in part of the very maneuverings around membership in the category. Official ethnonyms took on social lives of their own (Gladney 1991:299), and contestation took place primarily within the parameters of already established *minzu* (Harrell 1990:519). As the shifts in numbers suggest, the connotations of the Miao ethnonym, along with many others, by and large had shed the negative associations that they once bore. For the many who claimed "Miao" as their identity, the term was increasingly accepted and deployed in social life. The consequences for the putative cultural attributes of this identity, those that were implicitly consented to by virtue of membership, were manifold. How they took shape in popular cultural production remains to be discussed.

4

Internal Orientalism

Gender and the Popularization

of China's Others

On a visit to the nearest city — Kaili — during my 1988 field year in southeast Guizhou, I encountered an unexpected ritual. Or was it really so unexpected?

In 1986 a new six-story building had been constructed to supplement the mildewed older structure that had housed the city's No. 1 Guest House. Kaili was, after all, the capital of the Miao and Dong Autonomous Prefecture of Southeast Guizhou (Qiandongnan). It was the urban hub of the entire region, the destination for travelers laying over before venturing into the countryside, and the commercial center for peasants seeking to sell their local products and acquire cosmopolitan goods. Five hours east of the provincial capital, on a train line that connects Yunnan to Guangzhou, it was a meeting ground for all sorts of traffic, particularly tourist. With its mountainous and scenic but barely arable terrain inhabited by several minority groups, Southeast Guizhou had decided that its best hope for economic development was the promotion of tourism.[1] The new hotel complex had been renamed a "*Minzu* Guest House."[2] Teenage girls were recruited from the countryside to work as receptionists, waitresses, and chambermaids — and to showcase local culture. A representative sampling of different minorities, subgroups, and costume styles had been chosen, and each employee was to wear her ethnic headdress at all times to mark her uniqueness. Regular duties included not only the usual hotel drudgery, but also an occasional pose in full costume for foreign travelers' cameras and performances of song and dance to visiting tour groups.

The ritual I witnessed, however, was a variation on the packaging of ethnic performance for sale. Kaili had also been promoted as a site for domestic meetings of officials and scholars; that day, delegates to a regional conference of mayors convened at the hotel. The group of largely male, urban conferees assembled in the open parking area to be greeted with an elaborate and delectable form of local welcome. A glamorous set of maidens, adorned to the hilt in minority garb, displayed the rainbow of feminine variety offered by the prefecture. The young women serenaded the mayors with ethnic song. Firecrackers were set off to inaugurate the festivities. Then, in an adapted version of an indigenous custom commonly used to welcome guests from afar at the entrance to a village, delegates went through a receiving line in which the young women used chopsticks or their own fingers to pop local delicacies straight into the men's reluctant but curious mouths, then exhorted them to drink symbolic welcoming spirits out of the horns of bulls.[3]

Internal Orientalism

The mayors' reception, along with many other examples to be discussed in this chapter, may be referred to as "internal orientalist." I offer this term to denote a set of practices that occur *within* China, and that, in this case, involved, not international tourism, but the fascination of more cosmopolitan-identified Chinese with "exotic" minority cultures in an array of polychromatic and titillating forms. This intense fascination spawned encounters and images that were most commonly structured by a class/gender asymmetry in which minorities were represented chiefly by rural women, while Han observers appeared characteristically as male urban sophisticates.

Orientalism — as a critical concept — was proposed by literary critic Edward W. Said (1978). What Said described was the discourse of European colonial relations with the East, particularly with the Muslim "Orient," which was portrayed as a corrupted and decaying civilization, no match for European progress. Chinese characterizations of the frontier, by contrast, were more akin to European portrayals of the African continent as primitive and close to nature (McGrane 1989). In both cases, as suggested by the Comaroffs (1991), modern European self-consciousness was being consolidated: "In investigating the savage, the West set up a mirror in which it might find a tangible, if inverted, self-image. Non-Europeans filled out the nether reaches of the scale of

9. A rite of deference. Kaili *minzu* make offerings at a regional mayor's conference.

being, providing the contrast against which cultivated man might distinguish himself. On this scale, moreover, the African was assigned a particularly base position: he marked the point at which humanity gave way to animality" (1991:98–99). By the twentieth century, China's representing of internal others was implicated in a complex mimesis that both struggled with being the Orient to Europe's modernity and in turn echoed Europe's othering modalities in its own colonizing discourse. What we are engaged with here are the broad strokes of Said's theoretical intervention—the placing of the conjunction between power and representation in the context of colonial relations of domination.

   Rather than emphasizing the forceful and repressive character of colonial rule, Said borrowed Michel Foucault's notion of the productivity of discourse, maintaining that European orientalist representations were ideas and statements that constituted a hegemonic description of the object. Part of what Said aimed to do was to theorize the *"strength* of Western cultural discourse, a strength too often mistaken as merely decorative or 'superstructural'" (1978:25). There were two effects. First, the culture of the producers of such discourse "gained in strength and identity by setting itself off against the Orient as a sort of surrogate and even underground self" (1978:3). Second, European representations of cultural difference framed the colonized as deserving of domination.

By definition, then, orientalist practice actually produced the Other, in representations that appeared in art, in scholarship, and in an array of other media. But Said's insight has pressed a question asked repeatedly in subsequent scholarship: was orientalism a sufficiently pervasive order of representation that it may have come to structure other instances of intercultural representation as well? The focal point of *Orientalism* was the way in which northwestern Europeans represented the Muslim world. But what the original critique spawned in its impact on subsequent scholarship was a bifurcated mapping of the globe into the stable categories of East-West, and represented-representer, an approach that can conceal, as some have noted, the historical multiplicity of axes of domination even within the East. Some of these, despite being non-European, were decidedly colonial, such as Japan's presence in Taiwan (1895–1945); others, such as China's expansive "march toward the tropics" (Wiens 1954), were more broadly imperializing—or internal colonial.[4]

Pitting East and West as opposites in a dyadic, but unequal, relation stopped short at the conclusion that the East is muted and therefore, by extension, rendered incapable of othering. For Said, such silence was the crux of his argument about the nature of representation: "The exteriority of the representation is always governed by some version of the truism that if the Orient could represent itself, it would; since it cannot, the representation does the job . . . the written statement is a presence to the reader by virtue of its having excluded, displaced, made supererogatory any such *real thing* as 'the Orient' " (1978:21). Said is most compelling in his charting of a historically specific but globalized regime of representation in which the West made only its own voice audible. There is a risk, however, that in pursuing this formulation, one reproduces the muteness or invisibility of the agents of cultural production that might be operating within the so-called Orient.[5] As Robertson has pointed out, such critiques "both further privilege Euro-American intellectual and theoretical trends as universal and obfuscate and neutralize the histories and legacies of non-Western imperialisms and associated 'othering' practices" (1995:973).

What alternative do I pursue in proposing internal orientalism in

China? This chapter describes practices that can be located along the lines of class, ethnic, and gender difference within the domain of Chinese public culture. This approach resonates with Robertson's (1995) treatment of Japanese colonialism within Asia and to Harrell's (1995a) treatment of "civilizing projects" within China.[6] The "orientalist" is a figurative term that refers to those who produce representations that define others within the East. It is not that the modalities of orientalist representation are universally present, but that they underwent a historical course of dissemination precisely as a consequence of the West's securing the globe within its colonizing reach. The order of modernity, with its characteristic logic of representation — "understood as a presence standing for an absence which authorizes it" (Farquhar et al 1998:1) — was a particular artifact of the epistemic domain of the West. However, with the geopolitics of colonization and the increasing hegemony of the nation form, it was not exclusive to the West for long. Within Asia, forms of what has been called "subimperialism" (Chen 1994:700) or "colonial modernity" have been multiple and overlapping; crucially, "Asian modernities perform their own recordings of the discourses of modernity within a hegemonic capitalist world" (Barlow 1993:vi). Hence, the internal orientalism I describe was not an isomorphic parallel of East-West orientalism. It took place in an arena that was not spatially bifurcated and that was discursively cross-cut by imported modes of orientalist "knowledge" production, from Western anthropology to Soviet ethnology to transnational advertising. Myriad moments of disparate speech and practice occurred, unevenly deploying and "localizing" (Barlow 1991b) such imported modes, and variously drawing on premodern Chinese legacies of portraying others. Based on their contents and the social locations of their authors, such forms were selectively processed into dominant versions that managed to stabilize alteric identities.

The passion for boundaries, for boundedness, that marked the colonial order and the growing ubiquity of the nation-state was inextricably coupled with the authority of representationalism, as Mitchell has so convincingly argued: "Modern colonialism was constructed upon a vastly increased power of representation, a power which made possible an unprecedented fixing and policing of boundaries — an unprecedented power of portraying what lay 'outside.' . . . By establishing a boundary that rigorously excludes the Oriental, the other, from the self, such a self acquires its apparent cleanliness, its purity, its uncorrupted and undivided identity" (1988:167–68). For a China striving to position itself within a modern order of nations, the defining of what "lay outside" became a project of anxious urgency. It was not until the Maoist era that the fixing of boundaries, the codifications so indispensable to modernity, were realized in relation to the non-Han.[7]

In late twentieth-century China, I found at least five types of agents engaged in the manufacture of portraits of the self-in-negation: the Chinese state, Han urbanites, urban minority intellectuals, rural minority elites, and local villagers. The first two categories, especially Han urbanites, are the subject of this chapter. The representations that they produced were the result of power-laden encounters in which respective parties contributed differently to molding the outcomes. The chapters in the second section delve further into how Miao cultural production was implicated in the representational regime. While asymmetries — of status, economic resources, cultural capital, etc. — were inherent in these processes, it would be an oversimplification to suggest that the authority to speak was entirely unilateral. Classic critiques of orientalism relied on interpreting textual and visual media; hence, they were limited by what discursive material was available for analysis. To these sources, an ethnographic method adds observations of what happens at what I call the sites of the production of difference, when producers of representations encountered their objects face-to-face. At the moments of encounter, a more multivocal, less binarized picture emerged in which those whose images were being produced also acted to shape the process — whether by resisting, complying or taking up their own image-making practices. Hence, in my usage, Saidian orientalism, which emphasized only that those represented are silenced, their subjectivity denied, their power to speak for themselves of themselves usurped by imperialist discursive maneuvers, is considerably resignified.[8]

To pay attention to the practices of the represented is not to obscure the fact that severe inequalities obtained in the production of representations. Differential access to cash, to technology, to geographic mobility, to state authority, and even to literacy had a great deal to do with determining who crafted dominant representations. My point is that the more important question is not so much who speaks, or who produces otherness, but rather which representations, once produced, enjoy wide circulation in the larger society and beyond. Whose images and, more significantly, what kind of images appeared on television, in magazines, at tourist venues, etc.? The issue is particularly relevant in the internal orientalist context in which such representations were produced and circulated within the confines of a geographic territory also inhabited by their objects and therefore also consumed by those objects. Here, questions of power differentials emerged in sharp relief: certain sectors were able to make their voices hegemonic, while others were de facto muted by their relative lack of access to the channels of public culture. I suggest a more complex and cacophonous approach to the production of otherness — one obtained through ethnography — in which multiple versions were created, but only certain versions became dominant because of the uneven distribution of powers of dissemination.

Nationalism's Others

China's twentieth century saw dramatic upheavals in both minority and Han Chinese identities. Han perspectives on non-Han peoples were paradoxically both oppositional and incorporative as the non-Han came to constitute a part of what was seen as the Chinese people. Such shifts in the delineations of identity and otherness suggest still other qualifications of the orientalist paradigm. First, in the case of *internal* orientalism, those othered in dominant representation may simultaneously be considered an integral part of their representers' people or nation. Second, as was the case in the opening of China over the twentieth century, in the consolidation of identity, rather than a single other appearing locked in dyadic opposition to the nation, multiple contrastive others may be significant in defining the self. A complementarity between external and internal others is noted by Tölölyan (1991) as a characteristic feature of nationalisms that quest after homogeneity: "in [the nation-state] territory, differences are assimilated, destroyed, or assigned to ghettoes, to enclaves demarcated by boundaries so sharp that they enable the nation to acknowledge the apparently singular and clearly fenced-off differences *within* itself, while simultaneously reaffirming the privileged homogeneity of the rest, as well as the difference *between* itself and what lies over its frontiers" (1991:6). For China, it was the external West and the internal non-Han peoples that played the biggest roles in demarcating China's identity. But the peasant folk were also of crucial importance.

In the elaboration of Chinese national identity, like so many other

nationalisms worldwide, gender and sexuality emerged as key signifiers of difference. Maleness and femaleness, along with appropriate and
transgressive gender and sexual behavior, were regular means by which
insiders and outsiders were distinguished. Theorists of nationalism have
often located the ground for the iconography of national identity formation in the difference between men and women: "In the same way
that 'man' and 'woman' define themselves reciprocally (though never
symmetrically), national identity is determined not on the basis of its
own intrinsic properties but as a function of what it (presumably) is not"
(Parker et al. 1992:5). With tremendous historical regularity, then, men
tend to stand for national agents (Williams 1996:6), as determinants
of the fate of nations (Mosse 1985:23), in a metonymic relation to the
nation as a whole (McClintock 1995:354–55). By contrast, women function only symbolically or metaphorically (McClintock 1995:355) to mark
the boundaries of nations (Yuval-Davis and Anthias 1989:7), to conserve
tradition, and to serve as passive containers or vessels for male national
agency (Williams 1996:6, 12). Enloe identifies supporting or complementary roles in which women appear as handmaidens to masculinized
national agents in military conflicts: "as conquerors' mistresses, war-
time rape victims, military prostitutes, cinematic soldier-heroes, pin-up
models on patriotic calendars and of course as workers, wives, girl-
friends and daughters waiting dutifully at home" (1993:245). Feminist
critics have shown repeatedly that in the course of nationalist struggles,
women's agendas and women's experiences are set aside, subsumed
under nationalist imperatives. The image of rape to describe external
military/cultural/political incursions into national space is one of the
most classic examples. Not only is the trope of rape used as a metaphor for other forms of violation, but when it actually takes place and
the rapist occupies the position of national aggressor, the woman's gendered physical experience becomes a vehicle: "her female body is displaced by a nationalist agenda and denied the meaning of its specifically
female experience, for the nation decides all the meanings for it" (Liu
1995:198).

In terms of sexuality, the situation becomes a little more complicated.
Mosse (1985), who analyzed German and English nationalisms, emphasized manliness and a bourgeois ideal of respectability as the loci of
national essence. These nations promoted a heterosexual, reproductive,
and restrained sexuality subordinated to the national purpose. Con-

versely, others such as Chatterjee (1989) have focused on the situating of the nation in the body or idea of the woman — "a particular image of woman as chaste, dutiful, daughterly or maternal" (Parker et al. 1992:6). Here, the maternal is especially pivotal, for women are seen as reproducers of the nation's people both biologically through childbearing and socially through their inculcation of national traditions and values in the young. Alternately, their sexuality can be highly dangerous to the nation because of their potential power to contaminate the nation through asserting their agency in choosing foreign sexual partners and producing "miscegenation" (R. Chow 1995b). Hence, Eley and Suny point out: "Anxieties about the health of the nation, or its demographic future and productive efficiencies, or the stabilities of the social fabric, commonly translate into a politics directed to and against women, whether through systems of mother-child welfare, through rhetorics of family values, or by policy offensives around reproductive health, the regulation of sexuality, or the direct control of women's bodies" (1996:26).

A third strand in the relation between sexuality and nationalism is the emphasis on homogeneous sexual identity and practice as a figure of contrast with sexual excess or transgression. Often the internal or external others of the nation are portrayed as sexual misfits in a highly normative national sexual system. But as many have pointed out, following Foucault (1978), the very definition of the national system relies on the identification and classification of those who do not fit the norm (Berlant 1997),[9] and these may be people or groups who are already in the category of internal others, whether as women, minorities, or peasants. Let us turn to the others of Chinese nationalism.

Two Nationalisms, Multiple Others

Two types of nationalism antedate and inform contemporary Chinese concerns over identity. They can be referred to as Han nationalism and Chinese nationalism. Han nationalism was concerned with boundaries between peoples within the shifting territory of the Chinese polity, specifically between the Han and those they designated as "barbarians." Chinese nationalism rose in response to incidences of foreign imperialist aggression that prompted a unifying within the physical territory of China against the outside. As historian Prasenjit Duara (1995) has cogently argued, it is the advent of Chinese nationalism that is commonly conceived as the moment of the birth of nationalism in China, but this approach privileges a distinct moment of unified subjectivity that could emerge only in the so-called modern period. Duara has two quarrels with this portrayal. First, it assumes a consciousness of national community that is indeed unitary in unprecedented ways. Second, it marginalizes other forms of communal consciousness as premodern and therefore decidedly discontinuous with the global process that took place in the nineteenth century. He argues against a decisive break in forms of communal consciousness, suggesting instead that what is different in the course of the nineteenth century is the emergence of a world system of putatively commensurable nation-states. In the spirit of this critique, the following narrative pinpoints no single definitive moment for the appearance of nationalism in China.

What I call Han nationalism could be dated at least to the fall to Manchu conquest of the Han-ruled Ming dynasty in 1644 (at which time it probably is more appropriately referred to as Han "ethnicism").[10] Such sentiments crystallized in the Ming-Qing dynastic transition as a reaction against control of the center of the Chinese state by "barbarian usurpers," the non-Han Jurchen people from the north. These non-Han, now referred to as Manchu, had moved from the margins to the heart of the Chinese imperium, yet their otherness could not be effaced in the eyes of those loyal to the previous Ming dynasty. The superordinate political location of the usurpers, however, suggests some polysemy to the term yi, used by opponents to designate these alien rulers and conventionally rendered in English as "barbarian." An unequivocally pejorative association of the term with animality may need to be tempered if one considers that, in English, "barbarian" derives from a distinction between "those who spoke intelligibly and those beyond the pale of civil life whose language seemed simply reiterative mumbling" (Stocking 1987:10). Yi, then, at least in some instances, might be closer to a sense of barbarian as *foreign* rather than as bestial.[11] If the term encompasses both these significations, it is possible that considerable ideological work was at play in struggles over usage. Indeed, the case has been made that it may have been precisely the alien Manchu style of rulership in which relations were transacted with a "confraternity of princes" (Zito 1997:23) or a "multitude of lords" (especially Mongols and Tibetans in Hevia) rather than a singular lordship over uncivilized or bestial subjects that, at least in part, initially engendered Han boundary anxiety (Zito:36–39) about their monopoly on humanness/dominion. Later, with Manchu appropriation of Han-derived modes of civility, it became imperative for Han nationalists to recuperate a more racialized sense of *yi* that would render Manchu rule illegitimate.

Although its early voices were muted, in large part because of Manchu political censorship, strands of embodied Han ethnicism can be glimpsed in the philosophical writings of such renegade Ming loyalists as Wang Fuzhi (1619–1692). Wang's works analogized the distinction between "Chinese" (i.e., Han) and "barbarians" (implicitly Manchu) to that between people and things: "Chinese in their bone structure, sense organs, gregariousness and exclusiveness, are no different from the barbarians, and yet they must be distinguished absolutely from the barbarians. Why is this so? Because if man does not mark himself off from things, then the principle of Heaven is violated. If the Chinese do not mark themselves off from the barbarians, then the principle of earth is violated" (deBary 1960:544). Wang's writings did not gain popular currency until they were published two centuries after his death with the revival of anti-Manchu sentiment at the turn of the twentieth century (Gasster 1969:65–67). Revolutionary nationalist Sun Yat-sen recognized five "peoples" of China, including the Manchu (as well as the Han, Mongolian, Tibetan, and Muslim), but challenged the legitimacy of Manchu rule in the Qing dynasty on the basis of the putative purity and majority of the Han within China's territory. Sun's ideology deployed a myth of primordial homogeneity, asserting that China had been developing "a single state out of a single race" (Sun 1975 [1927]:6) since the Qin and Han dynasties (221 B.C.E.–202 C.E.).[12]

While internal divisions were Han nationalism's primary concern, a threatening overseas presence spawned what I refer to as Chinese nationalism. The figures of Western and Japanese power at China's shores tended to diminish the salience of interethnic issues in the domestic arena in favor of protection from territorial, political, and ultimately cultural incursions of what was construed as the Chinese nation.[13] In the wake of defeat in the Opium Wars and subsequent conflicts in the 1840s and 1850s, certain Chinese elites became committed to a movement for "Self-Strengthening," which entailed adopting military-industrial technology from the West while at the same time preserving a Chinese essence (*zhongxue wei ti, xixue wei yong*).[14] The subsequent shock of defeat in the Sino-Japanese War (1894–95), however, precipitated commitment to a more sweeping political and cultural overhaul, the ascendance of what Schwartz calls "the commitment to the preservation and advancement of the societal entity known as the nation . . . over commitment to all other values and beliefs" (1964:19)—specifically those associated with orthodox Confucianism.[15]

At this critical juncture in the first years of the twentieth century, an incipient political-territorial nationalism began to displace a Han-centered philosophy of unwavering loyalty to unreformed Confucian tradition.[16] The revolution of 1911, the overthrow of the Manchu regime, and the ending of the dynastic order in China did little to temper the mainstream Chinese intelligentsia's preoccupation with what they perceived as China's relative weakness and cultural bankruptcy. In the years surrounding the May Fourth and New Culture movements in 1919, intellectuals sought a new identity for China that took inspiration from the differences persisting among the Chinese people. At this point, burgeoning nationalism, sharpened by Chinese intellectuals' outrage at unfavorable treaty agreements at the Versailles Peace Conference, began to penetrate more thoroughly into the cultural domain, giving rise to an intense search for alternative sources of strength and vitality to be found among the Chinese folk (Eminov 1975:259-60). Both the "Going to the People" movement, which was spearheaded by Communist Party co-founder Li Dazhao and which advocated learning from as well as educating the peasantry, and the Folk-Literature movement, which consisted of extensive collection and celebration of the folklore of the rural masses, had their inception at this time (see Hung 1985).

In this iconoclastic climate of cultural transformation, along with the popularization of literature and the vernacular language (baihua) movement associated with such intellectual leaders as Hu Shi and Chen Duxiu, certain of the New Culture pioneers were discovering non-Han resources. Gu Jiegang, one of the main players in the folklore movement and an advocate of revamping Chinese historiography to include alternatives to the Confucian canon, saw the "barbarians" (referring to the Muslim peoples) of the inner Asian frontier as "perennial resuscitators of a cyclically decrepit Chinese culture" (Schneider 1971:14). He and contemporaries such as Zhou Zuoren pored over earlier folklore collections from the Ming and Qing dynasties and, convinced of the reinvigorating power of these popular forms, established a folk song collection bureau at Beijing University in 1918 (Hung 1985:22-32). This type of appropriation of non-Han cultural forms for national purposes has continued in various guises throughout the twentieth century.

Two apparently contradictory approaches to non-Han cultural material can be identified as having emerged from this historical moment. Coinciding with the two forms of nationalism described above, they differ in their perspectives on gender and sexuality. From the standpoint of Chinese nationalism, minority cultural production was a source of lost vigor and identity in an atmosphere of repeated humiliations by foreign powers. Accounts of strong women and less constrictive gender attributions promised ideological liberation from the Confucian straitjacket. From the 1920s on, a newly constituted group of (predominantly male) intellectuals (*zhishifenzi*) stridently advanced the trope of individuated, universalized woman (*nuxing*), cut loose from her former kin-inflected positionality, who would stand as a sign of New China's modernity (Barlow 1991a). Much-celebrated and often-recounted practices of non-Han courtship, romance, and free love suggested a passionate vitality that could revivify a stilted and suffocating Han urban culture.

Meanwhile, a subtext associated with these representations reveals the workings of a Han nationalism, soon to be recast in Maoist terminology as Han "chauvinism." Here, the identical material was employed otherwise—as evidence of Han superiority on a scale of "civilization": fluidity of gender roles became transgressive of the prescribed social order; openly expressed "love" became sexual promiscuity, a breach of morality. Certain cultural conservatives of the May Fourth period, for example, held fast to otherwise widely rejected gender practices precisely because they were seen as emblematic of Chinese tradition. The Western-educated scholar Gu Hongming, who published a short-lived journal, *The National Heritage (Guogu)*, was an unyielding apologist for footbinding as an important element of the Chinese spirit (Levenson 1967:276) and asserted that concubinage was "as natural as a teapot with several teacups making a tea set" (Chow 1960:62).[17]

In the folklore field, directives for collection betrayed both a repression of and a fascination with sex/gender practices. In 1918 students were urged to collect "folksongs concerning the customs and habits, the history and society of the respective places . . . songs of far-off soldiers, rustics, longing girls and sorrowful women, in so far as they have natural beauty and are not obscene" (in Eminov 1975:259). The Custom Survey Society in 1923 surveyed such "reactionary" old customs as "idolatrous processions and performances along the procession," "concubines and slave-girls," "brothel-frequenting," and "abandoned children" (in Eminov 1975:261).

Into these cultural upheavals, Shen Congwen, a writer of mixed Han, Tujia, and Miao descent from Western Hunan (Xiangxi), introduced a style of literary regionalism that valorized local language and lore as "building blocks for the New Culture, which would reinvigorate China through the cultures of all her people" (Kinkley 1985:165; see also Oakes 1995b). Raised as a Han in a military gentry family, Shen's works celebrated regional flavors and textures linked to the past and to non-Han peoples—including erotic evocations and frank accounts of sexual customs—even as his practice of writing distanced him from the non-Han and their practices and digested them for urban literate consumers of the 1920s and 1930s.

The 1930s and the Japanese occupation of coastal regions during the second Sino-Japanese War (1937–45) brought Chinese urban intellectuals—spatially—to the folk of the hinterlands. As we saw with Zhang Zhengdong, the flight of the personnel of several universities along with their students to Yunnan province in China's southwest resulted in much closer contact with the non-Han peoples. For those like scholar Wen Yiduo, who trekked on foot from Changsha west, proximity inspired admiration. The cultures of the minorities came even more to be conceived as a potential antidote to China's humiliating weakness. In 1939, Wen opined in the introduction to a book of Miao poems collected by his students on the march from Changsha: "You say these [poems] are primitive and savage. You are right, and that is just what we need today. We've been civilized too long, and now that we have nowhere left to go we shall have to pull out the last and purest card, and release the animal nature that has lain dormant in us for several thousand years, so that we can bite back" (in Spence 1981:317). Like those of so many other internal orientalists, Wen's comments had the effect of both appropriating and debasing minority cultural difference. By framing minority practices as merely the animalistic facet of a putatively unified cultural whole, he rendered them at once vitally constitutive of national identity and potently contrastive with the civility of the West.

In the Maoist and post-Mao periods, as we have seen, a minority policy emphasizing *minzu* unity as "fraternal" continued—except during homogenizing movements such as the Great Leap Forward and the

Cultural Revolution — to advocate the celebration of minority cultures as "resources" in the national "treasure house."[18] With the closing of the door to exotic foreign cultural products after 1949, the Chinese film industry and its audience had turned to the exoticism of minorities for an alternate form of escape from urban Chinese monotony (Clark 1987). Then, in the mid-1980s, with the revived import of unsettling foreign media, an anxious appetite for *minzu* color emerged in the works of the so-called Fifth Generation filmmakers (R. Chow 1995a; Gladney 1995; Yau 1989; Zhang 1997). Here, a nationalist appropriation of internal resources as contrastive with the West once again came into play. Fei Hsiao-t'ung, China's noted anthropologist who had conducted field research among southwest minorities between 1950 and 1956 (Arkush 1981:225–38), likewise contributed to reviving the notion of minorities as the antidote to a weakening China. In a foreword to a 1982 English translation of minority folk poems, he emphasized: "Only when contrasted to the vigor and vitality of minority peoples, can one be shamed into a sense of self-realization of one's own dull and feeble character. . . . While striving for economic modernizations, the Han nationality learn from other nationalities on how to combine arts closely with people's social life. Then we can turn the big family of various Chinese nationalities into a beautiful, blossoming garden" (in Alley 1982:ii–iii). As can be seen here, by the 1980s, reminiscent of the old legends chronicled earlier, the non-Han "barbarians," no longer so animalistic, had been transformed into brothers — constitutive members of the Chinese family.

In addition to the internal development of Chinese nationalism, foreign ideas also had affected the attention to folk and minority cultures over the course of the twentieth century. The missionaries who flocked to China from several Western countries lived among minorities and doubled as fastidious ethnographers. The growth of interest in folklore collection was partly prompted by the attention it received from resident foreigners and by the translation into Chinese of many Western language volumes on the subject (Hung 1985:18–21). The "Going to the People" movement of the 1920s and the ethnic classification project undertaken in the 1950s were prompted by Russian populism and Stalinist nationality theory, respectively. Foreign anthropologists lectured in China in the 1920s and 1930s, and several prominent Chinese anthropologists were educated abroad with such luminaries as Bronislaw Malinowski.[19]

After the founding of the People's Republic, Soviet influences were especially formative of what persists as Chinese ethnology to the present day (see Guldin 1992). This academic transfer extended to popular cultural domains with the cultural liberalization and growing transnational mediation of the 1980s. Young urbanites enthusiastically emulated such Western fads as modernist primitivism in art and the "roots" (*xungen*) movement, turning to minorities as objects of their imported fascination. Moreover, the rise of large-scale international tourism was met with great attention in many sectors of cultural production. Chinese hosts, in pursuit of foreign tourist revenues that had skyrocketed from US $263 million in 1978 to more than US $2.2 billion in 1988 (National Tourism Administration 1990:82), eagerly capitulated to visitors' insatiable desire for the exotic. Thus, paradoxically, while a nationalist ideology incorporated the domestic other to serve as contrastive with the outside, some of the practices and styles of othering used to highlight this contrast had, themselves, been imported and indigenized.

The notion of straightforward foreign "influence" on modes of Chinese nationalism and modernity has been resoundingly critiqued by Lydia Liu (1995) in ways highly pertinent to the problem of internal orientalism. To be sure, Chinese cultural elites have been in intensive dialogue with imported culture for at least the last century, and in the post-Mao era this kind of engagement has become popularly accessible through mass media. But this instance of what Clifford called "traveling culture" (1992) is by no means the uncomplicated transfer of meanings to the Chinese context. Instead, Liu favors a notion of translation (or what Barlow (1991b) called the "localization of the sign") to describe the process by which imported culture is agentively reworked in the host culture where it is subjected to "unexpected reading and appropriation" (1995:60). Liu's exhortation demands that analysts attend closely to the specificities of local uses, that, in the case of what we might call "translated orientalism," we ask *what these practices are doing* with reference both to internal Chinese social process and to the way in which China is taking its place in a global context.

Capturing Xijiang

As a peasant village, the community of Xijiang, where I did fieldwork in 1988 and 1993, was anomalous for several reasons. Nicknamed the

"Thousand Household Miao Village" (*Qian Jia Miao Zhai*) with a population of more than 5,000, its administration of about seventy "natural" villages[20] meant a significant state presence in the form of some 300 state employees, a government office building, a middle school, a post office, a bank, a courtroom, a grain depository, and other offices. It was oriented around a townlike main street, which was the terminus of a long-distance bus route and the site of a periodic market that drew peddlers and purchasers from far-flung counties. Despite its location in the remote mountainous region of Southeast Guizhou, Xijiang had an air of relative worldliness about it, of which its locals were proud. Young people could attend school right in town and could ride the bus to the county or prefecture seats for market. Older people who stayed home could keep up with current events by means of a public loudspeaker system, and with cultural trends by means of television or movies shown once or twice a week.

At the same time, Xijiang's reputation as a locus of "typical" (*dianxing*) Miao culture had been growing. In 1983, *China Reconstructs,* the slick English language magazine that circulates globally, chose Xijiang for a special feature article, "A Miao Village" (Peng 1983). A book introducing the Southeast Guizhou region boasted that Xijiang was "famed as a natural museum of ethnic customs" (Qiandongnan 1986:12–13). A 1990 compendium of Miao customs from all over the country (Pan 1990) featured Xijiang as the first of only ten photographs in the front of the volume and the only one that specified by name the locality pictured.

Despite its publicity, Xijiang remained closed to most foreign tourism throughout the 1980s and into the 1990s.[21] In the meantime, the community became one of the most popular destinations in Guizhou province for Chinese urbanites looking for a taste of the exotic and/or authentic. In the post-Mao years, Xijiang saw a constant stream of artists, photographers, journalists, ethnographers, officials, and tourists coming through in search of something—whether images or information—to take away from the Miao people that lived there. These were domestic travelers, but from as far away as Beijing, and they were primarily male. Where images were being made, the subjects were primarily female.

Travelers usually stayed in the government guest house and went out from there into the village in search of interesting angles. They often came back disappointed from these initial forays and sought me out as the "expert" ethnographer. One warm afternoon in June, a young man from Anhui province knocked at the door to my room in the guest house. He introduced himself, explaining that he was a teacher of art at the Jiangxi Education Institute and an oil painter himself. "I came to Xijiang because everyone said it was a good place," he complained, referring to his desire for native spectacles, "but actually you can't see anyone wearing *minzu* clothing around here. Do you know where I could go to see people in silver headdresses?" He had only just arrived on the noon bus, but he was so disappointed that he was thinking of leaving the next morning. He already had been around town taking some pictures, but there was, by his definition, nothing to see. The standard fare for many—dark wood houses built on piles and stacked into the steep hillsides, the brilliant green of the young rice in paddies terraced like steps up the mountains, women with hair twisted atop their heads beating laundry in the brooks or shouldering long poles that suspended baskets or water buckets—were of no interest. "I'm interested in images of real people, not just clothing and scenery. You can get this kind of material in magazines like *Minzu Pictorial*," he complained. "I'm in a bit of a hurry—I have to turn in my paintings in August for an exhibition at the Anhui Fine Arts Institute."

This artist's frustrations were typical of the reactions of outsiders when trying to make an image out of Xijiang. The local Miao people, they griped, were Sinicized (*Hanhua*): the women were in pants, and many of the people even wore Western-style clothing. Could I recommend a village in the region where they might see the "real" Miao? What they were referring to was the elaborately embroidered festival costume (*shengzhuang*) and silver headdress that they had seen for decades on magazine covers and television documentaries as "typical" Miao women's attire. When they discovered that what they sought was precious festival regalia reserved only for wear on special occasions, they frequently paid to have Zhou, the young Miao man at the local "Culture Station" (*Wenhua Zhan*),[22] organize a photo shoot. Carefully selected Miao young women would don their best costumes, marks of their beauty and emblems of their difference, and pose as directed for the replication of the images expected and craved by urban consumers. Gradually, the features of Xijiang's constructed typicality became canonized, reiterated over and over again through highly visible media means, such that the standardized popular image supplanted a more complicated picture on the ground.

I suggested to the artist that he was not likely to see what he was looking for on a regular afternoon in June. By the next day he had arranged with Zhou to make an excursion to take pictures in Gaiyong, a village about a half-hour's walk from Xijiang. Apparently Zhou had surmised that getting farther from the bus route, away from Xijiang's centrality, might be what the young artist was looking for. I decided to join them. Along the way I asked Zhou why he chose Gaiyong for travelers' visits. He said that the women photographed must "have good looks" and that Gaiyong girls were especially pretty. When we arrived at the home he had chosen, we were invited to sit on six-inch-high stools in the bare receiving room with a mother, a father, and a young woman. The father, a silversmith, was busy polishing silver. Zhou conversed with the family in Miao for a while as the artist grew more and more restless. He asked me to inquire whether Zhou had mentioned his purpose yet. Zhou responded by sending the artist to look at the frame full of family photos adorning the wall and to pick out what clothes he liked from those images. The artist chose a black embroidered outfit, and Zhou directed the young woman, whose hair was fastened back in a simple pony tail, to don the costume and comb her hair on top of her head. She disappeared to transform herself, protesting all the while that she did not photograph well (*zhao bu hao*). Zhou encouraged the artist to look at ancient clothing (*gufu*) while he waited, and the artist methodically laid out old embroidered squares from the family trunk and photographed them.

When his model emerged, he had her sit and stand in a variety of poses, always with her face turned demurely from the camera. "Now," he commanded, gesturing to a garment he had chosen from the family trunk, "put on this old embroidered jacket." The young woman refused embarrassedly, and her mother supported her. "*You* put it on instead," she poked fun at him. The artist protested that if it were men's clothing, he surely would be willing to try it on. Would the mother model it instead? She declined, referring to her old age as ugly, and asked him to sit down and take a break. As a diversion, she sent her daughter off to begin cooking dinner. Finally, after a great deal of urging, the mother reluctantly disappeared to put on the jacket. When she returned, her demeanor was very bashful as she posed for this strange visitor's camera. The cluster of children that had gathered laughed mirthfully at the sight.

As we walked home from the dinner that our Gaiyong hosts had served us, I asked the artist how he would use the pictures. "I'll hire a model at home for the face and body," he proclaimed. "The clothes will be the girl's. I want to paint in the classical style of Rubens, so the background will be very dark. . . ."

Two months later, Zhou told me that he was indignant at the bad manners of the young artist from Anhui. Zhou had arranged that the family would be compensated with copies of the photographs taken at their home. "He didn't send back one picture for the family that posed for him! This guy sure talks a good game—and he sure knows how to cheat people! It makes it awfully hard for me to carry out *my* work," he exclaimed bitterly. But, of course, the man from Anhui was long gone.

To capture Xijiang in representation meant engaging in multiple mediations. Nothing prevented urban cultural producers from poking about the village and documenting its raw and spontaneous appearance. But most were looking for something else. What was implied in the language of the "typical" was a certain undiluted intensity of folk color and an unbroken connection to the past. To obtain their image, they employed Zhou as ethnic broker, contrived the appearance of their representational objects, and often compensated models for their labors. It is not insignificant that the Anhui artist fulfilled his quest through the vehicle of the old family photos in which the subjects were groomed and posed. The mood of the resulting image-making was what Ivy (1995) has called the "elegaic"—performatively lamenting a bygone era. Yet even as its passing was mourned, folk flavor was preserved as vital. It was the persistence of the *minzu* past in the present that was to lend China its national distinctiveness and to afford urban Han their positional superiority.

Reading Domestic Encounters: Women and the Exotic

A closer look at the specific sites of the reproduction of difference in post-Mao China reveals the ways in which gender dichotomies framed both the interactions and the images that emerged from them. As I have said, visitors to the village of Xijiang were primarily male, and they came under various auspices. They hailed from major cities as distant as Beijing, Shanghai, and Guangzhou, although the majority were from Guizhou and neighboring Sichuan provinces. In some cases they were sent by their "work unit" (*gongzuo danwei*) — a newspaper, television station, or research institute with a specific agenda. In other cases, they were employed in unrelated occupations, such as factory or office work, and were personally interested in pursuits of the exotic, both experientially and for more utilitarian reasons such as making sales to foreigners or winning prizes in art exhibitions. Many visitors were from art institutes; it had become a common part of the curriculum of many art programs to send students "down" to minority areas such as Tibet, Xinjiang, and the southwest provinces for *shixi* (fieldwork) and to bring back "novel" material for their art products. Additionally, officials from various levels were regularly escorted by county bureaucrats to get a taste of the authenticity of Xijiang or, in some cases, to gather data on the lives of rural minorities.

These travelers brought with them, along with their easels, their tape recorders, and their preferred seasonings with which to doctor local food, a relatively unified metropolitan discourse by which they described their hinterland destinations. These places were "backward" (*luohou*), the ways of life "primitive" (*yuanshi*), and the people "simple, honest, unsophisticated" (*chunpu*). It was like going back in time; by visiting such outposts one could see the stages through which society had developed.[23] Most sought-after were locales that had "distinctive ethnic flavor" (*minzu tese*). When I asked why rural sites with minority inhabitants were preferred subjects, they explained that these were things they could not see at home.[24] Consequently, Xijiang with its jarring emblems of modernity — its three-story schoolhouse, its paved plaza where buses loaded and teenagers dribbled basketballs — was frequently characterized as having "not much worth looking at" (*meiyou shenme haokande*).

These distillations of difference were projected onto places, onto customs, and especially onto local minority women. Non-Han women constituted counterpoints to urban elite culture, signifying both a trajectory toward a modernity already claimed by the metropolitan class and evoking the "imperialist nostalgia" that Rosaldo (1989:68–87) has described in which one mourns the loss of precisely what has been destroyed through the "progress" one has wrought. Images were carefully orchestrated. One film crew hired local young women to act out net fishing in conjunction with the local Sisters Rice Festival (*Jiemei Fan*) that they had come to document in the river village of Shidong. They brought the peasants-turned-actresses to the riverbank, dressed in full festival attire, and painstakingly positioned them so that all would be visible and facing forward. To obtain the effect of ingenuous natural-ness, they chose camera angles that would reveal no houses or villagers, but only the scenic landscape in the background. These representational strategies effected transmutations in the meanings of the everyday prac-tice of their subjects. In this case, the banality of subsistence production was replaced by the romance of harmony with nature.

The oppositions of modern-backward, civilized-wild, then, were re-peatedly enunciated through the association of "the" minority woman with nature and with youth. In mass media images she appeared com-muning with animals or nestled among trees and flowers.[25] Luscious fruits abounded for the picking. Waterfalls and streams framed care-free, laughing teenagers. Youth was stressed not only by the physical appearance of the women represented, but also by their identity with the innocence of the natural. Childlike women were pictured, accom-panied by such companions as birds, lambs, or butterflies with which they seemed to be in direct communication.[26]

The effect was of infantilizing and trivializing.[27] Yet these represen-tations also were imbued with a kind of warmth — albeit patronizing — and an intense fascination. One team that visited Xijiang was making a video documentary on the region's atmospheric conditions and other natural phenomena for a meteorology institute in another province. The mystery of the "remote mountains and ancient forests" (shenshan laolin) of Xijiang and the surrounding area had been a long-standing object of interest for tourists and scientists alike (if not for the Anhui artist). Not content, however, with nature alone, this team decided that a bevy of local maidens would be the perfect companionship for their work and the perfect ornamentation for their meteorology video. They hired four local girls at nominal pay to accompany them on an arduous climb — filmed along the way — to a mountain pass 1,200 meters above the village. The girls were coached to look sharp. Despite the fact that it was a dank, chilly day with the mountain peaks enveloped in thick mist, they wore their best hair adornments and, shod in feminine plastic shoes with low heels rather than the rubber-soled canvas "liberation shoes" (jiefang hai) normally considered most practical on slippery slopes, they braved the steep, muddy path. As they climbed, they were stopped at strategically chosen scenic spots to perform such activities as washing in a stream or singing a Miao song on camera. The effect was to be of naturalness—the local women skillfully embedded in their wilderness environment.[28]

Joking and giggling characterized the mood of the climb as the filmmakers took pleasure in their ingenue escorts. When they reached the top of the pass, the girls sat with their employers, resting in the thick mist in an expansive clearing before beginning their long descent home. The filmmakers were to continue on to a more distant cluster of villages nestled in the next valley. One of the crew members held out a handful of candy—a seldom-eaten luxury for peasants in this region—in what the girls believed to be a gesture of gratitude and parting. They reached out to accept it, but he snatched his hand back. "Sing one more Miao song!" he demanded with gusto. "*Then* you'll get the candy!" "Too embarrassing!" they demurred, making excuses, stalling, and refusing to sing. Eventually, the filmmaker relented and gave them the candy without a song.

In this episode, minority women were subjected to a double objectification. On the one hand, they were arrayed among the massive trees and trickling brooks as part of the intriguing wildness that drew urban visitors. On the other, they were treated as ethnic automatons, expected to produce folk culture at a moment's notice for the reward of a mouthful of candy. This compensation dynamic is of course ubiquitous in ethnic tourism worldwide. But this instance represents, in effect, a proto-touristic moment in which peasants were being socialized to commodify their culture, to regard it as a discrete medium of exchange. In this case, however, the young women refused to comply, stalling, claiming embarrassment, and eventually persuading the filmmaker to give them the candy without a direct exchange. These practices exemplify ways in which local people confounded attempts at dominant appropriation, insisting that they and no one else define the contexts in which particular cultural practices were or were not appropriate.

A convergence of nature with culture was portrayed through the minority woman's ritual dexterity. Representations of minority customs portrayed non-Han women as servile and hospitable, anchored to the home, guardians of tradition. The reception of the mayors on the hotel plaza in Kaili, described earlier, was a classic example. Staged by the local tourism office and the management of the hotel (the local entrepreneurial sector), this welcome evoked for conferees a sense of lost culture intact. It was offered up, like the payment of tribute, to the governing elite in a manner that conveyed contented submissiveness. What better purveyor of this mood than the young minority woman, dressed exotically, in the receptive posture of greeting beloved guests? The ritual served to ignite delegates' fantasies of a cultural realm within China, brightened by marvelous costume and strange music, where ancient rites were not forgotten, and appropriate relationships were maintained.

While Chinese internal orientalism commonly classed minority women as natural, nonhuman or childlike, or as cultural conservators, this pigeonholing did not preclude their being very human objects of erotic fascination. In many contemporary art and media images, their bodies appeared voluptuous, and their expressions were unabashedly inviting. Sometimes their bodies would be more extensively revealed than would be appropriate for a Han woman; at other times, reminiscent of the French colonial postcards of Algerian women that Alloula (1986) described, the elaborateness of their costume operated like the veil, suggestive by virtue of its concealment and its excess.[29]

The imaginings that surrounded minority women, thus, constituted a powerful attractive force. Accounts that bespoke minority women's imagined availability were legion. Yet they were attended by a kind of repulsion, a repressive fear of the implied baseness and breaches of morality that made these women so other. On mentioning to a Chinese urbanite one's interest in minorities, it was not uncommon to be told in tones of confidentiality and admonition that, for example, the women "there" wore no tops, or that unmarried young people were said to have orgies during courtship festivals. In whispered lore as well as in bluntly scientific ethnographic reports and graphic documentary films, tales would circulate about non-Han courtship practices, freedom of choice in marriage partners, and especially sexual promiscuity. Tones of disapproval mixed with titillation characterized these furtively delivered anecdotes. They implied an ambivalently regarded double rupture in the conventional social order: unrepressed sexuality signified a relativizing of mores that was threatening but liberating, while strong, unrestrained women meant the hopeful but unnerving potential for transgression of constrictive gender roles.

10. Bookmarks for *minzu* voyeurs.

11. Postcard allure.

The Romance of Proximity

Many foreign tourists and Chinese urbanites were daunted by the prospect of hardship traveling in minority regions, but they still hungered for an experience of immediacy. This craving led to a demand for the "staging of authenticity" (MacCannell 1973) in the metropolis. One Han man, a regional native working as a musical director for the Guizhou Culture Bureau, watched the modalities of foreign tourism keenly and pioneered a "new" form of exhibition that was to become standard fare in ensuing years. It was a mobile display of words, photographs, and artifacts portraying Guizhou folkways accompanied by reenacted festivals in the form of a living museum. He forayed into the Guizhou countryside to recruit young people with particular talent and looks. They were instructed to bring with them not only their best festival attire, but also a song or dance typical of their locality. These "raw" materials were processed into a finely honed performance, carefully choreographed to be "realistic," that represented the songs, dances, and musical instruments of Guizhou folklife. The exhibition traveled to such major cities as Beijing, Xi'an, Tianjin, and Shenzhen.

While minority performing troupes have been commonplace in China for decades, what was seen as "novel" in this one was that the performers were minimally trained peasants from the countryside, holding out the promise of a kind of intimacy of (first) contact whose resonances with the lure of virginity were less than subtle. The director was the constructor and mediator of these desires, and he fashioned them out of the intensity of his own contact experiences. Among the recruits were two teenage women from Xijiang. The director had traveled to Xijiang and fallen head over heels into the embrace of Miao "hospitality." When I visited the traveling culture exhibition in Xi'an, he and his two Xijiang recruits recounted his initial visit to their hometown. At a meal prepared in his honor, he told me, he had dined among men while the women served him. His hosts had plied him with local liquor. The young women had approached him proffering bowls of libation and singing welcome songs. This treatment sent him into such reveries that he was struck by the muse. That night in Xijiang, he composed two original songs. Their lyrics capture the evening's atmosphere of sensuality and sociality:

I am a cloud in the sky; you are a spring in the mountain
I am mist in the forest; you are a lotus in the water

Xijiang, ah, Xijiang, would that I was a spring rain sprinkling upon
your fertile fields
Xijiang, ah, Xijiang, would that I could become the morning dew to
kiss your smiling face.

Through lyrical production, the object of desire was cast as a place,
beautiful and somehow inaccessible. The concatenation of images reveals the link between pastoral fantasy and romantic/sexual intimations.
The second song he created that night went even further in conflating
nature imagery with that of romantic desire. It was a veritable catalog of
the symbols most commonly used to characterize Miao culture. As the
verses developed, it became increasingly concerned with an unrepressed
and erotically charged passion associated by the Han with tabooed com-
panionate courtship practices — in this case the young woman's symbolic tying of a handmade sash on the musical instrument of the young
man she fancies in a ritual dance performed at certain festivals.

Isn't it delightful, Xijiang water
Mountain springs gurgle with a clear, crisp sound
Sweet as honey, it seeps into your heart
One sip from the clear spring makes you drunk
May I ask A Mei [a term of address to young women, meaning
literally "little sister"], whence comes the spring?
Every drop is a tear from the yearning between lovers.

Isn't it lovely, the Xijiang mountains
In the boundless forest, the bamboo is the most green
The sound of flying songs ["fei ge," a well-known genre of Miao
song], sung over and over
May I ask A Ge [a form of address to young men, especially by
younger women, meaning literally "elder brother"], for whom
are you singing?
It is for little sister embroidering inside the diaojiaolou [typical Miao
architecture of the region, consisting of wooden houses built on
piles with suspended balconies].

Isn't she beautiful, the Xijiang girl?
In splendid dress, her crown of silver shining in the morning light
Her smile is most full of affection [duoqing, referring to feelings
between members of the opposite sex]

On the *lusheng* ground, her dance is the most beautiful
May I ask A Mei, for whom is the embroidered sash?
[It shows] I wish to be together with A Ge forever.

These lyrics, charged with emotion and conceived by a Han man, demonstrate the intensity and vividness with which Miao culture and Miao sexuality had captured the urban imagination. Through his excursion to Miao country, the director had achieved the kind of momentary self-transformation so often sought after by tourists. A middle-aged man, he had found the romantic excitement of youth and drawn on it to fuel his own creativity. In his crafting of the festival show, however, passionate abandon was rechanneled as enthusiastic appreciation. The effect was of sanitizing, deftly repressing the sexual subtext and creating a safe domain for the controlled consumption of festival practices that in their original context might have been dangerously spontaneous and carnivalesque.

The Womanly Visage of Tradition and Modernity

Minority men, I should note, also regularly appeared in performances and images as objects of dominant consumption. But minority women, as emblematic of the natural, the traditional, and the erotically titillating, were not so subtly foregrounded in even these representations, with men serving as a foil to highlight the women's distinctiveness and allure. In images and accounts that dealt with minority courtship practices, for instance, the girl regularly appeared coy, but sassy and inviting; the boy gazed at or embraced her, functioning as a vehicle for the desire she provoked. In this way, minority men, in their intimate proximity to the desired object, focused and redirected the consumer's gaze from the indeterminate panorama of colorful culture to the minority woman-object.

It is less important, however, that minority women were specular objects per se than what they signified in the context of a profoundly ambivalent Chinese consciousness torn between the appeal of modernity and its threat of corruption. Following Lata Mani, I suggest that these women became the "site[s] on which tradition was debated and reformulated" (1987:153)—and in this case domesticated. As the work of Barlow (1991a), Beahan (1975), Chow (1991a), and Liu (1991) has amply demonstrated, for China the trope of woman has been a key signifier at historical junctures where modernizing was at stake. What "she" signified, however, was shifting and contested. In some contexts, she was the emblem of traditional China whose emancipation would be a marker of progress. In others, she was an object of desire, either a nostalgic desire that framed her as the bearer of an untarnished past, or a forward-looking desire that posed Western woman as the symbol of that which China longed for but did not have (cf. Chow 1991b:86). In all cases, however, she constituted a counterpart to a masculinist center/present. As Ong (1990) found for Islamic revivalism in Malaysia, subordinate women's gender propriety and sexual morality became battlegrounds for nationalist elites seeking to recuperate and entrench tradition as a mode of resistance to engulfment in the culture of global capitalism. In the Chinese case, situating the struggle squarely in the domain of the "other" woman freed would-be nationalists to pursue their own versions of the modern while purporting to defend the traditional.

A society's self-representation as modern often involves contrastive claims of what Laura Nader (1989), following Said, calls "positional superiority" over those constructed as less modern. Such discourses are commonly premised on the assumption of an improved position — however defined — of women within the society that is making claims to being more "advanced." In China, contemporary problems and reversals in the status of women were glossed over by focusing attention on "other" women painted as less civilized than the urban, "modernized" Han. As Nader puts it: "If progress is incremental then the place of women continuously improves, and evidence to the contrary is either minimized, or denied, or dealt with by turning the lens to the image of women in other cultures" (1989:342). Ironically, the image of sexual promiscuity and fluidity of gender roles commonly used to characterize minorities was misrecognized as a mark of backwardness in a metropolitan Chinese framework, which, despite being overtly progressivist, continued, despite itself, to assess "civilization" in terms of the fixity of Confucian gender/status hierarchies.

Since national identity was always implicated in these struggles over tradition and modernity, it was particularly fitting that the oppositional role was so often played by a non-Han woman. Her liminal character, as both of China and yet distinct from it, made her a much-traversed site for working through problems of Chineseness and its transformation. In the post-Mao period of reform, the presence of the minority woman as what promotional pamphlets called a "colorful element" in Chinese national culture was reassuring to cosmopolitan Chinese in two apparently contradictory senses. On the one hand, she was evidence of the uninterrupted existence of a well-preserved "traditional" culture in changing China. On the other hand, her intractable otherness made clear the need for the civilizing practices, however defined, of the "superior" Han. That an other existed on whom to carry out civilizing/modernizing projects mitigated the otherwise debilitating sense of the Han self as backward.

Internally Speaking

Earlier in this chapter we encountered, in the practices of Han internal orientalists, the active and selective framing of the Miao community of Xijiang as an emblem of minority otherness. In this process, Xijiang's undesirably "modern" look was elided (camera angles were chosen to conceal the concrete buildings that lined the paved main street), and its fictive typicality was reproduced in the distilled image of the colorfully dressed, smiling young woman—a young woman who was visibly and abjectly "different." The Miao, as a consequence, were feminized and rendered as symbols of the tradition-bound past, untouched by decades, even centuries, of change. For China, Miao and other minorities constituted an underground self that was internal, yielding an indigenous identity that allowed distinction from the West, while it simultaneously marked the modernity of Han urbanites by offering a "traditional" alter ego, as signified by the subordinate sex. In the anxious eyes of urbanites who consumed these images, China could take its place in a world of nation-states able to invoke a particular identity-bestowing history and also distance it.

As Bhabha notes: "The problem is not simply the 'selfhood' of the nation as opposed to the otherness of other nations. We are confronted with the nation split within itself, articulating the heterogeneity of its population. The barred Nation It/Self, alienated from its eternal self-generation, becomes a liminal signifying space that is internally marked by the discourses of minorities, the heterogeneous histories of contending peoples, antagonistic authorities and tense locations of cultural difference" (1994:148). It is my emphasis on ideological deployments of difference *and their consequences* that has led to my elaboration of internal orientalism. China's governance of non-Han peoples within its territory after Liberation may be structurally dissimilar from the classic colonial relations between Europe and the spatially distant "Orient," but its techniques of bounding and codifying strain toward the production of a nation commensurate with others worldwide.

This chapter has examined the multiplicity of practices and ideologies that constitute Chinese internal orientalism in order to make several arguments. First, the production and reproduction of difference is not a unitary project; rather, it involves a plurality of actors. It cannot be simplistically centered in state discourse or in the representational practices of a discrete dominant group. While these agents are key purveyors of the trope of cultural otherness, those who are commonly objects of representation also figure critically in the construction of contrastive identities. Competing interests (such as how prestige will be accorded) and convergent values (such as the thirst for modernity) intersect in this zone of cultural production. The fact of a haunting standardization in the images that constitute the "colorful minority" genre does not permit occlusion of the heterogeneity that characterizes the producers of these images. Ethnographic method can bring into focus that which solely textual approaches cannot gain access to—the active roles and vocalities of those who are ultimately rendered as mute icons.

Second, it was precisely the gendering of minority images that sanctified in social consciousness a set of perduring status inequalities with far-reaching material consequences. Collectively stamped as backward, the deftly amalgamated classes of minorities, women, and peasants, by virtue of their consociation in dominant representations, remained consigned to a secondary position in the Chinese social order—no matter how stridently their quaint practices were lauded in public discourse. It is this conjunction—between representation and structural inequality —that Said's work has been so influential in demonstrating, and that prompts me to extend his formulation to a contemporary "Eastern" site where political economy is likewise inextricable from discourse.

Third, it is in the circulation, not the creation, of images of difference that power asymmetries usually become determinative. In China, because the state and certain urban cultural producers were able to monopolize access to the means of dissemination, the content of their representations had the potential to become hegemonic. In a cultural climate that celebrated the trajectory toward modernity, infantilization, feminization, and stigmatization became normativizing strategies that condemned as retrograde those lifeways that transgressed the bounds of valorized tradition. Miao cultural producers, as seen in the second section, were themselves thickly implicated in the constitution of this order of difference. Chapter 5 carries this argument further, analytically reconfiguring discursive domination in China to account for a more polyvocal field of practices even in the manufacture of hegemonic outcomes.

5

Reconfiguring the Dominant

Xishuangbanna is rich in age-old traditions and fresh vitality at once. Remnants of socio-historical developments several thousand years ago can still be found here. Its natural scenery is diametrically different from that in the central and northern parts of China. Its distinctive features endowed by Nature unfold themselves before people [*sic*] eyes. . . . However what makes it even more attractive is the people here of various minority nationalities such as the Dais, the Hanis, the Bulangs, the Lahus, the Jinuos, etc. They have been living on this land generation after generation. With their industrious hands and creative labor, they have been contributing to the exploitation of the frontier, the creation of a long history and splendid culture of their motherland. Visitors to Xishuangbanna will doubtless be affected by their diligence, honesty, straightforwardness as well as their keen interest in dancing and singing.
—from "Our Beautiful Xishuangbanna," a tourism booklet

The text above, promoting the region in the southernmost tip of Yunnan province, catalogues features commonly associated with minority areas in China. It is a classic example of the language and images found in promotional literature of the post-Mao period. Xishuangbanna, a Dai autonomous prefecture, is portrayed as traditional, socially unevolved, diametrically different from China's center, endowed by nature, and full of frontier peoples contributing to the motherland who love to sing and dance. On the page following the introductory text is the first photo spread, which offers four images. Two photographs show characteristic architecture—rooftops and temple spires framed by bamboo and palm trees. The other two picture what is probably the most celebrated stereotype of this region—the wet woman.[1] In one photograph, five young women, arrayed at the banks of a sparkling river, hike up their sarongs to wade into the water. In another, a single young woman standing in water is photographed from above; she holds her sarong around her body in the manner reputed to be the local mode of bathing, but it is off her bare shoulders, and the bird's eye viewer can peek inside and almost see her breasts. . . .

Who is producing these statements about the region and its peoples? Despite the patriotic language of unity in diversity, this is not a state publication issuing from Beijing. The booklet was the product of eight photographers and the text copywriter; it was edited by members of a regional organization called the Photographers' Association of Xishuangbanna Dai Nationality Autonomous Prefecture, and it was printed in the coastal Special Economic Zone of Shenzhen, a city known for its free-wheeling enterprise and its remoteness from politics. Although not identified in the booklet's credits, some contributors were themselves likely members of minority groups. At least three of them are listed in the credits with names that are recognizably non-Han. Nonetheless, the glossy pages bursting with color, ritual, and images of nature feature wooden, sloganlike captions that seem to reiterate the terms of state minority policy: "Xishuangbanna is [a] great family of various nationalities. All these nationalities get along with each other on fraternal terms. Each of them has its own distinctive lifestyle and fine tradition." Why are minority cultural producers depicting themselves almost identically to the way that the state frames them?

This chapter weaves together the diverse strands that make up the dominant representation of minorities, women, and peasants. While the book argues that reified differences are the artifacts of multiple agents, this chapter takes up the problem of the formation of a dominant voice. What does it mean to talk about a dominant voice in China's cultural production? My account recasts conventional modes that have understood power in China as being strictly localized within the state in order to consider instead a wider discursive field. It sketches an uncoordinated but effectively unitary cultural production on the part of Han and Miao elites, both state and nonstate, who could claim a relative degree of worldliness. Their creation of imagings of Miao and other minorities was intimately enmeshed with international codes for portraying exotic others. At the same time, this creation was inextricably caught up with, even propelled by, Chinese nationalism and by a particular notion of

Chinese modernity. It was not a straightforward outcome of univocal state discourse speaking for a silent populace.

Freelancing in and Around the State

In post-Mao China the cultural producers whose artifice was primitivized images of minorities had varied and complex relations to the state. A close look at one of them reveals intricate entanglements of autonomy and affiliation.

Chen was a tall and urbane young man from Beijing who arrived in Xijiang in early September 1988. In the close heat of a late summer day, he dressed down, but he still marked his urbanity with tie-dyed shorts and a T-shirt sporting the words "Nouvelles Frontières." Full of self-promoting bravado, Chen presented himself as a self-directed and visionary artist. "Maybe you'll think this is immodest," he boasted, "but I think I am the photographer with the most promise in all of China." He went on to emphasize his worldliness and to distinguish his status by cataloguing skills and hobbies: "I know how to drive and how to ride a horse; I have climbed Mount Everest; I love music and can play a little flute and violin; and I love to swim and go fishing. . . ."

At a time when many students still awaited job assignments from the government, Chen described himself as unemployed, a freelancer. Here is his heroic self-portrayal: Upon graduation from the prestigious Central Academy of Art in Beijing, he had been assigned to work at a provincial publishing house, but he negotiated with his employers to let him shift his household registration back to Beijing so he could be with his girlfriend. Upon official approval of his request, Chen forfeited his iron-rice-bowl employment with the state and went out to make his own way. He described his situation as "very difficult" without a work unit. When he was in Beijing, he would do the shopping—buying high-priced rice since his lack of a work unit meant he had no allocations of coupons for state-subsidized grain—and then he would cook while his girlfriend went to work at a regular job. His status was that of one of the new entrepreneurs who had emerged after Deng's reforms in the interstices between state work units and new ventures. Chen did business with both, but he saw himself as resisting the drive for material gain and as evading the political scrutiny of the state. He acted as he did out of commitment to his art.

Chen's creative interest was in taking black-and-white photographs that he considered artistic. The subject of the pictures was not his primary concern; rather, he valued them for what he described as their aesthetic quality. He kept most of this work to himself, showing it only rarely. Meanwhile, he explained, he was traveling the country for a Swiss publisher, trying to take pictures that recorded the faces of all the regions of China. He already had published books on Tibet, Gansu, and Qinghai. He had decided, for political reasons, to stick to this kind of neutral photography. He had done pictures with political content for which *Time, Newsweek,* and the *New York Times Magazine* had offered him large sums of money, but he did not dare sell them right now. Instead, he complained, he was exploited by foreigners who knew he was just a young, unemployed fellow and paid him only fifty or sixty yuan for photos sold in small home exhibits. Working with such limited means, he lamented that he lacked the resources to do his own developing. He had friends with darkrooms in Beijing, but they could never handle the volume that he produced. Instead, he relied on foreign and Chinese friends to carry his film abroad and seek the best quality developing.

Despite his professed autonomy, one of the ways that Chen got his work done was by flashing forged papers from an influential state-run national newspaper. "It's better to tell locals that I'm a Beijing reporter rather than just a freelance photographer. It gives me more power because people are afraid I'm going to report back to the central government." Chen pursued his photography of China's minorities by going through official channels with his doctored papers. When he arrived in a new province, he would start at the capital, visiting social science academies, arts institutes, and nationalities research institutes. From these "experts" he would seek out recommendations as to which destinations were "good" and obtain introductions to state offices at lower levels in the bureaucracy. Then he would travel to county seats, again seeking out officials, this time at local culture bureaus; they would advise him as to specific locales that were optimal for photography and would supply him with additional introductions. When he arrived at villages, he would be equipped with names of specific contacts who, because of their obligations as state employees, would guarantee his success in gaining photographic subjects.

Chen's ambiguous status also brought him other benefits. His first evening in Xijiang he parlayed his officially sanctioned identity into an elite dining opportunity. A group of visiting state functionaries who were holding a meeting in town had contracted banquets to be served to them in a public hall. Chen managed to procure an invitation to eat with them. By joining outsiders whose food was specially prepared for them by the local guest house, he could avoid eating from the local food vendors or at the homes of peasants. Both of these options, he judged too unsanitary (bu weisheng).

"I'm not really interested in minorities," Chen demurred, "My own interest is in black and white art photography. But pictures of minorities in beautiful costumes are not controversial and they sell. I do this kind of photography to survive." One of his projects had been a wall calendar of Tibet commissioned by a Beijing firm that wanted a gift for clients. Why, I asked, did he think publishers and consumers liked minorities so much? "First of all, they are accessible to a wide audience. Second, China is very interested in things primitive these days." Why? He could not say.[2] The next day he arranged with Zhou of the Culture Station to pose young women in festival dress for photographs. In the evening he made tape-recordings of minge (local folk songs) to take back to Beijing, where a friend who had a computer would clean them up for better listening.

Chen was clearly a significant contributor to the panoply of depictions of minorities that were circulating in China's popular culture of the 1980s. He had published wall calendars and sold to magazines. He had distributed his work domestically and abroad. But Chen's practice lends considerable complexity to the question of how the unitary culture that displayed minorities came into being. Chen was not an agent of the state in the sense of being a state-employed official or functionary. He had forfeited the benefits of state employment and accepted economic insecurity and liminal status in order to have autonomy for his artistic production. Nonetheless, what Chen produced was not solely the expression of his independent spirit. His camerawork was guided both by the constraints of what he felt would insure his political neutrality in the eyes of the state and by the demands of foreign and internal-orientalist markets that were thirsting for exotic and "primitive" imagery. When Chen hired Xijiang locals to dress and pose for him, he was acting in concert with both state and public expectations for consumable images. In order to attain a level of visibility for his work, he capitulated to certain popular codes — the routinized celebration of ethnic cultures, the impenetrable surfaces of faces and colorful costumes, the calculated beauty of the feminine. His other, more individuated work, while central to his own understanding of his creativity, did not achieve popular circulation.

The same logic that guided Chen's camera and the public aesthetic toward images of minorities as feminized, tradition-bound, and picturesque subjects was also evident in the way that Chen conducted himself in his travels. First, Chen's deployment of simulated documents from a state-run newspaper indicated the authority that the state still held in giving him access to officials and to the local people he sought to document. Even though he wanted nothing of the actual affiliation, his impersonation of a Beijing journalist in effect accrued to the prestige of the institutions of the state's representational apparatus.[3] It was the institutional structures of the state — the minorities research units and the culture bureaucracy itself — that would shape the types of subjects he encountered and, in the process, restrict the types of images he might circulate. Second, when he arrived in town refusing to eat local food and insinuating himself into dining with visiting officials, his practices and "tastes" affirmed the distinction between himself as privileged urbanite and the peasants and local merchants from whom he refused food. This distinction was normative; even as he boasted of respect for local cultures, he judged Xijiang lifestyles to be diseased or dirty. The convergence of these representational practices with those of social distancing could not but contribute to constituting the hierarchy in which rural minorities were ranked — by virtue of the very lifeways that made them objects of fascination — far below state employees and urbanites. Third, the relations of representation themselves contributed to the differentiation of social strata. Equipped with cash, foreign cameras, imported film, state identity papers, mandarin Chinese, and Beijing residence, Chen had many bases for his privilege to appropriate the images of the people he sought to photograph. As we will see in this chapter and others, technologies, money, and access to spatial/cultural centers were key markers of status distinctions in the reform period. What is significant about this instance, however, is the fact that these assets translated simultaneously into status superiority for Chen (through his practices) and into conventionalized images that reinforced status inferiority for his photographic subjects (through his products). His confident masculinity, displayed as he expertly trained his camera on his feminine subjects, only heightened the status divide.

State, Society, and the Search for Autonomy

Was Chen working within or beyond the state? His representational practices seem to defy simple classification, yet this type of question is one typically asked of cultural production in China. To unravel the subtexts of this question, it will be necessary to take a critical detour into the ways in which politico-cultural process has been conceived in the Western academy. The state-society binary has very long lineages in the history of Western sinological scholarship. In depictions of China, this key split has tended to be offered as *the* salient distinction organizing social and political process. Such representations are usually explicitly or subtextually normative, contrasting Western societal models — of capitalism, parliamentary government, participatory democracy, free market — with those of Eastern authoritarianism. As formulated by Farquhar and Hevia: "Culture appears to condemn Others to totalitarianism or authoritarianism, and no indigenous institutional frameworks that might support popular participation in national politics can be perceived" (1993:502). It is, then, a staple of the social theory that contrasts the East with the West to figure the state as analytically central.[4] The direct control of the masses by a monopolistic state was the central theme both in Wittfogel's study of "oriental despotism" and in Marx's "Asiatic mode of production."[5] In this organization of production, the state or a centralized ruling elite with military backing extracted labor and tribute directly from primary producers. This image of a "state stronger than society" (Wittfogel 1981:49) was distinguished from the more spatially dispersed forms of extraction and control typical of European feudalism. It was characterized as a managerial state that "prevents the nongovernmental forces of society from crystallizing into independent bodies strong enough to counterbalance and control the political machine" (1981:49).

These representations, in turn, have structured Chinese minority studies spanning the Maoist and post-Mao years. When scholarly inquiries reach beyond microstudies of ethnically based cultural features, the most commonly posed problematics have to do with the state: How have minorities been classified by the state? How have they been represented by the state? How have they been marginalized or persecuted by the state? Or conversely, how have they benefited from state policies? Questions concerning the state as benefactor are less often entertained because of the implicit assumption that the state is an exterior—often despotic—power, the actions of which are not likely to be favorable for minority groups. In asking these questions, the state is characteristically conflated with the Han majority as a singular figure of domination.

Critics of the excessive power of the Chinese state, of the saturation of Chinese society with state control, have begun to offer notions of the growth of "civil society" and/or the "public sphere" as hopeful alternative social forms that might have begun to emerge in the post-Mao era (or much earlier). "Civil society" is characteristically defined as a domain distinct from the state, but also from the family and the individual; it is associated with the market and with private property, with nongovernmental associations, and with rational discourse.[6] The "public sphere," primarily associated with Jürgen Habermas (1989, 1992), denotes an arena in which members of society debate issues of societal concern independent of state intervention.[7] In commentaries on Chinese contexts, both terms are used—often almost interchangeably—to assess the possibilities for a public space distinct from if not oppositional to the state (see Whyte 1992, Gold 1990). The development of autonomous spaces has tended to be lauded by Western critics as tempering the absolute character of state power. Several assumptions here demand to be highlighted: (1) that there is, in fact, a sharp demarcation between state and nonstate sectors, and (2) that these sectors are by nature opposed; (3) that opposition to the state occurs in public practice, and the private is irrelevant; (4) that civil society and the public sphere are spaces potentially available to all members of society, and (5) that these notions, developed for Western societies, are exportable to the Chinese context. These assumptions will be considered in turn.

Advocates for the growth of civil society or the public sphere tend to emphasize the antagonism between the state and society. The nonstate public domain is promoted as a corrective that checks the excessive use of state power. It is seen as an arena for empowerment vis-à-vis repressive and totalitarian governments. Institutions and associations such as unions, clubs, churches, academic and cultural institutions, etc., are catalogued as measures of the strength of civil society. Autonomous

journalism, publishing, plural intellectual discourse, and entrepreneurial activity are also noted. However, while autonomy continues to function as an idealized diagnostic for these social forms, other commentators have pointed out that civil society and the state are enmeshed in
practice, have a "symbiotic" relation to each other (Saich 1994:260), or
are "bound together" in mutually limiting fashion (Shils 1991:4). This
was the situation, according to Duara (1995:147–75), in late imperial
China, where the rise of autonomous forms of power vis-à-vis the central state had a certain balancing effect, assuring the legitimacy of interdependence between society and the state. Pushing the point further,
social scientists working in Chinese and Indian sites during the 1980s
and 1990s have noted structural ambiguity (Yang 1989:39), state-society
interdependence (Goodman 1999), a blurring of boundaries, and the
notion that the state must be understood not only as a static institutional
agent, but also as something discursively constructed in the popular
domain (Gupta 1995). The difficulties in maintaining a hard boundary
between state and society put into radical question the otherwise unexamined assumption that civil society or the public sphere operates in
straightforward opposition to state control.

An emphasis on the public zone as one of free discourse that chal-
lenges state absolutism also marginalizes and depoliticizes a third term
— the "private." [8] Here, the assumption is that what happens in privacy
is insignificant for the larger society. Implicit in this equation is another
normative notion, that of the public as the exclusive site of contestation
and as the index of the political. A perceptual filter operates in which
nonstate practices are either seen as oppositional, resistant, dissident, in
some way directed toward the state, or they are not seen at all. Different
contexts, however, demand to be viewed in terms of their historical and
political specificity.

With regard to China, Philip Huang has argued that the historical
expansion of civic public association in the Ming and Qing periods (1368–
1644-1911) was dissociated from the assertion of civic power against
the state (1991:321). In the contemporary period, with China's emergence from the Maoist era of extensive state saturation of society, cultural movements may proceed precisely on the basis of "being removed
from the power/knowledge monopoly of the Chinese state" (Chicago
1992:534), of disengaging from political debate and focusing instead on
the cultural or the individual. This is comparable to what, in the Czech

context, Václav Havel advanced as "antipolitical politics" (1985:269). In societies that have been relatively state-saturated, therefore, the private also can become political simply by virtue of being out of the purview of the state's gaze or by producing discourses and values that elude particular state definitions of value. To carry on activities in private can itself become a kind of contestatory political action, even if the content of those activities does not fall within the categories of conventional politics.

The fourth assumption, that an autonomous public sphere can be accessible to all members of society, might be better thought of as an ideal. As Nancy Fraser summarizes: in Habermas's formulation "the public sphere connoted an ideal of unrestricted rational discussion of public matters. The discussion was to be open and accessible to all; merely private interests were to be inadmissible; inequalities of status were to be bracketed; power was to be excluded; and discussants were to deliberate as peers" (1997:72). Although such an ideal may have been promoted by those whose opinions stood to be registered in the public arena, in actuality it has been extremely difficult to realize since it depends on bracketing status distinctions that are constitutive of the social order. Drawing on revisionist historiography, Fraser argues instead that the public sphere described by Habermas was not only bourgeois, but also male and white supremacist,[9] and that it was based on promulgating a particular culture of civil society that was itself a strategy of distinction which effectively meant that women and minorities found it difficult if not impossible to make their opinions heard (1997:7). Despite the exclusions of women and minorities from participation in the dominant public sphere, however, these groups were not silenced, but instead they created "alternative publics" in which they pursued their aims according to different norms and cultural codes of public speech and action. That this sort of public voice could be accessible to all members of society, however, is still extremely optimistic. As Craig Calhoun points out, the democracy movement that resulted in the Tiananmen conflict, for instance, involved only a tiny fragment of the Chinese population together with a globalized media network. The vast majority of the Chinese people were left to silence and invisibility:

the Chinese democracy movement of 1989 never mobilized one percent of China's population. Some three quarters of the country's people are peasants. They have grievances against the government but the protesters did not speak to them directly. . . . One of the dangers of experiences like Tiananmen protests is that they make it easy to imagine that a particular crowd *is* the people. . . . This fact was sometimes recognized by leaders of the protest movement. . . . But this recognition was often belied by the rhetoric of the movement, which was monological and authoritative (1989:67).

The export of notions of public debate and autonomous societal process, then, have particular valences when the postsocialist societies of China, Russia, and Eastern Europe are the target recipients.[10] Theoretical export practices cannot help but be haunted by a legacy of cold war indictments of totalitarian regimes and an implicit if not asserted judgment as to the superiority of Western political norms. In the field of Chinese studies, the search for civil society spawned a spate of publishing by Western scholars in which the presence or absence of this social form was debated for periods as early as the late Ming dynasty.[11]

What are the implications of this kind of debate? Lydia Liu suggests that the search for equivalences, or what Eugene Eoyang (1993) calls "pseudo-universals," between different languages and cultures can indicate a kind of imperializing stance: "The subtle or not so subtle bias that informs certain comparative questions—Why is there no epic in Chinese? Is there a civil society in China? etc.—often says more about the inquirer than the object of inquiry" (Liu 1995:7). Following this critique, we might ask a number of questions: What are the agendas that inform Western discussions of the public sphere and civil society for the Chinese context?[12] What do social divisions and political processes look like in China if these primary categories are suspended? Does suspending the search for equivalences inevitably halt at reiterating the otherness of non-Western societies?

I propose to proceed neither by presuming to describe China in unique terms, nor by transferring categories in a way that smuggles in unexamined normativity. Rather, the analytical categories of Western social theory can be deployed with reflexive awareness as descriptive vehicles for inquiring into a context that is absolute neither in its difference nor in its comparability. China and other non-Western societies are not static and frozen in their difference. Political scientist Baogang He has sketched the variety of ways in which ideas of civil society were formulated by Chinese scholars in the mainland and Taiwan, concluding: "For Chinese intellectuals to talk about civil society is to search for a normative theory of democracy and the state, and to articulate a normative project for liberalization and democratization" (He 1995:53). As Barlow (1991b) has shown, when ideas—or signs—travel, they may be taken up in specific contexts as the mediums for internal struggles around the localization of imported meanings.[13]

A closer attention to signs is precisely what is needed in the debates about political contestation and rational communication. Suffusing the channels of public culture, touching and shaping the subjectivities of the populace, social meanings exceed the formal categories of political process and transgress the bounds of political locations. With a sense of the compelling power of representations to secure consent, a hegemonic formation emerges, and it becomes possible to envision a coalescence of perceived interests across the state-society divide.

State Images for Global Consumption

State imagings of Han and minorities reveal not only overlappings with unofficial cultural production, but also an acute attentiveness to a global order in which multiethnic states had become the norm. Filtered through Leninist-Stalinist nationality theory, images of horizontal fraternity abounded in official culture, fusing fashionable multiculturalism with the earlier trope of classless solidarity purveyed during the Cultural Revolution. Official renderings of Chinese-style interethnic solidarity can be seen as instances of what Leong (1989:76) has dubbed "national image-management." Despite being primarily directed abroad, these renderings also served to indoctrinate local citizens into a consciousness of the prescribed social order. Visual media and public ritual were two key venues for image dissemination.

For decades throughout the Maoist and post-Mao periods, the panorama of the dense, diversely attired, hand-holding throng encompassing all the nationalities of China was a staple in state presentations of the national visage. Beaming, exuberant, moving forward as if in a great wave toward the future, the tokens in these crowd scenes during the Cultural Revolution included a worker, a soldier, and a peasant in respective "class-status" garb. One such image, gracing the cover of a 1967 record album filled with ethnic songs in praise of Mao Zedong, pictured the

Chairman at the center of a crowd in which forty-four persons in pains-takingly detailed costumes oriented themselves toward their leader with adoring smiles. Mao, taller than anyone else, appeared dapper in a gray "Mao suit" under an ankle-length gray trench coat. To his immediate left was the worker-soldier-peasant triad, all males. The worker wore functional urban clothing, and the soldier wore a PLA uniform; the peas-ant, smiling through facial hair, sported a head-covering, a sash, and a fur-trimmed coat evocative of the styles of the rugged northwest prov-inces. Beside these masculinized vanguards stood the only child in the painting; a grinning, skirted girl in a costume from the southwest high-lands. She clasped the worker's hand trustingly, while a Tibetan woman with long, loose hair stood behind her, arm outstretched almost as if offering the child up to the guidance of the leadership. Over the girl's ornamental silver necklace was tied the unmistakable red kerchief of the Young Pioneers.

Having charted the ceremonies accompanying national sports com-petitions over the course of the twentieth century, Brownell (1996) found a significant shift with the move toward entertainment "value" in the post-Mao era. During the Maoist years, an egalitarian and martial body culture had come to dominate opening ceremonies. At the peak of the Cultural Revolution, minority sports (wrestling, horse racing, polo), which had been included in previous years, were omitted, as was any reference to gender differentiation. Performances of mass calisthenics and revolutionary songs were featured, and a full homogenization of China's peoples was the message. By 1982, a few years after the inaugu-ration of reform, the inclusion of gender and ethnic difference came to be considered a picturesque asset. Opening ceremonies featured dis-plays of folk traditions, and men and women were costumed to highlight distinctions. From then on, the national visage took on the aura of mar-ketable diversity, all the while underscoring the unity that subsumed differences (1996:233–37).

As codes shifted in the reform period, the throng symbolizing na-tional unity adjusted to a more entertainment-oriented image, but still one with didactic political content. Gladney (1994b) describes the four-hour television special aired on the eve of the 1991 Chinese New Year. On an elaborate stage, colorfully dressed minorities and Han appeared together described as "fifty-six different flowers." They moved among the darkly dressed members of the studio audience, singing in turn their native songs—Tibetan, Mongol, Zhuang, Uzbek, Korean, etc.— and offering, like tribute, cups of tea and minority gifts to their guests. The immensely popular program continued with ethnic song and dance performances, interspersed with those of the Han. Significantly, Han performers asserted their vanguardist modernity by eschewing a folksy look and appearing in Western-style suits and dresses (1994b:95–96).

Beneath the veneer of fraternal unity, many publicly circulated images revealed a more vertical vision of China's social order. In 1986 a billboard promoting development in southeast Guizhou loomed over the central traffic circle in Kaili. It showed two minority women in full festival regalia standing on either side of a Han male, taller and older, in worker's clothing that flaunted his vanguard urbanity. As Anagnost points out, in the official regime of representation, that which was excluded from state-defined modernity (i.e., local tradition) was not "disappeared," but rather rendered hypervisible in order to highlight, by contrast, the civilized character of the state: "Out of these practices is constructed an 'otherness' against which the Party can exercise its legitimating activism" (1994:231).

A 1984 wall poster marketed even in Xijiang's Xinhua bookstore relied on a generational idiom to emphasize the paternalistic role of the party. Literally infantilized minority children, rosy-cheeked and bedecked in full adult festival regalia, some holding toys and some holding musical instruments, along with one or two Han, were shown playing gleefully with, holding the hands of, or even embracing a fatherly Mao Zedong, Zhou Enlai, Liu Shaoqi, and Zhu De. Both this image and the development billboard invoked a Confucian vision of authority—the first employing the elder sibling/younger sibling relationship, the second conflating the father-child relation with that of the emperor-subject— to emphasize the ascendancy of the Han state. The spectacle—from rosy-cheeked cherubs to ethnologically accurate costumery—was itself what enabled the party to emerge in high relief—triumphant and progressive.[14] As Anagnost suggests, the state, constituting itself as center, may have purveyed such contrasts precisely to represent itself as a "modern, activist state opposed to all that is irrational, traditional and local" (1990:6).

12. A Kaili billboard, 1986. "Go all out to strengthen the country and struggle hard to develop Qiandongnan."

13. Charming *minzu* cherubs. Clockwise from upper left: Zhu De, Liu Shaoqi, Mao Zedong, and Zhou Enlai.

Ethnic Currency in the Reform Era

In 1980 new images began to be printed on the face of Chinese paper currency (*renminbi*). They replaced the industrial and agricultural scenes that had adorned the bills from the 1950s through the 1970s, displaying a different and perhaps more ambiguous message. The bills in use during Maoism had charted a modernizing progression in the ascent from the lowliest one-jiao (.10 yuan) to the ten-yuan note. The smallest bill featured perky, youthful peasants streaming to the fields with tools and shoulder baskets. In the background a flag fluttered in the breeze. Impressive buildings of several stories were enclosed by a wrought-iron fence. These imposing structures, evocative of commune headquarters, both symbolically harnessed peasant labor to the state and suggested the improved architectural standards achievable under socialism. The next largest bill was the two-jiao note, which featured a huge bridge construction project in the city of Wuhan, followed by the five-jiao note, which heralded the demise of menial labor promised by industrialization. The five-jiao note pictured a pristine, hygienic, and highly mechanized factory floor adorned with only three workers, all female, aproned and busy. The bills rose in denomination with motifs of a peasant woman on a tractor, a highland shepherd, a bulldozer at work in a quarry, a male welder. The ten-yuan bill, the largest denomination in common circulation at the time, was referred to as the *"Da Tuanjie"* (Great Unity). It pictured the Imperial Palace at Tiananmen Square adorned with placards proclaiming, "Long Live the People's Republic of China," and, on the flip side, a male worker, a male soldier, and a female peasant smiling and striding energetically ahead of a throng of diversely dressed minorities.

After the inauguration of reforms, this pictorial progression from scenes of economic modernization to the symbols of state leadership was replaced with a telling smorgasbord of the now more sharply individuated peoples of the nation. Each bill from the smallest through the ten-yuan note offered nationally famous landscapes on one side and two elaborately adorned heads of minority women, and fewer men, in full profile or semiprofile on the other. Looking off into the distance, with earnest faces, only some of which bore slight smiles, they seemed like neutral vehicles for the display of their varied and distinctive costumes.

14. Cultural Revolution currency: imaging socialist modernization. The worker-soldier-peasant alliance appears at top.

15. *Minzu* color on small denominations for the 1980s. The Miao appear on the left side of the bill in the center.

16. Who's in charge. A worker-peasant-expert alliance and party patriarchs on the large bills of 1980s currency.

Passed daily from hand to hand, these headdressed tokens visually re-iterated the multiethnic makeup of the Chinese polity.

The new 50-yuan and 100-yuan bills, however, told a superseding story. The 50-yuan echoed the worker-soldier-peasant alliance, except that the soldier was now replaced by a distinguished white-haired gentle-man with glasses and a Western tie, looking more like an intellectual or an expert. The 100-yuan note resurrected Mao Zedong, Zhou Enlai, Liu Shaoqi, and Zhu De, now in solemn profile. As with the posters and billboards above, the flurry of bills barraged the cash user with a sup-posed cross-section of China's heterogeneity, but the progression from small to large denominations recuperated relations of authority. Post-Mao state imaginings, then, made of the *minzu* a kaleidoscopic visage of ethnic inclusion, while at the same time coding them as subordinate.

Beauty and the West:
Negotiating International Codes

Over the course of the 1980s and into the 1990s, representational modalities adopted from the slick surfaces of Western advertising and satellite-transmitted music videos were processed into China's public culture. These merged with other strands of import, such as intellectuals' and artists' adoption of Western aesthetic styles from the paintings canonized in museums. Popular culture exploded with the erotically charged material that had long glutted the West. From artists oil-painting nudes in elite art academies, to entrepreneurs pirating foreign "yellow" videos and printing freshly penned popcorn porn, to bikinied bodybuilding contests, to state publications questing after readers through shocking seminude visuals, the fad caught on everywhere.[15] One outcome was that the allure of minority color was further sutured with the dynamic energy of the sexual. Influenced by Western modernist primitivism, artists creating products for the global market fashioned eroticized images designed to pique foreigners' interest while using visual conventions suited to Western tastes, thereby demonstrating that China was no longer isolated from an internationalized aesthetic system.

Debate generated by the mural "Water Festival, Song of Life" in the Beijing international airport demonstrates the multiplicity of players in and beyond the state that contributed to the shape of dominant representations and registered their concern for international image-management. The masterpiece of a Beijing Han artist, Yuan Yunsheng, the painting, completed in 1979, employed an aestheticized earthiness in its depiction of the productive activities, the tropical setting, and the ritual dances associated with the water-splashing festival of the Dai people of Yunnan, relatives of the Thai in Southeast Asia.[16] What was controversial was the "wet woman." Two Dai femmes fatales were pictured bathing completely in the nude.

A widespread popular version of the incident recounted that Dai elites were outraged at such a thing, and, arguing not only that nude bathing among their people was ethnographically inaccurate, but that even the intimation was morally degrading, they eventually prevailed in persuading the artist to paint clothing onto these contested bodies. While popular lore characterized the alteration of the painting as a matter of ethnic dignity on the part of the people represented, according to Joan

Cohen (1987:39–40) it was not only from Dai quarters that objections were made. Mainstream critics also voiced several complaints that had to do with China's identity vis-à-vis the West. They claimed that nudes were not part of the Chinese artistic tradition, nor was wall painting. Moreover, the fact that the subject matter was minority instead of Han made the mural an inappropriate self-presentation in a reception area for foreigners. Furthermore, artistic elongation of the women's bodies was considered to be an "ideologically impure" form of distortion. That Beijing critics espoused nationalist reasons for censuring the painting—defending Chinese artistic tradition on the one hand and assessing minorities' propriety as emblems of the state on the other—reveals how complex was the role of the minority woman as both symbol and other of China on the international stage. The controversy escalated, and the Beijing Dai leadership was summoned by state officials to pass judgment. They reportedly expressed *approval* of the work. A few months later, however, Dai leaders in Yunnan province were officially reported to have protested the nudity. In response, the painting was curtained off and then, in 1981, walled over. In the ensuing years it was repeatedly veiled and unveiled in response to changing political winds. However, it has never been painted over as the popular account would have it.

The particularly sharp and highly publicized controversy over the airport mural may have stemmed not only from its placement at China's cultural-political center, at a site that showcased China to outsiders, but as Lufkin's (1990:36) more formalist reading suggests, it may also have been a consequence of the confrontational quality of one of the nudes. Placed in the immediate foreground, close to life-sized, the figure was virtually able to interact with the space of the world. No longer in the guise of exotic culture, Dai women's nudity confronted viewers with a more unsettling eroticism, both in its frankness and in its erasure of the cultural difference that had made consumption of Dai femininity so permissible.

A greater degree of contextualization, a kind of ethnographic veil, creating a spatial-cultural buffer between the viewer and the unclothed women, might have been the necessary counterweight to an otherwise unnerving sense of proximity. Indeed, several years later, in the lobby of a new joint venture hotel for foreign visitors in Kunming, the capital of Yunnan, a province that has most actively commodified its minorities for tourism, nudity recurred in a large wall painting of what appeared to be a kind of "peoples of the world" amalgam. The mural, primarily concerned with the ritual, magic, and fantasy life of "tribal" people in various emblematic costumes and adornments, was a veritable catalogue of clichés. Hawaiians with flower leis, Native Americans with spears and stone implements, and several recognizable Chinese minority groups were intermingled with totem poles, pictographs, ritual instruments, and imaginary beasts. Female nudity appeared four times: twice in maternal postures of nurturing, once in the form of a line of identical nubile, beaded women flowing through the fantasy vision of a heavily muscled, dark-skinned, loinclothed man with loop earrings in ritual stance, and finally in the form of a Dai woman holding a sarong around her body, as if preparing to bathe, so that the garment only half-covered her breasts. Here, like Alloula's (1986:52) "ethnographic alibi" that enables the free play of fantasy, the bodies of non-Han women were safely couched within a context of barbarian wildness where they could be both desired and distanced through the dispassionate scrutiny of the ethnological gaze. Juxtaposed with a number of scantily clad male bodies, their otherwise provocative nudity shed its moral charge and was instead euphemistically rendered as simply a more primitive way of life. Reminiscent of the avid Western consumption of *National Geographic,* a highly self-conscious cultural relativism masked a kind of powered voyeuristic impulse in which looking on was acceptable where participating might have been frighteningly intimate, transgressive, or debasing.[17]

At least two nationalisms went head-to-head in the debates over images in which minorities appeared in states of undress. In regard to the Beijing mural, while some were concerned about how the national face of China should be presented to outsiders, others—especially Dai nationalist elites—were more sensitive to appropriate renditions of their particular ethnic group. In the actual debates, the female subjects whose bodies appeared for domestic and international visitors to consume were conspicuously absent. As the muted objects of dominant image-making, their silence affirmed their status inferiority. It was not a state-society division that structured the process; rather, it was urban elites, both Han and minority, both state and nonstate, that generated discourses about how ethnicized femininity should serve the nation and how sexuality should be contained.

Challenging Sexualized Representation

Another set of public debates shows a closer knitting together of state and minority elite agendas on the backs of the subordinated, sexualized ethnic other. In May 1989, at a moment of intense attention to the political activism associated with the student democracy movement taking place on Tiananmen Square, a parallel demonstration took place at the same site.[18] Earlier that year, the Shanghai Cultural Press had published a book, *Sexual Customs (Xing Fengsu)*, that took a round-the-world tour of sexual particularities in different cultures. The sections on Islam, among other things, imputed phallic overtones to minarets and debased Meccan pilgrimages as orgies that included homosexual relations and sodomy with camels. Muslims in major cities across China, including Beijing, Lanzhou, Xining, and Urumqi, were incensed at being the objects of a probing sexological discourse. They condemned the book as blasphemous, likening it to Salman Rushdie's *Satanic Verses,* which had been denounced by Ayatollah Khomeini of Iran. On May 12, some 2,000 to 3,000 students from the Central Nationalities Institute, Beijing University, Qinghua University, and other Beijing colleges marched downtown and presented petitions at the Grand Islamic Mosque and the Great Hall of the People, demanding that the book be banned. Significantly, the state was extremely complicit with the protest, providing permission, transportation, and protection from the Public Security Bureau. Even in other cities, where demonstrations eventuated in some violence and damage to state property, the state maintained a lenient stance by refraining from prosecuting demonstrators. The book was quickly banned, thousands of copies were publicly burned, and the authors and editor were tried in courts of law and sentenced to varying periods of imprisonment.

Western analysts have appropriated the protest as an instance of state-society conflict, of antagonistic resistance to state authority, or of counterstate ethnic advocacy to which the state subsequently capitulated. Gladney suggests that the state's acquiescence to the protest was a deliberate attempt to make a distinction between the legality of this state-recognized minority and the criminality of the democracy demonstrators (1994a:259). Mackerras sees the state acting almost opportunistically with an eye toward fragile international relations with a very powerful Muslim coalition: "It was an ideal opportunity to keep the minority nationalities happy and in support of the government, with a few daring scholars a very easy sacrificial lamb" (1995:126). What is stressed are utilitarian calculations on the part of a state primarily concerned with sociopolitical unrest and foreign affairs. Such instrumentalist interpretations elide meanings, ignoring the possibility that the struggle over representations was itself recognized by the state as significant.

I would like to read against the grain of such Western-derived analyses to entertain the possibility that the state and the Muslim protesters might have actually concurred on the issue of sexual propriety in discourse. Certainly, regulating sexual content in public culture was a practice in which the state had been intimately involved. Muslim indignation coincided with state norms for proper and wholesome public culture. The occasion of the protests afforded a moment for rectification of the desexualized image of minority citizens favored by this state-elite alliance. In the process, once again, elites, now allied with the state, affirmed their positional superiority by controlling representation.

Commodification and the Canons of International Tourism

The 1980s, with its official emphasis on diversity and tolerance, was a period filled with the excitement of testing the taboos that surrounded the beguiling but mysterious minority woman. She was brought in from the country to the city, domesticated, made into an object of consumption. Tourist and consumer appetites, both domestic and international, had set in motion a massification of "things ethnic." As folk material assumed a commodity form, an ever more speedy and comprehensive standardization of motifs took place.

Through media and advertising, the identification of the female body with sale was imported from the West and quickly naturalized.[19] The older minority-as-woman image encountered a commodity-as-woman marketing strategy, giving rise to an array of products that reworked raw, putatively traditional elements into portable, collectible, and purchasable forms. The now familiarly headdressed women proliferated on greeting cards, on shoulder bags, on bookmarks. A selection of decorated souvenir stones in a Guangzhou hotel tourist shop offered two feminine desirables side by side — a schematically represented minority woman (hand-painted) or a busty, tank-topped Han woman (photographed). A wall calendar promoting avant-garde fashions made from

batiked fabric adapted from Miao designs used models in *Vogue*-like postures, sporting leggings, pumps, and Western haircuts combined with
newfangled, ethnically marked outfits. Yunnan designers "blazing new
trails in Chinese fashion" adapted costume styles from a variety of minorities to produce "collections that were not only 'national,' but excit-
ingly original as well" (Wang Yongyao 1989:39).

An inevitable effect was that ethnic groups became increasingly indistinct and interchangeable. Certain signifiers—batik, headdresses, embroidery, sarongs, and prominent breasts and nipples—came to denote
a generic and palatable non-Han substance primed for popular inges-
tion. Regional and ethnic specificities—the stuff of daily life among
minority peasants—were increasingly irrelevant. However, specificity
could be recuperated when it served a market purpose. Visiting Yunnan
in 1988, I was struck by tourist shops filled with Guizhou handicrafts.
I assumed the craze for authenticity had made Guizhou pieces more
saleable since Yunnan's crafts had long been mass-produced. Guizhou
handicrafts would have been imported to Yunnan not only because they
were cheaper, but because the handiwork was more authentic. I asked
a shopkeeper for the origin of a piece I recognized to be the embroidery
characteristic of the Shidong region where a dragon boat festival was
held. I watched her eyes as she sized me up and apparently judged me
to be a tourist who would want something local, something specified in
terms of origin and ethnicity. "It's Yi, from the Kunming area," she replied with confidence. "Are you sure?" I queried, "It looks like Guizhou
Miao to me." "No, no; it's Yi from Yunnan," she insisted.

In promotional tourism literature the common rhetorics of international sightseeing came to streamline the way in which minority cultures were presented within China. "Many Dongs still wear their own
costumes and are well-known for their woodwork . . . ," enticed a bro-
chure from a Sussex, England, tourism agency. "We will visit a Miao
village to watch a costumed dance display and hear the bamboo lusheng
pipes being played." "Exchanging songs in front of a drum tower is an
important cultural content during the Dong's Spring Festival . . . ," Chinese promotional flyers parroted the foreign refrains: "The famous *lusheng* (a local musical instrument) dance, *caigu* dance, local folk song and
ballad as well as handicraft products like embroidery, wax printing and
bamboo weaving products, costumes and architecture all have distinctive local flavors." Critical to this type of discourse was the simulation

of discovery, the notion of untouched territory, uncorrupted culture, ingenuous natives, that is endemic to ethnic tourism worldwide. The Sussex brochures were peppered with comments such as "an area inhabited by ethnic minorities and hardly ever visited by tourists as it is so remote," and "we will eat local cuisine at one of the roadside restaurants which is so much more fun and tastier than tourist cuisine." Gaining access to the formerly inaccessible — i.e., the most other — became a value in itself. Media and tourism, then, collaborated to reposition minorities, excising them from revolutionary contexts and symbolically returning them to remote, wild, and putatively unclaimed territory.

Codes of acceptable representation clashed when the aestheticized native encountered the newly imported valorization of the authentic. When Guizhou provincial television came to Xijiang to make a "documentary" on Miao customs, they adopted a time-honored practice of featuring performers for their youth and attractiveness. A glamorous teenager, who identified as a member of the Bouyei *minzu*, was to simulate a Miao singer. They first made a high-quality tape recording of the full-bodied singing of a rounded, wrinkled Miao virtuoso at her place of work in the city of Kaili. They then transported the tape to Xijiang and played it for her Bouyei surrogate, costumed as a Miao festival dancer, to lip-sync before a panoramic sunset on the mountaintop. Despite the disgruntlement of the Xijiang villagers, the filmmakers left confidently, convinced that they had captured a special effect. Several months later, however, I was told that the leadership of the television station had criticized them for this attempt at simulation. Such fabrication was distorting, they were told, and they should stick closer to "reality" in future documentary work.

In Yunnan province the commodification of ethnic tourism had been developing for a longer time, and the numbers of visitors were far greater than those to Guizhou (Swain 1990). Foreign arrivals to Kunming numbered 121,312 in 1988, compared to Guiyang's meager 17,943 (National Tourism Administration 1989:41). Photo opportunities had become regular features at high-volume tourist sites. Outside the Stone Forest (Shilin), an array of stalls offered different styles of minority costume in which one could dress up for pictures. When I visited in 1988, the photo strip was mobbed by Chinese tourists, with hardly a foreigner in sight. One might transform oneself to resemble a member of the Dai, the Yi, or the Sanyi nationality. One could costume the whole family, or

17. Bouyei model lip-syncs for men with cameras. The vocalist looks on.

pose on the back of a camel. Best of all, one headed home with a visual
souvenir documenting one's cross-dressing adventure.

Experiential forays notwithstanding, tourism was rarely without its
boundary-drawing aspect, coded as ever in social-evolutionary terms.
A doctor from Beijing had come to Kunming because the city was her
husband's ancestral home. During their stay they had taken three days
for tourism and headed off to Dali, the heavily touristed center of a Bai
nationality region in western Yunnan. Animatedly, she told me her impressions. "The cultural level is very high," she reported with approval,
using the conventional connotation of "culture" as "education." "Lots
of people are leaving Dali to study. People's clothes and food are old-
fashioned, but that will change because so many foreigners and Chinese
are visiting there now." Although intrigued by the *minzu* distinctiveness
of the area, she was nonetheless comforted by evidence of modernization. Then with fascination she informed me: "You know I've heard
there are people west of Dali who live just like in ancient times, they
have a matrilineal system like society in the primitive stages of development." Acknowledging my research and distinguishing herself as one

sated by visiting only the modernizing city of Dali, she proclaimed: "It would be very interesting for *you* to go there."

Miao Men

The most salient configuration in the social order that represents and positions minorities is that between masculinized urbanites and the minority women for whom they speak. But the marking of minority otherness discussed in this chapter was not only the consequence of transactions between Han urbanites and minority women. Minority men also figured as key producers *and* consumers of "their" women as "ethnic." Such men, moreover, could never be equated solely with their ethnic attribute, for that attribute was always conjoined with their gender and class locations. Their tactics can better be understood as revealing split subjectivities, what Hall, following Gramsci, affirms in his assertion that "subordinated ideologies are necessarily and inevitably contradictory . . . the so-called 'self' which underpins these ideological formations is not a unified but a contradictory subject and a social construction" (1996b:439).

Men like Zhou of the Xijiang Culture Station operated as culture brokers, organizing formal photo shoots or staging ethnic events to present local lifeways to outsiders. In the course of his transactions, Zhou, who had little education but a degree of worldliness from having served in the People's Liberation Army for four years, had been gradually socialized into the expectations of the dominant culture in terms of what to deliver from his own. I asked him what skills his work entailed. "I know how to find the girls with looks (*maoxiang*) and figures (*shencai*)," he stated proudly. He also was the one who collected the money and distributed it to the models when they were hired. The function of the culture station, as an organ of the state, was in effect to monetize relations of cultural exchange between villagers and outsiders. The agent of this commodification more often than not, whether in Xijiang or elsewhere, was a Miao man.

Miao male elites not only facilitated *Han* consumption of their culture as embodied by their women, but they also engaged in a kind of ritualized objectification in which they themselves partook of stagings of their own "traditions." This practice was especially common among those Miao who had left the countryside for urban vocations and, living among the majority, separated in space from their home villages, had begun to cultivate a romantic nostalgia for their forgotten culture. The chief symbol of this still-recoverable past was the richly adorned Miao girl, usually in song. And Miao men's longing was tantamount to Miao women's interpellation, as young women were increasingly called on to act as hostesses and entertainers at official events convened by Miao elites. While male participants at formal events would wear urban Chinese or Western clothing, the young women who served them would glitter with the aura of the past, pulling festival costumes out of family trunks to commemorate this newer version of festival in which status was rehearsed in part through the dichotomization of males and females.

The practices of Miao men (and a few elite women) indicated that there were two increasingly differentiated modalities by which Miao engaged their tradition in the late twentieth century. One—usually assigned to women—involved the highly performative process of assuming characteristic roles and appearances to enact Miao culture through cloth, song, hair, and demeanor. The counterpart of this mode was activated through longing and through consumption. Miao men who partook of the native woman were not renouncing their cultural identity but recasting it as a form of subjectivity that remembered tradition fondly, took pleasure in gazing on it, but did not engage in it directly. This stance entailed the containment of Miao women in the category of native conservator, which was, in turn, implicated in the identity politics around their location in the Chinese polity. Trafficking in the ubiquitous categories of tradition and modernity, they effectively reiterated the state's progress narrative, the teleology that consigned their people to the economic backwater.

Harvesting the Discourse of Progress

It was late September, and although autumn was approaching, the weather was still muggy, the air heavy. The rice fields around Xijiang had turned to a gold that almost glowed with brilliance, even on overcast days. The turning of the rice from shimmering chartreuse to this more parched and mature color marked the drying of the water in the paddies and the readying for harvest of the grain that would sustain people through winter and spring. I spent day after day walking the narrow, elevated paths that ran along the tops of the mud walls which separated the rice fields, stopping at friends' invitations to pitch in with gathering the rice. Each day, more fields were peopled with harvesters—families and extended kin assembled to cut the rice at just the right moment. This year the moment was especially crucial since torrential rains earlier in the month had caused some of the rice stalks to collapse or begin to mold.

When a field was ready, a team would arrive with nothing more than a short scythe, some burlap sacks or shoulder baskets, and a huge wooden box about a yard square and open-topped.[20] To get the box to the fields was an undertaking for the fittest of men. He would hoist a box to shoulder level, with one corner secured over his head like a cap; then, with his arms extended upward to support it, he would trudge the distance to the fields, sometimes more than an hour into the mountains. Harvesting was almost always conducted by a team that moved from field to field, but never fewer than two people worked together. These were informal mutual-aid teams, a critical element of local social organization, formed out of various combinations of family members and in-laws. It was common for newly married young people to travel to help both sets of elderly parents, even if they had their own fields to tend. Brothers also regularly exchanged labor. The work was divided, starting with one or two people using the curved scythe to cut the rice stalks to a few inches from the ground, stacking the rice-laden cuttings in neat piles. The rest of the harvesters picked up hefty handfuls of stalks and, holding them at the opposite end from the rice grains, draped them over their shoulders with two arms until the stalks almost touched their backs, then in a swift motion raised and brought them down with a resounding thud against the inner sides of the wooden box. The hard impact would knock a generous sprinkling of golden-hulled rice grains into the box, and three or four hits would virtually clean off one handful of stalks. When the box began to fill, the rice grains were emptied into burlap sacks to be lugged back home at the end of the day.

"Beating the rice" (*da guzi*) was backbreaking work that took all one's energy. It strained the back and arm muscles to the limit, since the harder you whacked the rice, the more efficiently it would drop off the stalks. Moreover, because the fields were often a long walk from home, and since the harvest had to be done quickly so that the rice would not spoil, people worked long days with only a short break to gobble

18. Beating the rice for Xijiang's harvest.

handfuls of cold rice and chilis out of small bamboo lunch baskets. Xijiang peasants and development consultants alike saw no alternative to this method of harvesting. The rice terraces were small and scattered through the mountains; there was no way for any vehicles to reach them. Even mechanical threshers could not be transported to the fields because of the narrow, steep, and muddy paths that defied anything on wheels. Instead, from early September to mid-October the mountains reverberated with the rhythmic thudding of the rice stalks as they yielded grain to the peasants who worked them.

One day during harvest I was visiting the fields with a local *peitong*. Two young men approached us, cameras dangling from their shoulders so that we knew they were urbanites. Sunglasses, caps, and athletic shoes announced sartorial distinctions from the peasants bent over the rice in the paddies. They had come from the heavily industrialized northern metropolis of Tianjin, the two explained, and had chosen Xijiang to conduct the research for their graduating thesis (*biye lunwen*). Their specialty was Chinese traditional painting, but for this project they needed to do more than paint. They had to collect artifacts, write notes, and take pictures from which they would develop their painted works at home.

"We chose Qiandongnan because it is so *fengfu* [abundant, presumably in ethnographic novelty]. There's too much modernization in the cities! Do you know which places are really good, ones that preserve a lot of traditional customs [*baoliu chuantong de dongxi*]?"

Turning to my Miao *peitong*, they shook their heads, and one asked, "Is *all* the harvesting done by hand here?" The *peitong* assented, refraining from giving an explanation. "You should get some machines in here!"

Addressing me again, one queried, "Have you ever seen this type of agriculture before? It is very primitive (*yuanshi*). How does it compare to the U.S.?" And then to my *peitong*, "You know it's very wasteful to harvest this way. Too many rice grains fall off the stalks behind you as you put them over your shoulder."

Laughing awkwardly, the *peitong* protested with a feigned deference: "In this place there's no way around it [*meiyou banfa*]."

In this interchange, the techniques of agriculture, rather than appearing as a straightforward productive activity, were framed as indices of a lack, a shortfall in modernization that both fulfilled the visitors' touristic yearnings and privileged them to act as urbane judges. They performed their positional superiority by offering technical advice, and my *peitong* could not but listen docilely. His response, however, both acquiesced to their judgment and asserted the local exigencies about which they had betrayed their ignorance. Xijiang, in his subtext, was, of course, a place left behind by the turning wheels of progress, but it was not a place where the locals could be so ignorant as to have overlooked any viable opportunities for mechanization. Through such microinteractions, no less than through media, commodities, and tourism, we can see how peasant minorities and urban elites alike rehearsed again and again the rituals that patterned China's populace into social ranks. Despite their varying positionings, all affirmed the debased character of menial peasant work and the *minzu* association with it.

Popular Consent and Unitary Discourse

The superstructures of civil society are like the trench-systems of modern warfare. —Antonio Gramsci, 1930

Critical practices that privilege the state and its opposition to society, while on the one hand constituting crucial interventions in analyzing the Chinese social order, also have obscured other key divisions. Class-, status-, and gender-based differences become almost invisible when refracted through the totalizing lens of the state-society binary. Yet these differences are constitutive of China's current social formation and are salient in indigenous understandings of Chinese society. In the post-Mao era, as noted, key distinctions include urban elites versus rural folk, the intelligentsia versus manual laborers (both rural and urban), central places versus margins and peripheries, the cosmopolitan coast versus the remote interior, and market versus subsistence economies. Such differences have both structural and symbolic features and usually coincide with material inequalities. Peasants, for instance, can make great fortunes and still remain in a stigmatized social category.

The intersecting orders of inequality that organize Chinese society are both produced and buttressed by discourse. Agents and institutions of the state are among the producers of this discourse, but so are elites and even nonelites. Instead of assuming the state to be a source of control from which individuals and groups are striving for autonomy, it is also possible to envision the state working in tandem with cultural producers who are not formally state functionaries, but who share certain ideological stances with the state. A state-society approach, which emphasizes political process and eschews the circulation of meanings in popular culture, is ill-equipped to recognize the coincidence of interests revealed in the cultural domain. As a corrective, we might activate a more Gramscian notion of domination. For Gramsci, the pervasiveness of consent even across less-privileged class sectors was what was meant by "hegemony," which was both a political sensibility and a lived cultural system. Through ongoing cultural production, a particular social order presents itself as the "pressures and limits of simple experience and common sense" (Williams 1977:110). In China, the desirability of the modern—trumpeted as universally accessible—has become so hegemonic that it is sought after even by those constrained by the role of signifying its opposite. That modernity will be unevenly achieved, creating abjection and poverty for some, is naturalized as the inevitable liability of progress.

With the notion of a lived cultural system that operates hegemonically, it becomes possible to see that the emphasis on institutions and political contention assumed by models of the public sphere and oppositional civil society may not provide the whole picture. The material in this chapter shows that not only the state, but also urban Han and minority elites were involved in manufacturing discourses about the appropriate social order. While state images such as billboards, posters, opening ceremonies, and currency were geared more toward iconography supporting the authority of party patriarchs, these images also reproduced the ubiquitous tropes of polychrome, feminized, primitivized minorities as national ornaments. In other words, in popular culture, state and nonstate representations converged. The state appeared as much more complex, akin to Gramsci's formulation in which, in Hall's summary: "The state is no longer conceived as simply an administrative and coercive apparatus — it is also 'educative and formative.' . . . It is the point of condensation — not because all forms of coercive domination necessarily radiate outwards from its apparatuses but because, in its contradictory structure, it *condenses* a variety of different relations and practices" (Hall 1996b:428).

An emphasis on a dominant culture that permeates different levels and sectors leads us to a consideration of the role of media in social process and social hierarchy. Indeed, when Habermas authored the model of the public sphere, he lamented the rise of the electronic media — especially in its mass forms — for he held them responsible for the demise of the dialogic ideal of public debate. For Habermas, mediated society was one in which potential public participants had been turned into apolitical consumers under a "Don't talk back!" edict from the culture industry, which deprived them "of the opportunity to say something and to disagree" (Habermas 1989:170-71). Thompson argues, however, that this view of media is overly normative, refracted through the lens of Habermas's traditional model. Instead, Thompson suggests that mediated society be regarded as offering a new kind of publicness: "With the development of the new media of communication — beginning with print, but including the more recent forms of electronic communication — the phenomenon of publicness has become detached from the idea of a dialogical conversation in a shared locale. It has become despatialized and non-dialogical, and it is increasingly linked to the distinctive kind of *visibility* produced by, and achieved through, the media (especially television)" (Thompson 1995:132, emphasis mine). In this "space of the visible," "mediated symbolic forms can be expressed and received by a plurality of non-present others" (1995:245). This is a sense of public space not characterized by debate, but still encompassing the practices of a wide array of players. What is brought into visibility acquires a certain uniformity not because, say, the state is controlling what is disseminated, but precisely because of the high degree of visibility that certain images and discourses have achieved. These versions suffuse social process in hegemonic fashion, shaping the quotidian life in which they are repeatedly enacted.[21]

Portrayals of primitivized and feminized minorities are not only readable from static texts, but they also are a social process that takes place in the context of omnipresent mediation. Whether in offhanded comments of metropolitan visitors to Xijiang or in high-level debates about national image-making, the inferior status of women, minorities, and peasants was incessantly reasserted. When cultural producers made exotics of Xijiangers, they also made primitives of them in ways that were highly normative. The social and material consequences were palpable. Few Chinese at any level questioned the locating of these groups at the bottom of the prestige hierarchy where they had little opportunity to circulate counterrepresentations of themselves. As we will see in Part II, the cultural production they did engage in, while providing a range of opportunities and venues in which they might fashion a larger number of identities, more often than not ultimately affirmed dominant representation. Indeed, a point I wish to stress is that much of what minorities produced was itself *a part* of the dominant culture, the culture that extolled the virtues of modernity and disavowed the very "tradition" for which it pined. In the process, and in all the microinteractions that instantiated the prevailing ranking of the social order, the foundation was laid for the equation of poverty with primitive culture, for the exclusion of minority peasants from the prosperities and material comforts of reform on the grounds that their traditionalism prescribed economic stasis.

Part II

Identity and
Cultural Struggle

6

Songs for Sale

Spectacle from Mao to Market

Luo Xiuying was both a Miao and a woman of Beijing. That is where I first met her in 1982. I had been in Beijing for a few weeks, doing research according to the design of the Central Nationalities Institute in its early days of opening to foreigners. Each day I would sit in my room with a notepad. The *peitong* (companion) appointed to me by the Institute's Foreign Affairs Office would bring a Miao expert or two to lecture me on Miao culture, history, or language. The experts were senior scholars of the Institute, some of the highest-ranking Miao specialists in the country. Some were Miao, and some were Han who had, decades ago, been assigned to careers in Miao studies. Dressed in the somber cadre tones of Maoist days, they approached me with reserve, speaking from prepared notes. After our conversations—I learned months later—they were debriefed by the Foreign Affairs Office.

The day that Luo first came to see me was strikingly different. From the moment she crossed the threshold, she transformed my living space into a stage for her solo performance. Her voice was high, almost a permanent falsetto, and she moved about my room exclaiming mellifluously at the Hmong handicrafts I had brought with me from my research in Southeast Asia. She had dressed ethnic for the occasion, strikingly adorned with the mark of her native region—a sizable turban-like headdress that extended horizontally from her head ringed with coin-sized black pom-poms, plus sparkling silver earrings and an embroidered apron. Her arms, held out and away from her body, were in constant motion with the exaggerated gestures used to command an audience in large theater spaces. This rare meeting with a foreigner was to her a special opportunity to promote Miao culture, a practice that had been her vocation for her entire adult life. She was a famous woman, and she expected me to use her own name in writing about her. As the first among the many Miao who will people Part II, hers exemplifies one of the most elite stories. But she takes her place alongside many others whose practices contributed to shaping the cultural landscape of the post-Mao period and whose stories, at various levels and localities, follow.

Out of Maoism: Luo Xiuying

Luo Xiuying had come from a poor household in Guizhou province but had spent most of her life in Beijing as a star singer of her ethnic group. Hers is one of the less-told stories that were the outcome of the cultural policies of the Maoist era. Well before their national victory in 1949, the Communists who settled in the base camp of Yan'an in China's northwest were developing techniques for the use of folk material for revolutionary arts. Holm (1984) traces their theory of the pedagogical function of propaganda back to the Gutian conference held by the Communists in 1929 and to the period of Soviet advising of Communist and Nationalist parties in Shanghai in the 1930s. Two key anti-elitist strategies characterized the approach that emerged from the conference. First, propaganda messages were to be tailored to be accessible within specific regional localities and social strata. Second, older forms and local flavors were to be employed to make propaganda works appealing to the widely variegated masses. As Holm summarizes: "All pre-existing values, world-views, and modes of expression, all the forms of China's 'old culture' as they existed in the minds and collective experience of the Chinese people within particular social milieux, were potentially, at least, grist for the mill and could be linked to the new political ideals and manipulated for the furtherance of revolutionary aims" (1984:8).

This deployment of the arts of the masses for revolutionary ends was to be canonized in Mao's "Talks at the Yan'an Conference on Literature and Art" given in 1942 (see Mao 1967). These talks became the guiding programmatic statement for all officially sanctioned cultural practice for more than three decades. According to the Yan'an program, artists and writers were to process raw materials from the lives of the masses, refining them so as to communicate enlightening or mobilizing messages back to the widest audience. As Mao put it:

Revolutionary Chinese writers and artists, the kind from whom we expect great things, must go among the masses; they must go among the masses of workers, peasants, and soldiers . . . to observe, experience, study, and analyze all the different kinds of people, all the classes and all the masses, all the vivid patterns of life and struggle, and all literature and art in their natural form, before they are ready for the stage of processing or creating, where you integrate raw materials with production, the stage of study with the stage of creation. (in McDougall 1980:69–70)

Yan'an cultural producers, then, took seriously a process of immersing themselves in the daily lives of nonelites and of drawing on their cultural forms. This practice was vividly dramatized in the 1984 film *Yellow Earth (Huang Tudi)*, set in 1939, in which a Red Army soldier goes to live with peasants on the banks of the Yellow River in order to collect their folk-song melodies for reworking into revolutionary songs.

It was not only elites who were involved in cultural production, however. McDougall describes Mao's position on the role of the "masses" in artistic creation:

What is most strongly implied here is the validity of popular forms of literature as literature. The masses may be uneducated, but they are not idiots to be written down to; their art forms are primitive, but they still constitute art. Mao therefore recognizes their rightful demand to force writers to take into account their literary expectations, conventions, and beliefs, along with the fact that writers in practice invariably shape their means of expression with a preconception, however vaguely envisaged, of a given audience, however miniscule (1980:17).

The effect of such a position on policy was not only that arts of the masses were incorporated, but that nonelite *persons* were also brought into the domain of official cultural production. After the Communists came to power in 1949, people from less privileged walks of life, from peasant and minority backgrounds, were enlisted in amateur theater troupes in the provinces and summoned to urban centers as part of the revolutionary culture industry (Mackerras 1973). Some, like Luo, had nothing in their backgrounds that distinguished them. She told her own history with enthusiasm, pride, and a touch of nostalgia, remembering the humble beginnings of her career and where it had led her. She gave me copies of the lyrics to songs she had performed in different eras. Because we did not tape this oral history, told to me in 1988, I retell it in the third person, following the structure of her account and inserting contextualizing material.

Born in 1941 to a middle peasant Miao family in the Huishui region of south central Guizhou, Luo had dabbled onstage since the age of twelve. Her family had become impoverished because her mother had fled when Luo was only four and her father had managed the household badly. When Luo was six, her mother came to take her to Guiyang and put her in school. She began Chengdu Lower School but, because of economic hardship, went to work at age sixteen for a performing troupe back in her native region of southern Guizhou. By the time she was eighteen, she reminisced, she had become well-known throughout the province. As a consequence, she was chosen to represent Guizhou in a national competition in Beijing in 1959. From this competition she was one of a handful—and the only minority—chosen to perform for Chairman Mao and Zhou Enlai. She sang the following version of a Miao song:

Well-Being Comes with the Blossoming of the Gui Flower

Gui [sweet-smelling osmanthus] flowers grow on the gui cliff,
Gui flowers must wait for the v.i.p. to come,
Gui flowers must wait for the honored guest to come,
Only when the honored guest comes will the flowers bloom,
Ai, only when the honored guest comes will the flowers bloom.

The gui flowers are good like the heart of the Miao people,
The v.i.p. is the People's Liberation Army,
Chairman Mao is bright like the sun,
He shines brightness into the gui forest of the Miao,
Ai, he shines brightness into the gui forest of the Miao.

The mountains are all aflower with gui blossoms,
The Miao people emerge from hardship,
Chairman Mao walks before them,
The Miao people walk behind him planting flowers,

Chairman Mao walks before them,
The Miao people walk behind him planting flowers.

Chairman Mao is like a close family member coming,
Miao people's gui flowers bloom year after year,
With the blooming of the gui flowers comes well-being,
Well-being and Chairman Mao cannot be separated,
With the blooming of the gui flowers comes well-being,
Well-being and Chairman Mao cannot be separated.

Luo's first moment in the national limelight reverses the more well-known trajectory in which elites went to collect from the masses, processed their culture into streamlined versions, and offered pedagogical forms back to them. In Luo's case, by contrast, she *was* a member of a poor minority—those usually targeted as recipients of revolutionary culture—and she was offering her song to the highest leaders in a formalized performance that demonstrated both the gratitude of the Miao and their special contribution. From her perspective, this was not a form of tribute exacted from a reluctant subject of the new regime. Rather, Luo felt that this was a peak moment for her in which her ethnic culture was dignified and respected in urban venues that had denigrated the Miao for centuries.[1] Moreover, that she, as someone from a minority peasant background, and a woman at that, should be given this opportunity to present her ethnic specificity for consumption by luminaries the likes of these was an unimaginable kind of social mobility. Luo did not speak of her song as in any way inauthentic; she spoke of it as finally legitimate.[2]

The National Ministry of Culture (Zhongyang Wenhua Bu) made the decision to keep her on in the Central Song and Dance Troupe (Zhongyang Gewutuan). At that time, she recalled, Zhou Enlai paid great attention to minorities and insisted that she be well-trained (*peiyang*), young and pretty as she was, with such a lovely voice. One of her songs told of her special character and allure:

I am a Young Girl of the Miao People

I am a young girl of the Miao people,
My embroidered skirt is so, so pretty,

My round, round face is plump and full,
My whole embroidered outfit is sewn with my own hands,
Aiyi! The Miao people sing out a song of good fortune.

Luo's performance was clearly consonant with the gendered logic that we have seen. Her value in Beijing was indexed by the melding in her of youthful feminine attractiveness with folk distinctiveness. Interpellated in this way, what she offered the country's highest leaders was also a political ritual that could not but be structured vertically along gender and rank axes. Nonetheless, the ritual eventuated in her being chosen to train as a cultural professional, to assume the dignified stature of a Beijing urbanite. And she was to don this mantle of status on her own merits, not as the spouse of an employed male. This role sharply departed from the age-old practice among Miao peasants in which young men might go to towns and cities to seek labor opportunities, while women would invariably stay home to till the fields, possibly joining their husbands for a sojourn during slack season. Luo, by contrast, had escaped the menial work of farming entirely on her own. And in the process she had embarked on a mission that was to serve not only the revolution but also her people.

Training, for Luo, meant learning both singing skills and *wenhua* (culture, which connoted a general education, and especially Chinese language skills). While she made her way along the seemingly interminable path to Chinese literacy, she acquired a studied and controlled professional voice, one that enabled her to command greater audiences with the messages of her ethno-revolutionary songs. After a year at the Central Song and Dance Troupe, she moved on to three years of continued study at the Central Academy of Music (Zhongyang Yinyue Xueyuan), where she also was schooled in playing the piano. By now, she sang in the persona of a diva, theatrical and stylized.

After graduation, she married a Han man in Beijing. He was an intellectual, employed at the Ministry of Astronautics. They met in 1959 at a dance party celebrating the first ten years of the People's Republic. Captivated by a performance of hers, he courted her for five years before they were wed in 1964. Having studied at mainstream academies for performing arts, she was now assigned to a work unit more tailored to her role as ethnic messenger of revolution. Her first post was at the prestigious Central Nationalities Song and Dance Troupe (Zhongyang

Minzu Gewutuan). On arrival, she was promptly sent out to perform in Tibet and destinations along the silk road. Performing at 5,000 feet, she remembered, was a test of fortitude, and many of her colleagues and orchestra members fell, while she kept on singing unaccompanied. She had become a member of the cultural elite, now charged with bringing the hopeful spirit of liberation to other non-Han on China's periphery. Her songs would be entertainment for minorities in the hinterland who had not had the opportunities that she had. Her songs also were intended to demonstrate the respect that the Maoist government held for minority customs and the commitment it had made to fostering minority advancement. Luo's career meant not only her own fame, but the education of the masses who might identify with her.

Returning to Beijing after months of travel, Luo became pregnant on the eve of the Cultural Revolution. In late pregnancy, she made a difficult trip back to Guizhou, planning to have her baby and leave it with her mother so that she could continue her work unhindered. But she found she was unable to bear the idea of giving up her newborn son. She persuaded her mother to return with her to Beijing to help care for the child. The Cultural Revolution was in full swing now, and their travel was on trains besieged by Red Guards riding the rails for free at Chairman Mao's behest. The Cultural Revolution (1966–76) took aim at all forms of difference — whether class, gender, or ethnic — as vestiges of a society mired in feudal structures and practices. This meant that the folk traditions so caringly cultivated in earlier periods of Maoism were for the most part denounced as retrograde. Luo's stage in Beijing was smashed as a remnant of deplorable *"jiu wenhua"* (old culture). Nonetheless she remained in tremendous demand for political rallies and at universities. With as many as two or three performances a day, she had to give up breastfeeding and switch to milk powder for her baby. When the child was only six months old, she let her mother take him back to Guizhou.

Luo's songs in that period were, by political mandate, more generic Cultural Revolution fare, omitting special reference to the Miao and instead singing verses of Mao's poetry or his praises:

Chairman Mao Is the Golden Sun

Ai! Chairman Mao, Chairman Mao, the golden sun,
Shining with glorious radiance in every quarter,

Ai, shining with glorious radiance in every quarter.
He makes the mountains bright, he makes the oceans bright,
He makes the mountains bright, he makes the oceans bright.
The great doctrine of Communism lets off a red glow, ai,
The great doctrine of Communism lets off a red glow.
In the footsteps of our great teacher, Chairman Mao,
We go forward on the road without obstacles,
In the footsteps of our leader, Chairman Mao,
Our revolutionary determination is hard as steel,
Our revolutionary determination is hard as steel.
Ai, Chairman Mao, the golden sun,
Shining with glorious radiance in every quarter, Ai, shining with
    glorious radiance in every quarter,
Shining with glorious radiance in every quarter, Ai!

Propaganda, *Xuanchuan*, and Mass Arts

At this point, most Western readers will have concluded that Luo's work
fell squarely within the category of "propaganda." The notion of propaganda has been conventionally counterposed in the West to a more
popularly accessible and less didactic form of culture associated with
noncommunist states. Edelstein (1997), for instance, offers a veritable
catalogue of negative characteristics of propaganda: totalitarian, ideological, manipulative, moralistic. Moreover, it is simplistic in its messages, based on claims rather than knowledge, anonymous but reflect-
ing the concerns of those with authority, limited in who produces it,
and associated with control and censorship (1997:15).

These characterizations begin from the normative premise that propaganda is an undesirable and illegitimate cultural mode, harnessed too
tightly to certain types of interest. As Holm describes it:

Propaganda, unlike literature and art, is generally thought of as ema-
nating from organized political groups and is evaluated by the sponsor primarily on how effectively it changes patterns of thinking and
behavior in a target population—or, put more negatively, on how it
prevents people from thinking and acting in certain ways. Artistic criteria may of course play an important secondary role as a source of appeal; thus works of propaganda of a high artistic quality may be more

effective, as propaganda, than works that are, for whatever reason, less satisfactory artistically. . . . Nevertheless, in the eyes of the agencies commissioning or producing the propaganda, artistic quality is a means to an end rather than an end in itself. (Holm 1984:5)

This irreconcilability of art and ideology has been a staple in Western commentary on the arts under socialist regimes. Such commentary is premised on two founding distinctions, or even contradictions. The first, as the above passage shows, is that a specific regime or agency commissioning the propaganda desires to act on a population *separate from* itself. The second is that an inalienable individuality of the artistic creator is by nature in contradiction with designs that the commissioning agency might have for her/his work. Both premises are exemplified by the portrayal by Cyril Birch (1963) of the "burden" of the "writer under Communism":

With large areas of the field of writing closed to him — the literature of personal experience, the exploration of subjectivity, really incisive social protest — he must be constantly aware . . . of the propaganda requirements for his work. . . . The mere reporting of reality is, of course, no more acceptable from a Chinese writer than it would be from an English and American writer: but the *interpretation* of reality, there's the rub, must be made in accordance with what? . . . the Party's vision of the future. (Birch 1963:6)

It is not difficult to see the almost caricatured designation of heroes and villains in a passage such as this one. But I want to draw attention to a further assumption that appears less often or less overtly — that is, that the artistic creator is not only an individual but of a class/intellectual elite. This assumption manifests itself in two forms: (1) that the regime and the artist, both of elite stature, are locked in conflict over the hearts and minds of the masses or (2) that the creator, as a cultural elite, produces works that only appeal to or are only intelligible to other such elites, and that it is anathema to force creators to produce for a broader "target" population. In both cases, the emphasis is on the agency and creative work of a sociopolitical stratum distinguished from the masses, who serve only as a receptive audience or target population. One of the important moves that Mao made in the Yan'an Talks, by contrast, was to situate the audience at the center of the artistic process. In Maoist thought: "the writer loses his primary importance, while the audience gains immensely in relative status. The relationship is now defined as one in which the writer serves the people. . . . there is no longer even the theoretical possibility that writers may be on the side of the masses and yet write for a different audience" (McDougall 1980:16). The critique of propaganda, then, rests on the ideal type of the individualistic creator whose work is both antagonistic to the regime's ends and to the tastes of the broad masses. For Mao, on the other hand, "The first question is: Who are the people our literature and art are for?" (McDougall 1980:63).

Luo's story and Maoist cultural policy in general invite us to consider more complicated readings of the notion of propaganda than the Western ideal type presented here. The Western version relies on the assumption that ideology is tantamount to unmitigated repression as in the following passage: "in the Chinese Communist Party's brutal history of power struggles, ideology was deployed like the army: both were used as weapons of control" (Zha 1995:28). The Chinese word routinely translated into English as "propaganda," *xuanchuan,* however, is more conventionally used in Chinese to connote "disseminate," "propagate," or "give publicity to." In the context of revolutionary change, it was this spirit of dissemination rather than ideological control that was enthusiastically embraced by many cultural practitioners. This is how Luo Xiuying, never an elite before the party made her one, encountered the process. The social transformations wrought by Mao were profound and far-reaching and, in the eyes of its publicists, demanded to be recounted time and again for new audiences. Except for the fact that she had almost surrendipitously become an elite performer under state sponsorship, she felt little distinction from the audiences that she reached. A cultural system that raised awareness about the changes overhauling Chinese society and integrated ever more members of the populace into the process (whether nationalism, land reform, class struggle, or cultural production) was, for many in the new culture industry, a legitimate cultural system. A little poem from an amateur theater troupe in Anhui province illustrates just this thinking:

An amateur troupe is really good,
It is a great school.

Production, study and also propaganda,
The people's livelihood cannot but be improved. (quoted in
  Mackerras 1973:13)

Luo inserted herself into this system from a particular positioning that continued to condition her roles. Through her persona as ethnic woman from peasant stock, she propagated not only the standard messages of socialist transformation, but also a sense of hopefulness about possibilities for prestige and mobility for some women and minorities. Obviously, only a few of them would have careers like the one she enjoyed, but what she represented was the formal institution of such careers as part of state cultural policy. For Luo, her work was not about a loss of cultural autonomy, but rather about inclusion in a grand project on a national scale.[3]

In 1968, as the Cultural Revolution moved into the phase of reforming elites through agricultural labor, any cultural worker, even those who like Luo came from peasant backgrounds, came to be targeted as in need of a reeducation by peasants. First Luo's husband was sent to labor on an army farm (*junken nongchang*) in the south. In 1969 she, too, was sent to an army farm, but in the north. Their son remained in Guizhou. For several years the family was separated with only brief and infrequent leaves for family visits. Luo's special skills meant that she continued to perform, traveling around the region where her farm was located as well as laboring.

In 1974, when Luo was permitted to return to work in Beijing, she sought to change work units because interpersonal relationships had been strained by the Cultural Revolution. She secured a job as a Navy performer. Their son, aged nine, was able to rejoin them in 1975. In 1977, after Mao's death, she recalled with emotion, she was given an opportunity to do something for the people of her hometown. The story reveals the ways in which Luo had been able to parlay her privilege as employee of the central state into advantage and publicity (*xuanchuan*) for the plight of the kin she had left at home. She had traveled back to Guizhou to see her mother and discovered that officials were demanding that the peasants in her native village sell eggs at low prices. The villagers complained that they did not have enough to feed themselves, let alone chickens, and that as a consequence of their refusal to produce

eggs they had been accused of being disloyal to Chairman Hua Guofeng. On her return to Beijing, Luo wrote a letter directly to Chairman
Hua, and his reply made the news. His instructions were to be implemented immediately. In Luo's narrative, however, the details of the instructions were tangential, for the point of her tale was that she herself
was to be sent back to Guizhou with a coterie of officials to investigate
and to meet with the provincial governor and party secretary. She returned with great fanfare; it was the first time a car had ever come to her
hometown. Members of the Nationalities Song and Dance Troupe accompanied her, and they rigged up electricity so that they could put on
a glitzy performance right in the village. As the intensity of the homogenization push of the Cultural Revolution faded, the Miao came back
into her lyrics—lyrics still redolent with signifiers of transformation:

The Miao People Sing a Song for Offering Liquor

Lighting the bonfire and starting to sing,
Drinking songs fly out from the pit of the stomach,
The moon is so happy it becomes like smiling eyes,
The stars are so happy they fall down and fill the river.
Fall down and fill the river, ei.
The Miao village is paving a road of good fortune, ei,
And thanking the elder brother who did the surveying, ei,
The workers and the peasants are as close as close relatives, ei,
Please drink of the fragrant rice wine, ei,
Ayei-ei, ayei-ei,
The fragrant rice wine is waiting for you to drink, ei.

The Miao village is building a hydro-electric power station, ei,
And thanking the elder brother who did the surveying, ei,
The Miao and the Han are one family, heart linked to heart, ei,
Please drink of the fragrant rice wine, ei,
Ayei-ei, ayei-ei,
The fragrant rice wine is waiting for you to drink,
Ayei-ei!

The song was framed by the cultural idiom of offering liquor, the
quintessential Miao hospitality ritual. It took the scenario of the loving

reunion in which friends and family greeted each other with drink and song and transposed it to the scale of Miao-Han relations. The Han, as in most representations, had become the elder brother in this interchange as well as the benevolent bestower of technology and modernization. Even as Luo mobilized state power to benefit her natal village, she simultaneously affirmed state authority in her song of asymmetrical but harmonious reciprocities.

Altogether, Luo stayed with the Navy for six years, and then, on turning forty and past her prime as a youthful performer, she transferred to the Central Nationalities Institute to become a singing teacher. During the 1980s she still had frequent opportunities to appear on stage, however, and she even was sent to Japan in 1985. In 1987 she was appointed head of the newly founded Central Nationalities Institute Art Troupe (Zhongyang Minzu Xueyuan Yishu Tuan), charged with organizing performances and pursuing opportunities for travel—especially abroad. This was one of many newfangled ventures, burgeoning in the period of cultural liberalization, that was geared toward commodifying arts for profit and especially for enticing foreign revenues. Over the years of reform beginning in 1979, Luo watched her career as a state professional gradually lose its luster as the market increasingly structured cultural production. In 1982 her songs had been a centerpiece of the formal program of the Siyueba Miao festival at the Institute; in 1988, however, she did not perform at all, her popularity supplanted by the fascination with new genres and country customs that constituted the focus of proceedings that year.

But Luo's spheres of activity, despite her relative marginality in the Beijing Miao festival, were far from outmoded. On the contrary, she had been facile at keeping pace with the times, and the reforms of the 1980s held many entrepreneurial opportunities for her. When I went to see her in 1988, it was at her home, the bans on foreign visits to Chinese residences having gradually been relaxed. Home was a spacious, multiroomed apartment at her husband's work unit, cluttered with new appliances including a television set, a VCR, and a video camera. She flaunted a pants suit boldly patterned in blue, pink, and white that she had bought from a Guizhou batik factory. Topping a henna-tinted wig was a matching hat to complete the ensemble. Now, her fashion statement exclaimed, she could display her membership in the economic

19. Luo takes center stage at Beijing's Siyueba, 1982.

elite by being a consumer of the ethnicized fashion that was being designed for tourists, and, at the same time, she could proclaim her continuing ethnic pride. Describing her family's economic status with the thumb's-up signal, she spoke with pride of the high salaries that she, her husband, and her son were able to draw, of how they had enhanced their riches when her husband spent four years in the United States. They had invested in a piece of land in Guiyang on which they had constructed a building to rent out for additional income. Most important, in 1988 she had just founded her newest venture, the Guizhou Arts Company (Guizhou Yishu Gongsi), a multipurpose enterprise out of Guiyang with all manner of offerings, including the organization of performances, song-and-dance lessons, a makeup salon, lighting services for performances, a beauty parlor, and a restaurant. She was seeking foreign investment for the firm and thinking of calling the joint venture the Chinese-American Art Company.

Luo's contemporary practice was one version of assuming modernity, one that dovetailed with government policy toward the pursuit of profit in the 1980s. It was a modernity shaped by and articulated with globalized capitalism. Its indices were wealth and all its accompanying material trappings along with a cosmopolitan outlook premised on a kind of universalism. But this notion that all modernity was unitary was abutting a rival vision structured by particularism. Luo was encountering a world of capitalist consumption saturated with desire for the unique, the raw, the traditional, the unprocessed. The professional finesse, the trained skill, the slickness of packaging of streamlined ethnic culture that she offered, all were in diminishing demand. It was a competing version of modernity, one built on difference, one that marked itself through the disavowal of a past, which was now fetishistically gazed upon rather than suppressed.

The fascination with lived local forms had everything to do with recovering locality as China underwent an explosion of urbanization and rural-urban migration. A unidirectional movement out of rural villages and peasant statuses toward the promise of the metropolis took place throughout the 1980s, burgeoning with the policy change in the late decade that permitted high school and college graduates to seek work by themselves rather than waiting for state job assignments. As fewer students of rural origin returned home after graduating, they increasingly desired a more symbolic form of return through the nostalgic imagination. Under this new aesthetic regime, *jiagong*—the term that denoted processing or reworking—became a pejorative, the antithesis of "real" culture.

An example of Luo's work in the 1980s shows that she emulated this studiously depoliticized nostalgia, but she deviated from the new canon of identitarian authenticity in offering a folk tune from the north despite her origins in the south:

I lower my head toward the mountain gully,
Chasing after the months and years gone by,
The boundless sand blown by the wind fills the mountain valley,
And I cannot see my childhood years.

I raise my head toward the clear blue sky,
Searching for a distant past,
White clouds wander idly to their hearts content,
Not one thing has changed.

The wild goose has heard my song,
The little stream has kissed my face,
The *dandan* flower in the mountains has blossomed and fallen,
Over and over again.

My dreams are left in this place,
This song carries my feelings away,
The stars are tiny points in the sky,
And I will long for them forever.

Luo had been a vanguard of her people and had achieved a great deal of fame, but this cultural sea change was destabilizing her position of artistic authority and licensing whole other domains of cultural production. What was called for in the 1980s was ethnic uniqueness and an equivalence between the performer and the genre that they represented. The rest of this chapter describes activities that other Miao cultural producers, most of them far less elite than Luo, were undertaking in their attempts to make culture turn a profit.

Staging Ritual Authenticity: Kaili's Success

In 1988 an invitation was received for an arts troupe to travel to Italy to participate in an international folklife festival. Departing from the older practice of favoring the elite center as the standard-bearer of quality, Chinese authorities chose to send the Southeast Guizhou—not the Central—Song and Dance Troupe. One of the leaders in charge of organizing the trip, a deputy director of the Guizhou Art and Literature Federation, told me that the troupe was chosen because its members' fidelity to local style pleased foreigners' tastes—that foreigners did not like too much *"jiagong."* Ever more canny about what Western critics have described as the lure of the primitive for metropolitan consumers, tourists, and art connoisseurs (Clifford 1988; Price 1989; Torgovnick 1990), Guizhou entrepreneur-artists intensified their folksy character, grooming it for the burgeoning market.

20. Rural festival takes to the stage in Kaili, 1985.

Re-creating ritual was becoming the practice of multiple nationalities gewutuans (song and dance troupes) scattered across China from Beijing to every medium-sized city where minorities were concentrated. As we saw with Luo Xiuying, official organizations were composed of trained performers, composers, directors, choreographers, etc., mostly from minority backgrounds, together with a few Han. Their performances since the 1950s had been made up of didactic themes, in keeping with the Stalinist slogan, "National in form, socialist in content." [4] Their audiences were largely domestic; performances had the dual role of ideologically educating the masses and entertaining high leadership through the repackaging of official messages in exotic wrappings. In the earlier 1980s the Southeast Guizhou Gewutuan put together a performance that bespoke contemporary tensions between tradition and modernization. A dance that hewed to the "National in form, socialist in content" line was performed by four girls dancing merrily as batik artists with props evoking the craft, while behind them hung a large batiked backdrop with a symbol of one of the four modernizations — agriculture, industry, science and technology, and the military — in each corner. Meanwhile, another dance in the same show staged the Chiguzhang ceremony, that most important and serious (*longzhong*) of ritual events, whose content was the worship of ancestors. This was not seen as a corruption, but as a celebratory reformulation that remade Miao culture into a medium of exchange that could fuel development. Simultaneously, it presented an image of themselves with a unique heritage, one that was, in Tilley's words, "self-consciously not of Western modernity, but of a vibrant culture independent of it. What is being explicitly rejected here is that a desirable future will owe nothing to the past" (1997:84).

As the reform era moved into the 1990s, the Southeast Guizhou Song and Dance Troupes, more versatile than their big-city colleagues at retooling themselves for nostalgic consumption desires, garnered engagements in clubs in Shanghai, Shenzhen, Beijing, and other sites, as metropolitan consumers rejected the predictable codes of Maoist days in which experts like Luo Xiuying had molded their ethnic material into socialist professionalism. One older Miao musician-turned-entrepreneur in Kaili started an independent arts company (*Yishu Gongsi*) to supplement his long-term job at a state-supported troupe. He hired untrained teenagers from the countryside and charged them with dancing wildly to such motifs as courtship and flirtation. The romance with wildness was also extended to the literally animal in another ritual performance. In one of its most lucrative ventures, water buffalo were loaded onto the train to Beijing where a rural festival was staged, complete with bullfights, in an outdoor auditorium. Beijingers paid dearly (by Guizhou standards—five yuan a seat) to witness this display of carnality. When demand continued unabated, the troupe enhanced its profits by selling off the animals, leaving them in the national capital for a lifetime of clashing horns to titillate metropolitan audiences.

Noble Salvage: Jin Ou

Jin Ou had had a career path similar to that of Luo Xiuying. He had been performing with the Central Nationalities Song and Dance Troupe since the 1950s. A Miao man from Southeast Guizhou with a humble peasant background, in the 1980s he boasted of being the only Miao Level One (*Diyi Ji*) performer in the entire country. For decades, Jin Ou performed highly choreographed dances based on motifs from Miao folk culture (one of the most famous was "*Dou Ji*," in which he and another male performer enacted a chicken fight). His repertoire also included dances of other nationalities. His costumes had been fabricated in Beijing, in bold performer's colors, with a token pattern from Miao or other ethnic dress incorporated to designate nationality.

Jin Ou was proactive in adapting his artistic motifs to the tastes of the reform era. During 1988 he left Beijing to travel to Guizhou at least twice. One trip was to purchase festival costumes handcrafted by rural Miao women. The other trip was to follow up on the purchase of brand-new bamboo reed pipes (*lusheng*), which he had commissioned from a well-known and recently rehabilitated master craftsman. This kind of collecting was far from unique. Performing troupes all over the country were overhauling their props to include genuine minority festival attire and musical instruments. Enormous amounts of funds were being allocated to acquire rough-hewn artifacts; in turn, many village Miao enthusiastically rummaged through family heirloom chests to cash in on the new demand. When I asked Jin Ou how much he had to spend for costumes, he would tell me only that they were "extremely expensive."

One innovation which Jin Ou reported proudly was his recasting of the kinesthetics of the shaman. In the mid-1980s he started making trips to the countryside to collect materials and inspirations. When I met with him in 1985, he proudly showed me a Miao shaman's ring, a large metal loop strung with smaller coin-type discs to make a bell-like sound when shaken; he had recently brought it back as a prop. His design, now that liberalization had made some shamanic practices permissible again, was to choreograph a dance that re-created the jerky, convulsive movements of the shaman in trance as its central motif. Such a motif, according to Mackerras, also was seen in a Mongol dance called *Andai:*

> Its basic structure is the waving of handkerchiefs with accelerating foot movement rising to an exciting climax. The vigorous waving of the handkerchief was originally part of a religious ritual which aimed to drive evil spirits away from a sick person and so effect a cure, but in the course of time came to represent any plea to the spirits, such as sending drought-breaking rain. The reformed, professionalised *Andai* dance retains the handkerchief waving and the exciting climax, but disposes of the religious significance. (1995:197)

To the extent that they offered amusement, Jin Ou's moves also had the effect of sanitizing and secularizing popular ritual. Indeed, in my research area, shamanic rituals were some of the few remaining ritual practices that, despite being revived on a large scale, were still carried

21. A shaman in trance performs a healing rite. She holds a "shaman's knife," an accessory used by Miao and Hmong shamans all over the world. (*Below*) 22. Shaman choreography.

out under the cover of darkness, privately and somewhat furtively. Jin Ou's representation of them through the medium of his art, then, had a latent political significance. Although the state was officially opposed to shamanism as "feudal superstition" (*fengjian mixin*), when constructed as a remnant of minority traditional custom (*chuantongde fengsu xiguan*), legitimate spaces could be created for its perpetuation.

Prosperity for Posterity

Jin Ou's strategy — of consolidating Miao culture precisely through its production as a palatable consumable — echoes what Friedman has described for the tourism project of the Ainu of Japan as "a manifestation via a commodity form of a larger constitutive process of cultural identity, one that must, of course, be manifested for others if it is to have any real existence" (1990:321). Projects of cultural preservation under the banner of commercialization also were common in rural sites that had been developed for ethnic tourism. A major state initiative in the reform period, this strategy, from the state's perspective, is summarized by Oakes:

> Ethnic tourism is seen as having both economic and propaganda benefits for Guizhou. For domestic tourists, it encourages investment from other provinces in ethnic commodity production. For foreign tourists, it generates precious foreign exchange and opportunities for investments and joint-venture proposals. According to Deputy Minister Rong Mu of the State Tourist Bureau on a 1986 visit to Guizhou, tourism can also propagandize the multinational unity and stability of China. (1993:59)

Upon the state's opening of rural villages to foreign travel and its adoption of policies promoting the conversion of local customs into revenues, minority villagers in certain key areas joined ethnic elites like Luo Xiuying and Jin Ou in presenting their local flavors for consumers' cash. These projects were always fraught with tensions over who should keep the profits. State tourist agencies vied with locals for control of what tourists spent — and of what was offered for them to spend it on — as the tourists indulged in folk culture experiences.

Several special "tourist destinations" (*luyou dian*) had been established by the China Travel Service in Southeast Guizhou; these included the

Miao village of Shang Langde. Shang Langde had been chosen by the authorities because it had been the home of Yang Daliu (1830–72), one of the most famous of Miao rebels against administrative abuses perpetrated by the colonizing Qing state (1644–1911). Now canonized as a class protorevolutionary, he had been enshrined by the state, which put up money for the picturesque paving of dirt paths with small stones and for the construction of a small museum and reception building. Local residents had converted their productive lives to include tourist entertainment and, in the process, had entered into a dynamic of ethnic subjectification. Here, at any time of year, tourists could experience an entire reception program from the moment they stepped off the bus. Colorfully dressed young women, having been notified ahead of time to assume their most formal appearance, waited at a faux doorway that signified the entrance to the village. They pushed ritual welcome wine encased in the horns of bulls to the lips of hapless visitors. In a hall erected for the purpose, they performed hospitality, serving a feast made with local ingredients. Along with feasting, a tour of the museum in which old weapons used by Yang Daliu were housed, and signing of the guest book, the centerpiece of the program was the simulation of Miao New Year processional dancing. Thirty or forty ethnically costumed local women danced around musicians playing drums and *lusheng.* Tourists could look on at what in other villages was an annual harvest rite but in Shang Langde had become a daily labor. Local girls then took them by the hand, beckoning them to join the processional.[5]

Despite the state tourist agencies taking large cuts of paid admissions for these ritual events, locals saw their participation as a highly desirable source of cash income. According to Oakes (1995a:313), in 1993, for instance, 3,945 tourists visited Shang Langde, earning villagers more than 43,000 yuan in fees. Indeed, Miao from other villages in the region harbored jealousies about the sudden windfall that residents of Shang Langde had received, while young people angled to court with these newly prosperous marriage targets. At the same time, key employees in Shang Langde were aware of the inequities of their protoproletarianization and voiced concern that their share in tourist dollars was so pitiful.

In other cases, and especially in sites that had not been developed by the state for purposes of tourism, local Miao culture producers and entrepreneurs had more control over earnings. In 1988, Zhou of

Xijiang's Culture Station set up a small display of local handicrafts in his office in the local government building. He recruited the most well-crafted and representative older pieces from elderly women and promised to sell them on consignment, should interested travelers pass through Xijiang. He also commissioned some small souvenir-sized *lusheng* to include in the exhibit.

In some ways the commodification endeavor stimulated cultural preservation that might otherwise not have been a concern of peasants struggling with the exigencies of the privatizing economy. The rehabilitated artisan commissioned by Jin Ou had learned *lusheng*-making at a young age. During the Cultural Revolution, however, his father had been so badly persecuted that after his father's death the younger man had refused to carry on the family tradition. Only after a great deal of urging and an offer of wage employment on contract with the Leishan county Culture Bureau had he been persuaded to renew making *lushengs* in the late 1980s. Seeing the new political correctness of his practice and the returns on sales of the instruments, he left the county post and returned home to go into business on his own. When I visited his comfortable village home in 1988, he said he was backed up for six months with orders to handcraft instruments for performing troupes, research units, cultural and foreign affairs offices, and nationalities affairs bureaus all over the province and beyond.[6] His popularity derived from his skill at producing quality instruments in the ancient style. And his humble workshop boasted a rural rarity: a television, acquired with his new wealth, which he played continuously as he worked.

In addition to sponsoring individual artisans like the *lusheng*-maker, the state also was instituting mass production and marketing of Miao handiwork. Locally crafted costumes and embroidery pieces were bought in huge volume and sold for hundreds, sometimes thousands, of yuan in tourist shops in smaller cities like Kaili and in the craft shops of major tourist hotels in the metropolises like Beijing, Shanghai, Guangzhou, and Chengdu. Production and distribution of standardized commodities were variously organized. In the city of Anshun, a batik factory commissioned designers and hired wax applicators, but it contracted the messy process of indigo dyeing to peasant households. The batiked squares, shoulder bags, wall hangings, clothing, and other items produced in bulk were sent out for sale in craft shops throughout the country. In the town of Taijiang, a workshop was set up in which several

23. Rehabilitating *lusheng* craftsmanship to TV accompaniment.

silversmiths worked for salaries, producing uniform jewelry items to be sold at subsidized prices in a government-run shop whose chief clientele were local Miao people.

These commodifications of culture, marking as they did the transformations in the cultural regime entailed in emerging from Maoism and variously entangling with global capitalism, were the subject of considerable consternation among Chinese observers and participants in the process. One perspective often conveyed to me is that it was only the funds from the state's patronage and from the plethora of nostalgic desires that served to preserve these ancient customs. The local people, I was told, were so concerned with modernization that they would let many of these practices go if no profit was to be had from them. Two Miao intellectuals from Guiyang debated these considerations with me in 1993. Miao culture, they explained, was undergoing *shangpinhua* (commodification). For example, they reminisced, according to customary regulations (*guiding*), the playing of the *lusheng* and the beating of the ritual drum were restricted to agricultural slack season (*nongxian*) and could be done only after the playing was initiated by the *lusheng tou* (the elder in charge of *lusheng* rites). Now, with the coming of tourists, accommodations were being made and the *guiding* had been smashed (*dapole*), especially in Shang Langde. I asked them what they thought of this change. "Smashing the customary regulations is a violation of Miao ethnic dignity [*minzu zunyan*]!," one exclaimed. But the other disagreed. "Commercialization is vital for ethnic development [*weile minzu fazhan*]," he protested. Both spoke to what was best for the Miao, and in the process they addressed the contradictions generated out of reliance on the market to invigorate culture.

Festival Tours: Longchuan Jie

The site of Longchuan Jie (The Dragon Boat Festival) was Xijiang's neighbor county, Taijiang, which had officially been opened to foreign travel in 1987. The Qingshui River, which is viable for boat traffic and flows eastward to Hunan province, has given rise to a special subculture and economic life for those Miao who live along its shores. In former times the trade in timber was an important link with more populous Han areas in Hunan, accounting for the relative prosperity of the area compared to mountain-bound Xijiang, whose trickling stream provided water sufficient for a large community but no opportunity for transporting goods. Longchuan Jie takes place in several communities along a short segment of the river that marks the present boundary between Taijiang and Shibing counties. In no other place in Guizhou province are dragon boat races performed either by the Miao or the Han (deBeauclair 1970:30,52).

A relatively anomalous festival has been cast, through mass publicity, as one of the stereotypical features of China's Miao. Longchuan Jie's spectacular marketability was one of the chief reasons that the state opened the county for tourism relatively early. Even before opening, however, the pageant of the dragon boats, with its dramatic and agonistic elements, had become popular among Chinese media and tourists as well as for foreigners who obtained special permission to attend. The majority of these visitors focused on highly visible elements, only some of which were deliberately offered up for outside consumption, leaving others to be quietly carried out by local villagers.

Early on the first morning, in the already oppressive heat and humidity of July, the ritual of putting the boats into the water took place in villages all along the river. Each narrow wooden boat, long enough for thirty-eight oarsmen to stand in pairs along its length, featured an elaborately carved and painted dragon head mounted on its bow. A ritual expert, his assistant, and other village men assembled on the riverbank.

They made offerings of liquor to an anthropomorphic spirit that is said to live in the highest mountains, then to the mountain dragons to call them to come protect the boats and the village. A rooster, which had to be white for purity, was killed, and a branch from the gallnut (*wu-beizi*) tree was stuck into the ground. Gallnut was mandatory because of its abundance of white sap; since the mountain spirit was a breast-feeding mammal, it was appropriate to give it this "milk." On the top of the branch was fastened a bannerlike set of white paper strips splattered with chicken blood. New clothes were provided for the spirit — once a ragged beggar — to don so that it would not be ashamed to enter the village. A parasol also was essential, seen as a mediator between the ritualist and the spirits.

This offering ceremony took place early in the morning and went undocumented except by me, by several culture workers, and by reporters from relatively local work units within Southeast Guizhou. Once the boats were in the water, the festival became decidedly more public and recreational. The boats spent several hours of the first day paddling upstream and receiving greetings of firecrackers and gifts of ducks, chickens, pigs, and goats at villages along the way. Ducks were hung by their feet along the extended neck of the dragon, and other animals were put into a companion boat that traveled alongside. This extensive gifting mapped the networks of extended kin that knit families together across the river and straddled the county line.

By midday, the boats had converged at the village of Pingzhai in Shibing county, the most upriver village taking part in the event. Oarsmen docked, received more gifts, and feasted with their hands on sticky rice, fat meat, and liquor. In turns, they rowed a little farther upstream and, orchestrated by an older man playing a wooden drum and a younger boy beating a gong in the bow of the boat, both in festival costume, they practiced their speed for the following day. A third man periodically shot off gunpowder.

On the riverbank a huge market was under way. Long lines of people were walking into Pingzhai along the riverbanks from all over the region, and stalls selling food and miscellaneous goods were packed with customers. Young people predominated in numbers, for Longchuan Jie also was an important courtship opportunity. Youths in single-sex batches of from two to eight clustered in the market and cruised the river's edge, hoping to meet members of the opposite sex from other villages. At one point, some younger oarsmen, dressed in the customary jackets of shiny brown homespun cotton, metal-link belts, and cone-shaped straw hats, debarked and attempted to get some antiphonal courtship songs going with local girls. Peasant spectators circled around and pressed in on them, forming a crowd so thick that the singing was squelched by the confusion and scrutiny. But the promenading, the joking and getting acquainted, continued throughout the evening.

This first day of Longchuan Jie was a massive regional Miao event in which local attention was directed toward the boats, and reciprocal gazes were exchanged between potential marriage partners. While a sprinkling of reporters and other Chinese tourists had bought river passage to Pingzhai on the small overloaded boats that wended their way upstream from Shidong (Taijiang County) that day, their presence had little impact on the course of events. The focus for visitors was the township (*zhen*) of Shidong, which was more accessible by long-distance bus, and where, on the second day of festival activities, the locale would be transformed into a stage. The people of the township, by 1988 already highly experienced in the theatricalization of Longchuan Jie, had undertaken large-scale preparations to receive these visitors.

As with peak season in any resort, the local guest house had doubled its prices for both Chinese and foreign guests for the duration of the festival. Two exhibitions of embroideries and silver jewelry from all over Southeast Guizhou, advertised in English as well as Chinese, had been mounted to satisfy the appetites of tourist shoppers. On the street outside the guest house, two additional stalls selling handicrafts appeared on festival day alongside those selling snacks and miscellaneous goods. Such handicrafts, including older costume items and newer products designed for display rather than wear, were never seen in rural markets frequented only by peasants. Some struggle took place over who would profit from sales to big-spending outsiders as local peasants circumvented the officially sponsored exhibitions and approached visitors to independently offer crafts at cut-rate prices. In addition, the local middle school had assembled an exhibition of local paintings, photography, and calligraphy—with price tags attached.

The domestic visitors attending Longchuan Jie represented the Chinese news and culture industries as well as the burgeoning ethnologically oriented institutions. These included Guizhou Television, Chongqing Television (Sichuan province), the Culture Bureau of Southeast

Guizhou, the Taijiang County Culture Bureau, the Taijiang Nationalities Affairs Committee, the Taijiang Government, students from the Beijing Film Institute, and the Art Departments of both Guizhou Teachers' College and the Guizhou Nationalities Institute, as well as a great number of independent photographers and filmmakers from across the country. A province-wide conference on Miao folklore also had chosen the Shidong Longchuan Jie as its site, adding dozens of folklorists and culture bureau personnel to the ranks of spectators.

The list of foreign visitors included ten American women on a tour; a French photo-journalist, along with his soundman, making an ethnographic film; nine independent travelers from France, Germany, England, Holland, and Japan; seven Hong Kong travelers collecting embroideries; two British teachers of English from Kaili and their parents; and an American anthropologist (me) and spouse.

The key attractions for outsiders were the assembling of dragon boats in Shidong and their late afternoon races. About 2 P.M., spectators were guided to the riverbank. A large, concrete, steel-roofed reviewing stand, built in recent years for the reception of such dignitaries, was prepared with place cards, and tea was brewed for some of the honored Chinese guests. The reviewing stand was decorated with four large red posters welcoming, respectively, leaders from all levels, media personnel, foreign friends, and Hong Kong and Macao compatriots. From the stand, using a public address system, the master of ceremonies called the races.

In sharp contrast to the disorderly mingling of people at the Pingzhai market the previous day, the Shidong event was characterized by a strict bifurcation of space that sought to distinguish those who watched from those who participated, thus creating the conditions for a unidirectional gaze. The presence of white foreigners huddled in the segregated shade of the reviewing stand, however, gave rise to a great deal of reverse reviewing. Uniformed public security officers kept a constant vigil to hold back the crowds of spectators that gravitated to the spot in front of the stand in order to get an eyeful of these pale strangers from faraway places. Public security also did crowd control at the guest house, barring entrance to nonguests, but their efforts did little to discourage the crowds that were clustered outside for a glimpse of a white visitor passing through the reception area. For many of the region's peasants, the novelty of seeing foreigners was a far greater attraction than the dragon boats themselves.

On the river that afternoon, the boats assembled, docked, received gifts, and the oarsmen feasted before they rowed in competition as they had on the first day. Unlike the first day, however, now when the boats went racing by, they were dogged by motor boats with cameramen on their bows, filming the action. The shallows around the docking sites were filled with photographers up to their knees in water getting close-ups. One dragon boat even added a fourth man to the collection on its bow — a photographer from the Kaili Culture Bureau. With the bifurcation of space disrupted, the scene developed into one in which no space distanced performers from spectators; the processes of cultural consumption became an integral part of the production.

The formal competitive races did not begin until about 5 P.M. By that time, spectators were restless. The American tourists were herded off to board a bus heading out of town, and the attention of the locals was shifting to the market street where young people were gathering for an evening of courting. The pageant element of the event had upstaged the importance of the actual boat competition to such a degree that by the time the boat race took place it passed almost unseen by many who ostensibly had come to watch it. By dusk, most of the spectators had left or retreated to the guest house and Miao villagers reclaimed the space that had been the site of outsiders' scrutiny during daylight hours.

As the curtain closed on Longchuan Jie's theatrical segment, self-display gave way to a more symmetrical form of scrutinizing practice — that of young people checking each other out in search of desirable partners. The street was packed solid with teenagers walking up and down in single-sex groups, examining each others' faces under the direct glare of a flashlight, and gathering to chat, joke, or, in rare instances, initiate antiphonal courtship singing with members of the opposite sex. Promenading and boisterous play went on throughout the night, and fatigued young people could still be seen wandering about when dawn broke at 6:30.

In Longchuan Jie, outside visitors' spectating practices did not negate the festival's other central meanings — particularly around the social ties affirmed through offering gifts to the boatmen as well as those ties formed in courtship encounters. But because, like any periodic market in the region, Longchuan Jie already had a public/anonymous aspect, it was fitting material for commodification, especially if locals stood to gain economically from doing so. It was a multicommunity happening

24. Boy in festive attire beats the gong on the dragon boats.

that thrived on *renao* (exciting, densely peopled, carnivalesque), and the
attention it received from high-status, affluent outsiders only enhanced
this atmosphere. The packaging of Longchuan Jie for consumption,
then, far from being seen as corruption of ancient purity, was viewed
as consonant with its embrace of the logics of spectatorship.

There was one contest over meaning in which I encountered a tension between Longchuan Jie's putatively private backstage and its public
appropriation. One of the most popular images for photographers and
media producers to capture was the young boy in elaborate festival regalia adorning each boat. His costume, resembling that which today is
usually seen only on girls, was sensationalized in mass representation as
a mysterious form of cross-dressing by those who sought cultural curiosities to make their material more marketable. Local Shidong elders,
however, insisted to the contrary that this practice was a holdover from
ancient times when males as well as females dressed elaborately for festival. Their version offered a memory of gender equality that challenged
the dominant representation of the practice as gender transgression.[7]
This rival view, however, was not widely circulated, as it was much less
palatable than ritual transvestism to consumers with an appetite for the
exotically other.

Conclusion: A Lue's Demise

The stories in this chapter reveal how, in effect, shifts in the Chinese economy and in state policies toward the arts selected different Miao to become cultural producers. They also show that what determined whether one's products would have wide circulation had little to do with individual artistic styles per se. The professional histories of Luo Xiu-ying, Jin Ou, and other Miao who rose to prominence during the Maoist period hinged very little on opportunities for individual creativity or constraints upon it. Rather, their accounts were about participation, about class mobility, and about contributing to *xuanchuan*.

It is also clear from these stories that both the state and the market were incitements to particular kinds of cultural production. Presuming the value of autonomy—both for the arts and for ethnic cultures—Western critics have been quick to lament these dual processes. Mackerras, who has written extensively on minority performing arts in China, compares marketization unfavorably to even state professionalization:

> More and more of the professional troupes target their performances not at their own people, but at tourists and people from outside their region. . . . The Kaxgar Song and Dance Troupe contracts out no less than 70 percent of its annual performances to organizations such as tourist hotels. The good troupes go abroad as much as they can or spend quite a bit of time in areas of China other than those where they live. . . . The professionalised traditional song and dance forms of the minorities are thus tending to become reduced to a tourist attraction. (1995:197)

That cultural production for tourism should be portrayed as a "reduction" implies a particular normativity for nonelite or ethnic producers, one that defines their authenticity in contradiction with market exchange. On the other hand, ironically, those who would take aim at propaganda are in the position of naturalizing, or rendering invisible, just such market normativities. As Marcus and Myers (1995) describe it, the modern Western sense of art has been defined by that art's contrast to anything like the production of *xuanchuan*, for the artist's subsumption by larger processes would be the negation of art itself. "In modernity . . .

art has had a privileged position in social and cultural critique. A strong sense of the autonomy of art in modernity, on which its authority depended, even for avant-garde experiments and social criticism, could be preserved as long as no one participating in the art world looked at their own conditions of production and relationship to structures of capitalist society like market dynamics" (1995:23). This was one sense of artistic "freedom," but it was built on effacing the market, something Miao cultural producers emerging from Maoism never could have done.

On the other hand, speaking of the role of the artistic producer under Soviet rule, art historian Boris Groys has described another kind of "freedom"—the exhilarating sense of power experienced by state-supported cultural agents.[8] He identified at least three types of freedom as contrasted with the situation of artists in capitalist systems who experience the constraints of the market. First, the state artist is free *to be the same,* not to worry about producing something novel or unique in order to outsell competitors. Second, with state funds at her disposal, she can command tremendous resources and marshal huge amounts of labor for grandiose art projects. Third, access to a wide public audience does not have to be sought out but is provided as part of the job description. Thinking in these terms, it is easy to see how Luo Xiuying and others might have cherished the prestige and even the power of their state jobs and how they have encountered market reforms with trepidation. Interestingly, what the reform era market demanded was that Miao cultural producers "be the same" in quite another way: they were to be identical to what was imagined as their essential cultural identity, to engage in a mimesis that was "the creative imitation of that which is constituted as [their] 'nature' once it has been produced in representational forms for them" (Adams 1996a:18)—or they were to face economic ruin. The story of A Lue is a sobering instance of how this transition played out.

In 1993, when the commodification of all genres of ethnic culture already was firmly established, I visited a middle-aged Miao woman in downtown Guiyang. I had been to her home village, stayed in her natal household, and knew several of her relatives, one of whom was now performing Miao culture at the Splendid China Folk Culture Villages, a theme park in cosmopolitan Shenzhen.[9] A Lue was a performer retired from her active role on the stage. The apartment she lived in was crammed with belongings, occupied by more people than it was intended for. A Lue reminisced about her days of glory. Like Luo Xiuying, she had been chosen out of her rural village in 1950 as a representative (*daibiao*) to travel to Beijing. There she had had the honor of singing and dancing for Mao Zedong, Zhu De, and other key party leaders. She even once sat across the room from Mao, she recalled with pride, and presented him with Miao clothing and silver ornaments.

A Lue had been invited to stay and work in Beijing, but she decided to return to her home province and to work with the Guizhou Song and Dance Troupe (Guizhou Gewutuan). She had had a long career there as a singer, dancer, and choreographer. Now in her late fifties, she had achieved such a stature that she recently had been honored with a five-year term as a people's representative to the National People's Congress (Renmin Daibiao Dahui). Interestingly, this distinction affirmed the political import of her career in the stage arts, making of a minority peasant woman a leader empowered to speak to the center about the concerns of people in her province. At the same time, it transmuted her work into a vestige that shimmered with an aura of prestige but that was no longer vital to reform China. A note of regret sounded in A Lue's pride about her political attainment, for she was no longer acclaimed for her specialized skills.

Members of the Guizhou troupe to which she belonged complained that they no longer had any mission (*meiyou shenme renwu*). In the Maoist days, they had been given assignments to travel the country, performing for various political and didactic functions. They had been well-supported by the state, and their work was busy and meaningful. With reform, their iron-rice-bowl guaranteed salary was withdrawn, and they were required to make their cultural products turn a profit. But this was the Song and Dance Troupe of the *province*, not a group explicitly associated with minorities. Tarnished by the mark of their former utility as agents of *xuanchuan*, aesthetically stigmatized for the formal, controlled style of their offerings, and without the exotic appeal of the "*minzu*" troupes with which they had to compete, they were having a hard time getting contracted to perform anywhere. Scrounging for enough cash to live on from month to month, this collection of former cultural elites was now adopting a common survival strategy among former state employees whose vocations were no longer supportable in Deng's marketized economy; they had gone into a petty venture to garner some basic income. After managing to purchase a collection of tawdry billiards tables, they had placed them in the spacious court-yard of their once-eminent work unit. By turns, they served the newly affluent and newly idle young entrepreneurs of their little metropolis. Collecting a few yuan from each player, they stood by, gazing vacantly through the clouds of smoke that hovered over the pool players, to a distant vision. Their daily lives amounted to treading financial waters; what they awaited was another opportunity to sing and dance.

7

Scribes, Sartorial Acts, and the State

Calling Culture Back

About midway through my Xijiang fieldwork, Zhou, the young Miao man in charge of the Culture Station offered to accompany me to interview an old man who was reputed to know a great many folk tales. The offer was at Zhou's own iniative, and he repeatedly urged me to bring my tape recorder. On the appointed day, he showed up with a boom box of his own and a tangle of wires for a microphone as well as an AC adapter, should current be flowing in that part of the village that day. We hiked up the hill and with great fanfare set up and settled in for a taping session. Quickly it became clear that my questions were irrelevant, that Zhou was doing the eliciting, and that stories were going to be spoken briskly in a highly colloquial Miao that was beyond my comprehension. Several hours later, we left with my having had little to do with what had transpired. I realized that I had been incidental in Zhou's making his own folklore collections. The event revealed how complicated was my state-assigned role as legitimate scribe of the Miao people. In this case my function had been to lend authority to the project as a foreign researcher present at the taping. My residence in Xijiang may have heightened awareness of cultural preservation because of the common stereotype of ethnology researchers as collectors of curious and near-extinct lore; but, in this case, what my presence inspired was collection by an insider for insider consumption. Months after the taping expedition I learned that Zhou had been laboriously translating the stories into written Chinese versions for his own use and for submission to the county Culture Bureau.[1]

25. Auto-ethnology?

Collecting the Canon

They [the moderns] want to keep everything, date everything, because
they think they have definitely broken with their past. The more they
accumulate revolutions, the more they save; the more they capital-
ize, the more they put on display in museums. Maniacal destruction
is counterbalanced by an equally maniacal conservation. Historians re-
constitute the past, detail by detail, all the more carefully inasmuch as
it has been swallowed up forever." (Latour 1993:69)

Documentation and collection efforts were central to much of the cultural recovery project of the mid-1980s. In this era of rapid change,
"Collector Fever" (*Shoucang Re*) struck many urbanites, prompting the
systematic hoarding of all manner of artifacts from old furniture and
musical instruments to grain coupons and model cars (Anagnost 1997;
Liu Yuping 1992:51–55). In more academic domains, folklorists focusing on minorities spent a great deal of energy recording customary
lore (*minsu*), folk songs (*minge*), and stories (*minjian wenxue*).[2] Fieldwork
(*shidi diaocha*, or on-site investigation) became central to this endeavor,
effecting a symbolic return to the putative source of "extant tradition."

Zhunque (accurateness) was a critical element in evaluating field data and determining which items or versions should be included in published works or research reports. A major criterion for determining *zhunque* was authenticity, usually defined by key experts as that which was typical (*dianxing*) or had ancient historical origins (*gulao*). As collections were made, materials put in order (*zhengli*), museum exhibits mounted, and volumes edited and published, a gradual streamlining took place in which such experts designated what legitimately constituted any given nationality's culture or Chinese culture as a whole.

What I have called "key experts," i.e., university-educated specialists in folklore techniques, were not the only actors in the collecting project — as this chapter will show. With meager means, minority people in widely scattered locales also engaged in an effort at documentation to forestall permanent loss in the seemingly inexorable process of modernizing change. The salvage sensibility that infected so many people in the years of the unraveling of Maoism was what Lavie and Swedenburg have called "a process of selecting one of many possible sets of experiences from their history, in order to narrativize it linearly, and frame it as the 'authentic representation.' Tradition, folklore, and realism are authenticity's preferred modes of enframing. Yet," they continue, "we wish to stress not only that such modes conceal hybridity, but also that hybridity is equally 'authentic' " (1996:164). The self-appointed scribes who chronicled fading customs should not be seen as simply recording the cultural practices of their people; rather, they should be viewed as cultural producers themselves. Their practices blurred the lines between producers/consumers and between production/reproduction as they crafted hybrid products that fused local material with contemporary modes of cultural intercourse and representation.

The abundance in Xijiang and beyond of multifarious scribe/producers draws attention to two important trends. First, cultural conservatorship was linked to the authority of the written word. Soon after I arrived in Xijiang I had made arrangements to interview an old cadre who also was known to be a ritual expert. Before our meeting could take place, he had circumvented the indeterminacy of our dialogue by presenting me instead with a seven-page handwritten account of Xijiang's festivals (*jieri*), an account he had copied and recopied for numerous ethnological collections. Textualized versions of tradition had become like maps or guidebooks of how to stay essentially Miao. Even for some peasants, movements of recovery took place in increasingly dialectical entanglement with written words.

These texts, however, were little read by most local people, and it is notable that they were written in Chinese. There had been some small-scale publications in the script that had been devised for the Miao language in the 1950s, but the second trend I want to draw attention to here is that Chinese had become the language of choice for inscribing ethnic lore.[3] The production of such written accounts, then, had a dual character. The use of written Chinese designated the producers as modern participants in a national, state-sponsored preservation project carried out with unified standards in the majority language (cf. Anderson 1991). A collection of Miao courtship songs (Guizhou Sheng 1991) opened, for example, by invoking the following 1984 directive from the State Council: "The ancient lore [guji] of the minority nationalities are a part of the precious cultural heritage of the fatherland; to salvage [qiangjiu] and put in order the ancient books of the minority nationalities is a relatively important work."[4] At the same time that minority scribes affiliated with the national objective, the content of their works valorized their ethnic distinction. Classically characteristic of a nostalgic structure of feeling, Miao modernity was asserted *through* the process of representing the yearned-for past in an ever more formalized manner.

Art, Nostalgia, Heritage

Li was a fifty-year-old Miao man with a vision. He lived with his family in a shack in the compound of the Transportation Company of Kaili, the capital of the Southeast Guizhou Miao and Dong Autonomous Prefecture. He had grown up in a small mountain village, but in 1959 he had gone to serve in the army. After his return, he did not go back to rural life but instead was assigned work as an administrative cadre (*xingzheng ganbu*) in the transportation company where he had been working for twenty years when I met him. In 1988, Li got restless. Office work, so coveted by peasants and workers in China, was too suffocating for him. He switched to selling tickets on the long-distance buses that traversed the dusty, unpaved roads through the mountains where he had grown up. He retained his enviable urban residence, but he traveled daily to the hinterlands that filled his tender memories.

Besides ameliorating his restlessness, Li was working on something else. He had always been interested in art, and he had apprenticed himself several years earlier to a well-known local artist. Under that artist's tutelage, he studied drawing, painting, and woodcut printing. Then, in 1986, he undertook, on his own initiative, a massive project of recording the patterns in the embroidery and silver jewelry of the Miao in the region. When he traveled to the countryside, he photographed actual costumes from families' collections and returned to the city to re-create them with felt-tip pen or paint. By 1988 he had collected seventy or eighty patterns. Some were enlarged details from an embroidered sleeve or an ornamented shoe. Each was painstakingly detailed, lovingly colored, and carefully marked with an explanatory phrase. I asked Li why he chose costume patterns as his subject instead of something else. He said that he feared they would be "lost" (*shichuan, shidiao*) forever if he did not document them.

Li's own life had followed the nostalgia trajectory, from a rural childhood to a desk job in the drabness of the city, to a yearning for his country roots and an attempt to recover and re-create what he had lost through the production of images of it. He also began making woodcut prints that recorded local life. His subject matter was standard fare in the modernist mode of representing the pastoral: scenic village panoramas, peasants and draft animals heading into the mountains at dawn, and lively festival scenes in which costumed locals danced and played characteristic Miao instruments. His project bespoke the unresolved tension between city and country, as he had literally crafted his products out of his occupational movement between sites. On the other hand, as a Miao man from a peasant background, his enterprise undercut the alterities we have seen so far—those of foreigners questing for remote China, of Han elites exoticizing the customs of minorities, or urban intellectuals romanticizing the countryside. Not immune to the commodification logic that saturated reform era life, neither can his efforts be described as wholly incited by the market. But what concerns me here is less the forces of the market per se, but how the nationwide impulse toward cultural recovery manifested itself among Miao in differing social locations. Li's works (and other instances in this chapter) involved minorities adopting dominant modes with which to formalize fragments of their own culture before it disappeared—an impulse that had everything to do with emerging structures of prestige.

26. Li Wenzhong's woodcut print. Parasoled crowds watch a *lusheng* procession. Title reads: "*Guzang* Festival."

Gender and Hybridity

The efforts to fix certain elements of culture, and to fix them on certain practitioners, placed Miao women in complicated positionings in which hybridity was deeply implicated. Projects of cultural recovery, as chapters 4 and 5 showed, were usually gendered such that they foreclosed the scenario of rural women themselves pursuing modernity. The marking of their physical appearance — their costumed elegance — with the sign of tradition generated for rural Miao divided subjectivities in which questions of embodiment and sartorial decisions were especially at stake. What did the gendered regime of cultural recovery entail, then, for those most regularly its objects?

Miao women who went to Han-dominated cities expressed intense ambivalences that emanated from their "different" looks. Women told me of visiting relatives now working in Guangzhou and Tianjin and of the conflicts they underwent in deciding whether to put their hair up in characteristically Miao style. At first, they did it out of habit, but after enduring the curious stares of urbanites on the street, they decided to take their hair down and braid it when they went out. The young women working in the *Minzu* Guest House in Kaili told me that they would prefer to wear their hair down, living as they did in the city, but that they were required by their workplace to comb it up in ethnic style. When they were seen on the street after working hours, they often appeared indistinguishable from Han urban residents in their more Western clothing and hair styles. I interpret this adjustment less as a desire for cultural assimilation than as a tactic by which they sought to avoid provoking attributions of backwardness.

These dilemmas prompted two different types of internal conflict for Miao women. For rural women sojourning in cities for short periods of time, dressing like the Han felt like putting on a costume, a kind of denial of self. On the other hand, women working long-term in cities, such as those employed in tourist hotels, or traveling performers, faced the converse paradox. While their work brought them to the metropolis and accustomed them to its ways, it also required them to maintain their otherness as the basis for them having salaried work in the first place. As minority peasants, their rituals and customary dress had been matters of everyday convention with significations of their own, not simply vestiges of the past. To cast such practitioners as "cultural artifacts . . . [which are] attributed only a historical referentiality" (Kligman 1988:259) was to freeze them in time, denying them the longings for modernity that had gripped the rest of the country.

In contrast, how did Miao women remaining in the countryside come to terms with their imaging as quintessentially ethnic? The prestige associated with symbols of modernity was no less significant in rural areas than it was in the cities, but rural and especially minority areas bore the double burden of questing to modernize while being frozen in time by the representations and implicit injunctions of urban culture. The vast majority of rural young women were peasant daughters living in settings more isolated from circuits of communication than those of most of the Han peasantry. Their interactions with Han Chinese were rare. Many of the outlying villages were without electricity and consequently without television; mail was delivered over the mountains on foot, and the occasional newspaper or magazine that arrived was scarcely glanced at by young women because of their widespread lack of literacy. Their choices to adorn their hair or wear ethnic clothing were governed by regional standards, which as a rule called for everyday dress of simple Miao style but did not necessarily disdain more Western-style clothing. Decisions were made on the basis of local pressures toward conformity and were unconcerned with image-management vis-à-vis the larger society. Unlike those living in cities, then, these women rarely gave a passing thought to dominant expectations that they would enact cultural distinctiveness.

Only in the larger, more central villages — sites of periodic markets or important bus routes and popular destinations for domestic tourism — did the heavier volume of traffic by Han and more cosmopolitan Miao bring a heightened encounter with Miao women's gendered visage in mass culture. In Xijiang, young women knew that a handful among them would be chosen to pose for artists' canvases or to sing for folklorists' tape recorders. Gossip circulated about who was picked and for what reasons, and a range of responses were offered to this display element of their existence. Many young women, professing shyness, eschewed cameras and other forms of scrutiny under all circumstances. Some of them confided to me their indignation at being at the receiving end of such an exploitative gaze. Others complied reluctantly and were occasionally even cajoled into putting on "better" clothes for photographs. And a handful of young women routinely accepted remuneration in exchange for much more formal labors in the creation of "authentic" images. Some had become so accustomed to this commodification of their bodies that they had altercations with visiting journalists. When they demanded pay toward the end of a trying photo shoot, the photographers balked, claiming that they were producing good publicity (*xuanchuan*) for Xijiang that would result in social and material benefits for the community. The models, impervious to arguments about the wider advantages of their cooperation, insisted through Zhou, their advocate, that they be compensated. Extended negotiations ensued, and the women eventually prevailed.

Meanwhile, young women's own social and aesthetic codes powerfully shaped their engagement with dominant cultural producers. When hired for photo shoots, they sometimes failed to show up at the appointed time, or they simply did not show up at all. They dragged their feet in assuming required poses or did not keep still, requiring photographers to use greater quantities of film to obtain the "perfect shot." If asked to sing, some burst into giggles midverse, holding their hands to their mouths and piercing through the solemnity of the contrived moment to expose the artificiality of the context. And when photographers imposed their aesthetic of female beauty by attempting to surreptitiously rearrange group shots to foreground the "prettiest" among them, they balked at being ranked according to photographers' notions of attractiveness.

Resisting versus submitting to their repres" er's demands were not the only modalities by which young women negotiated their designated cultural slot. Clearly, much of their agenda concerned the assertion of their subjectivities as formative in the process. Sometimes this meant that they were the initiators of material exchanges. Young women's demands for payment defied the use of their adorned bodies, their smiles, and their time in the service of an amorphous community principle. They also invoked a China-wide protocol that called for compensation whenever requests of visiting urbanites interrupted peasant production. In this way, they refused to submit themselves unilaterally to the service of their locality or their people, just as they withheld themselves from the urban gaze until they were sure of remuneration. Self-commodification, far from being equivalent to objectification, was tantamount to establishing their subjecthood.

One night in Xijiang, a few local young women showed up at the

27. Struggling for a formal tableau.

guest house to visit Chen, the Beijing photographer described in chapter 5. Having befriended him in the course of posing during the day, the women had agreed to sing for him that night. The relationship now took on a new valence, replacing dispassionate transaction with mutual curiosity and sociability, trading the normative space of the village for the liminal zone of the guest house lounge. Marked as a site of modernity, and of the traffic of outsiders, the guest house offered the anonymity of an extra-local domain. Here, the young women could refashion themselves with relish, singing for Chen's tape recorder coyly but willingly amid laughter and tentative chatting, and collaborating in the documentation of their lore. After a while, however, the guest house director appeared in a rage as the guardian of cultural propriety. He was an older man, originally from one of Xijiang's outlying villages, and was widely known as conservative about tradition. He shooed the young women home, scolding them for "luan chang" (i.e., singing indiscriminately outside the appropriate cultural context). They obeyed with demonstrations of deference, but I heard later that they had made arrangements to meet Chen the following night for more recording in a less monitored public venue — the courtyard outside the empty schoolhouse.

These young women exemplified a widespread strategy of both rural and urban Miao. Entering into a seemingly overdetermined relationship, in which they, as women, presented themselves as exemplars of tradition, they nonetheless took hold of it in such a way as to call the exploitative relation into question. By willingly pursuing Chen's recording of their melodies, they were carving out a third modality, one in which they could enact a modern subjectivity neither by adopting the trappings of metropolitan style nor by becoming scribes themselves. Instead, they actively undertook to make their own cultural production visible, containable, performable. That their male elder objected to this move suggests that it had a transgressive charge. In the process of defying him, they came to occupy a kind of hybrid zone in which they acted both as producers of raw culture and as participants in its salvage.

Recovering Ritual

The preservation enterprise became, over the course of the 1980s, a concern of the majority of Xijiang villagers, just as it was for so many urbanites. Their avid recuperation of family and community rituals consequent upon the liberalization of policy following the Cultural Revolution was described by one Xijianger as "zhuzhong yichuan" or "honoring one's heritage" — literally, "laying stress on heredity." But the recovery of fragments from the past was also a rendering of those fragments as heritage. It could not help but be — in the words of postcolonial critic

Homi Bhabha—an "act of cultural translation" that, in its very artifice, "denies the essentialism of a prior given original or originary culture, [such that] we see that all forms of culture are continually in a process of hybridity" (1990:211). In the Xijiang of 1988, I recorded a dense ritual life packed full of events, some of which were only being revived for the first time more than a decade after the end of the Cultural Revolution. A brief sketch:

Xijiang's Ritual Calendar

— The year began with a relatively small-scale celebration of the Han Chunjie (Spring Festival) in which feasting and the making of sticky rice patties called *baba* was accompanied by fireworks, reciprocal hosting and guesting, and much inebriation.
— At the end of March, the Lu clan within Xijiang performed a Jing Qiao (Offerings to the Bridge) ceremony in which ducks, colorfully dyed eggs, liquor, rice, "money paper" (*qianzhi*), and other offerings were given to the bridge within the clan territory after it had been maintained or repaired. The clan's important tree also was honored.[5]
— In April, timed with the Han festival of Qingming, descendants tended their ancestors' graves, or in special cases, they erected new gravestones in a ceremony involving shamanic offerings, firecrackers, and animal sacrifice.
— Soon thereafter, several of the clan groups in the community performed Zhao Long (Calling the Dragons), which will be discussed at length later. The rite entailed climbing to the highest nearby mountain and, using sticks mounted with white paper cutouts of human figures, marking the way back for auspicious dragons and souls of unborn children. This ritual was followed by offerings to the dragon by a shaman and twelve elders and offerings to trees and communal feasting by all of the participating families.
— In midsummer, when the first kernels of rice began to appear on the stalks, all of Xijiang was caught up for about a week with Chixinjie (The Festival of Eating the New) to be described in chapter 8. It began with each family making offerings to ancestral bridges, both in the fields and within the village, and to the ancestral shrine within the home. On market day the festival took on an entirely different quality with young people gathering by the bridge in town for court-

ship games and antiphonal singing that would go on throughout the night.

— In late fall, male household representatives individually made half-day treks into the mountains to make offerings to certain powerful stones. Large boulders were offered incense, money paper, and chickens killed on the spot to supplicate them for fertility, prosperity, and other household needs.

— After harvest, the community began gearing up for the largest-scale ritual of the year: Miaonian (Miao New Year), the Han Mid-Autumn festival having passed with only minimal acknowledgment. The Miaonian celebrations were in three installments spanning a month: Tounian (the First New Year), Danian (the Great New Year, also called Zhongnian or Middle New Year), and Weiba Nian (the Tail End New Year). Here, Miao animism was highly evident in offerings that had to be made to powerful boulders high on the mountaintops and at the river's edge. Bridges, ancestral shrines, and other important places in the home also received their due. In some villages in the region it was the year for Chiguzhang, an ancestor worship ritual held only once every twelve years. In this case, offering requirements were made stricter and more demanding. Ancestors had to be included in each meal over the course of two and a half days, and several animals were sacrificed, including the mandatory pig, which, in an effort to reduce wasteful expenditure, had replaced the cow of olden days. Guesting also was intensified, filling the villages with the sound and smoke of firecrackers and necessitating feast after group feast.

— As winter approached, individual subvillage groups within Xijiang conducted the Saozhai (Sweeping the Village) ritual to rid their residences of evil spirits. This rite began at the hearth, moved to the edge of the village where offerings were made, then to the edge of the river for animal sacrifice by a group of elders, followed by distribution of the meat from the slaughtered pig. Each participating family brought food for feasting on the riverbanks to insure that undesirable spirits would be well-fed there and not tempted to enter village homes.

— In addition to more communal events, evidence of small family offerings could be found all about the village and beyond. Homemade incense was a regular staple at market, as was money paper, and they were used regularly for offerings placed over entrances to ward off spirits that caused quarreling, alongside mountain paths to resolve romantic problems, and on auspicious boulders. Shamanic trance rituals to cure the ill also burgeoned in the 1980s.

— Life-cycle rituals were also undergoing renewed elaboration. Weddings, funerals, and births were occasions of feasting, ceremonial activities, and much reciprocal exchange. Corollary events also were revived, such as the return of a young woman to her natal home after marriage (*hui niangjia*), a mourning feast for the deceased some time after burial, and a "Manyue" feast for a new baby after it had survived its first month of life.

The State's Hand

Ritual plenitude, then, had once again become a staple of village life as the first decade of reforms came to a close. But how was the state positioned in relation to rural revivals?[6] With deep antecedents in Maoist and even earlier twentieth-century projects, the state's self-production as modernizing force against the irrationality and local idiosyncrasy of ritual had come to be a key element of the social context in which people were reclaiming culture.[7] During the Cultural Revolution, Miao ritual had been a special focus of didactic representation. A revolutionary opera entitled *Miao Ling Feng Lei* (Wind and Thunder in the Miao Mountains)—in which a heroic Miao woman archer teams up with a noble Red Army soldier to drive out Han bandits and liberate the region— played to the masses. The story line was peppered with what were characterized as "superstitious activities used by reactionary leaders to cheat and oppress the masses" (Miao Ling 1976:3). In one instance, the Miao "reactionary leader" extracts hefty debts from villagers in return for making collective offerings to the tree spirit on their behalf. In another, a riot is instigated in the guise of making offerings to the village. In a third, the Miao tyrant threatens the heroine with cutting out her heart and offering it to the tree spirit. The opera's line was abundantly clear: ritual offerings were vehicles for socioeconomic exploitation, particularly through the shrewd manipulation of Miao dupes.

By the 1980s, modes of representation had shifted. Ritual events, rather than being entirely suppressed, were being discursively recast. The state maintained its hostility toward "superstition" (*mixin*), but less in terms of class/ethnic exploitation than in terms of its purported antimodern character. An authoritative 1981 volume introducing each

28. A ritual elder makes offerings at Saozhai. A recycled Pepsi bottle holds the home-brewed grain alcohol, and the anthropologist's tape recorder documents his incantations.

29. A Xijiang funeral. Guests shouldering an offering of a slaughtered pig approach the home of the deceased. The casket is placed on display (right).

of China's nationalities protested in reference to the Miao festival Cai Huashan (Stepping on Flower Mountain—performed in more westerly Miao areas) that "although it has superstitious content, it is at the same time a traditional festival amusement of the Miao people" (Zhongguo Shaoshu Minzu 1981:448). This purging of danger, in which putatively retrograde religious (gloss "superstitious"—*mixin*) practice was secularized in portrayals that suggested its eligibility for conservation as "tradition" (*chuantong*) and its social value as "recreation" (*yule*), infused nationalist cultural production.

To imply, then, that tradition-bound Miao villagers immune to cultural transformation exploited policy ambiguity to reinstate subversive local rituals would be to remain in a state/society, domination/resistance binary that at best oversimplifies and at worst entirely distorts the working out of meanings around cultural production during the flux of the 1980s. It also would perpetuate a notion of cultural inertia whereby practices are assumed to continue on their own momentum, disappearing only because of external suppression. To the contrary, the role of the state, particularly in the more public of rituals, extended well beyond simply permitting or prohibiting their renewed florescence. In many cases, state involvement may actually be characterized as productive of both meanings and practices. In varying degrees, most events embodied not simply an accommodation between state and local interests, but an *interlocking* of state programs with the projects of Miao actors.[8]

In December 1985, I got off a bus in a town called Fumin for an exploratory visit to Miao villages in the Yunnan countryside. It was local Party officials who, not expecting my visit, volunteered to rush me over the mountains to a Christian "Thanksgiving Worship" (Xian'en Chongbai). Local clergy, descendants of Miao who had been Christianized in western Guizhou around the turn of the century, had reclaimed their church building that had been used as a grain storehouse during the Cultural Revolution. For three days, services were held around the clock, beginning inside the church and eventually, when the crowd swelled with the arrivals of pilgrims from all over the region, moving to a makeshift amphitheater outdoors. Donations of grain were taken for the church, and communal meals were provided. Everywhere, young girls dangled shoulder bags in which they carried Bibles and hymnbooks printed in the "Pollard" Miao script developed for them by the Western missionary who had converted their predecessors to Christianity.

30. A *lusheng* processional for Miao New Year in the Leishan
county seat.

These materials had been published under official auspices in Kunming
as part of the state's commitment to bilingualism and more freedom of
religious worship. Indeed, Christianity was the only Miao practice that
was classified under the official designation of "religion" (*zongjiao*) as
opposed to "superstition" (*mixin*). Indicating its new centrality as an official marker of Miao identity, a 1982 annual yearbook listing of China's
nationalities, under the heading of Miao religion, offered only: "A few
believe in Christianity" (*New China News* 1982:18).

Funding was often the specific form of the state's involvement. The
staging of the *lusheng* processional dancing that accompanies Miao New
Year, for instance, required considerable resources. In 1988 many communities in the Xijiang region declined to undertake the processional
at all since they had not been designated as recipients of state subsidies.
That the event might be held as an autonomous, community-based rite
did not come in for consideration, indicating how naturalized the state's
involvement in the staging of local ritual had become. Conversely, in
a village outside the Leishan county seat, county officials had decided
to promote the event and had provided prizes and supplies. There, it
took on mammoth proportions and a decidedly public face, attracting
visitors and documentarians from as far away as Beijing and the provincial capital. State fiscal support, then, usually entailed the submission

of certain elements to the exoticizing gaze, the gaze that restructured ritual as spectacle for the consumption of those not privy to its internal meanings.

Calling Back the Dragons

The early spring ritual of Zhao Long (Calling the Dragons) was not an object of canonization or commodification.[9] Devoid of music, dance, or special costume, it did not fulfill external consumption desires. Nor had it drawn state attention, either for promotion or for censure. Unique to a Miao subgroup in the immediate Xijiang region, almost nothing had been written on it (I have found only a handful of published descriptions, cf. Wan 1991:86–95, Yang 1985:376). Zhao Long went unmentioned in both the seven-page description of Xijiang festivals handwritten for me by the elderly cadre and the locally mimeographed account of *Xijiang Fengqing* (*Xijiang Customs*) prepared by a committee of village experts. One reason for Zhao Long's lack of canonic routinization may have been that its performance, as I was told, was episodic—at intervals of anywhere from five or six to ten to thirteen years or when needed for the resolution of specific crises.

In 1988 several of Xijiang's villages revived Zhao Long on the auspicious days of April 2 and 11 (the sixteenth and the twenty-fifth of the second lunar month). Practitioners in one of the villages said they had not done it in more than thirty years because of the previous decades of turbulence. The villagers' demeanor throughout was one of jubilant recovery. The resurrection of Zhao Long was done quietly and without advance fanfare, but it had no aura of secrecy. My presence, and my documentation practices, were regarded matter-of-factly, rather than as any kind of special access. Zhao Long was one of the rare cultural practices whose recovery was at village hands; it had not been incited by state support or by commercial spectacularization.

The reasons for performing Zhao Long in a given year included poor harvests, lack of rain, infertility, high child mortality or illness, or the progressive thinning of trees. The aim of the ritual was to coax back the dragons—who had retreated to the mountains because people had neglected the making of offerings to them—so that they would protect the village, its children, its crops, its animals, and its trees. It was the natural village (*zirancun*) unit, of which there were eight clustered together in Xijiang, that undertook Zhao Long.[10] Each had its own *"di-pan"* (territory) in the landscape that surrounded Xijiang—the purview of their village dragons.

Yangpai's Zhao Long On the morning of April 11 the male elders of Yangpai village met to discuss the route to be taken to call the dragons back. Homemade incense was prepared, and money paper was crafted by making semicircular cuts in brown paper rectangles to suggest copper coins. Several hundred images of people, cut out of white paper by an experienced elder, were mounted on bamboo sticks about three feet tall. Each Yangpai family had contributed two or three yuan and about a *jin*[11] of sticky rice for making the sweet fermented-rice wine called *tianjiu*.

In the early afternoon, two groups of young and middle-aged men headed to the mountains, each group carrying a live duck, money paper, incense, a canteen of liquor, some uncooked rice, and the bamboo sticks decorated with paper people. Two children eagerly trailed behind, constituting one of the few spectatorial acts, other than mine, in the entire ritual. The delegation walked without ceremony to the two highest points in the village's territory. Highest points were important, I was told, to call back the biggest dragons. The elder in the group summarily set some incense and money paper to burn and sprinkled some liquor around the spot, while the younger men began staking out the area with bamboo sticks. They then returned down the mountain at a hasty clip; along the path, the young men placed sticks over which the elder sprinkled rice.

With each handful of rice scattered, the elder murmured some incomprehensible incantations. The paper people, it was explained, were *"shentong"* or spirits of children who had to be coaxed back to the village along with the dragons and given rice along the way. Zhao Long's fertility agenda, then, was addressed not only through the dragon's protection of children, but through direct appeals to their unborn spirits. Meanwhile, the duck was periodically forced to walk, dragged on a leash threaded through the nostrils in its beak, for the duck, it was explained, represented the dragon, and a dragon, of course, would be too big to be carried.

The route back was complicated, departing from the regular paths and cutting through rice fields and patches of thick forest. It ended at a shrine just above Yangpai village where an offering table had been set up and elders had killed chickens and put out incense and money paper to burn. The groups then headed back to the site where all the villagers would congregate. This spot, of which each natural village had one, was called *"fengjingshan"* or "scenic mountain" spot. It was collectively held and fastidiously conserved, its trees harboring a unique sacredness. The returnees from the mountain expedition joined some elders to inspect the state of the trees.

Much had taken place while the two groups of men had been in the mountains. Representatives, primarily women, from Yangpai's 214 households had come to plant new trees. Each family, I was told, should plant three seedlings, but others told me that there was no clear-cut rule, and some individual heads of household said that they had no time to plant trees at all. Some of the tallest trees in the territory had been scaled by skilled climbers, and a ten-foot bamboo branch with banner-like white streamers attached to the top had been fastened to the highest tree branch that could support it. It stretched well above the treetop.[12] Beckoning toward the sky, the banner was a signal to the gods that all was not well below. Once, long ago, a great fir tree had reached clear to heaven; but humans climbed it too often and bothered it too much so Thunder (Leigong) struck it down, leaving humans only this recourse for communicating with the gods.

Meanwhile, a pig purchased with the villagers' donations had been killed, and several men were preparing its meat. A long table was set up, and offerings of *tianjiu,* bits of meat, fat, liver, innards, fish, eggs, and balls of sticky rice were laid out in twelves along its length. The head of the pig was placed in the table's center; a ritual expert (*guishi*) stood opposite it in a full-length blue robe — the only participant dressed specially for the event. He burned incense and money paper and spoke to the dragons, conveying that this was a day of abundance and inviting them to come and dine. Two assistants cast bits of each type of food and drink on the ground beside the table for the dragon to eat, then twelve male elders partook of bits from the twelve piles of food and gathered up the rest to keep. The elders — identified as men from prosperous households with males and females in each of three generations — ate and drank to accompany the dragons.

After this ceremony was completed, firecrackers were set off, summoning the rest of the village. Villagers began pouring up to the site

31. Incense, eggs, and bits of meat are offered to the most revered trees at Zhao Long.

with baskets in their hands. They clustered around several of the largest trees in the grove to take turns making arboreal offerings (*jing shu*). They burned incense and money paper and put out bits of fish, dyed eggs, rice, and meat at the foot of the trees. Surplus dyed eggs as well as other leftovers from the offerings were given to children to eat. *Tian-jiu* was offered in toasts to some of the important elders, while other villagers who had brought their own liquor settled into little groups to drink. Some curious art students who were visiting from the provincial teachers' college were in no way shunned as interlopers but welcomed as guests into these family groupings. Meat from the pig and handfuls of sticky rice were distributed according to a name list of contributors. Careful written records had been kept. Four paper people were given to each household to take home and stick up in the family shrine. Close to dusk, people returned to their own abodes to eat a celebratory meal.

The recovery of Zhao Long after a several-decade hiatus was a self-conscious reinstatement of what one practitioner called *chuantong wen-hua* (traditional culture) or *minzu xinyang* (roughly: ethnic beliefs) after its long suppression and silence. At the same time, several concerns of more recent vintage also found expression in the course of events. Zhao Long affirmed the continuing potency of the natural village, a collectivity that had been important before and during Maoist times (as an exogamous extended kin entity and then a production unit). That importance, however, had been undercut by current policies of household responsibility in agriculture and the supersession of the *xingzheng cun* (administrative village) in official management. In Zhao Long's structured donations and redistributions may also have been an iteration of an ideology of collectivism otherwise forgotten in the rush of atomized households to get ahead economically. Interestingly, in keeping with conventional gender distinctions, it was men who attended to the *dipan* and the village-level ritual responsibilities, while women represented households in planting and making offerings to trees.

While Zhao Long was overtly focused on dragons, in many ways the trees were the more important concern. Some explained to me that the dragon's return is to protect the trees, which in turn protect the village, hence warranting reverent propitiation. Indeed, Miao lore of this region holds that a maple tree was their earliest ancestor; it gave birth to two butterflies, which, in turn, produced twelve eggs, one of which hatched a human. During this Zhao Long, however, several educated young people put a more materialist twist on the reverence for trees. Timber had been an important industry in Southeast Guizhou, and in recent years deforestation had become a matter of serious concern in the region. With decollectivization, the uncultivated land around villages was divided into household plots, and it was forbidden to cut firewood at random. In 1982 the great forested mountain ridge that rose above Xijiang was officially cordoned off as a Nature Preserve (Ziran Baohu Qu), within which it was illegal to tamper with any plant or animal. The tree-planting element of Zhao Long was highly resonant with government-sponsored movements for reforestation. But, as these young people explained, Zhao Long was an even more effective way to inculcate conservation consciousness, for no one would dare to cut down trees once they had been made sacred through the ritual.[13]

Codes, Control, Conservation

To me, the meanings of Zhao Long were plural and sometimes contradictory. I found shards of state presence scattered throughout the content of the ritual, and throughout local interpretations and commentary on its meanings and effects. Cultural revival was enacted as a reaction against the recent past, not against the contemporary state, which was perceived as similarly committed to the revival agenda and to the repudiation of the destructive past.

The more pertinent fracture in cultural recovery was that between community-directed practices and those that were produced primarily for outside consumption (see chapter 6). Zhao Long was a ritual occasion that did not address itself to the outside; even guests from other natural villages within the Xijiang community were not invited. But Zhao Long was not immune to the outside. Its practitioners did not hesitate to craft the ritual into a form that both satisfied desires for continuity with their reinvented cultural past and, simultaneously, worked through dilemmas of its articulation with their socioeconomic present. Both conflicts and conjunctions emerged. Expressing a gap between central policies and rural actualities, one of the men on the mountain hike acknowledged that the fertility desires enacted in Zhao Long contravened state birth-planning policies. However, he did not see these pursuits as deliberately transgressive; rather, he said, *"nongcun"* (the countryside) wants many children, while *"zhongyang"* (the center) opposes *"renkou fazhan"* (population growth). On the other hand, in the case of the trees, Forestry Commission and villagers' agendas were consonant; revering the trees helped to preserve them against deforestation, and this initiative in turn strengthened the legitimacy of the ritual. Its lack of a public face notwithstanding, Zhao Long's incarnation in the 1980s was thickly intertwined with extra-local concerns.

At the same time, dominant cultural trends persisted in misrecognizing such hybridized revivals in the quest for the protection of past purities. Replacing a modernity defined by the state as the rejection of feudal superstition was the growing enactment of nostalgia. An aesthetic of naturalness was both demanded by the market and defended by Miao cultural producers. Xijiang villagers, in turn, were prompted to assert claims of authenticity. After a photo shoot in the center of Xijiang in which several young women in full festival dress took part, an elderly shopkeeper grumbled to me that the womens' clothes were meant to be worn only at festival time. When a delegation of Singapore photographers was scheduled to visit, heated disagreement took place among the leaders and elders involved in planning their reception. Twenty girls were to be dressed in festival costume, but the problem was whether to play *lusheng* to greet the delegation, for Xijiang's *lusheng* masters usually refused to violate custom to play at other than conventional times. Likewise, although no objection was raised to my having taped courtship songs, most Xijiang people were reluctant to translate or explain the cryptic and figurative language of the songs or to play them in the company of preadolescent children. Codes of protected authenticity were being forged at the intersection of two complementary trends: an appropriative dominant practice that produced valorized tradition to exoticize it, and a proprietary subordinate ethos that recovered and conserved tradition to shield it from the corruption that dominant appropriation entailed. The agent of appropriation was decidedly not designated as the state, but rather, as something more akin to the market. For the state was not external to any of these processes; rather, it appeared as a sometimes promoter, sometimes suppressor of revival, and as a supporter of marketizing change.

The insatiable appetites of the global market, the urgency of delineating a national cultural essence, and the impulse to expurgate the excesses of Maoism all converged in the nostalgia impulse. The cultural fragments that became objects of recovery were not simple vestigial gems but instead were strewn with elements of all these structuring presences. They can be situated in the "third timespace" that "goes beyond the old model of culture, but not as another fixity—it designates phenomena too heterogeneous, mobile, and discontinuous for that, on the one hand, while remaining anchored in the politics of history/location on the other" (Lavie and Swedenburg 1996:166; see also Tilley 1997:86). Even as certain fixities—Xijiang as quintessential village, Miao women as intact tradition—were actively being produced, we shall see that the differences they implied were highly mobile in their ascriptions.

8

Displacing Subalternity

The Mobile Other

In 1988, members of the Miao intelligentsia in Guizhou province formed the Guizhou Miao Studies Association (Miaoxue Yanjiu Hui) and convened its inaugural meeting.[1] The event, officially titled the First Academic Conference on the Occasion of the Founding of the Guizhou Miao Studies Association (Guizhou Sheng Miaoxue Yanjiuhui Chengli Dahui Di Yi Ci Xueshu Taolun Hui), was held in November in a Southeast Guizhou county densely populated by Miao. It was deliberately timed to coincide with a *lusheng*-playing festival in the nearby village of Gulong. Delegates — not only from far-flung academic institutions, but also from government and party offices in Miao regions — were drawn from a cross-section of the polyglot Miao leadership. Only a handful of token non-Miao were invited (including a few senior Miao specialists and me). Organizers had made this strategic exclusion since one stated purpose of the association was to "strengthen nationality unity" (*jiaqiang minzu tuanjie*) — in the unorthodox sense of forging solidarity among the Miao rather than between different nationalities.[2]

Miao Studies Imbibes Tradition

The conference intermingled intellectual production with cultural consumption. Sited in the heavily Miao county of Huangping in Southeast Guizhou, it lent itself to auto-touristic indulgence, to an oscillation between participation and spectatorship. During the days, conferees filed into a hall postered with slogans such as "Support Ourselves, Strengthen Ourselves, Respect Ourselves, Love Ourselves"(*Zili, Ziqiang, Zizun, Zi'ai*), and "Establish a New Type of Socialist Ethnic Relations" (*Jianli Shehuizhuyi de Xinxing Minzu Guanxi*). Proceedings

32. Cover of *Guizhou Pictorial:* Communist Party
General Secretary Jiang Zemin receives an offering of
liquor from a Miao maiden on his visit to Guizhou.

included the election of officers, formal speeches, and presentation of
academic papers about Miao culture, history, economy, education, language, modernization, etc. Titles of studies ranged from "An Overview
of the Miao Lusheng Dance in Weining" (*Qiantan Weining Miaozu Lusheng Wudao*) to "An Exploration of the Distinctive Features of the Miao
Rural Pattern and a Strategy for the Comprehensive Reform and Opening of Miao Regions" (*Shilun Miaozu Nongcun Moshi de Tedian He Miaozu
Diqu Quanmian Gaige, Kaifang de Duice*) to "A Preliminary Exploration

of the Common Psychological Qualities of the Miao" (*Miaozu Gongtong Xinli Suzhi Chutan*).[3]

At regular intervals the official formalities were intercut with banquets in which the spontaneous and egalitarian etiquette of Miao reciprocal drinking and singing prevailed. Then, by night, conferees flocked to highly theatricalized performances of ethnic music and dance at a theater in town. Finally, on the last day of the meeting, conferees enacted the ethno-touristic fantasy of gaining access to culture-in-the-raw as they boarded tour buses to travel as camera-equipped spectators to the *lusheng* festival under way in Gulong.

Of most significance here was the very first event of the conference. On a dank, drizzly autumn day, conferees were crowded into buses and cars to travel from points throughout the province to this site of reunion. Conference organizers orchestrated a special welcome to soothe travel-weary bones and delight their guests' senses with the charms of Miao hospitality. Piling from their vehicles at conference headquarters, conferees were greeted by elaborately garbed, smiling Miao young women who refused to let the visitors pass until they had imbibed ritual spirits from the horns of bulls. This version of a hospitality ritual used to welcome visitors at the threshold of Miao villages had been widely re-created for domestic and international tourists to the region. Structured by a gender asymmetry in which women as emblems of traditional culture made deferential offerings to the primarily male conferees, the packaged ritual replaced the more balanced reciprocity of peasant Miao sociality — in which hosts and guests exchanged toasts one for one — with the enactment of unequal statuses between cosmopolitan visitors and their country hosts. Indeed, the conference version of this ritual was identical to that described for the *non-Miao* mayors at the beginning of chapter 4. The format had, significantly, become canonized through glossy tourist brochures promoting the region and widely installed in the reception protocol for foreign tourists. Like the nationalists who produced Chatterjee's "derivative discourse" (1986), Miao elites had adopted this ceremony of urban privilege as a means of partaking in their own culture in intimate and bodily fashion at the same time that they ranked themselves above its local and feminized forms through ingesting it as consumers.

Displacing Subalternity

Conferees' arm's-length consumption of their own culture suggests that the Miao as an aggregate were ill-described by any fixed attribute of subalternity. Miao cultural production was so thick with negotiations of subalternity that the group as a whole could not simply be made to stand for the counterpart of Chinese modernity. Rather, we can see the other produced by Chinese definitions of modernity as mobile, repeatedly displaced by those seeking elite status through practices of marking themselves off.

Before considering this process in greater depth, I want to look more fully at what is meant by subalternity. The term, variously employed in multiple contexts, has come to have a range of significances. In recent postcolonial studies, scholars of South Asia working under the title of the Subaltern Studies Group developed a specialized field and a serial publication around what they designated as "subalterns." Theirs is primarily a project of social history concerned with recovering the silenced stories of those subordinated by imperialism and, later, by national elites. Historian and political economist Ranajit Guha prefaced a selection of these works by extending the dictionary (and British military) definition of subaltern as "of inferior rank" to mean "the general attribute of subordination . . . whether this is expressed in terms of class, caste, age, gender and office or in any other way" (1988:35).

A strength of Guha's definition as a starting point is that it allows for multiple axes of subordination and, implicitly, their intersectional relations. But in this formulation, he still emphasizes structural categories without adequately considering their ongoing constitution in social process. We need to go further and view elite versus subaltern positionings as created precisely in their relationality. The line dividing these binarized poles can shift, depending on perspective and in the course of cultural and political struggle. Following Antonio Gramsci, Guha nuanced the condition of subordination by suggesting that subalterns had the potential either to affiliate with dominant political orders or to produce cleavages, or "formations," out of which variant forms of historical agency might emerge.[4] Highly attuned to the ways in which subalterns might divide and coalesce, Guha argued that what on a larger scale might have constituted an aggregate group of subordinates was also composed of various regional or local elites. Hence, "the same class or element which was dominant in one area . . . could be among the dominated in another" (Guha 1988:44).

Within twentieth-century China, the nation's status of subordinate vis-à-vis the rest of the world was assiduously displaced onto peasants, minorities, and women, consolidating a masculinized urban elite that could disavow its painful subalternity on the global scale by redirecting the focus onto internal difference. Barlow (1991b), in an article comparing the Chinese intellectuals (*zhishifenzi*) of the early twentieth century to those of the post-Mao reform era, has lucidly analyzed this process. *Zhishifenzi*, she argued, universalizing themselves as modern subjects through their deployments of imported signs of modernity, "made native Tradition an internal other within a localized 'Western' discourse," and "this habit of demonizing the past charged 'culture' not just with the powers accorded tradition in any modernist discourse, but also with the power to infect" (1991b:213). This kind of thinking, in which tradition is encountered as mobile, as ever threatening to contaminate would-be moderns, is precisely what drives so much of the anxious cultural production around it. The containment of tradition in any number of rituals, commodities, performances, and costumes is also about circumscribing tradition socially, about disavowing its presence in those who pursue modern subjecthood. Disavowal appears as a dense and continual social project, one that spawns myriad performances of modernity. As this chapter will show, even among the Miao and among Miao women, such disavowals took place as part of everyday social life.

Subalternity, then, might be more fruitfully thought of in terms of the *mobility* of otherness in which sites of subordination are anxiously reconstituted by those seeking to evade them. China historian Gail Hershatter has suggested the image of "nesting" to describe this process: "for most groups in China, it is important to keep in mind the possibility of multiple, relational degrees of subalternity. I am tempted to label these as 'nested' subaltern statuses, in which some groups go to great pains to distinguish themselves from and speak for those 'below,' while allying themselves with and speaking to those 'above' " (1993:111). In cultural production on and by the Miao, what we also see is not only the practice of "speaking for" but also the practices of "speaking of"— in the sense of representing—and of consuming. One technique for disavowing subalternity in the post-Mao era was to assume the role either of authoritative representer or of pleasured consumer of Miao cultural

fragments. Invariably aligned with the traditional, these ostensibly treasured essences were in turn cast as the abjected substances against which
elite aspirants could define themselves in their quest for alliance with
more prestigious sectors.

Needless to say, those who were placed in the position of delivering Miao culture were speaking neither of themselves nor for themselves. Their status as subordinate was symbolically constituted by what
appeared as their mute and rote repetition of time-honored conventions, no matter how contrived. This brings us to Gayatri Spivak's subtle
discussion of subalternity. In her notorious essay, "Can the Subaltern
Speak?" (1988a), Spivak offers a searing challenge, from a feminist perspective, to the notion that subaltern voices could be effectively recovered and made to speak in the historical (or ethnographic) records.[5] To
pursue such a project, she suggests, is to be complicit with empire, for
it reflects the conceit of Westerners and of bourgeois nationals who demand that voices be audible in the dominant register. But for Spivak,
neither the voices of postcolonial intellectuals nor those of any active
kind of subordinate resistance can be described as subaltern. Rather,
"the subaltern is the name of the place which is so displaced from what
made me and the organized resister, that to have it speak is like Godot
arriving on a bus" (1990:91). Spivak's notion of subalternity, then, hinges
on displacement. It is precisely the quality of being unheard that marks
out the domain of the subaltern. Conversely, at the moment a subordinate voice begins to be heard in the dominant arena it ceases to be
subaltern.[6] What I would add to this persuasive formulation is that being
unheard does not amount to invisibility, to being unseen as well. Indeed,
subaltern positionings are often characterized by a kind of mute hyper-
visibility. In many cases, it would appear that being speechless is often
a necessary condition of being the gazed-upon, a point that feminist
critics have long stressed.

Such a configuration raises questions about the methods of historians, literary critics, and anthropologists, and about their differing
encounters with subalternity. While literary critics' focus on the textual-
discursive domain that is demarcated precisely by its exclusion of subalterns, social historians and anthropologists may recover other kinds
of practice. The approach advocated by China historian Gail Hershatter
(1993:119–21) is to read against the grain of dominant representations
of subalterns to find traces of the activities and strategies of those who

never set pen to paper. Another approach — one pursued in many parts of this book — is for the ethnographer to participate in social process in venues where the formation of subalternity is taking place. Here, the negotiations of dominance and subordination, the mobility of otherness, become apparent beyond the purview of language, at least that language which is recorded in print.[7] Let us turn now to one of these venues.

Pageants and Country Cousins—A Multivalent Gaze

The Siyueba — or Fourth Moon Eighth Day — festival, held on the campus of the Central Nationalities Institute, was a politically charged and simultaneously joyous occasion, the largest-scale annual celebration for Miao in Beijing. Performed every year since 1981, Siyueba drew upon some 900 Miao residents in the greater Beijing area (Xiong 1993:259), including scholars, students, workers, cadres, People's Liberation Army soldiers, and the inhabitants of a small migrant agricultural community in the suburbs. In the overall population of the city their numbers were infinitesimal, but enough were there to gather together and stage a festival steeped in nostalgia. Meanwhile, the event also served as an opportunity for Miao from the provinces to visit the capital and perform their local cultural specialties. Non-Miao participants included some relevant Han dignitaries and a handful of foreign "friends." I attended in 1982 and 1988.

The primary form of Siyueba was derived from state political ritual and entailed high theatricalization. It consisted of the display of leaders — including both Miao and Han, in academic as well as government posts — arrayed before an adulating audience and pampered with hot tea, peanuts, and candy. Speeches by these luminaries were followed by performances of music and dance by trained performers. Afterward, the performer-spectator format turned into a more communal one as members of the audience were drawn into processional dancing, followed by a great feast. These events were critical to consolidating the cultural amalgam that defined the Miao in the 1980s and 1990s. As Litzinger has put it, they "provide a window into the production of an imaginary totality predicated on a discourse of cultural plenitude . . . to produce an image of one diverse yet unified ethnic culture" (1998:230).

May 23 of the Western calendar, a warm spring day in Beijing, was the date for the 1988 celebration of Siyueba. Experts explained to me that historically the occasion was to honor a famous Miao martyr who died defending his people, but in Beijing this commemoration had little to do with the content of the event whose more clearly articulated aim was to foster pan-Miao solidarity. In 1988, Miao planners were especially proud that many Miao hailing from outside Beijing, particularly from the Xiangxi subgroup of western Hunan province, were included in the celebration.

Under Maoism, the Miao of Xiangxi had been weakly integrated with the locus of national Miao leadership in Southeast Guizhou and with the leaders that the latter region had produced and sent to Beijing.[8] Their representation in the Siyueba festival was momentous for a number of reasons. The Xiangxi Miao, while politically remote from their Southeast Guizhou co-ethnics, had been less isolated from the avenues to wealth opened up by economic reforms. Situated within the borders of more affluent Hunan province, the Xiangxi Tujiazu Miaozu Zizhizhou (Western Hunan Tujia and Miao Autonomous Prefecture) had bene-fited from a more elaborate provincial infrastructure than obtained in Guizhou, and some sizable revenues had been garnered from local ven-tures. When organizers had appealed to regional Miao centers to con-tribute donations to the national event, Southeast Guizhou, politically significant but economically depressed, had been able to give a mea-ger 100 yuan. Meanwhile, several counties in Xiangxi, where new local businesses, cash crop production, and joint ventures had been burgeon-ing, had together given a staggering 4,000 yuan. In return, organizers invited performers from each of the donor counties, as well as a deputy county head, a representative from a culture bureau, some members of "ten-thousand yuan households," and some ordinary peasants. The sizable donations would support both the day's activities and a week of sightseeing for the Xiangxi delegation. While the country folk imbibed the flavors of the big city, Miao urbanites at the metropolitan center would have an opportunity to gaze upon their newly wealthy fellow Miao from the rural hinterland.

Overall, organizers hoped this coming together would be an opportu-nity to effect pan-ethnic unity, precisely through constructing an event that bridged class and occupational statuses as well as Miao subgroups. On the appointed day the auditorium filled with spectators, only a hand-ful of whom wore clothing denoting their Miao identity. After a long table on the stage had filled with officials and Institute scholars, the Xiangxi delegation entered ceremoniously from the back of the room, proceeding down the aisles to the scrutiny and resounding applause of the audience. They took designated seats in the front row.

The formal program of events reflected the particular form of admixture that characterized the late 1980s. Introductions were made by a Miao deputy secretary of the Nationalities Institute Workers Union (Gong Hui), who extended welcomes to leaders and guests—as well as to Beijing Television, which had come to do a news spot. Thanks were given to the many units that had contributed money for the festival. The Miao as a people were praised in sloganlike formulations— as a nationality that was ancient, industrious and brave, honest and sincere, and patriotic toward the fatherland. Additional speeches followed, replicating the format of combining presentation to the outside with presentation of the Miao self for insider consumption. These two inseparable motifs informed the entire proceedings; in an event organized around spectatorship, the subject of the Miao was at once the object of two gazes—that of the other and that of identification.

After the official speeches, amateurish performances by members of the Xiangxi delegation were offered. There were singing, horn playing, and a kind of drum dancing in which two young women stood on either side of a suspended wooden drum, 3 feet in diameter, beating it while they danced in synchrony. The performances appeared rehearsed, but not with the finesse in which professional Beijing artists had been trained. A great deal of onstage tinkering took place to get the drum just right. The female deputy county head broke off her song midverse and ran offstage, apparently overcome with embarrassment. Such momentary ruptures punctured the smooth surface of performance, exposing the troubled accommodation of Miao cultural practice with the formality of the staged setting and offering up instead the coarseness of rural authenticity. Coarseness versus theatrical finesse, of course, was one of the axes along which Beijing Miao were to displace subalternity upon their provincial counterparts.

The Xiangxi segment was followed by a polyglot set of numbers in a wide range of genres. The performers were largely Beijing Miao. More Miao singing was followed by Chinese singing. Chinese instruments were played as well as Western-style rock 'n' roll. And martial arts were demonstrated by a young man in flashy white athletic wear. The overall effect was the portrayal of hybridized cultural futures for the Miao people, an inclusive vision of modernity that was neither hostile to the incorporation of non-Miao styles nor entirely renunciative of what stood for the Miao past.

While the Siyueba festival was characterized by a clear-cut distinction between spectator and performer, complete with stage, darkened audience, and applause, the event's contents in some ways complicated the power binaries that have been under consideration here, bringing class and culture into a different alignment. The fascinated gaze cast upon the Xiangxi Miao objectified them as tradition, but also exalted them for their wealth. Transposed into the sterility of the urban context, these Miao from the proverbial provinces had become objects of riveted attention. Spectators were looking across imagined chasms of difference — not only the cultural difference that separated Miao subgroups, but also the difference that ordered so much of Chinese experience — that between the country and the city. But the urban-rural prestige hierarchy was cross-cut by the newly acquired wealth of these country folk who had been able to enrich themselves entrepreneurially in the marketized economy. That these country cousins were those among the Miao who had most effectively embraced capitalist modernity, achieving a position of fiscal charitability toward the urbanites, constituted an even more mesmerizing difference. Given their economic status, it was difficult to consign the Xiangxi visitors to a position of lower prestige. Hence, on the one hand, their quaint musical numbers exacted for the pleasure of urban dwellers lent the urbanites a smug sense of cultural advancement, enhanced by the fact that the Xiangxi performances were mostly by women, while other newfangled performances by Beijing Miao included many men. On the other hand, the Xiangxi visitors simultaneously displayed economic "progressiveness" for all to envy (cf. Anagnost 1989). In that celebrated otherness, Miao spectators were looking to find a version of themselves that not only retained cultural particularity, but also amassed new wealth. This new self, of course, was what Dengist reform policy was scripting for all Chinese — a conservation of cultural uniqueness united with a market-oriented economic overhaul.

Miao urbanites, then, cultivated by the central authorities in Maoist times, and gripped with class mobility longings in the reform era, had come to assume the gaze of China's prestigious metropolitan elite. This type of gaze bears much in common with the "second sight" that Gyan Prakash (1992a) described for Indian colonial elites in their encounter with British museums and exhibitions. The elaboration of a form of spectatorship that conjoined a Western "scientificity" with a kind of wonder distinguished from the "superstition" of the "native" "opened up an ambivalent space for the subjectivity and agency of Western-educated Indian elites" (Prakash 1992a:163–64). Prakash found two effects. First, the colonizer-as-subject/colonized-as-object binary was disrupted by the necessity of constituting the museum-going Indian as knowing subject rather than as object. Second, there opened "an incommensurable gap between elites and subalterns that could never be accurately measured or closed" (1992a:168). Likewise, once some Miao had become spectators, gazing reflexively upon others, "The Miao" could no longer be a simple category of dominant objectification. In turn, the shifting production of the boundary between elites and subalterns over the 1980s undermined the clarity of both the East-West and the Han-Miao binaries. Miao urbanites took up the business of display in such a way as to view themselves from an informed distance, and also to reproduce the categories of the dominant order. Entering into what Tony Bennett (1994) has described as the "exhibitionary complex," they became viewers who were subjected to societal normalization precisely through their viewing of conventionalized and orderly presentations of themselves. In the Miao case, the presentations they viewed were ordered precisely through the imported categories of status-bestowing modernity.

Constituting Difference in Marriage Strategizing

The displacement of subalternity discussed above was by Miao urban elites onto Miao provincials. But it was not only in urban settings that gazing upon "traditional" culture had become an increasingly desirable practice. Miao peasants in the Guizhou mountains also effected displacements, at once living their culture and holding it at arm's length in laudatory appreciation. In the process, subalternity was further circumscribed as rural people strove to situate traditionality in "even more rural" people and in women.

Rural young women were not simply cultural conservators, and their acute longing for "modernity" was especially evidenced in their marriage strategizing, for they had considerable latitude in choosing their partners. Historically, although subject to certain strictures of clan and village exogamy and to parental interventions, such unrestricted courting was a custom by which they distinguished themselves from the Han. From the Miao perspective, the Han custom of parentally arranged marriage was, I was told again and again, an austere and unfeeling practice.

Market days and annual festivals when young people traveled out from their home villages were the most common times for getting acquainted with potential partners. Miao young women participated actively in market day courtship practices, "shopping" and mingling by day and promenading on Xijiang's main road with flashlights after nightfall. What they looked for reflected finely honed calculations of hypergamy. Strategies for marrying up were distinctly spatialized; villages were evaluated according to size, proximity to the road and to long-distance bus routes, presence of a periodic market, availability of goods, electricity, and television, etc.[9] Aspirations tended toward the relative center, wherever that particular center stood in the hierarchy of places that organized the social landscape.

Linguistic usage reflected such calibrations. Going to a social center, whether Xijiang or Beijing, was referred to as "going up" (shang), whereas the compound that denoted the countryside (xiangxia) had the meaning built into it of "down, lower, inferior" (xia). Long-standing practices of patrilocality determined that young women would be the ones most concerned with spatial distinctions because they would be expected to uproot and accustom themselves to living in a new locale among strange and demanding in-laws. Xijiang young women, for instance, usually said that they would never marry into the outlying villages that were far from the road; they would be interested, however, in marrying into smaller villages as long as they were on the bus route and closer to the county and prefecture seats. Those from small villages, on the other hand, wanted very much to find a partner who resided in an economic and social hub like Xijiang.

Post-Mao changes added some new dimensions to these considerations. With economic liberalization in the reform era, many young men were leaving villages to find temporary labor in factories, road construction, lumbering, etc. Many young women felt that, despite such a move entailing a life with new in-laws in the long-term absence of one's spouse, marriage to a man with such unprecedented access to cash was preferable. Any suitor who had salaried work (*you gongzuo*) was preferable to a simple peasant (*nongcunde*); those who had permanent official employment with the state (*gongzuo renyuan*) were even more desirable. The fact that marriage to a worker did not change the wife's official designation as "agricultural personnel" (*nongye renyuan*), and that such marriages entailed long separations, was not enough to deter young women from ranking these potential partners as highest on the ladder of socioeconomic mobility. Indeed, parental pressures for arranged marriage had intensified since the end of the collective period as family members considered the benefits to be gained from marrying someone with cash income, with superior comforts in everyday living, with access to transportation, etc. In terms of marrying up, all these considerations weighed far more heavily in young women's minds than did, for instance, the notion of intermarriage with the Han, about which their feelings were very mixed.

Grooming, as we shall see, became critical in such a finely calibrated marriage market. Body types and practices—heavily inflected by class gradations—were tailored for the particular rural codes of attractiveness that all in the region recognized. To be "*pang*" (fleshy), for instance, clean, and of fair skin was highly desirable. To be skinny (*shou*) and dark (*hei*) was associated with excessive labor, which in turn implied poverty and exposure to the sun. This standard of beauty was made poignantly clear to me when my spouse came to visit from the United States during the summer months. For weeks, I was troubled that a close friend—a nineteen-year-old woman who had visited me regularly earlier in the year—never came to visit. After what seemed an incomprehensible several weeks of absence, she came abashedly to our door, apologizing that she had stayed away so long. She confided to me that she had been ashamed (*bu hao yisi*) to be seen by my spouse because her hard outdoor work (*ganhuo*) had blackened and emaciated her. Even minority women in the remotest parts of China, then, were thoroughly enmeshed in the nationwide system of valuation that attached superior status to urban workers over the stigmatized peasantry and to mental over manual labor (Potter 1983).[10] I turn now to a courtship context in which these considerations came into play. As will become clear, cruising for a mate was not unlike consuming festival color in that it had everything to do with instantiating class distinctions and displacing subalternity.

Watching Chixinjie

It was a sultry evening in July, and, even though in summer Guizhou is one of the coolest places in China, the air was close and heavy with humidity. The residents of Xijiang had finished a lavish dinner for Chixinjie — the "Festival of Eating the New." Celebrating the promising appearance of that season's first rice pushing out of the bright green stalks, the festival was an occasion for ancestral offerings, guesting, and feasting. In 1988 the entire event took place over the course of five days — July 11–16. On the first day, young people — chiefly young men — made pilgrimages to family bridges in the rice paddies, dispatched by their elders to make offerings of liquor, fish, eggs, and a live chicken. Feasts were held after offerings had been duly made at doorways and household shrines. By the fourth day of the festival, most people were still dining on pork, or on special five-inch-long fish that they caught by plunging bottomless baskets into the water of uncultivated rice paddies. If the ring of straw entrapped one or more fish, they were easily snatched out by hand. By now, adults had imbibed abundant quantities of locally brewed spirits and were relaxing or drinking on into the evening. Some sought the entertainment of a free movie projected outdoors on a sheet suspended on the facade of the schoolhouse. For the screening, a standing audience of all ages packed the basketball court that doubled as the site of the periodic market. This diversion suited the teenagers just fine, for they were preparing *their* part of the festival, which would not get under way until after midnight.

For the past few days, guests and relatives had been arriving in Xijiang from neighboring and distant villages, some in other counties. Most had come on foot, navigating the tiny paths that criss-crossed the mountain ridges, and descending past the rice terraces into Xijiang's densely peopled riverside ravine. Looking at the steep slope across from my window, I had seen the side of the mountain become animated by a steady stream of visitors in single file, some with hefty shoulder poles suspending baskets full of goods, negotiating the switchbacks that got them down into town most quickly. Some others had arrived on the bus that connected the town to the nearest big city and to counties beyond walking distance. Of course, before public transportation, Miao from these counties would simply walk, even for several days, staying with

33. Cruising Xijiang-style.

relatives along the way, to attend a big festival like that held in Xijiang. Courtship opportunities were the chief reason for their effort.

Chixinjie was not highly commodified like the Miao Dragon Boat Festival (Longchuanjie) described in chapter 6 or the Water Splashing Festival (Poshuijie) of the Dai in Yunnan that we encountered in chapter 5. Nonetheless, Chixinjie had received the attention of an array of domestic cultural producers and was canonized in the handy book-length *Survey of Guizhou Nationality Festivals — Reference Table*,[11] the *Brief History of the Miao (Miaozu Jianshi* 1985), and the *General Survey of the Southeast Guizhou Miao and Dong Autonomous Prefecture (Qiandongnan Miaozu Dongzu Zizhizhou Gaikuang* 1986). In 1988, when I was living in Xijiang, the festival received only slight attention from outsiders. A lone Japanese scholar dropped in for an overnight stay. Then Guizhou Television showed up unannounced in the hopes of covering rituals of sociality for a documentary on the region. But they had arrived a day too late for the feasting. The TV producer ceremoniously convened a meeting with the local leadership, cajoling them to spend money to stage a "realistic" celebration in a peasant's home, complete with food, liquor, and guests (including the American anthropologist). Local Miao cadres, put off by this contrived, big-budget approach, steadfastly declined to bend the ritual calendar to support such a project. It was just too late, they demurred, and local people had "already eaten" (*yijing chiguo le*).

Chixinjie was always timed to coincide with the periodic market. Market in Xijiang fell on the fifth and twelfth days of the twelve-day animal calendar. After five days, a small market was held; then, after a seven-day layoff there was a big market. Within the region, the town operated as a typical market of the kind described in Skinner's central place theory (1964–65). People came to sell and acquire goods, to visit with kin, and — in the 1980s — to do administrative business, for Xijiang's hub status had been reinforced by the establishment of a *qu* (district) with jurisdiction over seventy villages in a space roughly coterminous with the older market district. Metropolitan goods entered Xijiang and, in turn, trickled to the region's outlying villages through the funnel of the periodic market.

The market was the site of a multiplicity of contradictions. As Stallybrass and White suggest, "a marketplace is the epitome of local identity . . . and the unsettling of that identity by the trade and traffic of goods from elsewhere" (1986:27). On the pig and horse days of the animal calendar,[12] Xijiang became the intersection of many of the categories that organized local life within the Chinese state. The loci of the traditional and the modern, the center and the periphery, the spectator and the participant, the alien and the indigenous lost their fixity, shifting under local practices of signification.

For Xijiang residents, the experience of identity was both heightened and unsettled by the presence of foreign goods and the traffic of outsiders. The market brought Xijiang locals into proximity with their "less fortunate" neighbors who hailed from villages not only physically distant but classed as remote in the prevailing social categorization of space. Outlying villages, despite their widely ranging features, were uniformly described by Xijiang inhabitants as "backward" (*luohou*), "poor" (*qiong*), "small places" (*xiao difang*). Their villages were "dirty," often for lack of water, "dark" for lack of electricity, more reliant on homemade products (whether food, tools, or clothing), less sophisticated in their technologies, and less savvy about the ways of the world. Xijiang villagers looked (down) on these outsiders — many of whom were also kin as a result of marriage or migration—with a commingling of fascination and revulsion. Peasants from "small places" signified the lowest level of a social hierarchy in which Xijiang residents were positioned at or near the top. Constructing the regional spatial hierarchy, and assuming an elite position within it, were means by which Xijiangers strove to cast off their subalternity vis-à-vis the larger society.

Yet these remote neighbors were not only *stigmatized* as subalterns; they were also attributed special knowledges that rooted them firmly in the past. Folklorists and ethnographers from the city routinely favored outlying sites over centers like Xijiang, believing that these *"shenshan lao-lin"* ("dark mountains and ancient forests") held the mysteries (*shenmi*) that they had come to uncover. This system of value had permeated local structures of feeling as well. During Chixinjie, visitors from the periphery had been accorded a familiar niche, regarded with both contempt and appreciation as the gendered guardians of tradition virtually untouched by the turning of the wheels of civilization.

At the same time, visitors from outlying villages turned a reciprocal gaze on Xijiang. Many made the pilgrimage to the "center" on market day—and only on market day—with no intention of buying, selling, or courting, but simply to *"kan renao"*—to experience the excitement, the pulse of cosmopolitanism evoked by the crowds and the appearance of riches. They also came for a vicarious taste of the higher standard of living (*shenghuo hao*) enjoyed by the more fortunate inhabitants of this "big place" (*da difang*). Xijiang's "good life" was measured by a variety of indices: the bus, which allowed for commerce and greater circulation of goods; local meat and tofu for purchase on a daily basis; electrification, which enabled machine-hulling of rice, milling of wood, and, perhaps more importantly in local assessments, the availability of television in the evenings. On top of these things, there were movies—occasionally even foreign ones—played in Xijiang's auditorium-style movie theater. In 1988 an enterprising *getihu* (household business) had even set up a video shack in which martial arts and other movies were played continuously—paid admission only.

In the post-Mao era, the marriageable youth of Xijiang stood at dead center of the tensions generated out of the interface between imputed traditionalism and desired modernity. Young men made offerings on the first day of festival, telling me they did so in the name of *chuan-tong* ("tradition"), because "their ancestors had always done so." They

34. Bridge offerings for Chixinjie. A sacrificial chicken's blood is dribbled on a stone that crosses the family's irrigation ditch.

carried out their duties conscientiously, albeit unceremoniously. From their perspective, however, the festival peaked on the day that coincided with the periodic market. On that day, material modernity would be most conspicuously present in the form of enticing commodities such as cassette tapes, wristwatches, and name-brand cigarettes brought by peddlers from afar.

Xijiang's youth, then, envisioned a "modern" Chixinjie, one that merged nostalgia with novelty. A basketball competition had become naturalized as a central element of the festival and was followed with great interest by members of the community. The elder who handwrote the account of Xijiang's festivals had included it on a list along with bullfighting, cockfighting, horse racing, and singing. Its legitimacy went unquestioned; indeed, when I attended Chixinjie in a smaller village and expressed incredulity at being told that an archlike feature of a household shrine symbolized a basketball hoop for spirit children to play with, my disbelief provoked offended indignation.

It was after night fell on Chixinjie's steamy market day, after a long day's encounter with metropolitan products and wholesome team sports, that young people reclaimed the market space in the wee hours of the night, crowding Xijiang's public areas in single-sex clusters on the make. At anytime on that midfestival July night, were you to climb the slope to a perch above Xijiang, the ravine could be heard echoing with a resounding roar created by the bustle of activity typical of this special evening. In the houses, dimly lit by electric bulbs, young women were preening. They had donned their best and newest casual attire (formal festival costume was reserved for daylight processional dancing on more solemn occasions such as Miao New Year), and they had made an effort to keep it clean from the dust that rose off the paths and from the grime of cooking. For most of these young women, the casual outfit meant a side-fastening top in any number of solid colors—pink, white, red, baby blue—decorated with a band of embroidery along the cuffs and along the line of the blouse's front panel. Some had added a colorfully embroidered apron that covered their front from chestbone to waist. Favoring synthetic fabrics, they completed the ensemble with polyester pants of darker colors. This year, however, fashion pioneers sported dresses, swaying skirts, or even shorts and button-down Western-style blouses, announcing their trendiness with sartorial symbols of urban or imported culture. Those pushing the limits went sleeve-

35. Xijiang's main street: Haute couture goes to market.

less, exposing the formerly taboo upper arm. It was paramount to them
that clothing be new and in good condition, and that clothing materials appear distinct from homespun textiles and dyes. On women's feet
were any number of dressy shoe styles, including sandals and platforms,
always with a significant elevation for the heel, regardless of how far
the young women had had to walk to reach Xijiang. Some shoes even
had spike heels. Women of marriageable age paid special attention to
the grooming of their hair. For most, it was combed up and twisted into
an elaborate vertical knot (*jiujiu*) that stood four to five inches above
the crowns of their heads. In it were placed adornments such as artificial flowers, silver ornaments, and ribbons. At the back of their heads,
lodged in their hair just below the topknot, was a bright-colored comb,
always of manufactured plastic rather than the home-crafted wooden
ones like those that their mothers and grandmothers wore. Some of
them had loosed the emblematic Miao *jiujiu* and let their hair flow down
their backs, occasionally gathered with a bright ribbon. The crowning
adornments were wristwatches or gaudy, store-bought earrings. Sartorial statements claimed modernity in two ways. On the one hand,
they displayed affinity with what was considered urban fashion. On the
other, they demonstrated a kind of economic status as evidenced by the

248   Identity and Cultural Struggle

young woman's ability to purchase clothing rather than rely on what could be made at home.

In the hours of making ready, young men were busy, too. Less concerned with dress, they sported Western-style short-sleeved shirts or sleeveless T-shirts atop pants of army olive drab, dark blue, or black. Some of them had purchased polyester slacks from the market to replace their daily cottons for special occasions. After perfunctory hair-combing, young men would drink with the older men, or join neighbors to watch one of the handful of television sets that had been acquired by the more prosperous Xijiangers. Others began to position themselves with studied casualness outside in the street, clouds of smoke from their cigarettes wafting upward from their tight clusters. Some were readying their technology.

Two technologies became critical to the courtship scene in the newly commodity-driven reform era: the flashlight and the tape deck. Bulky flashlights powered by two D batteries had long been standard possessions of all rural families in the region. Nighttime activity was common in all villages, whether going from home to home, feasting and drinking, or meeting for family or government business. But during Chixinjie, the flashlight had a specialized function. As the evening progressed, and despite the late hour, the road winding out from Xijiang's main street, across a bridge, and up the hill into the mountains became increasingly crowded with young people in quest of a *duixiang* (or target) for her or his affections.

One of the first steps toward making overtures was what I have dubbed "flashlighting." Young men, and to a lesser extent young women, promenaded in small groups up and down the road, aiming the beams of their flashlights directly into the faces of those about whom they were curious. Lights beamed between strangers and as a means of recognition between friends and acquaintances. To turn away from the lights blinding one's eyes would be unthinkable, for flashlighting was the means by which tentative matches were made. Not only the physical appearance of the person under scrutiny, but also their responsiveness to the attention might influence whether a conversation ensued from the initial spectoral encounter. If a tentative match was made, then roadside chatting might begin in earnest, or the clusters of young men and women might begin to sing antiphonally the songs of courtship for which Miao have been known for centuries.

In this centuries-old genre called *duige,* a group of young men and a group of young women stood facing each other. Each group took turns stating their interest through the oblique imagery of improvised serenades crooned in a low tone, almost conspiratorially. Sentiments of flirtation, desire, and unrequited love were poetically conveyed through natural metaphors and techniques of indirection. Dense with telescoped and ambiguous language, the lyrics to one published song (Li Tinggui 1991:29–31) translate roughly as follows:

Boys: Although we aren't your iron and fire,
         Although we aren't your boyfriends,
         Bring out your most precious to sell,
         Bring out your mouth to sing;
         Come and we'll smoke a cigarette before we go,
         Come and we'll have a chat before we go,
Girls: Let's smoke a cigarette,
         Let's have a chat,
         Why are you so anxious to get together [*cheng shuang*]?
         Jiyue [appellative for boyfriend]
         After you've paired off you'll be back to fool with us,
         Do you know what my partner is like?
         If you say you're not paired off, I'll go with you.
Boys: Only when the fields collapse does the water call the
           mountain flooded,
         Only after getting together will I call you
         Guomu [appellative for girlfriend];
         I am still single,
         I still am not paired off, *Guomu.*
Girls: Wait until the fields have collapsed and then the water will
           call the mountain flooded,
         Wait until we've gotten together and then you tell me;
         Your children are all grown,
         You are deceiving us, *Jiyue.*
Boys: The paddy at the base of the village, the sweet potato plot,
         The girls of this place all talk this way;
         I am lonely in my mother's house,
         I am lonely in my father's house, *Guomu!*
Girls: When I don't see you I just stay at home,

When I've seen you my heart is on fire;
Dirty water can smother fish to death,
Stuffiness will suffocate me to death,
Do you know on which honest person bad luck will fall?
I fear the most unlucky will be me.

Boys: *Guomu,* if you don't go I'll be the same,
I want you, I can never forget you,
If I eat bitterness, I'll still want you, if I eat sweetness, I'll still
    want you,
Every day I want you,
I won't dodge if I see the red-hot iron,
Who is hiding oneself, *Guomu!*

Girls: The cold water bucket shouldn't seal in the water,
The hive shouldn't hold in the honeybees;
Old Grandma in the West, don't lock in our *Jiyue,*
Let our *Jiyue* come play with us,
Why would you want to lock our *Jiyue* up?
Why not let us play.

Boys: To build a water canal, it must be long and winding,
To make a human heart, it must be long and broad,
You and I together until we're old.

Girls: The water in the fields goes through bend after turn,
To be a human heart, heart must be connected to heart,
You and I together until we lose each other in death.

Displacing *Duige*

In the post-Mao years, *duige,* much romanticized in the literature on the
Miao and nationally recognized as a symbol of Miao culture, was regarded with considerable ambivalence by Xijiang youth. In many ways,
young peoples' struggles over modernity were activated in their approaches to *duige.* Despite their differential participation in the singing,
all regarded it with intense interest. But when asked if they were going
to sing, young women and men from Xijiang proper declined embarrassedly, explaining that only the people from the countryside (*xiangxia*)
knew how to sing. To them, "the countryside" meant those villages in
the farthest reaches of Xijiang district and beyond. These were the sites
to which a migrating otherness had been attached. Nonetheless, Xijiang

youth were transfixed by the virtuosity of their "country cousins" at Miao song, listening avidly night after night in tight spectatorial clusters around those cultural custodians against whom they distinguished themselves.

Young men had devised an additional modality for participating in the evening exchanges, and here their playing with the potentialities of the modern and the urban was most apparent. Constructing themselves as poachers on the terrain of tradition, they activated their second form of technology, the tape recorder, cradled in their arms like babies and aimed at young women in song. This practice, they explained, would give them a souvenir of the girls they had met. Culture was once again transformed into a gendered vestige of the past, the control and possession of which functioned in turn as a sign of the modern, allowing Xijiang men to eschew their own subalternity.

Young male suitors, capitalizing on a context in which their techno-appendages constituted a status marker, also used their recordings of village song as props for flirting with other girls. Their tactic was to impress precisely through their adeptness at transposing tradition to a contemporary format, to woo through their mastery of the medium of mechanical reproduction. In the process they established their identity with more "advanced" (*xianjin*) sectors of Chinese society, constructing themselves as relatively worldly sophisticates counterposed to the far-flung villages and unabashed singers of the raw "countryside." The struggle for the modern enacted in the taping of *duige,* then, effected in one stroke the replacement of the formal symmetry of the antiphonal genre with the incipient status *and* gender asymmetry that was saturating much of everyday life in the 1980s and 1990s.

Modernity Mobilized

Through the production of these distinctions, Xijiang youth came to know themselves as particular class- and gender-inflected types of Miao. "Modernity" was seen as distributed over space, finding its greater concentrations in places thought of as more central. But the modern was not only statically distributed in fixed sites; it also could be generated and displayed as a form of symbolic capital. In this way, Xijiang peasants sought to displace subalternity onto their technologically muted neighbors. Positioning themselves as spectators and as manipulators of technology, Xijiangers, like the Beijingers at Siyueba, generated a distance between themselves and those they watched—the putative "country folk."

Interpreting the vignettes in this chapter permits some generalization about the features that had come to characterize modernity for Miao cultural practitioners. To "be modern" was to consume or reproduce rather than to produce, to watch rather than to do, to be urban rather than rural, masculine rather than feminine, to do things mechanically or with machines rather than with one's body, and to standardize or routinize rather than to improvise. As I have suggested, Chinese popular conceptions of modernity were also defined by contrasting them with a constellation of features such as the childlike, the natural, the female, the peasant, the non-Western, and the minority. These valuations of the modern and nonmodern, however, were fraught with ambivalence. Boundaries were continually renegotiated as people struggled for particular identities as well as for a more universalized prestige. Thus emerged the kind of mobile otherness seen in events such as the Miao Studies conference, Beijing's Siyueba, and Xijiang's Chixinjie. In certain domains of cultural production and at different historical junctures, as we will see more clearly in chapter 9, what constituted the modern mode was subject to what might be called turf contestation. Subalternity, then, could rarely be fixed squarely on the shoulders of any particular social sector; disavowing it through myriad maneuvers of cultural reformatting and status struggle was precisely what it was about.

9

Performances
of *Minzu* Modernity

It was February 1988, just after the celebration of Chinese New Year, and I was to attend my first Xijiang wedding. This would be a special occasion for all of us because never before — or at least since 1949 — had a Xijiang wedding featured a foreign guest. Much deliberation had gone into what gift I should give. Local officials who had appointed themselves as advisors on the decision debated whether I should give the customary money and a bolt of cloth, or something unique, such as a wall calendar brought with me from the United States.

Doing Things with Weddings

At the appropriate time in the late afternoon I arrived at the home of the groom's family, announcing my presence like other guests with the staccato din of firecrackers and a cloud of smoke. The home was in the level area of Xijiang, near the banks of the river. The floor was packed earth, and its wood and bamboo walls were papered with old newspapers and other printed material. At a family shrine — a kind of shelf mounted on the wall and covered with paper cutouts and money paper — food offerings were laid out and incense was kept burning at all times. The three rooms allocated to feeding the guests were already crowded, and more newcomers were still squeezing in.

The bride was cloistered in a bedroom, into which women were permitted to inspect her presentability in the best of Miao clothing. This was one of the moments in a Miao woman's life for which she spent years of her youth preparing a lavishly embroidered costume. The approval of her new in-laws was a matter of considerable importance. This bride was different, however, for she was from a Han family. She came from a village two counties away that was a mixed Han and Miao population. In the characteristic manner of a neophyte daughter-in-law, she spoke to me of her homesickness, lamenting that although Miao was spoken in her home village, the dialect was different and she understood little of what was said in Xijiang. Her costume was borrowed from the groom's family, and she had worn it for the requisite promenade through the village, accompanied by two little girls, also fully bedecked, from among the groom's relatives. Earlier that day she had performed the mandatory rite of subservience in which she knelt by a basin outside the house and did the entire family's wash. Her attire for the chore was that of a youthful peasant of the 1980s—a padded, off-red jacket over a green sweater and a white-collared shirt, dark blue pants, and brilliant red faux-leather pumps. When she and her new husband went to dry the clothing at the riverbank, she stood out among the other young laundresses because of her thick bangs and shoulder-length hair pulled into a modest pony tail at her shoulders rather than twisted atop her head in local Miao fashion.

While women inspected the bride, older male guests arrayed themselves around a long table in the main room of the house. Ornamented with the head of a pig slaughtered for the occasion, the table was the central spot where monetary gifts were being publicly tabulated by one of the younger, better-educated clansmen. Nearly 300 guests, including children, would pass through this wedding event, and their gifts totaling several hundred yuan had to be painstakingly recorded in notebooks, lest anyone's level of generosity be forgotten. When it was time for dinner, the guests were segregated by gender and rank, with elder men remaining in the central room, elder women in a side room, and younger men and women of lower status in relation to the family divided in two rooms at a neighbor's house. The youngest women—those who had the job of attending to the guests—stood around informally. Except for a brief toast in which she appeared in costume to inaugurate the drinking, the bride remained sequestered in the bedroom. For dinner, large hunks of pork, porkfat, and liver from three freshly butchered pigs were passed out by hand from big serving baskets, while guests helped themselves to soup and vegetables on the tables. Later, fried tofu and innards were offered straight into guests' mouths, using specially fashioned disposable bamboo chopsticks that a relative of the groom's family had cut that morning.

The main event, one that would stretch through the night till nearly dawn, was the ritual drinking of home-brewed grain liquor and the singing of reciprocal wedding songs between members of the extended family. Toasts were offered in strictly codified fashion, with seniority, gender, and proximity to the groom's family determining the sequence at first, followed by a general and less scripted series of exchanges initiated by men and women alike. The air was solemn during the brief opening speeches, then shifted to an atmosphere of revelry. Celebrants approached each other proffering drinks and singing a verse or making a short speech before forcing the liquor to their recipients' mouths and tipping it up to insure that the harsh intoxicant flowed down their gullets. Never would one put a shot glass or a drinking bowl to one's own lips without it being offered.

Varieties of inebriating interchange were regarded by most Xijiangers as the central substance of all rituals of sociality. From impromptu meals for visiting relatives, to life-cycle rites such as weddings and funerals, to the feasting that accompanied both Miao and Chinese New Year celebrations, liquor was exchanged through highly conventionalized modes that bound people in dense relationships. The phrase *"he jiu"* was not limited to its literal meaning of "drink liquor"; rather, it connoted a range of activities—celebration, commemoration, mourning. For these purposes, being drunk to unconsciousness was entirely permissible, an indication of one's appropriate spirits. Evasion also was allowed, as a strategy for prolonging one's endurance for marathons that demanded the bodily enactment of the social fabric through one's sustained chemical alteration. Conversely, a person who drank alone was immediately classified as an abuser.

That reciprocal drinking was a constitutive aspect of social life was taken for granted, then, but not, as I learned, unreflexively. During the formal toasts to which everyone attended at the outset of the feasting, self-appointed informants explained to me, *"Women Miaojia jiushi zheyangde . . ."* ("We Miao people are just this way"), or *"Women shaoshu minzu shi zheyang he jiu"* ("This is the way we minority nationalities drink"). That evening as the wedding progressed into the wee hours, more and more guests and hosts alike staggered toward me, hands clasping bowls containing shots of liquor, pushing them to my mouth and coaxing me with the justification: *"Women shaoshu minzu xiguan!"* ("Our minority nationality custom!"). Sometimes the statement was varied to *"shaoshu Miaozu xiguan"* ("minority Miao custom")—a grammatically playful way of claiming the ethnic distinctiveness of the rites.[1] One celebrant announced, "Ana! This is our minority nationality custom — what do you think?" (*"Ana! Women shaoshu minzu fengsu — ni you shenme ganjue?"*).[2] When two long nights of feasting and drinking were over, an educated young man asked me to evaluate (*pinglun*) the wedding, give my reactions, and assess whether it was good or bad. When I paused, searching past my anthropologist's suspension of judgment for a judicious answer, he interjected impatiently, "Whether it's good or bad, we have to do it. It's our *minzu* custom!"

What do these comments and queries, standard fare at most of the events I attended, indicate about those who posed them? And what is the significance of their being uttered at all? And to me? Such statements might be read in several ways. First, they indicate that moments of ritual were marked with the stamp of ethnic identification. Whereas Xijiangers experienced their daily life of agricultural production *as peasants,* these intermittent moments of Dionysian indulgence were, conversely, ethnicized. And second, they were ethnicized in the language of officialdom, as "minority nationality" practices. Such speech was highly charged; it acknowledged the stigma that the state had attached to certain "wasteful" practices as ritual excess and intoxication, especially as seen in references to the evaluation expected from me. In a sense, then, as the addressee to whom many of these comments were directed, I stood in for an officialdom that promoted efficiency and production as equivalent to modernization and that scorned the indulgences of ritual abandon. But there was something parodic about these solicitous bids for my adjudication, since it was clear that my opinion made no difference whatsoever to whether the practices would take place. In the 1980s, Miao embraced their rituals with the confidence that the modernizing state (for which I proxied in those Xijiang instances) would not interfere. Indeed, the labeling of the practices as *minzu xiguan* not only marked their stigma, but simultaneously emphasized their official protection under the category of minority nationality customs. In these utterances, then, Miao commentators spoke themselves through the language of the modernizing state.[3] And it was according to the state's categories that they demarcated themselves as Miao.

What, then, could we say that these comments do? My third reading is directed more at the moment of speaking, at what was being accomplished in the uttering of these statements and questions to me in those particular contexts. What were the celebrants making of themselves through these acts? This is the theme of this chapter: I ask what was being done when Miao took up their culture and remarked on, observed, consumed, and critiqued it self-consciously from some measure of distance.

In the 1980s, as we have seen, Miao cultural practice abounded in forms of distancing. Through nostalgia, traditions were historicized, consigned to the past. Through mediation, culture was rendered as a slick surface of images. Through commodification, culture was alienated from embedded social process. And through formal staging — whether for tourists or for themselves — rituals became transactions between spectators and performers. Marking these shifts is not to imply that culture was unreflective and universally practiced before this era. Duara has argued cogently against the notions, derived from Hegel and from nationalism theorists,[4] that modernity is a unique form of self-conscious awareness and that a sense of community defined by culture is a unique property of the modern nation. He counters: "There were large numbers of people in agrarian societies who were conscious of their culture and identity at multiple levels and, in that sense, were perhaps not nearly so different from their modern counterparts" (1995:54). What I am suggesting here is not that Miao came to consciousness for the first time in this moment of transition, but rather that the cultural politics of this moment were such that enacting a reflexivity and a distance from one's traditions, even as one embraced them, had potent significations and not only as a fashioning of self for the inquisitive foreign anthropologist.

Throughout this book I have given examples of how the prevailing social order was instantiated through cultural production and through cultural struggles. What I would like to draw attention to in this penultimate chapter are the moments in which an indigenously and variously defined modernity was repeatedly constituted through acts that could be called *performances*. From off-handed comments at ceremonial events to scripted acts on stage, Miao were negotiating their location in relation to the social categories that typed them. But, I will argue, they also were rearticulating those social categories through these acts. Performing modernity works in tandem with the displacing of subalternity discussed in chapter 8. Many of the instances detailed there could also be considered performances of modernity. This chapter pushes further in interpreting what, for the purposes of the larger social context, it is that such performances do.

Performativity Theory—and Practice

Performance theory, or performativity, has been elaborated in many fields, but—with the influence of Judith Butler—it has become especially prominent in gender and queer studies.[5] Building from the linguistic theories of J. L. Austin (1975), who suggested that utterances might be performative in the sense of *doing something* rather than just describing or expressing things, Butler developed a notion of gender as a consequence of the enactment of social norms. When people repeatedly acted out the conventions for maleness and femaleness in a given society, they made the male-female polarity seem real. The significance of this argument lies in the notion that there is no essence, origin, or reality prior to its enactment in a multiplicity of performances. It is only their recurring performance that gives certain social norms their authority, their aura of inevitability.

Nowhere is this better demonstrated than in the putative correspondence between biological sex and definite gender behaviors. Butler suggested that not only the absolute difference between two types of bodies, i.e., "male" and "female," but also the naturalness of the heterosexual union between them, were actually social constructs that acquired their reality precisely through the regularity with which gender differences were enacted. The repetition of hegemonic gender norms, then, she calls—following Derrida—"citationality."[6] Citation is in turn akin to that which Lacan referred to as the "assumption" of normative sexed positions: "The force and necessity of these norms . . . is thus functionally *dependent on* the approximation and citation of the law. . . . If 'sex' is assumed in the same way that a law is cited . . . then the 'law of sex' is repeatedly fortified and idealized as the law only to the extent that it is reiterated as the law . . . by the very citations it is said to command" (Butler 1993:14). Hegemonic cultural orders, in other words, rely for their authority on being repeatedly reproduced in an array of minute social processes—"citations."

Performance theorists, however, are not only interested in how prevailing social categories are *reified* through conventionalized performative acts. As Diamond, introducing her collection *Performance and Cul-*

tural Politics, suggests: "In performance . . . signifying (meaning-ful) acts may enable new subject positions and new perspectives to emerge, even as the performative present contests the conventions and assumptions of oppressive cultural habits" (1996:6). Debates around the social and ideological consequences of performativity have centered on the issue of whether any subversion takes place. Many scholars have tended to focus on such practices as drag, transvestism, or cross-dressing as paradigmatic instances of cultural artifice in which prevailing social categories might be parodied or transgressed.[7] Challenging those who stress the destabilizing character of such artifice, some ask: if cross-dressers work with, even exaggerate, the roles that are scripted for the opposite sex, don't their performances both on and off stage serve only to reinforce those binarized roles as the limits of possibility? Lancaster, reviewing the interpretive literature, suggests that either/or analytics of performance are premised on an artificial mutual exclusivity. Considering a male transvestite performance by a young Nicaraguan man named "Guto," he argues that theories "put before us a set of dreary options: either Guto was making fun of women, or he was celebrating femininity. . . . Either Guto was transgressing gender forms, or he was intensifying them. . . . An interpretive apparatus, an analytical technology, hums its familiar noise: parody or praise, subversion or intensification, deviation or norm, resistant or enabling, play or serious. . . . But what if a dramatic moment *en cours* is overwhelmed by nuance and ambiguity?" (1997:568). Nuances, then, become the stuff of ethnographic investigation, where theoretical options become blurred.

One way that performances become nuanced is through the very social relations that surround them. Performances of gender or cross-dressing do not happen in the solitude of a dressing room; rather, they occur between people with variant takes on the presentation. Kath Weston suggests that these social relations are central to the way performance works because gendered presentations occur in contexts of differential power and differential material circumstances. "When performance theory does away with the gendered subject, it inadvertently displaces and fetishizes gender by relocating gender in the hair, beads, muscles, trousers, shoes, mascara, and fingernails that people draw on to create their gendered presentations. What this tendency to perceive gender as a physical property of possessions . . . obscures is gender's character as an aspect of social relations" (1993:14). In some cases different spectators will respond differently to a performance; in other cases, all involved are performing, and what matters is the particular way in which these acts become entangled in social interaction.

Pushing further in nuancing the meanings of performances, observers have noted the other axes of difference that intersect with gender at every moment. The notion of performativity need not be confined to the production of gender norms. Other categorical differences—such as race, ethnicity, or class—could also be argued to acquire their inexorability through an accumulation of verifying performances or to have their essential aura eroded by crossover performances.[8] Aiming to broaden the range of differences that could be considered performative, Lancaster proposes to look at a broad category of what he calls "crossover desires" (1997:574–76) in which an explosion of costumery renders all sorts of privileged and not-so-privileged positions the substance of masquerade. Carnival and other rituals of inversion are classic instances in which gender, sexuality, race, class, and ethnicity are all objects of theatrical play; Carnival is "the occasion for remembering, interrogating, and *playing with* the history of systems of domination" (1997:573–74). A great deal can be learned from the moments in which people do not reiterate prevailing structures and conventions, but rather appear to contravene them, to upend them, or at least to mock them. But as the advocates of nuance continually remind us, a durable outcome is not to be expected from these giddy festivities. "To destabilize is not to subvert," cautions Weston (1993:17).

Many of the persons encountered in this book could be considered performers. I have characterized them as performers of modernity in a way that connotes their crossover desires. That feminized Miao emblematize tradition and backwardness within China does not mean that they routinely perform only that. By extension, the practice of noting in ethnographic analysis that they emblematize tradition should be vigilantly scrutinized to avoid becoming part of the apparatus that scripts backwardness as their only role, their only positioning in the Chinese social order. Hence, I end this book by focusing on the ways that Miao, contrary to dominant expectations, *performed modernity;* and I suggest some of the social effects of these performances. These acts ranged from formal, onstage versions to the highly informal, but they usually involved making culture an object of reflection. Just as gender and its attachment to certain bodies might come under question with performative acts, so cultural traditionalism and its attachment to members of certain social sectors or ethnic groups might seem less tenable with these acts of crossover. Stated most boldly, by performing modernity as *Miao*, these actors confounded their consignment to the role of impoverished, rural, tradition bearers and strove to make membership in the prestigious category of modernity less exclusive, more negotiable. But paradoxically, they simultaneously reiterated the prestige of modernity as the very hegemonic cultural system that stigmatized them.

The Posture in the Gift

It was late September dusk during my return visit to Xijiang in 1993. I had climbed up the winding paths, crossed over streams on makeshift planks, skirted a menacing barking dog, and reached a home perched near the top of Xijiang's steep hillside where a wedding was to take place. I found things already well under way. Amid firecrackers, guests were arriving bearing shoulder poles of gifts—pork, sticky rice, home-brewed liquor, quilts, fabric. Some items were contributions to the several days of ceremonial that were to ensue. Others were household goods for the bride and groom to keep. The couple getting married were educated Miao youth with good jobs—she an elementary school teacher in a neighboring village, he the manager of the subcontracted state dry goods outlet in the center of Xijiang. The bride stayed in the nuptial chamber while the groom circulated, mediating between his relatives and the urbanized young people they had invited from their educational sojourn in Kaili. Guests, of which there would ultimately be several hundred, were received in the central room of the groom's natal home and offered a simple meal and some perfunctory shots of home brew while they waited for the more formal meal to be served in the evening.

I settled in the nuptial chamber where the bride was hanging out with a couple of young female relatives. Languorously, she made up her face with powder, blush, lipstick, and eyeliner, then dressed in Miao finery— the full-length, pleated skirt layered with a circle of embroidered bands, the jacket laden with brocade, appliqué, and silver panels, then chokers and chain necklaces of delicately handwrought silver. Her hair was thickened with extra strands and combed upward into a topknot dense enough to support the weighty silver ornaments that would complete the ensemble. Just then a group of city friends arrived, classmates from

36. A "modern" wedding gift.

the days when the couple had attended high school in the prefecture seat. The firecrackers they set off were so noisy as to put those of the local village guests to shame. Then, the pièce de résistance—the gift born on shoulder poles. It was an ostentatious framed wall hanging behind glass, a photographic decoration slated for the walls of the nuptial chamber. Other guests had also presented such articles for interior decoration—framed reproductions of Chinese watercolors or fanciful embroideries. This particular picture, however, in a bizarre juxtaposition with the bride, even upstaging her, was of a blonde model in a hot-pink G-string bikini reclined atop a snazzy racing car. Lovingly, the hanging was given front center placement among the other gifts—heaps of quilts and household goods—on display in the nuptial chamber for guests to review.

The gift materialized a conjunction between youth and a special form of modernity as it was displayed in an abundance of social encounters in the post-Mao period. While bride and groom undertook their hometown rituals of betrothal with solemnity, they also created a space within

37. An urbane parlor in a country home.

which their urbane distinctions were enacted. Sporting a white tailored shirt and red necktie, the groom, tall and affable, alternately received his village guests and repaired to a side room that had been done up as a receiving parlor with upholstered chairs, teacups, and a tray of peanuts, candy, and sunflower seeds as snacks. Here, youthful visitors from the city were playing cards, smoking cigarettes, and resisting the otherwise mandatory alcohol exchanges. One of these young people hung a beeper from his belt, despite the fact that no phone would be available on which to return calls during his stay in Xijiang. Another wore a T-shirt with images of Western women and their printed names emblazoned across his chest. Like the red pumps of the Han bride with whom I began, these minutia of sartorial marking took on heightened significance in a context characterized by their relative scarcity.

The voluntary spatial segregation of these guests along with their distinctions in dress bespoke more than an intergenerational chasm asserted by the young. It also mapped the divide between villagers and those upwardly mobile metropolitans who had left the villages and adopted lifestyles that were accorded greater prestige in the current social order. Far from rejecting the quaint customs that they had grown up with, they indulged in them with a kind of ironic ardor, but at the same time they shaped them as venues for displaying their acquired status. The socially charged segregation of activities was mirrored by the bride's use of *her* designated space. Instead of the nuptial chamber being a place where she was sheltered and cloistered, the bride had made it a world unto itself in which she exhibited her newfound status through decor.[9] While incense placed by the groom's father burned auspiciously outside the closed door, a step across the threshold ushered one into a personalized interior. The couple, with the relative affluence of two salaries, had been able to acquire a handsome set of furniture. The floor space was monopolized by a double bed layered with eight or ten luxurious quilts presented by wedding guests. One entire wall was filled with matching dresser, wardrobe, and cabinets that reached almost to the ceiling. A large mirror was the centerpiece of the ensemble. All of the components, which had been commissioned from a woodworker in Xijiang, were decoratively painted in a manner uncharacteristic of peasants' wood furniture. The color that the couple had lovingly chosen was a faint sea-green with black trim. On a side table an imposing multifunction tape deck blared Chinese pop music, while another surface was occupied by an aging television set. A brand-new standing fan offered relief from the heat to a degree that most Xijiangers never dreamt of, especially because electric current was unreliable. Arrayed on the shelves were ornamental trinkets such as artificial flowers in stylish vases and porcelain animal miniatures, luxuries rare to peasant homes.

The image of the G-stringed Western woman was welcomed into this space, not as eroticized flesh for male titillation, but as an emblem of the boldness of exposed skin, of unconstrained canons of dress, and of the material abundance signified by the flashy car. Depictions of the West, during the transitional period in which China was opening its doors wider and wider, introduced a measure of modern style into any space they adorned. Through giving the framed picture, the urbane guests flaunted their sophistication, their taste. And by cherishing it, the couple themselves demonstrated a streak of cosmopolitanism. Speaking from a Western feminist standpoint, I asked a young woman if this kind of picture would be considered offensive in a bedroom. "Not at all," she replied, "the woman is beautiful and fast cars mean wealth. This is what young people like to look at."

In *Distinction* (1984), Bourdieu argued that people mark off their class positions not only through the direct accumulation of wealth, but also

38. Bride, groom, and nuptial interior.

through the ways in which their consumption displays "good taste," "aesthetic value," and the like. Clearly, distinctions were very much at work in the practices of the young bride and groom and their urbane guests, but what is not so clear is whether it was strict divisions *between* social sectors that were being demarcated. The carefully chosen adornments of the nuptial chamber asserted a particular aesthetic of decoration distinct from local village conventions. Moreover, many of these accoutrements bespoke the pleasures of consumption itself, of the whole complex of commodity desires and pursuits that were becoming so fashionable in the period of market reform. The newlyweds were noticeably proud of their acquisitions as the effects of advanced and improved style. Likewise, the presenters of the framed girlie/sports car picture were announcing a counteraesthetic to that of flowery wall decorations and sumptuous quilts. But the distinctions which they affirmed did not necessarily mean that they thought of themselves as any less Miao, or as somehow outsiders to the practices that were taking place during the course of the wedding.

These consumption practices, then, were like a script that young people designed for how everybody could become modern Miao. The fact that young people affirmed the value of modernity and urbanity was by no means a clear-cut indicator of their crossover into a discrete social sector such as "urbanite" or "non-Miao." Rather, I think it can be interpreted as an affirmative statement that the prestigious styles which marked modernity and urbanity were also cherished among the rural Miao, despite the inability of the majority to gain access to them. That they, as Miao villagers themselves, chose these styles was precisely the point. The effect at another level of reading was to call into question Han urbanites' monopoly on the accoutrements of modernity.

A Youth Performance

If the practices of consumption, gift-giving, and interior decorating were one way that Xijiang youth performed modernity, the production of their own culture was another. Life in 1980s Xijiang was punctuated by multiple instances of the literal staging of culture, usually sponsored by the Culture Station. Equipped with the requisite technology to mediate and amplify, the Culture Station provided the means by which to render culture a discrete and compartmentalized activity. A big tape deck, amplifiers, speakers, and a microphone made it possible to throw dance parties and to put on performances (and in the 1990s, to sing karaoke).[10] This performance component, complete with audience, had a different valence than that discussed in earlier chapters. What it asserted in many ways was the ability of the rural participants to take hold of, contain, and manipulate "culture" employing "modern" formats.

Shortly before Chixinjie, the summer courtship festival, Zhou of the Culture Station came to me with big news. He proudly explained that he had been able to procure just enough funds to purchase prizes that would allow him to sponsor a youth performance. On a high festival afternoon, on the stage of the local movie house, groups of children and teenagers from throughout the district would have a chance to give amateur performances. The structure of the event was established by Zhou. Spectators would assume their role by purchasing tickets beforehand. Audience and performers were strictly separated by the spatial arrangement of Xijiang's movie house, which featured an elevated stage and a sloped, darkened seating area. Performing groups were framed as contestants, even though each participant, not only the winners, was to get a prize. Indeed, Zhou maintained that the event's success was contingent on the awarding of prizes to motivate the participants. With this in mind, he had approached six county-level offices for supplementary funds. None had granted him a cent, so he had only thirty or forty yuan to work with. He regarded the prizes that he was able to award—lipstick, handkerchiefs, and the like—as inconsequential. With more funds for better prizes, he claimed, they might have been able to stage a real competition.

At two o'clock on a steamy afternoon midway through the festival, those of us who held tickets presented them at the door and filed into the dingy movie house. The space of the theater strained to accommodate this newer genre, while revealing the traces of other formats in which messages were conveyed more unidirectionally through the medium of the government-approved moving picture. The painstakingly contrived ambience of festive performance rubbed coarsely up against the functionality of the otherwise little-used public room. The movie house walls were painted in two tones, pale green and faded white. The stage was unadorned, except for the prominent technology arrayed at its edge. Some long wooden boards, which no one had bothered to remove, were stacked at the back of the stage. No scenery had been rigged on the wall behind, although a white sheet had been hung to cover over some government-issued posters. The audience was of mixed ages, with young people and children in the majority. Cigarette smoke wafted upward and hovered in clouds above the expectant but irreverent crowd. Spectators had come to see their friends and family members; they squirmed under the implicit injunction to maintain the requisite decorousness.

Seventeen numbers comprised the afternoon program, led off by Zhou who convened the event with an introduction. An MC mediated the material, introducing each element of the program and designating each set of performers in terms of where they came from and a relevant work unit if one existed, as in the case of the kindergarten groups who represented their respective schools. A gong and drum signaled for applause. Four performing groups were of kindergarten age. The sets of performers came from far-flung villages, all within Xijiang district and all with a proud sense of representing their native place. In some cases, however, the performing collectivity was formed not by a natural village but by the production brigade (*dadui*) to which they had belonged before decollectivization, revealing how local identifications were still shaped by the fast-disappearing institutional structures of Mao's era.

Using innovative bricolage, performers fashioned their renditions to demonstrate both their mastery of contemporary material and their fluency in Miao styles. Their means were song, dance, music, props, and costume. Flouncy pink skirts and skintight leggings mingled with PLA jackets. Performances spanned both the songs of Han popular culture and versions of the notorious Miao drinking songs (*jiuge*). Those who included indigenous tunes in their medleys punctuated their endings with loud whoops, canonizing a custom associated with the rowdiness of social drinking. Some of the older performers flaunted their urbanity through the use of makeup, the microphone, or recorded Chinese popular music. Others choreographed dances intended to represent Miao styles. Recorded music blared from the tape deck, alternating with the live melodies from a small orchestra to one side of the stage that included an accordion, string and wind instruments, and a drum.

Costumes for the Miao look were studied imitations of the ones worn by the official song-and-dance troupes that these young people had seen perform: a skirt in a solid color such as red or pink ringed with a couple of decorative ribbons to designate embroidery, side-fastening tops in

39. A youth performance for Chixinjie.

pastel colors, an occasional sash to punctuate the waist, or an embroidered apron for added flair. The look was significant because it required a special crafting of appearance, not in accordance with the customary rural Miao look, but resembling instead the widely publicized and professionalized *minzu* performers. Other young women simply wore standard festival attire of polyester pants under a Xijiang-style jacket. Unassuming white sneakers were worn by almost everyone. Young men, for the most part, presented themselves in everyday dress. Almost all the performers kept their hair in quotidian style; for men this meant a simple short cut, while for women it meant the regional *jiujiu* topknot, sometimes with an extra adornment or two. Through their attention to costume, youthful contestants neither repudiated their traditions nor perpetuated them; rather, they packaged them in ways that demonstrated the artifice through which they were maintained. Playing the Miao part indicated to them both respect for their ethnic heritage and a forward-looking management of its expression.

The kindergarten groups were a special attraction and sported specially designed costumes. The girls wore crisp white dresses with flashy diagonals of red and black. The boys wore suspendered pants over white shirts and colorful masks or hats that simulated roosters' combs. They sang and danced with ardor in well-oiled routines that school discipline had imparted to them. The audience was delighted.

No ranking was imposed with regard to the indigenous or borrowed nature of the contestants' material. What was important here was that culture was an object of self-conscious display and hence control. The result was a homey replica of professional song and dance routines, a kind of sterile counterpoint to the evening "performances" in which young men and women would actually seek lovers through antiphonal singing. The event amounted to a pageant in which Xijiang Miao could demonstrate to themselves the shape and the viability of their contemporary polyglot culture loosed from its moorings in everyday or ritual life. As emblematized by the spatial polarization into stage and audience, the performance served as a form of containment in which carefully selected elements of culture were arrayed like pinned butterflies for the detailed perusal of spectators who were also local Miao. It was not publicized other than by word of mouth, and it was not directed at any outside audience. To the extent that performances drew upon dominant styles, we may say that it represented a coming to terms with the outside. At the same time, it identified the performers as producers. As members of a putatively backward minority group, commonly portrayed as unselfconscious and tradition-bound, they performed in ways that marked them as active and aware, in charge of defining themselves, dominated neither by their weighty past nor by the subsuming mainstream. Additionally, the sale of tickets and the fact that each performance was compensated with a token prize demonstrated the participants' complicity with the growing logic of marketization in which culture was commodified, broken up into little bits suitable for exchange.

Festival Meets the Academy: Siyueba

By isolating and valorizing "culture" as something produced and consumed, the participants in the youth performance were enacting a particular way of being modern, one in which their ethnic lifeways were compartmentalized, associated with the domain of leisure, and rendered as cherished objects for preservation. These themes were likewise variously dramatized in Miao performances that took place in Beijing. One occasion was Siyueba, the Fourth Moon Eighth Day Festival, dis-

(Above) 40. Festive identities. Miao *lusheng* processional at the Central Nationalities Institute, Beijing. (Left) 41. Entranced by Miao adornment.

cussed in chapter 8, which was held annually by Beijing Miao on the campus of the Central Nationalities Institute. Throughout the Maoist period and beyond, nationalities institutes had functioned as sites for the forging of permissible alteric identities. What students and cadres-in-training learned was to "be ethnic" within the parameters of state cultural policy and the expectations for urban ethnic personae. Orchestrated by Beijing Miao elites, the Siyueba event condensed many of the themes seen in the Xijiang youth performance. The overall effect was the portrayal of hybridized cultural futures for the Miao people, an inclusive vision of modernity that was neither hostile to the incorporation of non-Miao styles nor entirely renunciative of what stood for the Miao past.

Dancing the Past Away

Among the numbers in an afternoon revue of performances of Miao song and dance—intercut with demonstrations of martial arts and of Han and Western music styles—was a solo dance by a young Miao woman. The slender dancer entered the stage dressed conservatively in an urban-style pale-pink shirt and black pants, her hair braided simply down her back. Her movements were graceful, reserved, dignified, her face expressionless. After a few moments, she discovered in a heap some Miao silver jewelry and a flame-red diaphonous skirt in a pattern evocative of the stereotypical Miao pleats. She approached tentatively and began to try on the jewelry. As she adorned herself, her enthusiasm seemed to grow, and she quickly donned the rest of the ornaments and pinned her hair up in characteristic Miao style. She danced with the skirt as prop and then put it on, too. Now her movements became bold, flamboyant, confident. She seemed to have been somehow freed. The tempo picked up. She beamed with an expression of childlike mischievousness. She twirled to make the skirt flare triumphantly. Then, as if pulled by an inexorable force,[11] her movements gradually slowed, and she reluctantly began to shed her ethnic attire. One by one, she removed the Miao articles from her body. When the garments were returned to a heap on the floor and her hair again hung braided down her back, her urbane look was restored and she brought her dance to a close by *fleetingly covering her face with her hands.*

Both the dancer and her dance suggest multiple themes. The dance was created by a young Miao woman whose own life path had taken her out of peasant/ethnic status and placed her in her country's capital as an urbanite drawn to conform to the norms of Beijing's prestigious metropolitan culture. In the case of this dancer, her own past, symbolized by ethnic dress, became the subject of romantic longing, even as it was inevitably renounced. Renunciation, however, did not mean complete eradication, and in this light the dance can be seen as enacting the recuperation of an underground sensibility. The dance encapsulated the tensions generated out of the cultural climate that valorized the color and beauty of non-Han ways, but condemned them as retrograde. It expressed the problematic articulation of the Miao self, a self even more fractionated by urbanity and its pained relation to the rough vitality of the countryside. In contrast to the villagers' performances in Xijiang, the content of the dance was more directly concerned with the tribulations of migrating from Miao rural origins.

When I watched this performance in Beijing, I saw the final gesture — the dancer covering her face with her hands — as an expression of shame, a retrospective condemnation of her momentary transgression. I interpreted it in a postmodern frame, assuming that what the dance dramatized was a structure of feeling characterized by ambivalence in which standards of beauty and contours of identity were unsettlingly shifting and indeterminate. It seemed particularly characteristic of the fragmented nature of crossover subjectivity. But a Miao scholar with whom I later discussed the dance read her message in terms of a more modernist teleology: her final gesture was one of mourning (*beixin, tongku*), expressive of the tragic but inevitable break (*tuoli*) with "traditional culture" entailed by the exigencies of progress. The interpretive disjuncture between my version and that of the Miao scholar highlights that ambiguity, as well as ambivalence, is the stuff of Miao performance culture.

Refracted through the lens of gender, this ambiguity can be seen in the way that the dance both reproduced and ruptured conventional representations of the modernist teleology. Without a doubt, the dance, with its emphasis on the central theme of costume, worked within the paradigm in which minority women were consigned to the position of conservators of tradition through dress. But, because the dancer as a *woman* portrayed herself as moving between the less ethnically marked, urban, more gender-neutral positioning (pants, Western-style shirt, and the single braid down the back reminiscent of the Qing dynasty male queue as well as a ubiquitous women's style during Maoism) and that of the typical colorfully dressed Miao woman, she in effect challenged the prevailing social categories that placed minority women unilaterally in the rural/traditional category. The dance, then, substituted movement and flux for the static attributions of Miao character that were the staple of dominant cultural production. Indeed, the interpretation of the Miao scholar noted above suggested a literal drama of movement metaphorized by the changing of clothing. In his view, the putting on of Miao attire signified the happy return of a college student to serve her country home (*gaoxingde wei jiaxiang fuwu*) as teacher, whereas the shedding of ethnic dress indicated her subsequent — and reluctant — return to the city, which, according to his reading, had been prompted by her parents' concern that her personal advancement would be hampered by remaining in her home village.

A Song of Vanguardism

The conjoining of notions of progress and participation in China's development with ethnic pride and self-promotion was epitomized by a song composed and awkwardly but intently performed by a group of nine Miao graduate students at Siyueba. These students were the most highly educated of the Miao in the most prestigious location in China. And they were all men. Their dress had the Westernized urban look that was the standard for young Beijingers concerned with status — collared shirts and blazers, jeans, athletic sweats, glasses, leather shoes with chunky heels, even a necktie. Their song was written and performed in Mandarin. As the lyrics show, these male students had appointed themselves pioneers in the effort of bringing about Miao modernization and of controlling powerful but unruly tradition. The ambivalence, the sense of being torn between identities that had been the stuff of the dancer's act, was virtually absent as they looked toward the future:

The Vanguard of the Miao People

In the capital of Beijing, there is gathered a group of the finest sons and grandsons of the Miao people,
The development of [our] *minzu* and the task of the four modernizations rests entirely on our shoulders,

Brothers, we must study diligently, unite, and keep active, earnest,
and energetic.
It is our style, brothers, to be intense in our work, to struggle
through adversity, and to advance bravely,
Our traditional way is like the waters of the Yangzi River, surging
tempestuously
To elevate [our] *minzu* to a standing in the world, to advance to a
new era, to advance,
We are the vanguard of the Miao people.

Like the other instances we have seen, what was presented here was
a vision of the Miao future uplifted by modernization but never at the
expense of ethnic loyalty and solidarity. More fundamentally, it was a
vision that refused the script devised for the Miao in more dominant
representations — that of economic stasis and cultural continuity. Gone
was the very fraught oscillation between the charms of home and the
demands of the city that the dancer struggled with. The young men's
self-assurance contrasted sharply with the doubt and hesitation that the
female dancer had expressed. Reading these two performances against
each other once again compels us to closely examine the nuances by
which the gender distinction was recuperated to mark off the contours
of modernity. Although the femaleness of the dancer was not a simple
equivalent to tradition, it was she who had to struggle with its persistence in her life, while the young Beijing men "advanced" as if never
once looking back.

The lyrics of "The Vanguard of the Miao People," were far from
assimilationist. They asserted that movement, transformation, and advance could be consonant with, even critical to, Miao identity. Indeed,
the performance, despite its apparent self-assurance, captured the complex and even contradictory positionings of Miao elites in flux. The
image of the vanguard borrowed from China's revolutionary past, while
the Yangzi River was more a symbol of the Chinese nation as a whole,
having little special significance for the Miao. Meanwhile, their ostensibly unassuming couture located these young men in proximity to the
Westernization that Beijingers so characteristically flaunted. Overall,
it was as if to protest that the Miao, far from simply being backward,
were, like other Chinese, candidates to travel on the unitary road to
"progress" — here meaning higher education and a kind of struggle on

the model of the People's Liberation Army from which some of the slogans in the song were adopted.

In the vision of the vanguards, then, progress was not antithetical to the pursuit of more ethno-nationalist interests. The song resonated with lyrics of other college songs of the 1980s, such as those recorded by Brownell for Beijing athletes: "Facing the world, facing the future,/We give our best in the struggle for national unity./We give our best in the struggle for national dignity" (1995:164). That the Miao version was an ethnic appropriation was subtly conveyed by the polyvalent use of the term "*minzu.*" Appearing twice in the song, it was technically ambiguous whether the term referred to the Miao specifically or to the Chinese people in general. This semiotic slippage had a great deal of political freight, for it undercut the more authoritative version in which only the Han occupied the role of vanguard. A Han intellectual with whom I shared these lyrics was discomfited by this apparent ambiguity, although she acknowledged that the context made it obvious that it was the Miao who were to be promoted. Protesting that she had no prejudice (*qishi*) against the Miao people, she nonetheless held that theirs was an illegitimate use of the term "*minzu,*" which, in the absence of the qualifier *shaoshu* (minority), should have been reserved for all the peoples of China as an aggregate. Her resistance suggests that minority adoption of "*minzu*" for particularistic usages, however commonplace it had become, still had a transgressive charge. Not only did it poach on the language of officialdom, reshaping conventional usages, but it also enunciated a rival nationalism to the one that was to unify China in its collective struggle toward modernization. Although far from a secessionist or even oppositional impulse on the part of the student vocalists, alternate modernizing nationalisms threatened subversion of the order of the unitary Chinese state.

Performing the Future, Complicating the Present

The figure of the vanguard is an apt metaphor for all Miao performers of modernity. From wedding celebrants to stage performers, and many others throughout this book, the common ground for these cultural practitioners was a kneading and refashioning of tradition in order to engage it with a kind of nostalgic retrospective while they moved forward along the modernization trail. Earlier, I described the way in which differences can come to acquire an aura of inexorability through an accumulation of verifying performances. In the instances described here, and in so much of Miao cultural practice, what was rendered as inexorable was precisely the advance toward the modern in its varied and multiple incarnations. Each time a wedding guest commented on a drinking ritual or presented an unconventionally urbane gift, each time tradition was taken up and reprocessed on stage, the players reiterated this trajectory. Likewise, as we have seen again and again, each time a Han urbanite framed Miao women through the gendered lens of the camera, or imbibed Miao customs as pleasured spectators, they temporalized these fragments as holdovers from a fanciful but fading past.

The apparent unity of meanings among Han and Miao performers of modernity emerges as fractured, however, when their different locations in the social order are taken into account. Miao performers, in addition to affirming the value of modernizing, could also be seen as parodying the stigmatized ranking it implied for their people. The shape of the imagined future sketched in the visions of the self-appointed vanguards was one structured by the logics of consumption and spectatorship in which culture was a domain of entertainment. But it also was one of revitalized ethnic strength built on a secure base of education, skills, prosperity, material possession, and other indices of progress in the post-Mao era. By claiming this as their vision, these performers of modernity made the sharpness of the categorical distinctions that equated Miao with backwardness and Han with progress a little more fuzzy. Appropriating the label of vanguard was highly significant here since, of course, the Han, the urban elite, the party member, etc., were characteristically featured as the quintessential vanguards. No monopoly on modern identity was permitted in this field of polysemic performance in which so many Miao made appearances.

Nonetheless, even though Miao performances can be read as mocking their own consignment to the role of rote practitioners of custom while Han urbanites left them behind, they cannot be interpreted as presenting a challenge to hierarchizing orders per se. As we saw with the displacing of subalternity, the social ordering of so many Miao cultural events still entailed framing certain Miao as unreflexive traditionals who needed to be led into the future. Performances of modernity, then, in their various oblique and direct ways, reiterated the system of ranking that was indexed precisely through quantifying the modern. In those instances that were gendered as well, hierarchization became even more naturalized as they rehearsed yet again the alignment of minorities with women and with rural backwardness. Even as class mobility was extolled, the widening spaces of class difference were upheld.

10

Conclusion

Why talk about culture as production? I conclude *Minority Rules* by recounting a tale the likes of which recurred throughout my fieldwork but which so far has remained peripheral to this story.

It was the day of the 1988 Miao Siyueba festival in Beijing. I was at the Central Nationalities Institute on a sojourn from my Xijiang site. Miao colleagues and friends were eager that I join the festivities, especially now that I had become a resident of the Miao countryside instead of just a foreigner.

Siyueba began for me with the arrival to my room of an older Miao woman to help put my hair up in Southeast Guizhou Miao style. She had been recommended by Miao colleagues because she hailed from Xijiang. She combed great quantities of oil and hot water into my hair, darkening it through wetness and giving it a slick sheen. She meshed a long strand of hair that she had brought with her into my own locks to thicken them, then twisted it all into a complicated *jiujiu* knot on the crown of my head and adorned it with roses we had picked from the garden outside. I put on a dressy version of the everyday clothing worn by Miao in the Xijiang region. Atop simple pants, I wore a jacket with embroidered borders and over that an embroidered apron, both of which had been gifts from friends in Xijiang. Fully groomed, I headed over to the school auditorium where the festival was to take place. My arrival was greeted with excited stares from Miao gathered outside. At the door of the as yet empty auditorium, two people in charge asked me whether I was going to perform. I declined and took a seat in the front row, one that positioned me, in keeping with my liminality, between the audience and the dignitaries who filed onto the stage.

The afternoon proceeded with ritual and performances, as described in chapters 8 and 9. Spectatorship and the display of culture in polyglot formats structured the proceedings. As the program wound to a close, the MC took the microphone and stood center stage surveying the darkened audience. It was to be the grande finale, a simulation of the solemn processional danced at Miao New Year in which a cluster of men walked in a circle playing *lushengs* while a long line of women, and some men, followed with understated but highly scripted dance steps. In the Beijing version, repeated at every Miao festival held in the capital city and at every tourist village where the ritual was enacted for visitors, the audience would be invited to join the dancing. But the MC had a surprise: "We have a Western Miao among us!" he exclaimed. Not identifying the referent at first, I confusedly realized that he was beckoning to me, that I was to head up the procession as the first dancer following the *lusheng* players. Awkwardly, I accepted his outstretched hand of solicitation and climbed the stairs to the stage. Summoning up my somatic memories of participating in village festivals, I began a shuffling dance alone behind the musicians. Cameras rushed to train their lenses on this anomalous sight. The next day, friends told me animatedly that they had seen a clip of my dancing on national television.

Nation/Abjection/Struggle

James Clifford has written: "Cultural action, the making and remaking of identities, takes place in the contact zones, along the policed and transgressive intercultural frontiers of nations, peoples and locales. Stasis and purity are asserted—creatively and violently—*against* historical forces of movement and contamination" (1997:7). The material that I have presented in these pages could be read as shot through with contaminations and their corrections. Hmong in the West, or some of them, do not recognize the Miao about whom I write as part of their ethnic group but rather as an amalgam that has subsumed their people. The Ge in Southeast Guizhou likewise resist as a political artifact their categorization under the Miao rubric. A Beijing dancer toys with donning Miao attire, but she ultimately sheds it with reluctant resignation. A Han peasant dresses ethnic as she marries into a Miao family, all the while voicing her cultural homesickness for her hometown. And what in the world was *I* doing dressing up as a Miao as if to disavow my Western whiteness or, for that matter, to join in the romanticizing of Miao cultural purity?[1]

The Miao, then, are in part constituted precisely out of the transgres-

42. Posing as a "Western Miao" with friends in Beijing, 1982.

sions and policings of just that category, as this book has attempted to show. Conversely, those people nominally inhabiting the social space that is referred to as Miao are made — their subjectivities shaped and incited — by the social force of the term. What is critical is that we are talking here not only about repressive force, not only about the patrolling of cultural borders and the imposition of policies from above. The process that makes the Miao is tremendously productive, involving ongoing cultural work, invention, improvisation, admixture — and struggle. It is a process that extends back many centuries.

Attempts at Miao genealogy uncover a deep history of manufacture as an unfixed population was coarsely designated, framed in paintings and texts, chronicled in military accounts of violent rebellions, but left no written records in its own words. In the twentieth century the political valence of the Miao term shifted, as Miao designees were incorporated into a national unit that conferred social existence in exchange for people assuming their assigned role as minorities. At the same time, Miao words and texts acquired a new significance, for they began to speak, to represent and canonize themselves in the discourses of history and ethnology. It was a kind of self-crafting that implicated the Miao directly in the large transitions of the era. Classical frontier/colonial relations gave way to nation forms, routinizing structures more akin to internal colonialism in which minorities were solicitously included while being subject to myriad extractions and modes of governmentality.

The structural relations in which Miao were located had everything to do with the crafting of difference in which Miao and non-Miao were likewise engaged. For earlier dynasties in the Chinese imperium, Miao had marked the edges of civility, even of humanity. That they should be subdued, and that they would evade attempts to do that, was in effect prescribed by the perceived intransigence of their cultural otherness (Sutton n.d.). In the twentieth century an excruciating longing for modernity took hold in China, resituating the central kingdom in relation to other potent national powers that flaunted their wealth and technology in encounters that were often fiercely military. The global positional superiority of the West was never divorced from the struggles around difference within China's borders, for the modern had become a hegemonic value that drove the production of otherness at all scales.

What does it mean to say that the striving for modernity was hegemonic, but at the same time that what it produced was differences?

Conclusion   283

Listen to Stuart Hall: "I have always understood hegemony as *operating through* difference, rather than *overcoming* difference. . . . People imagine that the subordinate groups in a hegemonic formation must be reconstituted in the image of the dominant formation. On the contrary, hegemony is an authority which can be constructed *only* by continuing to recognise difference. . . . Hegemony is the process, never complete, of trying to create some formation out of persistent, contradictory differences which continue therefore to need the work of 'unifying' . . ." (1995:69). The formation that prevailed during the years in which I did fieldwork was one in which the Miao were firmly consolidated as ethnic agents within the Chinese polity. They were slotted as peasants, as irremediably rural peoples whose lands and labors were to bear fruit for the nation. Miao territories held prized resources, and these were to be delivered up to the governing bodies that had provisioned them with an ethnic slot. As the policies of post-Mao years developed, those governing bodies retrenched their social responsibility toward peripheral peasants, instead entrusting that the hegemonic values of modernity and prosperity would drive these people to get "ahead." If they did not, as Hall suggests, their exclusion from affluence became recognized as the distinction that constituted them. Such recognition — or misrecognition — was formulated in cultural terms, and this is a key reason for my attention to cultural production. To the extent that Miao material lives fell outside the triumphant economic miracle purportedly sweeping China, the alibi given for their lack was backwardness (*luohou*), a clinging to customs and an immunity to progressive change. Han urbanites could enjoy their relative affluence and cosmopolitanism with impunity, reassured that tradition was alive in the economic periphery.

In fact, tradition was being vigorously recuperated by Miao cultural practitioners. Indeed, it had become a crucial axis along which Miao, through an intricate politics of local culture, were generating their own highly mobile others. In other words, contests for positional superiority organized not only the minority-Han relationship, but also the intraethnic status struggles that inflected Miao cultural production. Portrayed as caught in the web of valorized tradition and stigmatized backwardness, women and peasants were symbolically assigned subordinate rungs on a myriad of ever-reproduced status ladders. Even Miao peasants trafficked in this version of hierarchy as they romanticized but looked down upon other Miao peasants, those farther from the putative center(s) that structured the spatialized hierarchy. Through their multiple performances of modernity, they ossified its gendered counterpart of backwardness, even as they eschewed association with it. As gender, status, and ethnicity were conflated over and over, a particular vertical arrangement was ratified.

The Feminine Hinge

Gender—the trope of the feminine—becomes a particularly critical hinge in this process. For minorities to be peasantized, mapped as earthbound agriculturalists onto the remoter corners of the rural-urban landscape, was not so inconsistent with the configurations of space and the divisions of labor that had characterized China for centuries. But for minorities to be feminized required a different order of symbolic work. For minorities to be assigned the subordinate role in a dyad essentially defined by a lack of parity entailed invoking the most pervasive signifier of incommensurate difference around—gender—and often activating the potent force of eroticism as well. In turn, for the feminine to be called up again and again where peasant minorities were concerned only reinforced that femininity stood unquestioned as the inferior rank in a vertical social ordering. This bifurcation, in which both woman and non-Han occupied that vacuous, inert domain around an active masculinized center, was inseparable from a discourse of modernity premised on what could be called its abjected counterpart. As Judith Butler explicates the social contours of abjection: "we get a kind of differential production of the human or a differential materialization of the human. And we also get, I think, a *production* of the abject. So, it is not as if the unthinkable, the unlivable, the unintelligible has no discursive life; it *does* have one. It just lives within discourse as the radically uninterrogated and as the shadowy contentless figure for something that is not yet made real . . ." (Butler in Meijer and Prins 1998:281).

Images such as "shadowy" and "contentless" may seem to ill-describe the profusion of colorful cultural production that has filled these pages. The key, however, is that the discursive, almost theatrical, social existence of minorities is consonant with their being boxed into static peasant slots that are unlivable, undifferentiated, uninterrogated; moreover, that rural term inserts itself as the feminine into a national order of hardened differences.

By "national order" I mean two things. First, what is being constructed in the cultural proliferation of the post-Mao period is not only social hierarchy but also national identity. China, through the innumerable practices of its various cultural elites, is being assembled to assume a position alongside other parallel national entities, each with their own managed forms of diversity and each with their role to play in global capitalism. One of China's roles is to sell both its gendered labor and its cultural curiosities cheap on the world market. Conveniently, fostering cultural curiosities is, at the same time, just what appears to consolidate China's defense against the ferocious onslaught of Westernization. Indigenous heritages, whether Han or otherwise, have a double life as inner essences that keep Chineseness intact *and* as increasingly desirable and lucrative commodities.

Second, as I have said, a national order composed of finely graded class and status distinctions, of center-periphery relations of extraction, and of vigorous discursive othering is being actively sustained. Critiques of Western modes of orientalizing continue to risk eliding the practices and struggles that make up cultural/power asymmetries outside the West. I have emphasized this point not to assert that internal colonial or internal orientalist relations are isomorphic with West-East modes of domination. Instead, it is about reckoning with the complexities of the co-implication of China's internal cultural politics and those beyond its borders, and it is about, as Rey Chow has advocated:

> acknowledging that the West's "primitive others" are equally caught up in the generalized atmosphere of unequal power distribution and are actively (re)producing *within themselves* the structure of domination and hierarchy that are as typical of non-European cultural histories as they are of European imperialism . . . we [must] move beyond the seemingly infinite but actually reductive permutations of the two terms—East and West, original and translation. (1995a:194–95)

Invoking "orientalism" in a discussion of othering practices within China is, as I see it, part of the project of what Dipesh Chakrabarty has called "provincializing Europe" (1992:20–23). What may appear initially as a universalizing statement that uses a paradigm developed for Europe as a blueprint for discussion of non-European practices has, in effect, the consequence of decentering Europe as the sole subject of history. The idea of co-implication allows us to better read the complexities of what might otherwise have appeared as an open-ended identity play in which a white Western woman cross-dresses as a Miao and makes it onto national television in China as a curiosity. Much as it might have been broadcast as an anomaly, being dressed up as Miao was a routine part of my fieldwork, and rarely at my initiative. Sometimes it was done privately, in Miao homes where I was a visitor or a guest, for the entertainment of those present; sometimes it was under the voracious gaze of the news-mongering journalist, as organs such as the *People's Daily*, the *Guizhou Daily,* China Central Television, and many, many more captured and transmitted my ethnically made-over image. In most cases I was cheerfully complicit with those who wanted to momentarily transform my visage, for I was convinced that this was part of a kind of identity production that was central, not tangential, to my research.

Why were my cross-dressed images so newsworthy, so desirable, so consumable? I suspect that it was precisely because the structures which constrained Miao and Chinese lives were barely permeable that a chimera of voluntarist boundary-crossing was so compelling. In the 1980s and 1990s, mainland Chinese were ever more confronted with their subaltern positioning in a world still dominated in many ways by the West. Likewise, Miao were reminded again and again that their class/status positioning was on the inferior side of an ever-widening social rift within China. In a climate of modernizing and liberalizing in which, suddenly, the effort to get ahead was no longer condemned as counterrevolutionary, the incontrovertible obstacles to just that effort produced a kind of dissonance that was hard to bear. What was anomalous was that a relatively unhindered white Westerner should apparently elect to transgress racial, national, and ethnic boundaries in a downward direction. What made it intelligible, I suggest, was my femininity: as a woman, my subordinate gender meshed relatively smoothly into the associational network that aligned it with minority and peasant statuses. The image, then, of my ostensible transgression, pleasurable as it may have been, was eminently recuperable into the national order that—relentlessly deploying the female signifier—kept disparities in place.[2]

National Modern

Minority Rules has argued for an analytical reconfiguring of domination in post-Mao Chinese society—and by extension in other societies that have been typed by the West as state-saturated or despotic. An authoritarian state binaristically opposed to an oppositional civil society, apt as it may seem to many Western analysts, is not an adequate framing for the intricate social hierarchy that orders China and that has lineages both in the Maoist and in earlier eras. But understanding the way in which social rank operates within late-twentieth-century China requires placing it within a global order that prizes the modern, however variously that modern may be defined. Marilyn Ivy writes of Japan: "Correlated with the historically located transformations that have accompanied the rise of capitalism and nation-statehood in the twentieth century, modernity implies a structure of consciousness and subjectivity with a peculiar relationship to temporality, one in which continuity (the continuity of "tradition," for example) can never be taken for granted within the upheavals of capitalist commodity relations. Places or origins, displaced, subsist as traces of loss that reinfiltrate modernity's present" (1995:242).

It is such a cultural apparatus of advance, loss, and longing that permeates the state, the nonstate elites, and the populace within China. Its hold on subjectivity can be aptly described as hegemonic, for it is both popularly consented to and also strategically valuable to those who are able to situate themselves over others by invoking it. This coalescent promotion of modernity, and the concomitant exclusion of its denigrated counterparts, indicates a bloc-like alliance between the state and urbane cultural producers. These historical agents are not the only players in the work of fashioning China's social order, but they are the ones who stand to gain the most, both materially and in terms of prestige. None, however, can escape an exquisite sense of loss, for within a modernizing global order national identity is also at stake. Thus arises the plenitude of cultural production that fills these pages and that draws Miao, other minorities, Han elites, and state organs into interlocking systems of identity and difference.

Notes

1 Introduction

1 Fei Hsiao-t'ung (Fei Xiaotong), born in 1910, studied sociology in China, and anthropology under Bronislaw Malinowski at the London School of Economics. With an academic background in rural fieldwork and anthropology, he became affiliated with the Central Nationalities Institute after 1949, where he served as its vice president. During the 1950s Fei was involved in extensive social surveys and classifications of minorities, with a special responsibility for Guizhou province. He fell into political disfavor during the Anti-Rightist Campaign of 1957, but his internationally recognized stature was resurrected in force with the reforms of the 1980s (Arkush 1981; Guldin 1994; McGough 1979). See additional discussions below.

2 "Major Data of the 1990 Census: Population of China's Ethnic Nationalities," *Beijing Review* 33 (52) (December 24–30, 1990): 34. (See Table of Populations, p. 70.)

3 See Michaud (1997) for a recent condensation of the literatures on Miao migrations.

4 Millward (1996:123–24) describes the main features of the internal frontier process as (1) indirect governance by indigenous chiefs, (2) Han sojourning and in-migration, (3) an attempt to maintain cultural and physical boundaries between Han and non-Han groups, and (4) regulation of the dealings between Han migrants and indigenous peoples.

5 For more on Miao and opium, see Geddes (1970, 1976) and Grandstaff (1979). See Kemp (1921) for a firsthand account of poppy cultivation in the Guizhou mountains in the early twentieth century.

6 Dikötter (1992:8–10) holds that this classification had very deep roots in classical texts, and that the binary also referred to whether the peoples in question ate their food cooked or raw. Citing a twelfth-century reference to African slaves, he mobilizes the raw-cooked distinction as evidence of racial thinking in which actual physiological differences were implied:

"They [the Africans] eat raw things. If, in captivity, they are fed on cooked food, after several days they get diarrhoea . . . they sometimes fall ill and die" (1992:9).

7 DeBeauclair (1970:65) reported that the term *"sheng"* was still used in Southeast Guizhou at that time but that it had become more of a subgroup designation than a political classification, a holdover from the eighteenth century when the Miao there were first "subdued." She also found the term *hua wai sheng Miao* used for Miao "outside the range of Chinese civilization" during the Ming dynasty (1368–644).

8 Compare Mullaney (1983) who distinguishes the European late Renaissance sensibility — of wondrous curiosity toward cultural otherness — from the twentieth-century passion for inquiry and systematization, now connoted by the term "ethnography."

9 Military commander Zhu De, then a member of the party politburo, recorded impressions of Guizhou in a notebook as he passed through: "Peasants call selves 'dry men' — sucked dry of everything. . . . Three kinds of salt: white for the rich; brown for the middle classes; black residue for the masses. . . . Poor hovels with black rotting thatch roofs everywhere. . . . People digging rotten rice from ground under landlord's old granary" (Salisbury 1985:108).

10 See Snow (1978:192, 268). The loyalties of certain Miao notwithstanding, Dreyer conjectured that, at the same time, the hostilities which the Red Army encountered in many minority regions were severe enough that the earlier promise of the right to secession came under reconsideration for fear that many might actually exercise it if given a chance (1976:67–72).

11 Anna Tsing's (1993) ethnographic account of the politics of marginality in Indonesia is useful for comparison here; however, her treatment overprivileges spatial margins — what she calls "out-of-the-way" places — when much of what she describes is relevant to political marginality in central spaces as well, as Bhabha shows.

12 This stretches Lancaster's usage somewhat. What he was describing was something often thought of as one element of culture — the system of machismo as it operates in Nicaragua. For Lancaster, what was important was the *system* of relations of inequality between men, women, and children, one that operated by its own internal logic and thereby imperceptibly reproduced itself by virtue of appearing "natural" or "normal" (1992:20).

13 Of course, many different ways to typologize the different senses of culture have been in use over the course of the twentieth century. For a critique by anthropologists of the distinction between culture "Out There" in the Third World and elite "culchah" "Here" in the Eurocenter, see Lavie and Swedenburg (1996), which draws on the discussion in Williams

(1983:87–93). See also Manganaro's (forthcoming) book on the culture concept. Farquhar and Hevia (1993) offer a groundbreaking treatment of the roles that the culture concept has played in American sinological historiography.

14 Note, however, that Tylor's definition, although often credited with being the inauguration of the later anthropological culture concept, did not in Tylor's sense connote the plurality that came with Boas (Stocking 1987:302–3).

15 We also can think here of Renato Rosaldo's modified version of the holistic definition: "Culture . . . refers broadly to the forms through which people make sense of their lives, rather than more narrowly to the opera or art museums. It does not inhabit a set-aside domain, as does, for example, that of politics or economics. . . . Culture encompasses the everyday and the esoteric, the mundane and the elevated, the ridiculous and the sublime. Neither high nor low, culture is all-pervasive" (1989:26). Rosaldo, however, ultimately shifts the emphasis away from undifferentiated totality to account for conflict, inequality, and what he calls "cultural borderlands" where subjects cross cultural boundaries.

16 In fact, a glance at the HRAF description of the Miao of South China, however, reveals such diversity within respective categories of ethnographic description that it belies the very typologizing process which it purports to purvey. Miao, for instance, are mountain swidden farmers, but some are wet-rice cultivators; they are patrilineal in descent, but not always; and "religious behavior reflects the centuries of contact . . . between the Miao and the Chinese, the Tibeto-Burmans, and Tai" (Lebar 1964:66–70).

17 This distinction is taken up by Stuart Hall (1994) as the "culturalist" versus "structuralist" paradigms in cultural studies. He associates the culturalist paradigm with the work of Raymond Williams and to a lesser extent with E. P. Thompson, the structuralist with Lévi-Strauss and Althusser.

18 See Farquhar (1996:250–51) for a lucid contrast between Chinese Communist and Western mass cultural forms.

19 In the interdisciplinary field of cultural studies some key figures who pursue reception studies include Ang (1985, 1991, 1996), Radway (1984, 1988), Fiske (1989a, b, and c), Morley (1980, 1986, 1991), and Willis (1990). Within anthropology — although it has not always gone by the name "reception" study — exciting work has begun to examine how people use media products and meanings in India (Appadurai 1996; Das 1995; Mankekar 1993a, 1993b), China (Rofel 1994; Yang 1997), Egypt (Abu-Lughod 1995, 1997), Trinidad (Miller 1992), the United States. (Ortner 1998), and other sites. See, by contrast, Modleski's (1991) critique of ethnographic reception studies.

20　See, for instance, Fiske (1989a, 1989b), Gilroy (1987, 1993), Ginsburg (1991), Hebdige (1979), McRobbie (1991), Willis (1990).

21　Janice Radway makes a related point in her incisive critique of the tendency of academic readers of texts and audiences to emphasize the speaking moment or the moment of enunciation of the text as starting point. She suggests "we may need to rethink the process of cultural circulation from a new point of view — now not from our point of view as speakers, but from a point of view we share with others in our everywhere-mediated society, the point of view of the active, producing cultural worker who fashions narratives, stories, objects, and practices from myriad bits and pieces of prior cultural productions" (1988:362). I will go further and ask whether it is only "cultural" productions that constitute the bits and pieces, or whether indeed structural work takes place in this process. This is not to imply that "structural work" is necessarily readable as resistance, but to complicate the overdrawn dichotomy between culture as a site of subordinate agency and structure as an exterior mode of determination.

22　My discussion here follows Guillory's excursus on the work of Bourdieu. Guillory maps Bourdieu's concern with capital as distinguishing between a premodern symbolic capital in which "the economy in the narrow sense is 'socially repressed' " (1997:387) and a capitalist market in which honor has been replaced by material goods as the "pre-eminent form of capital" (1997:388). He then outlines a third type (which corresponds to reform-era China) called a mimetic market, one in which "there is no attempt to conceal the mutual convertibility of cultural and material capital; on the contrary, agents are deliberately and even enthusiastically interested in reconstructing cultural spheres as practices of rational accumulation and assured convertibility. This market corresponds to the advancing frontier of commodification . . ." (1997:388). The most useful aspect of this description is its unmasking of the separation between culture and economy as a particular conceit of European society and theory.

23　See useful discussions in Watson (1984).

24　See, however, Anagnost's (1997:40–43) suggestion that Billeter's analysis could have gone further if he had acknowledged the very act of representing notions of class and status "as an instituting moment on which all other functions depend" (1993:42), as well as the importance of such a system of representation in the "context of cold war politics and . . . the coalescence of a national subjectivity that was no less salient for the postrevolutionary period" (1993:41).

25　This is the point that Judith Butler (1990a, 1990b, 1993) has made about gender difference: that it is elaborated from the unexamined binarity of two sexes, which in turn is derived from the presumed naturalness of heterosexual complementarity.

26 This process of subject formation is closely linked by Foucault to the emergence of a certain kind of state: "I don't think that we should consider the 'modern state' as an entity which was developed above individuals, ignoring what they are and even their very existence, but on the contrary as a very sophisticated structure, in which individuals can be integrated, under one condition: that this individuality would be shaped in a new form, and submitted to a set of very specific patterns" (1982:214).

27 This is another instance of what is characterized as the poststructuralist move. Note that Butler eschews a vocabulary of structures in favor of a notion of power that is more fluid, more productive, and more dispersed. This move has been portrayed as an infinite decentering of power such that determination is unimaginable (Hall 1985; Hartsock 1990; Sangren 1995); however, the compulsory character of power in theories of subjection should be clear from this discussion.

28 Likewise, if such a contingency is taken seriously, the possibility also arises that certain forms of individual subjectivity or collective identity may *not* emerge in given historical moments or configurations of power, as Roger Rouse affirms (1995).

29 For more on this process, see Schein (1999).

30 Anthropologists also have applied notions of cultural production to national identity-formation in more ethnographically rooted instances (Fox 1990). Handler's (1988) study of Quebec was similarly processual, focusing on the ways that culture is objectified by both nationalists and social scientists who presume the boundedness, continuity, and homogeneity of the nations that they construct. Brackette Williams's work (1989, 1990, 1991) has been particularly noteworthy for its dynamic treatment of the intertwining of culture with race in the construction of "myths of homogeneity and purity." For Williams, a key effect of nationalist cultural production is that culture becomes racialized, that it acquires a rigid "aura of descent" which permits the exclusion of groups whose divergence from the mainstream causes them to be classed as impure by virtue of inheritance. Such classifications, however, and the hegemonic systems of prestige and dishonor to which they become wed, remain objects of recurrent cultural struggle.

31 The feminine figure in national construction, it should be emphasized, also has signified danger and excess, often appearing as the specter of transgressive or ungovernable sexuality, threatening national integrity through miscegenation or through insufficient domesticity.

32 Anthropologists have begun to investigate in more microethnographic

terms specific incarnations of modernity in particular non-Western sites. Rofel's (1999) account showed how a post-Mao Chinese modernity was pursued and realized in a Chinese factory site rife with its own historical conditionings but also hyperaware of the West as somehow emblematic of the modern. See also Pigg (1996) on Nepal and Mills (1997) on Thailand for other accounts of local modernities. See Ong (1996) on the notion of "alternative modernities" in Asia and *Public Culture* 11 (1) 1999 on "alter/native modernities."

33 See chapter 6 of Schein (1993) for an extended interpretation of how I was perceived and its social significance.

34 Based on figures I was given in 1988, there were 5,862 residents in Xijiang, of whom thirty were Han, five were Dong, and one was Bouyei. Twenty-five of these non-Han were government employees, compared with 411 Miao working for the state. The administrative domain that Xijiang governed—a commune converted into a *qu* (district) by 1988—comprised about seventy villages totaling 26,179 people. Some 92.3 percent of these were Miao, with the remainder primarily more recent Han immigrants clustered in four villages.

2   Of Origins and Ethnonyms

1 See Jensen (1997:22–25) for a lucid defense of the notion of manufacture to describe historical cultural production.

2 For those who would posit the continuity of the Miao back to earliest times, the argument is supplemented by the assertion that during the centuries in which no references were made to the "Miao" per se, they were subsumed under the broad category of Nan Man (南蠻, often translated as "southern barbarians"). Occurrences of other phonetically similar ethnonyms, particularly Mao (variously written 髦, 髳, 毛), are also claimed to be references to the Miao. These inferences are based largely on the assertion of consistency in geographic positionings. This is the approach in the *Brief History*, which depicts a continuous and discrete ethnic group, either coming into conflict or being mistakenly classified together with other such discrete groups. When "Miao" came to have a broader sense during the Ming and Qing periods, the book offers the explanation that the Miao received particular attention from the imperial authorities because of the expanse of lands that they controlled and the extent of their influence; thus, smaller ethnic groups such as the present-day Bouyei, Dong, and Shui were subsumed linguistically in official records while remaining separate culturally (1985:5–6).

Some authors (cf. Ruey 1967:53; Wiens 1954:69) have considered the argument that the terms "Miao," "Mao," and "Man," together with the names by which many Miao refer to themselves, i.e., "Hmong," "Hmu," were all variants of a single ethnonym, confused over history because of their phonetic similarity. Liang Qichao, a late Qing scholar, took this position in contradiction to Zhang Binglin, who held that the present-day Miao were descended from the Mao, a group he thought were entirely distinct from the Miao of ancient records (cited in Ruey 1967:53).

3 As Ruey (1967:50) recounts, over time commentary has differed on the relatedness of the so-called San Miao to the Jiuli; the theory came under question in the Qing Dynasty, but it was then reaffirmed by twentieth-century scholars such as Zhang Binglin and Liang Qichao. Ruey himself concludes that the Jiuli were the ancestors of the present-day Li people of Hainan Island and were unrelated to the contemporary Miao. Wiens (1954:17) assembled sources which suggested that the Miao "constituted an alien ruling group" over the Jiuli.

4 The missionary Samuel Clarke recorded a variant of this tale among the "Hei" (Black Miao) around the turn of the twentieth century. In this version, however, it was only the Miao who traveled southward, determined to move because the Chinese were "too cunning for them." In crossing the wide river, they swallowed a great deal of water and with it all their characters, and they have been without writing ever since (Clarke 1904:198). Significantly, this earlier account does not claim equality for the Miao but reproduces their resignation to an inferior status. It is possibly relevant that the later (1956) version coincided with the heyday of state sponsorship of research on minority languages and cultures and specifically with the development of new scripts for otherwise unwritten dialects.

5 See Tapp (1989) for an extended treatment of the metaphor of sibling rivalry to express contest between ethnic groups.

6 Kinkley also conjectures that the author Shen Congwen, a Han-identified writer who was half-Miao by blood, romanticized the Miao as bearers of a simpler culture and vitality once possessed by the Han as well, seeing the "Miao way [as] that of the Chinese race when it was young" (1987:11). This interpretation suggests a more symbolic sibling relationship in which the trope of youth lends the Miao the distinction of vitality as well as the stigma of immaturity.

7 While the Miao are almost nowhere reported in print to have had a pan-Miao political organization governed by a ruler equivalent to an emperor or a king, Miao lore to that effect is legion. These supreme rulers appear both as mythic and historical figures in the form of Chinese-appointed headmen under the *tusi* system or as leaders of rebellions against the Chinese state (cf. Graham 1978:34, deBeauclair 1970:132). Jamieson, writing

in 1923, spoke of "overlords," referred to as "kings," among the Guangxi Miao (1923:380). Bernatzik (1947:66–71) found Miao in Indochina to have vivid and highly elaborated memories of kingship and chieftainship in former times. Contemporary times reveal ongoing reincarnations. In the 1980s I encountered the convention of referring to the Miao governor of Guizhou as the *"Miao Wang"* (Miao King). Vang Pao, the CIA-backed general who led the Hmong secret army in Laos during the Vietnam War, also has been titled a king of the Hmong people. Tapp (1982, 1989), who analyzed Hmong myths of monarchy in Thailand, regards these claims as a consequence of the felt contradiction on the part of the Hmong and other minorities between (dominant) state and (their own) stateless society.

8 Expanding on Savina, political philosopher Quincy, who has pieced together a popular history of the Hmong at the prompting of those in exile in the United States, stresses phenotypical difference as a key diagnostic, as we saw in the short quotation at the start of this chapter.

9 Cao Cuiyun, personal communication, 1985.

10 This vision of world diaspora from a Chinese center was aptly imaged by a Hmong refugee in the United States who chose to represent the members of his sublineage not as a family tree, but as a descent wheel in which successive generations radiated out from a distant grandfather born in China (Hang 1986).

11 The Yellow Rain controversy raged for several years in the 1980s. Hamilton-Merritt (1980, also 1993:413–60), a journalist, publicized it as a deliberate chemical-biological form of ethnocidal warfare being waged specifically against the Hmong in Laos. Others (Evans 1983) were more skeptical about the politics surrounding the allegations, and Harvard University scientist Meselson and colleagues developed a countertheory to the effect that the material falling from the air and causing people illness was in fact bee feces (Robinson 1987; Seeley 1985).

12 In the late 1800s the missionary Edkins (1870:74) reported the popularity of books of these illustrations in Beijing and Shanghai revealing that "the customs and mode of life of the Miau tsi [*sic*] [were] by the Chinese regarded as very curious and amusing." Some of the Miao albums have been republished by Ruey (1973a, 1973b), and some were translated by Bridgman (1859). David Deal (n.d.), Laura Hostetler (1995), and Norma Diamond (1995) have also conducted studies of the albums.

13 See chapter 7 for further discussion.

14 See chapter 3 for discussion of the classification of dialects.

15 Having resoundingly critiqued the reifying effect of national character studies, the last two decades have brought the practices of fieldwork, colonial representation, and ethnographic writing under close scrutiny within

the anthropological discipline (Asad 1975; Boon 1982; Clifford 1988; Clifford and Marcus 1986; Fabian 1983; Stocking 1983, 1987). Several points about how ethnographic writing can shape selves and cultural others emerge from these works. First, ethnographic reporting risks homogenizing and reifying the culture of the group being studied. Second, proceeding from the assumption of unilinear "progress," many accounts implicitly position the other in an earlier time. Third, these accounts tend to elevate the producer of ethnography to a position of superiority bolstered by global power asymmetries. I raise these points at this juncture in order to stress that the systematically presented modes of ethnography cited here are not exempt from the considerations of authority and representation that are raised elsewhere in this book with regard to Chinese ethnology under Maoism.

16 In addition to the 7.39 million Miao within China's borders, Yang (1993: xvi) compiled the following population figures for Hmong worldwide: 400,000 in North Vietnam (1986), 200,000–300,000 in northern Laos (1991), 80,000 in northern Thailand (1992), 40,000 in Thai refugee camps (1991), several thousand in Burma, 120,000 in the United States (1992), 11,500 in France (1992), 1,500 in French Guyana (1992), 650 in Canada (1989), and 650 in Australia (1992). This yields a worldwide total of considerably more than 8 million; one Miao scholar from China believes the number more likely approximates 10 million because of the "traditions" of Miao/Hmong having large families and routinely underreporting births to the state.

17 "Delayed transfer" refers to a form of marriage in which, in a patrilocal system, the wife only takes up residence in her husband's home months or years after the wedding ceremony has taken place.

18 Simon Cheung, a U.S.-trained Hong Kong scholar, takes issue with Jenks's solidarity thesis on the grounds that instances of overt cooperation do not necessarily rule out ethnic difference, or even strife. Emphasizing that the rebellion ultimately failed, he cites mainland historiographers who pointed to disunity among the insurgents as a chief cause. His argument rests on the assertion of fine-grained ethnic differences in the Southeast Guizhou region — differences that fall out of the picture if the historian relies on the official categories of Qing or Maoist classification. "I suggest that intergroup cooperation among insurgents of diverse ethnic, social, and religious backgrounds, even if it was based on common grievances, might be out of expediency under rational consideration; and that intergroup divisions among them, based either on emotional hostility or on rational competition, might have hindered their cooperation and contributed to their final failure" (Cheung 1996:54).

19 See Catlin (1981) for an ethnomusicological discussion of this skill.

20 The Republican period (1911–49) can be thought of as a transitional era between the more bifurcated imperial vision of a civilized center surrounded by innumerable others and the more hardened and bounded enumeration of a set of "nationalities"—or *minzu*—arrayed in parallel within the nation-state that was instituted in the Maoist period. Simon Cheung's study (1996:70–124) details the discursive struggles of this transitional era, especially the efforts of Miao elites to obtain formal political inclusion. These efforts entailed challenging the description of the Miao as primitives who could be assimilated through sinicization, demanding instead their political recognition as a culturally distinct component of the Chinese polity—another minority alongside the already recognized Mongolians, Tibetans, Manchus, and Muslims. These discursive moves coincided with the arrival of Western anthropology to the Chinese ethnological landscape and with the spread of missionary influence on ethnic designations.

21 On the use of HRAF and other anthropological information for U.S. strategic national interests, see Ford (1970) and Price (1998).

3 Making *Minzu*

1 See also Litzinger (1999) who deploys Althusser (1971) and Butler (1993) to describe the way in which the state's act of naming produced ethnic subjects in China.

2 See Rudelson (1997:34–38) for a comparable analysis of the Xinjiang region in terms of internal colonialism.

3 The other provinces in order of importance were Yunnan, Shaanxi, Gansu, western Henan, western Hubei, and western Hunan (Kirkby and Cannon 1989:9).

4 Based on the Seventh Five Year Plan (1986–90), the coastal region comprises the provinces of Liaoning, Hebei, Shandong, Jiangsu, Zhejiang, Fujian, Guangdong, Guangxi, and the cities of Beijing, Tianjin, and Shanghai. The western region is made up of Xinjiang, Gansu, Ningxia, Shaanxi, Qinghai, Sichuan, Guizhou, Yunnan, and Tibet (Yang 1990:248).

5 See Unger and Xiong (1990) for a fine-grained account of the way that government policies of "betting on the strong" in the awarding of credit and land contracts exacerbated the discrepancy between new prosperity and the majority who were becoming increasingly impoverished. As of mid-1988, the authors concluded that "in almost all aspects of the rural economy . . . some advantaged families, often with government assistance, are gaining near-permanent control over local assets" (1990:8).

6 Guizhou, of course, had garnered other forms of outside attention, espe-

cially earlier in the twentieth century when missionaries worked all over the province and ethnologists such as Ruey Yih-fu and Inez deBeauclair did extensive fieldwork and publishing on the region. What distinguished the post-Mao moment was that dealings with foreigners were far more commodified.

7 De facto, in the 1980s and 1990s the term *minzu* was employed only to designate minorities. It came to connote "ethnic" or "folk," terms that were disavowed by the Han. In popular parlance, then, *minzu*, as an adjective, denoted colorful features of the non-Han, while the qualification *shaoshu* (minority) almost completely dropped out of use.

8 It is difficult to determine what proportion of the trainees and eventual specialists were women, but their widespread inclusion in the project was already significant in and of itself. One of the leaders of the 1950–51 delegations to minority areas, Li Dezhuan, was a woman who chaired the entire south-central team (Moseley 1973:41). See also Guldin (1994), who gives accounts of women in post-1949 Chinese anthropology. My impression from the 1980s was that perhaps one-third of the *minzu* experts I met or heard about were women. By contrast, the 1990s saw an increasingly prevalent assumption that city-based women were incapable of withstanding the rural hardships entailed in minorities work.

9 Note that this was by no means the first time that efforts had been made to collect and record the folk customs of China's peasants. See chapter 4 for a discussion of efforts earlier in the twentieth century.

10 The Minority Nationality History Surveys were a particularly in-depth form of study. The project began in earnest in 1956, although preliminary efforts had been underway since 1950; at its peak, the project involved more than a thousand fieldworkers. Researchers regularly stayed in the field for three years or more, were expected to participate in daily life, and often worked in the respective minority languages. Local histories were taken, artifacts collected, and detailed reports written. Those involved recall the surveys as invaluable for their own teaching as well as for making policy recommendations. For a fuller account, see Guldin (1994:135–42).

11 See the *Miaozu Jianshi* (1985) for a detailed application of stage classification. See Chao (1986) for a critical treatment of its use for several southwest Chinese minorities.

12 Chen Qiguang, personal communication, April 7, 1982.

13 Chen Qiguang, personal communication, April 7, 1982.

14 All were related to the three major self-appellations Qoxiong (western Hunan), Hmu (eastern Guizhou), and Hmong (Sichuan, Guizhou, and Yunnan). See Strecker (1987) for a new comprehensive classification of what he calls "Hmongic" languages based on reform-era linguistic research.

15 See Anderson (1983) and Gellner (1983) for discussions of the ways in which linguistic uniformity spawns national sentiment. Both authors emphasize the rise and circulation of print and other media as critical factors in creating recognition between co-nationals.

16 See chapter 6 for an extended discussion of Yan'an cultural policy.

17 See Wu Zelin (1982).

18 Yau (1989) had found similar themes in what she calls the "National Minorities Genre" of film during the early years of the PRC (1949–65). Particularly resonant with contemporary state cultural productions was the "inflexible presence of a male Han cadre" (1989:120) and the presentation of non-Han women as convenient sites for displaced sexuality (1989:122).

19 Zhang was assigned as my academic adviser during my 1988 field year in Guizhou. Even semiretired, he was a lively and demanding intellectual interlocutor. He had an avid interest in anthropology, and, although we always spoke in Chinese, he had learned a great many technical English terms in the social sciences. He regarded my project with tremendous seriousness, and he went out of his way to advocate for me in terms of research plans and permissions. Early in my stay in Xijiang, he arranged to visit me there — despite the fact that such a trip represented considerable hardship at his age — because he was concerned about the progress of my research. It was with a great sense of regret and loss that I learned of his passing away in 1997.

20 See Rudelson (1997) for an extended treatment of another kind of contestation, that of Uyghur intellectuals acting against the Chinese state, while simultaneously Uyghur peasants and merchants assumed identities as Chinese citizens. For Gladney (1991:7), a rise in ethnonationalism among Hui Muslims in the 1980s was also closely related to the tension between self-perceived identity and state definition. These forms of oppositionality, also more evident in Tibet, diverge in some ways from the forms of contestation around categories that I am discussing here.

21 Interestingly, though the Miao term had been chosen to eliminate bias and to be appropriate for all of the people it referred to, a Western language publication of the time railed against the elimination of the old names (given as Red, Black, Yellow) and criticized the government for undermining pan-Miao unity by promoting linguistic dialect classifications (*China News Analysis* 1958:3).

22 Although in the areas where I conducted research a two-child policy was in effect, as it was in many rural Han areas, it was applied much more leniently than in Han areas and adjusted according to local factors such as population density.

23 See Wu (1989) for a detailed discussion of the "branches" (*zhixi*) of the Miao nationality.

4 Internal Orientalism

1 Qiandongnan, or Southeast Guizhou, was established as an autonomous Miao and Dong prefecture in 1956, based on its dense population of minorities. It comprised fifteen counties and the new city of Kaili, which has grown only since it became the prefecture seat during the Third Line military-industrial buildup. In 1986, Miao were the most populous ethnic group, constituting 37 percent of the prefecture population and a full 60 percent of Kaili's population. The Han made up 32.5 percent of the prefecture population, and the Dong followed at 24 percent. The remaining 6 percent included pockets of Bouyei, Shui, Zhuang, Yao, Yi, and several other nationalities (Qiandongnan 1986:1). For reasons of numbers as well as history, the region has come to be regarded as a locus of Miao identity and determinative of what is considered Miao culture, despite a great deal of variation among subgroups both within the region and scattered over the rest of China (cf. Cheung 1996; Diamond 1995). As a consequence, Qiandongnan is where people look to find the "typical" (*dianxing*) Miao. For a comprehensive study of Qiandongnan's tourism development strategy, see Oakes (1998). See Cheung (1996) for an extended study of ethnic politics in the prefecture.

2 The term *minzu* has several senses when used as an adjective in proper names. When used for such work units as "Nationalities Institutes" (Minzu Xueyuan) or "Nationalities Song and Dance Troupes" (Minzu Gewutuan), it denotes actual participation by members of various nationalities including the Han. By popular connotation, however, it operates as a shorthand for the term *shaoshu minzu* (minority nationalities), and it designates ethnicities other than that of the standard Han. In this case, it may have referred specifically to the fact that the guest house is in a minority area, and thus have been intended to play to tourists' presumed interest in the exotic. The term also may indicate that the construction of the building was at least partially funded by the Nationalities Affairs Commission (*Minzu Shiwu Weiyuanhui*) as an extension of policy designed to develop minority areas. See chapter 3, Crossley (1990) and Harrell (1996) for general discussions of the *minzu* term.

3 See my discussion in Schein (1996b:93-96) for an analysis of the gendering of drinking/hospitality rituals in terms of social hierarchy.

4 See Hind (1984) for a review and critique of literature employing the concept of internal colonialism; for a collection of rigorous case studies, see the special issue on internal colonialism edited by John Stone, *Ethnic and Racial Studies* 2 (3), 1979. See also Hechter (1975). Millward (1996:116-17), discussing the Qing dynasty, classifies the "southwestern highlands" as an "internal frontier" where "Qing military power, Han population

pressure, and opportunities offered by New World food crops encouraged Han farmers to develop or encroach upon lands in macroregional peripheries." Cannon (1989) also uses the notion of the "internal frontier" to describe an ongoing process of colonizing by which territory and resources have been expropriated from minorities who were defined as part of China but branded as inferior and left behind in terms of economic development. As early as 1940, the cultural geographer J. E. Spencer applied "internal colonialism" specifically to China's Guizhou province to describe the complex of features — political/military control and persecution, underdevelopment, and ethnic stratification — that could account for the continued poverty of both the peasant Han and the "tribes-people" there (1940). This usage has been carried forward by more recent critics (Goodman 1983, Oakes 1998). Under state socialism, Gouldner (1977–78) held that the entire Soviet peasantry was subject to internal colonialism in the form of unequal exchange with and cultural discrimination by the urban power center, a position echoed in Bulag's (1998:50) treatment of Mongolia under Soviet rule and in Sulamith Potter's (1983) analysis of the stigmatized position of Chinese peasants in the contemporary era. For non-Han peasants, these conditions especially obtain, ever buttressed by portrayals of their cultural inferiority and remoteness from the center.

5 See Barlow (1991b), whose discussion of the "localization of the sign," drawing on Benita Parry's (1987) critique of colonial discourse theory, strives to refocus inquiry on the strategic appropriation of imported discourses in non-Western contexts so as not to mute the speaking subjects who perform such appropriations.

6 My usage is distinct from another class of revamped "orientalisms" such as Heng and Devan (1992) on "internalized orientalism," Ong (1993) on "petty orientalism," Tang (1993) on "self-orientalization," and Chen (1995) on "occidentalism." These formulations stress the assumption of Western orientalist logics for self-representation in the course of Asian processes of identity production — processes that reinstantiate the East-West configuration in the guise of counterrepresentation.

7 What Harrell (1995a) describes as the "civilizing project" undertaken by the People's Republic since 1949 has deployed regulatory techniques that resonate with the disciplinary practices that Mitchell (1988), in his analysis of the colonization of Egypt, considered hallmarks of the Western "power to colonise." For Mitchell (1988), these methods of control included the creation of armies, the commodification of labor, the rebuilding of towns and villages to be orderly and hygienic, the disciplining of bodies, and above all the introduction of compulsory schooling. In China, during the collective period, the most apparent analogue was the meticulous organization of production and the quantification of agricultural

labor (see Potter and Potter [1990] for a detailed account of commune functioning and Rofel [1999] for an urban factory case). Education in a standard Chinese curriculum and promulgation of norms of hygiene were other ubiquitous measures. The Miao section of a 1981 compendium on minorities boasts of a Miao mountain village that became a model of hygiene under a "campaign of patriotism and sanitation" in which "all cattle and pigs were given pens, all houses were given privies, all wells were covered and sealed, there were regular clean-ups and work attendance was over ninety-five percent"; it concludes: "One after another, new Miao villages are emerging that are clean, healthy, and literate" (Zhongguo 1981:457). In the 1980s the birth planning policy entailed heightened surveillance and supervision of women's bodies. A further refinement in the form of the Civilized Village (*Wenming Cun*) campaign inculcated specific protocols of proper behavior and pushed for the eradication of practices condemned as "feudal superstition" (*fengjian mixin*) (see Anagnost 1994, 1990). Historically, as well as in the present, civilizing has entailed incorporation into a centralized system of rule and the bestowing of "culture" (*wenhua*), in the sense of education, particularly Chinese literacy. For the Communist Party, the project also involved socioeconomic development, not only to improve the living standards of minorities, but also to bring them into the putatively most advanced stage of human history, a stage held to have already been obtained by the Han—that of socialism.

8   Even in his 1985 "Orientalism Reconsidered," in which he makes a strong pitch for the recuperation of subaltern voices in a more decentered discursive present, Said continues to emphasize the silencing power of the orientalist production that was the subject of his original treatise. See Bhabha (1983) for a critique and nuancing of Said's unilateral paradigm. See Carrier (1992) for "occidentalist" counterrepresentation.

9   See, for instance, Murray who asserts that, in Martinique, "homosexuality is crucial for the maintenance of state cultural authority and the popular ethic of hypermasculinity" (1996:252).

10   A related sense of physical difference between those of the "civilized centre" and those of the "barbarian periphery" was to strongly inform the sense of loyalty to a territorial "central kingdom" (*zhongguo*) that developed in response to aggression from the Khitan and Jurchen peoples during the Song dynasty (960–1279). It is in this period that Trauzettel (1975) and Tillman (1979) identify the emergence of the first Chinese nationalist feelings.

11   This usage is suggested by Hevia (1995:120–21), who would dispense with the "barbarian" translation in his analysis of Qing guest ritual.

12   See Gasster (1969:65–105) for an extensive discussion of the anti-Manchu

thought of Sun Yat-sen and his contemporaries. Additional treatment of Sun's Han nationalism and its relevance to non-Han peoples within China may be found in Gladney (1991:81–87). For a synopsis of Nationalist historiography of the period and its contradictions, see Wakeman (1975:225–28).

13 At this point, the ancient dichotomy between "inner" (*nei*) as civilized (*wen*) and "outer" (*wai*) as barbaric (*ye*) (cf. Wiens 1969:2–3) had to give way to the subtler bifurcation of "inside barbarians" (*neiyi*) versus "outside barbarians" (*waiyi*), the latter of which, according to Dikötter (1992: x), included Westerners and Africans who were distinguished by their striking phenotypical discontinuity with the Han.

14 The phrase translates roughly as "Chinese learning for substance, Western learning for practical application." See Wakeman (1991) for an account of the subsequent emergence of the National Essence (*Guocui*) movement in 1903 and its development into a quest to discover and define Chinese "national character." Liu (1995:242–45) shows that the very concept of national essence was itself a co-authored product of Western orientalists and Chinese scholars.

15 On the periphery of Sun Yat-sen's Revolutionary Alliance, there were voices of cultural conservatism, especially that of Zhang Binglin, who advocated overthrow of the Manchus for the purpose of restoring the integrity of Han culture. Reviving texts from seventeenth-century Ming loyalists like Wang Fuzhi, Zhang espoused a kind of "racial nationalism" which held that a fundamental distinction existed between Han and Manchu, manifested in cultural differences, and that the flowering of superior Han civilization had been thwarted during the centuries of Qing rule. China's hope, then, lay not in cultural overhaul, but in a return to the Han heritage (see Grieder 1981:172–80; Levenson 1958:96–97; Wakeman 1975:240–41).

16 My concept of "Han nationalism" overlaps to a degree with what has been called "culturalism" by Levenson (1958:95–108) and other scholars concerned with issues of Chinese identity. But whereas culturalism emphasizes commitment only to the purity, integrity, and centripetal tendencies of "Chinese culture," Han nationalism suggests a more political and relational ideology, a concern with ethnic boundaries and the control of state power even before the advent of a "modern" nationalism that sought to situate China in a world of nation-states. Han and Chinese nationalisms are best thought of as variants of one ideology, each achieving salience at different moments in history, depending on whether the particular challenge was territorially internal or external. My thanks to Ethan Goldings for suggesting this clarification. For a discussion of the concept of Chinese culturalism and a critique of the argument that it preceded and gave

way to nationalism, see Townsend (1992). Duara (1995:56–61) also takes up the problematic of culturalism.

17 See also Schwarcz (1991) for further discussion of Gu's brand of conservatism.

18 Phrases such as this one, which construct colorful culture as a resource to be prized by the nation, commonly pepper contemporary publications on minority customs. A 1987 book on Guizhou ethnic festivals makes four such statements in the first two introductory pages: "Guizhou's traditional ethnic arts are a great treasure-house (*baoku*) waiting to be exploited (*kaifa*);" "Guizhou is a treasure-land (*baodi*) of our great fatherland which is in the process of development (*kaifa*);" "the human landscape (*renwen jingguan*) is an important aspect of Guizhou's cultural treasure-house and of its tourism resources (*luyou ziyuan*);" and "[ethnic festivals] constitute a component of this cultural treasure-house" (Zhang et al. 1987). Interestingly, this particular work issues from the provincial center rather than the national one; it thus exemplifies not an appropriating discourse, but what Williams (1990:116, 1991:131–47) calls a discourse of "contribution," in which Guizhou cultural producers market their province as a gem to be desired and consumed by the nation and by the international tourist, in turn raising revenues for the nation and winning Guizhou a place of prestige in a hierarchized cultural economy.

19 As late as 1933, Beijing's Qinghua University was the only academic institution with a formal department of sociology and anthropology (Arkush 1981:37). The American-run Lingnan University in Guangzhou also hosted many foreign instructors in the social sciences (Guldin 1987:761). Among the most influential foreigners to lecture in Beijing were the University of Chicago sociologist Robert Park, British social anthropologist A. R. Radcliffe-Brown, and the Russian Sergei Shirokogoroff; the works of Franz Boas, Robert Lowie, and Alfred Kroeber also were widely read (Guldin 1988:8). Other visiting scholars included Davidson Black, Johann Anderson, Eliot Smith, C. G. Seligman, Richard Henry Tawney, Wilhelm Schmidt, Karl Wittfogel, Leslie White, B. W. Aginsky, and Reo Fortune (Wong 1979:20).

20 The term "natural village" (*ziran cun*) is used by way of contrast with "administrative village" (*xingzheng cun*) and refers to distinct villages as they are perceived by local people independent of government administrative designations. In the Miao areas of Southeast Guizhou, natural villages are usually separated from each other by space and by norms of exogamy; administrative villages, which are the reform-era replacement of the former commune brigades, comprise several of these smaller units.

21 Reasons I was given for Xijiang's remaining closed were (1) its continued poverty, (2) the unreliability of transportation and difficulty of access,

(3) its lack of infrastructure for foreign tourist reception, and (4) the lack of training on the part of Xijiangers in hosting tourists.

22 Outposts of the Ministry of Culture, the culture stations were the lowest in a bureaucratic hierarchy with offices in Beijing, provincial capitals, prefecture seats, county seats, and hub towns such as Xijiang (cf. Grant 1995 on Soviet culture bases). The center itself served a multitude of purposes, offering a community room that housed a lending library of games and comic book reading on market day, maintaining a display case outside with revolving exhibits of magazine pages and local art, conducting ideological campaigns among peasants, and sponsoring recreational events such as basketball tournaments, performances, dances, films, and other leisure activities. In Xijiang, Zhou also was responsible for facilitating the activities of outside visitors, especially helping them obtain access to local "culture."

23 Lewis Henry Morgan's *Ancient Society* (1877) and Friedrich Engels's *Origin of the Family, Private Property, and the State* (1972 [1884]), disseminated through Chinese nationality policy, had molded popular perceptions of minorities in terms of the fixity of evolutionist stages. For more detailed discussion of the importing of these approaches and their contemporary applications in China, see chapter 3 and Gladney (1991:66–96), Guldin (1987, 1992), Harrell (1991), Litzinger (1995), McKhann (1995). For a critical discussion of such temporalizing moves in anthropology, see Fabian (1983).

24 Not all tourists to Guizhou were seeking ethnic attractions. Spectacular scenery was also a big draw, especially the much-touted Huangguoshu waterfall in western Guizhou. Chinese visitors to Guizhou, whether of domestic or overseas origin, tended to be primarily interested in scenic attractions, while Westerners and Japanese favored remote ethnic villages and primitive customs (Oakes 1995a:254). See Blum (1992:269–70) on relative disinterest in minorities on the part of some Han Chinese.

25 I use the singular "she" here and throughout to evoke the unitary and homogeneous character imputed to minority women through the standardizing of representations of them.

26 Historically, so strong was the association of the non-Han with the non-human, that the radical component of the characters used to designate groups was in many cases that of a dog (犭) or an insect (虫). Miao was then written as follows (犭苗, 蟊). Only in the twentieth century were the characters revised to omit these indignities.

27 I am indebted to Ann Anagnost for pointing out that the furrowed faces of elderly minorities, both male and female, were also common subjects of representation, and that this may have been an artifact of the Maoist glorification of labor as literally engraved on the body.

28 In addition to the local young women, the filmmakers were eager to have me join them on the hike. Indeed, despite the apparent strangeness of the scenario, they often encouraged me to enter their camera frames. This was consonant with the tremendous desire that I encountered throughout my fieldwork for the production of representations of the white Western woman (Schein 1993, chap. 6).

29 Alloula, in his treatment of the ways in which the postcards intimated the orientalist fantasy of the harem, saw the elaborate over-bedecking of the female models as metonymically related to erotic overindulgence: "Bedecked in this manner, decorated so to speak, these Algerian women in full regalia . . . are ecstatic icons, passively submitting to their cosmetic makeover, readied for the *other scene,* for a feast of the phantasm, whose secret is known only to the photographer. The model and what she signifies (the Algerian woman) are effaced to become no more than the purport of a *carnivalesque orgy*" (1986:62).

5 Reconfiguring the Dominant

1 Probably the festival that most regularly emblematizes Xishuangbanna, and the one to which most tourists flock, is the Water-Splashing Festival (Poshui Jie) of the Dai. Image after image of Xishuangbanna displays young women in sarongs with basins or buckets of water, splashing each other and getting soaked.

2 While Chen did not identify it, he was commenting on the moment, touched on earlier, in which Chinese intellectuals were caught up with the "*Xungen*" or Roots-Seeking Movement. Zhang Xudong describes this as a moment of aesthetic modernism in which cultural producers "tried to stretch their subject matter into a cultural anthropological rediscovery of the Chinese language and way of life through an aesthetic incorporation of the global. This maneuver reveals its politics in transcending the immediate cultural order rooted in the past experience of the Chinese revolution and Chinese modernity" (1997:140). Reaching beyond the recent history of revolution, in other words, Chinese literati were questing to construct a postrevolutionary utopia that was both essentially Chinese in its folk forms and unequivocally cosmopolitan in its deployment of them. See also Jing Wang (1996).

3 Indeed, Chen's performative display of state authority raises questions about the character of the state itself. If Chen impersonated a state official and was received in that way, could we say that the state, or its prestige and clout, operated as symbolic capital wielded in social situations to secure status? What does it tell us about the boundaries of the state

when a person who regards himself as oppositional in spirit to state control also presents himself as a state agent? See Anagnost (1985, 1997) for provocative discussions of high-profile impersonations in the reform era.

4 Eric Wolf, for instance, states: "It has long been customary in the West to counterpose Western freedom with Eastern despotism, whether this was done by Herodotus with reference to the Greek city-states in their struggles with Persia, or by Montaigne and Voltaire counterposing societies based on the social contract with societies characterized by multitudes groveling under despotic rule" (1982:81). Wolf's study *Europe and the People Without History* (1982) attempts to correct this dichotomization; following Samir Amin (1976:45), he groups so-called Eastern modes together with Western feudal modes under the rubric of the "tributary mode of production."

5 For an excellent genealogy of these concepts, see Perry Anderson's chapter, "Asiatic Mode of Production," in *Lineages of the Absolutist State* (1975: 462–549). Anderson traces the notion of oriental despotism through Aristotle, Montesquieu, Adam Smith, Hegel, and others, and he discusses at length the "Asiatic Mode" in the work of Marx.

6 The notion of "civil society" traces to such social thinkers as Hegel, Adam Ferguson, and, much later, Antonio Gramsci. See Shils (1991) for a genealogy of its earliest usages. Shils (1991:3–6) also associates the elaboration of an autonomous and market-based civil society with Adam Smith and Karl Marx, and of a certain code of civility in public conduct with Montesquieu; none of these are credited with developing the concept by name. More recent discussions from a range of perspectives can be found in Keane (1988), Taylor (1990), and Chatterjee (1990). The Gramscian development of the concept (see Gramsci 1971; Hall 1996) will be addressed later in this chapter.

7 For extended discussions of the notion of the public sphere and its current applicability, see Calhoun (1992) and Robbins (1993). Mayfair Yang's (1999) volume represents some of the most recent applications of the concept to contemporary China.

8 Multiple meanings of private, of course, are linked to how the public is conceived; moreover, the lines between the two are constantly shifting (Robbins 1993:xv). Thompson distinguishes two basic senses of public/private that have been current in the West since the Middle Ages. The first had to do with the distinction between institutionalized political power in the hands of the state (public) versus the domains of economic, familial, and personal activity that fell outside it (private). The second was a dichotomy that had more to do with visibility: "What is public, in this sense, is what is visible or observable, what is performed in front of spectators, what is open for all or many to see or hear or hear about. What

is private, by contrast, is what is hidden from view, what is said or done in privacy or secrecy or among a restricted circle of people" (Thompson 1995:123). This second sense of private coincides with the feminist reading of the private as the domestic and familial space to which women so often have been restricted. For more on the meanings of public/private, see Habermas (1989, chapter 1), Landes (1995), and Robbins (1993).

9 Obviously, Fraser is here extending Habermas's focus to contemporary Western societies; hence, the emphasis on white supremacy. In non-Western contexts, the practices of exclusion through which the public sphere is formulated and effectively policed might attach to different dominant social groups, such as the Han in China.

10 For examples of this type of discourse, see the articles by Rupnik, Szucs, Vajda, and Pelczynski in Keane (1988).

11 Most notable among these studies are Rowe (1989), Rankin (1986, 1990), and Strand (1989). See also Duara's more recent discussion of this historiography (1995:147–75). For overview assessments of the issue of whether China ever evidenced civil society or a public sphere, see Huang (1991), Rowe (1990), and Wakeman (1993). See also Perry (1994) for a more general survey of the problematics of state and society relations in China.

12 Farquhar and Hevia suggest a sobering answer to this question, one with which I am in considerable sympathy: "Concern with the 'public sphere' has, it seems, returned a China-centered history to the discovery of a single trajectory of modernization, posited, miraculously, as empirically present in history. What motivates efforts to pick out the trembling origins of civil society in treaty ports, self-governing societies, or tea houses?" (1993:500).

13 Duara has employed this approach in an iconoclastic rewriting of the history of the notion of civil society in the Chinese context — and in the interpretation of its purported decline or absence in the twentieth century. To the historiography on civil society and public sphere in the late Qing dynasty that documented a thickening associational life, the expansion of economic networks, and the growth of popular print, Duara adds a discussion of the discursive functions of the notion of *fengjian* or "feudal." This discourse, sanctioned by Confucianism, was propagated by reformist literati "as a critique of imperial power's encroachment upon the locality and community" (1995:153) and called for a more localized and autonomous form of governance that involved local elites and public opinion in decision-making. The narrative of *fengjian* was part, Duara argues, of a hybrid discourse in which this indigenous strand was entwined with the exogenous Enlightenment narrative of history such that feudalism appeared as a historical stage in the evolution toward an ever more popular sovereignty. Ultimately, however, societal initiatives were to be

limited by still another global discourse—that of the modern nation-state, which came "in the early twentieth century to sanction the precedence of state over society and led to the demise of the effort to mobilize civil society toward the creation of a modern nation" (Duara 1995:159). That the global nation-state system demanded of China that it recuperate a strong state and dispense with its indigenous movement toward more societal autonomy presents an eminently convincing case for the historically deep imbrication of China's social forms with global discourses and geopolitics.

14 Compare Heng and Devan's (1992) analysis, in a powerful reading of Singapore's state discourses, which found that a recent selective appropriation of Confucianism as antidote to the (now) contaminating West likewise advanced the homology between family and state in ways that legitimated governmental authority. Heng and Devan proposed the term "internalized orientalism" to describe the careful and rationalistic crafting, by a largely Western-educated political elite, of an idealized "Chineseness" consonant with a modern market economy and a patriarchal order that the authors called "state fatherhood."

15 On the institutional specifics of the production of sexually charged material at a slightly later date, see Schell (1994) and Zha (1994). Brownell (1995:265-77) has analyzed the rise of bodybuilding in relation to gender dynamics and "obscene bodies."

16 Reproductions of the mural can be seen in Cohen (1987).

17 That the fantasy of participation was never entirely displaced, however, became clear in the 1990s with the rise of a thriving ethnic sex industry sited in none other than Xishuangbanna. So lucrative was the trade that Han women from other provinces routinely donned sarongs to make a fast yuan off johns with exotic appetites (see Hyde forthcoming).

18 My account here is condensed from several versions including *Beijing Review* (1989), Gladney (1994a), and Mackerras (1995).

19 See Pollock (1987) for a discussion of the significations of the female body in Western art and advertising. Pollock argues that the desirability of an object for purchase in Western commodity culture is suggested simply by the co-presence of a woman, in most cases partially clad. See Notar (1994) for an analysis of images of women in early 1990s Chinese television advertising. Notar found not only a preponderance of young women, but that motifs of sexiness and domesticity coexisted.

20 This wooden box was replacing another kind of receptacle, the *luokuang*, a gigantic basket used in a similar way.

21 For extended discussions of the relation between media and the notion of the public sphere, see Garnham (1992), Habermas (1989:159-75, 181-211), Thompson (1995), and Warner (1993).

6 Songs for Sale

1 Other treatments of representations of minorities in centers of state over the course of Chinese history have interpreted them less favorably than did Luo (see chapters 4 and 5). In analyzing the function of "tribute illustrations"—paintings of peoples who paid tribute to the throne—in the Qing dynasty, Hostetler asserts: "Compiling representations of peoples that participated in the tribute system was a means of recording their politically subordinate position" (1995:182). This perspective could most certainly be applied to Luo's presentation of culture to Chinese leaders, but instead, she regarded it as a kind of honor unprecedented in Miao relations with China. See Hevia (1995) for an extended rethinking of the tribute process and of the problem of "representation" of others in the Chinese imperial center.

2 David Wu (1993) also has written on the topic of professional ethnic performance in Beijing. His account presents performers as hapless tools of a state bent on distorting preexisting cultural forms. My account is intended to demonstrate that a more complex subjectivity among ethnic performers and a less dichotomized relation between state cultural policy and minority cultural production prevailed in this professionalized domain.

3 This is not to dismiss issues of autonomy for cultural producers in the Maoist era. Certainly, a considerable intellectual elite experienced *"xuanchuan"* policy as a pernicious control on their artistic expression. What I draw attention to here is the fact that this intellectual elite is far from coextensive with the body of cultural producers that should be considered in such contexts.

4 See Connor (1984:202) for a discussion of the history of this program.

5 Just as it has been heavily visited by tourists, so Shang Langde has been extensively studied. Other accounts can be found in Oakes (1998:193-204) and Cheung (1996:124-29); Cheung describes the dynamics of a visit of Miao elites and Hmong refugees from abroad in the course of a Miao studies conference.

6 The following list gives a sense of the magnitude of this demand. Specific work units ordering *lushengs* included at the level of Guizhou counties, districts, and prefectures: the Huangping County Cultural Center, the Taijiang County Federation of Trade Unions, the Zunyi District, the Bureau of Broadcasting and Television of the Huaxi District of Guiyang, the Nationalities Affairs Commission of the Southeast Guizhou Prefecture, the Song and Dance Troupe of the Southeast Guizhou Prefecture, the Communist Youth League of the Southeast Guizhou Prefecture, and the Song and Dance Troupe of the Southwest Guizhou Prefecture. At

the provincial level these units included the Guizhou Nationalities Affairs Commission, the Guizhou Nationalities Song and Dance Troupe, the Guizhou Foreign Affairs Office, and the Guizhou Group for the Collection of Historical Relics. Beyond the province, instruments were ordered by the Rongshui Autonomous County in Guangxi and the Southwest Nationalities Institute. Orders also were received from musicians in the counties of Kaili, Leishan, Rongjiang, Jianhe, Taijiang, Sandu, and Huangping.

7 A more extended discussion of these types of disjunctures can be found in Schein (1996b).

8 Comments are from his seminar at Rutgers University Center for the Critical Analysis of Contemporary Culture, January 28, 1998.

9 See Schein (1994).

7 Scribes, Sartorial Acts, and the State

1 It may be that Zhou hoped to earn "publishing fees" by submitting the folktales to a research journal. During that era and into the 1990s there was a rush to produce publishable ethnological materials since publishing offered one of the few opportunities, short of starting an enterprise on the side, for intellectuals to supplement their income.

2 A sample of some titles gives a sense of the explosion of publications after the liberalization of policies. Since 1979, just on Miao folklore, I collected the following volumes: *Miaozu Minjian Gushi Ji* (A Collection of Miao Folk Tales), Yunnan Nationalities Press, 1988; *Miaozu Shishi* (Miao Epic Poems), Central Folk Literature and Art Press, 1983; *Miaozu Wenxue Shi* (History of Miao Literature), Guizhou People's Publishing House, 1981; *Miaozu Minjian Gushi Xuan* (Anthology of Miao Folk Tales), Shanghai Literature and Art Press, 1981; *Miaozu Guge* (Miao Ancient Songs), Guizhou People's Publishing House, 1979; *Miaozu Minjian Gushi Ji* (A Collection of Miao Folk Tales, 2 vols.), n.d. In addition, Miao folklore appears in numerous collections of Guizhou, Yunnan, and Chinese minority folklore. Several volumes concerning Miao history and language have also come out. A spate of periodicals such as *Minjian Wenxue Luntan* (Folk Literature Forum), *Shan Cha — Minzu Wenxue Jikan* (Mountain Tea — A Folk Literature Quarterly), and *Guizhou Minzu Yanjiu* (Guizhou Nationalities Research) also carried articles on folklore and folklife.

3 When Miao script was used for publications, it usually appeared in tandem with Chinese characters. Publications exclusively using Miao script were rare. I saw the bilingual format in small local newsletters, in text-

books for primary school education, and in recent major folklore collections (cf. Guizhou Sheng 1991; Yang 1991).

4 Significantly, the term *guji* usually refers to textual materials, literally meaning ancient books that have been passed down over time. Since the author was referring here to courtship songs, we can only surmise that he might have been attempting to dignify this improvised, oral tradition with a textual connotation.

5 Both the bridge, associated with fertility, and the dyed eggs, associated with children, suggest that this may have been what the elderly cadre, in his handwritten account of Xijiang's customary rituals, called "Bao Tong Shou Ri" (Day of Protecting the Lives of Children). This annual event, according to his description, involved offerings to trees, bridges, and stones in the hopes of children growing swiftly without illness. Dyed eggs also were prepared specially for the children to eat. The Lu clan Jing Qiao, however, was on a larger scale, and I was told that it was only done this way every thirteen years.

6 The politics of such a hearty revival — one that was taking place among both Han and minorities — have been subjected to much interpretation in Western scholarship. David Wu (1990), for instance, writing about the Bai nationality in Yunnan, suggested that the post-Mao ethnic resurgence was a form of compliant political participation, a manipulation of ethnic identity actually triggered by shifts in state policies that offered political and material rewards to minorities. Gladney (1991) argued for a more dialectical model in his consideration of Hui ethnic nationalism, seeing state policy as critical in molding the Hui *minzu*, but asserting that this process was accompanied by a more bottom-up attempt in Hui communities to preserve their own ethnic integrity. Both these approaches propose that revivals comprised responses to state policy shifts. Rudelson, writing a half-dozen years later (1997), saw Uyghur cultural recuperations as imbricated in nationalist politics among Uyghur subgroups jockeying for national hegemony vis-à-vis other groups as well as the Chinese state. Bulag (1998) went further, suggesting that Mongol cultural revival was inspired by a mode of thinking based on notions of purity derived from the rise of modern Chinese nationalism.

At a more local level, Potter and Potter (1990:337), interpreting the return of ritual in Guangdong Han areas, made the materialist argument that it was the renewed post-reform importance of the household and village economic base and social structures that inspired their symbolic expression on the ritual plane. Rituals cemented relations with relatives that were of renewed importance under household production responsibility; larger-scale events like dragon boat races expressed village solidarity and lineage competition (1990:258–59). In contrast to the emphasis on reinstatement of socioeconomic structures through ritual, Siu (1989) suggested that, for Han in the Pearl River Delta, original meanings having to do with the consolidation of new social networks, the identity crises of youth, and the pleasure of secular spectacle were being infused into "recycled" ritual practices. Likewise, Anagnost (1990), taking her data from Han activity in the Fujian area, found the return of ritual to be a virtual metaphor for the struggle over the state's appropriation of the signifying function of "the people." In her notion of ritual displacement she interpreted contestation over ritual spaces such as ancestral halls as enactments of local people's efforts at decolonization—as refiguring the particularity of the local in opposition to the totalizing power of the state voice.

    While analysts have differed over the resistive character of revival, perhaps the one who has gone furthest is Litzinger (1999), who argues that the resurgence of ritual and "tradition" among the Yao minority in the post-Mao context stages conversations about the appropriate relationship between the state and local people. Yao culture becomes a zone in which the potential compatibility of party and local ideals is enacted, while tradition and modernity embody multiple and reformulated meanings over time and across reconstituted divides of ethnic difference.

7 See Anagnost for further discussion of how the party defined itself in part through the "oppositional category" of "feudal superstition" and how this, in turn, created "the potential to express counterhegemonic sentiments" (1994:224). Duara (1995:86–113) gives a historical account of the campaigns spanning the twentieth century in which the Chinese state sought modernity through eradication of popular religion.

8 A distinct form of hybrids that had proliferated in Xijiang since Maoist days were rituals initiated by the state that marked particular institutional, technical, or productive transactions. In 1988, I attended formalized inspection tours of irrigation canals and waterways, expeditions with a tea-planting advisory team from the city, an inauguration ceremony for a newly constructed hydroelectric power plant in a nearby river, an evaluative inspection tour of primary school education, the founding of a senior citizens' center to serve Xijiang's elderly, etc. Each episode was accompanied by a standardized component of feasting, speechmaking, and toasting, usually in a manner which merged more communal and network-oriented reciprocal exchanges that stood as a hallmark of Miao sociality with processes by which relations of authority were enacted (positioning local cadres vis-à-vis villagers in terms of prestige and vis-à-vis senior government officials or technical advisers in terms of deference). Each evinced a tension over hierarchy, as a universalistic state for-

mat was domesticated through Miao villagers' practices such that local contestations over and of particular ranked relationships became part of its content.

9 See Schein (1989) for an extended comparison of Zhao Long with the commodified Shidong Dragon Boat Festival.

10 See chapter 4 for an explanation of natural village units. Other than the occasional residual importance of the *"dadui"* (brigade), which had been grafted onto the natural village during the collective years, this was one of the few times when I saw the importance of this social-organizational unit communally affirmed.

11 A *jin* is equivalent to half a kilogram.

12 In some ceremonies, the space around the tree had been staked out with paper cutouts of children placed on sticks, incense and money paper had been burned, and liquor had been sprinkled around the spot, marking the trees themselves as worthy of honor. In other ceremonies the same bamboo branch had been stuck in the earth on a mountain crest above the village.

13 See Leepreecha (1998) for a comparable analysis of a tree-conserving ritual among Hmong of Thailand.

8 Displacing Subalternity

1 This followed upon the transfer of an influential senior Miao scholar from his post as professor at the Central Nationalities Institute in Beijing to take over the position of president of the Guizhou Nationalities Institute. His move was significant in terms of cultural conservation and nostalgia because it was motivated, according to him, by a desire to be closer to his childhood roots and to do more in-depth field research in the Miao countryside. It was this nativist impulse that made him willing to go against the grain of current preferences, which favored movement "up" in the spatial hierarchy that ranked Chinese places. One of his first initiatives upon his return had been the establishment of the provincial Miao Studies Association. Gregory Guldin (1991:19) recorded the founding or revival of a great many such academic societies in the post-1978 period. These societies are usually connected with a particular academic *danwei* and are independent from central supervision by the Nationalities Affairs Commission or the State Education Commission. See Litzinger (1998) for a provocative discussion of a comparable meeting convened by the Yao intelligentsia, also in 1988.

2 By 1993, according to an informal conversation with one of its record-keepers, the association had seen significant growth. Membership had

increased from the hundred official members who had attended the 1988 meeting to about a thousand. Two additional meetings had been held since the Huangping inauguration, one in Anshun with about 300 in attendance and one in Kaili with 500 attendees, including some Hmong from the United States. Branch associations had been established in Songtao, Anshun, Bijie, and Sinan as well as in the provinces of Hunan and Yunnan. About 8–10 percent of the membership was from outside Guizhou. Only 5 percent were non-Miao.

3 *"Xinli"* here, although conventionally translated as "psychology," probably refers to the category "common psychological make-up" in Stalin's scheme for identifying ethnic groups. In conventional usage, this phrase denoted common *cultural* sensibilities and had been imported via Japan where it had been closely tied to national character.

4 In "Notes on Italian History," Gramsci detailed an approach to the thorough investigation of subaltern histories: "it is necessary to study: (1) the objective formation of the subaltern social groups, by the developments and transformations occurring in the sphere of economic production; their quantitative diffusion and their origins in pre-existing social groups, whose mentality, ideology and aims they conserve for a time; (2) *their active or passive affiliation to the dominant political formations,* their attempts to influence the programmes of these formations in order to press claims of their own, and the consequences of these attempts in determining processes of decomposition, renovation or neo-formation; (3) the birth of new parties and dominant groups, intended to conserve the assent of the subaltern groups and to maintain control over them; (4) *the formations which the subaltern groups themselves produce, in order to press claims of a limited and partial character;* (5) those new formations which assert the autonomy of the subaltern groups, but within the old framework . . ." (Gramsci 1971:52, emphasis added).

5 See also Spivak's introductory essay (1988b) in *Selected Subaltern Studies* in which she raises more pointed methodological and epistemological questions about the project of recovering subaltern histories.

6 China scholars have noted that the notion of speechlessness is complicated by the role of state-induced speech by subalterns in the making of the Maoist revolution. Here, in what Hershatter calls "official subaltern-speak" (1993:108), peasants and members of other oppressed groups such as women were encouraged to "speak bitterness," to recount their own oppressions in the interests of creating a recognition of their collective conditions. As Anagnost describes it: "speaking bitterness solidified an authorized structure of feeling as a means of making individual experience socially available for the launching of revolutionary subjects defined by class" (1997:32–33). One could think here in terms of a more productive

function of the subaltern category—instead of repressing the subaltern as the negation of discourse, in this instance, subalternity was aggressively called into discourse, generating new subjectivities in the process. The relation, then, between state discourse and the subaltern in revolutionary contexts may pose ongoing questions for theorizing subalternity.

7 The privileged gaze of the anthropological observer, however, must come under scrutiny, for, as I argue, watcher and consumer are positions assumed by those who would disavow subalternity. What this argument forces, then, is the question of the role of participant-observers in themselves constructing subalternity.

8 Southeast Guizhou became consolidated as a political center under Maoist governmentality through the recruitment of key Miao personnel for work in Beijing, either in administrative or cultural posts. Central authorities paid particular attention to incorporating the region because of the density of its Miao population and its infamous renegade status in earlier centuries as culturally and politically unsubdued. This policy focus, in turn, engendered research focus, and Southeast Guizhou gradually became emblematic of Miao society and culture.

9 Lavely (1991) has reported that, even in the collective period, the landscape had become so hierarchized as to induce consistent strategies of spatial hypergamy even when incomes were relatively undifferentiated. See also Croll (1984), who found that the rural-to-urban move persisted as a desirable marriage strategy throughout the Maoist period and that within the rural sector wages and access to transportation and to relatively level and fertile land also were valued in a potential partner.

10 Indeed, the Miao countryside had even seen some strictures of patrilocality come under challenge with the emergent class differentiations. In rare cases, a woman's employment in Xijiang, for instance, would determine the couple's residence since her cash income was increasingly viewed as critical to the household economy.

11 "Guizhou Sheng Minzu Jieri Gaikuang—Lanbiao," 1984, unpublished.

12 "Pig day" and "horse day" refer to two of twelve days in what Skinner (1964–65:13) has described as the duodenary market cycle. In each twelve-day period, there were two market occasions, but unlike Skinner's model, they were not separated by six days each, but instead by five days and seven days, respectively. In Xijiang, this cycle was consulted in the designation of auspicious days, festival days, and important agricultural junctures as well.

9 Performances of *Minzu* Modernity

1 Since the term *shaoshu minzu* was a way of distinguishing the fifty-five minorities *as an aggregate* from the majority Han nationality, to say *shaoshu Miaozu* technically made no sense. However, it can be read as a way of appropriating official language to refuse the Han-minority bifurcation, replacing it instead with the particularity of Miao identity. See Harrell (1996) for a discussion of *minzu* terminology.

2 Ana was the Miao name I had been given in Xijiang.

3 On the way in which the state is spoken through local subjects, see the insightful discussions by Anagnost (1990, 1995, 1997:17–44).

4 Duara specifically meant to critique Ernest Gellner's *Nations and Nationalism* (1983) and Benedict Anderson's *Imagined Communities: Reflections on the Origins and Spread of Nationalism* (1991). What he objected to is that "Gellner and Anderson regard national identity as a distinctly modern mode of consciousness: the nation as a whole imagining itself to be the cohesive subject of history" (1995:54). Duara, as we have seen, advocated thinking in terms of a less-definitive break in our understanding of the historical passage into so-called modernity.

5 The fields in which performance theory has genealogies include philosophy and linguistics (Austin 1975; Benveniste 1971; Derrida 1988; Searle 1969), performance and theater studies (Conquergood 1991, Schechner 1985, Taussig 1993), sociology and linguistic anthropology (Goffman 1959; Hymes 1974), and in the interfaces between the anthropology of ritual and the study of performances (Conquergood 1991; Schechner 1985; Tambiah 1985; Turner 1986).

6 See "Signature Event Context" in Derrida (1988).

7 Pursuing the subversive potential of parody, Butler writes in *Gender Trouble:* "The notion of gender parody . . . does not assume that there is an original which such parodic identities imitate. Indeed, the parody is *of* the very notion of an original . . . parodic proliferation deprives hegemonic culture and its critics of the claim to naturalized or essentialist gender identities" (1990a:138).

8 Many chapters in Butler's second book on performativity, *Bodies That Matter* (1993), deal with the interplay of race and gender.

9 I am grateful to Zhang Xudong for first drawing my attention to the importance of interior design as a consumption practice that has tremendous political freight in the post-Mao period, a time in which materially indexed lifestyle practices and the personalization of space have become important social signifiers. See also Tang (1998) on the recuperation of the subject through interiors.

10 By comparison, see Adams (1996b) for a fascinating discussion of the role of karaoke and cultural performance in Tibet.

11 Growing up, conformity, modernity?

10 Conclusion

1 An extended discussion of my dressing Miao for public spectacle can be found in Schein (1996c).

2 That male geographer Tim Oakes (1998:1–7) was also dressed up as a Miao while doing fieldwork in Southeast Guizhou does little to compromise this point since, when he was adorned by sportive villagers, it was *as a woman*. Indeed, that his border crossing into the Miao category also entailed crossing into femininity further displays the associative logic that I am describing.

Bibliography

Abu-Lughod, Lila. 1991. "Writing Against Culture." In *Recapturing Anthropology: Working in the Present.* Richard G. Fox, ed. Pp. 137–62. Santa Fe, N.M.: School of American Research Press.

———. 1993. *Writing Women's Worlds: Bedouin Stories.* Berkeley: University of California Press.

———. 1995. "Movie Stars and Islamic Moralism in Egypt." *Social Text* 42:53–67.

———. 1997. "The Interpretation of Culture(s) After Television." *Representations* 59:109–34.

Adams, Vincanne. 1996a. *Tigers of the Snow and Other Virtual Sherpas: An Ethnography of Himalayan Encounters.* Princeton, N.J.: Princeton University Press.

———. 1996b. "Karaoke as Modern Lhasa, Tibet: Western Encounters with Cultural Politics." *Cultural Anthropology* 11 (4):510–46.

Alley, Rewi. 1982. *Folk Poems from China's Minorities.* Beijing: New World Press.

Alloula, Malek. 1986. *The Colonial Harem.* Minneapolis: University of Minnesota Press.

Althusser, Louis. 1971. "Ideology and Ideological State Apparatuses (Notes Toward an Investigation)." In *Lenin and Philosophy and Other Essays.* Pp. 121–73. New York: Monthly Review Press.

Amin, Samir. 1976. *Unequal Development: An Essay on the Social Formations of Peripheral Capitalism.* Brian Pearce, trans. Sussex: Harvester Press.

Anagnost, Ann. 1985. "The Beginning and End of an Emperor." *Modern China* 11 (2):147–76.

———. 1989. "Prosperity and Counter-Prosperity: The Moral Discourse on Wealth in Post-Mao China." In *Marxism and the Chinese Experience.* Arif Dirlik and Maurice Meisner, eds. Armonk, N.Y.: M. E. Sharpe.

———. 1990. "The Politicized Body." *Stanford Humanities Review* 2 (1):86–102.

———. 1994. "The Politics of Ritual Displacement." In *Asian Visions of Authority: Religion and the Modern States of East and Southeast Asia.* Charles

Keyes, Laurel Kendall, and Helen Hardacre, eds. Pp. 221–54. Honolulu: University of Hawaii Press.

———. 1995. "Who Is Speaking Here? Discursive Boundaries and Representation in Post-Mao China." In *Boundaries in Chinese Culture.* John Hays, ed. London: Reaktion Press.

———. 1997. *National Past-Times: Narrative, Representation, and Power in Modern China.* Durham, N.C.: Duke University Press.

Anderson, Benedict. 1991 [1983]. *Imagined Communities: Reflections on the Origin and Spread of Nationalism* (Revised and Expanded). London: Verso.

Anderson, Perry. 1974. *Lineages of the Absolutist State.* London: New Left Books.

Ang, Ien. 1985. *Watching Dallas.* London: Methuen.

———. 1991. *Desperately Seeking the Audience.* London: Routledge.

———. 1996. *Living Room Wars: Rethinking Media Audiences for a Postmodern World.* London: Routledge.

Appadurai, Arjun. 1996. *Modernity at Large: Cultural Dimensions of Globalization.* Minneapolis: University of Minnesota Press.

Arkush, R. David. 1981. *Fei Xiaotong and Sociology in Revolutionary China.* Cambridge, Mass.: Harvard University Press.

Arnold, Matthew. 1994 [1869]. *Culture and Anarchy.* Samuel Lipman, ed. New Haven, Conn.: Yale University Press.

Asad, Talal. 1975. *Anthropology and the Colonial Encounter.* London: Ithaca Press.

Austin, J. L. 1975. *How to Do Things with Words.* 2d. Ed. Cambridge, Mass.: Harvard University Press.

Barlow, Tani. 1991a. "Theorizing Woman: *Funu, Guojia, Jiating* [Chinese Women, Chinese State, Chinese Family]." *Genders* 10:132–60.

———. 1991b. "*Zhishifenzi* (Chinese Intellectuals) and Power." *Dialectical Anthropology* 16 (3–4):209–32.

———. 1993. "Editor's Introduction." *Positions* 1 (1):v–vii.

Beahan, Charlotte L. 1975. "Feminism and Nationalism in the Chinese Women's Press, 1902–1911." *Modern China* 1 (4):379–416.

Beijing Review. 1989. "Muslims Get Book Banned." *Beijing Review* May 22–28: 13.

Benjamin, Walter. 1969. "The Work of Art in the Age of Mechanical Reproduction." In *Illuminations.* New York: Schocken Books.

Bennett, Tony. 1994. "The Exhibitionary Complex." In *Culture/Power/History: A Reader in Contemporary Social History.* Nicholas B. Dirks, Geoff Eley, and Sherry B. Ortner, eds. Pp. 123–54. Princeton, N.J.: Princeton University Press.

Benveniste, Emile. 1971. *Problems in General Linguistics.* M. E. Meeck, trans. Coral Gables, Fla.: University of Miami Press.

Berlant, Lauren. 1997. *The Queen of America Goes to Washington City: Essays on Sex and Citizenship.* Durham, N.C.: Duke University Press.

Bernatzik, Hugo Adolf. 1970 [1947]. *Akha and Miao: Problems of Applied Ethnography in Farther India.* New Haven, Conn.: Human Relations Area Files.

Bernstein, Thomas. 1977. *Up to the Mountains and Down to the Villages: The Transfer of Youth from Urban to Rural China.* New Haven, Conn.: Yale University Press.

Betts, Geo. Edgar. 1900–1901. "Social Life of the Miao Tsi." *Journal of the North China Branch of the Royal Asiatic Society,* 33:85–105.

Bhabha, Homi K. 1983. "The Other Question . . . Homi K. Bhabha Reconsiders the Stereotype and Colonial Discourse." *Screen* 24 (6):18–36, November-December.

———. 1990. "The Third Space: Interview with Homi Bhabha." In *Identity: Community, Culture, Difference.* Jonathan Rutherford, ed. Pp. 207–21. London: Wishart.

———. 1994. *The Location of Culture.* London: Routledge.

Billeter, Jean-François. 1985. "The System of 'Class Status.'" In *The Scope of State Power in China.* Stuart R. Schram, ed. Pp. 127–69. London: School of Oriental and African Studies.

Birch, Cyril. 1963. "The Particle of Art." In *Chinese Communist Literature.* Cyril Birch, ed. Pp. 3–14. New York: Frederick A. Praeger.

Bliatout, Bruce Thowpao. 1982. *Hmong Sudden Unexpected Death Syndrome: A Cultural Study.* Portland, Ore.: Sparkle Enterprises.

Blum, Susan D. 1992. "Ethnic Diversity in Southwest China: Perceptions of Self and Other." *Ethnic Groups* 9:267–79.

Bo Gua. 1975. "Opium, Bombs, and Trees: The Future of the H'mong Tribesman in Northern Thailand." *Journal of Contemporary Asia* 5:70–81.

Boon, James A. 1982. *Other Tribes, Other Scribes: Symbolic Anthropology in the Comparative Study of Cultures, Histories, Religions, and Texts.* Cambridge: Cambridge University Press.

Bourdieu, Pierre. 1984. *Distinction: A Social Critique of the Judgment of Taste.* Cambridge, Mass.: Harvard University Press.

Bridgman, E. C. 1859. "Sketches of the Miau-tsze." *Journal of the North China Branch of the Royal Asiatic Society* 3:257–86.

Broomhall, Marshall, ed. 1907. *The Chinese Empire: A General and Missionary Survey.* London: Morgan & Scott.

Brownell, Susan. 1995. *Training the Body for China: Sports in the Moral Order of the People's Republic.* Chicago: University of Chicago Press.

———. 1996. "Representing Gender in the Chinese Nation: Chinese Sportswomen and Beijing's Bid for the 2000 Olympics." *Identities* 2 (3):223–47.

Bulag, Uradyn E. 1998. *Nationalism and Hybridity in Mongolia.* Oxford: Clarendon Press.

Butler, Judith. 1990a. *Gender Trouble: Feminism and the Subversion of Identity*. New York: Routledge.

——. 1990b. "Performative Acts and Gender Constitution: An Essay in Phenomenology and Feminist Theory." In *Performing Feminisms: Feminist Critical Theory and Theatre*. Sue-Ellen Case, ed. Pp. 270–82. Baltimore: Johns Hopkins University Press.

——. 1993. *Bodies That Matter: On the Discursive Limits of "Sex."* New York: Routledge.

——. 1997. *The Psychic Life of Power: Theories in Subjection*. Stanford, Calif.: Stanford University Press.

Calhoun, Craig. 1989. "Tiananmen, Television, and the Public Sphere: Internationalization of Culture and the Beijing Spring of 1989." *Public Culture* 2 (1):54–71.

Calhoun, Craig, ed. 1992. *Habermas and the Public Sphere*. Cambridge, Mass.: MIT Press.

Cannon, Terry. 1989. "National Minorities and the Internal Frontier." In *China's Regional Development*. David S. G. Goodman, ed. Pp. 164–79. London: Routledge.

Cao Wei. 1992. "When Nationalities Get Together." *China Reconstructs* 41 (7):10–12, July.

Carrier, James. 1992. "Occidentalism: The World Turned Upside-Down." *American Ethnologist* 19 (2):195–212.

Catlin, Amy R. 1981. "Speech Surrogate Systems of the Hmong: From Singing Voices to Talking Reeds." In *The Hmong in the West: Observations and Reports*. Bruce T. Downing and Douglas P. Olney, eds. Pp. 170–97. Minneapolis: Center for Urban and Regional Affairs, University of Minnesota.

Chakrabarty, Dipesh. 1992. "Postcoloniality and the Artifice of History: Who Speaks for 'Indian' Pasts?" *Representations* 37:1–26.

Chao Wei Yang. 1986. "Evolutionary Theory and Cultural Diversity: A Study of the Ethnology of China's National Minorities." Ph.D. diss., University of California, Berkeley.

Chatterjee, Partha. 1986. *Nationalist Thought and the Colonial World: A Derivative Discourse*. Minneapolis: University of Minnesota Press.

——. 1989. "Colonialism, Nationalism, and Colonialized Women: The Contest in India." *American Ethnologist* 16 (4):622–33.

——. 1990. "A Response to Taylor's 'Modes of Civil Society.'" *Public Culture* 3 (1):119–32.

Chen Kuan-Hsing. 1994. "Positioning *positions*: A New Internationalist Localism of Cultural Studies." *positions* 2 (3):680–710.

Chen Xiaomei. 1995. *Occidentalism: A Theory of Counter-Discourse in Post-Mao China*. Oxford: Oxford University Press.

Chen Yongling, ed. 1987. *Minzu Cidian (A Dictionary of Ethnic Groups)*. Shanghai: Shanghai Dictionary Press.

Cheung, Siu-woo. 1996. "Subject and Representation: Identity Politics in Southeast Guizhou." Ph.D. diss., University of Washington.

Chicago Cultural Studies Group. 1992. "Critical Multiculturalism." *Critical Inquiry* 18 (3):530–55.

China News Analysis. 1958. "Languages of the Minority Peoples." *China News Analysis Weekly Newsletter* 234:1–7, June 27.

China Reconstructs, ed. 1984. *China's Minority Nationalities (I)*. Beijing: Great Wall Books.

Chow, Rey. 1991a. *Woman and Chinese Modernity: The Politics of Reading Between West and East*. Minneapolis: University of Minnesota Press.

———. 1991b. "Violence in the Other Country: China as Crisis, Spectacle, and Woman." In *Third World Women and the Politics of Feminism*. Chandra Mohanty et al., eds. Pp. 80–100. Bloomington: Indiana University Press.

———. 1995a. *Primitive Passions: Visuality, Sexuality, Ethnography, and Contemporary Chinese Cinema*. New York: Columbia University Press.

———. 1995b. "The Politics of Admittance: Female Sexual Agency, Miscegenation, and the Formation of Community in Frantz Fanon." *The UTS Review* 1 (1):5–29.

Chow Tse-tsung. 1960. *The May Fourth Movement: Intellectual Revolution in Modern China*. Stanford, Calif.: Stanford University Press.

Clark, Paul. 1987. "Ethnic Minorities and Chinese Film: Cinema and the Exotic." *East-West Film Journal* 1 (2):15–31, June.

Clarke, Samuel R. 1904. "The Miao and Chungchia Tribes of Kueichou Province." *East of Asia Magazine* 3:193–207.

———. 1907. "The Province of Kweichow." In *The Chinese Empire: A General and Missionary Survey*. Marshall Broomhall, ed. London: Morgan & Scott.

———. 1911. *Among the Tribes in Southwest China*. London: Morgan & Scott.

Clifford, James. 1988. *The Predicament of Culture: Twentieth-Century Ethnography, Literature, and Art*. Cambridge, Mass.: Harvard University Press.

———. 1992. "Traveling Cultures." In *Cultural Studies*. Lawrence Grossberg, Cary Nelson, and Paula Treichler, eds. Pp. 96–116. New York: Routledge.

———. 1997. *Routes: Travel and Translation in the Late Twentieth Century*. Cambridge, Mass.: Harvard University Press.

Clifford, James, and George E. Marcus. 1986. *Writing Culture: The Poetics and Politics of Ethnography*. Berkeley: University of California Press.

Cohen, Joan Lebold. 1987. *The New Chinese Painting, 1949–1986*. New York: H. N. Abrams.

Comaroff, Jean, and John Comaroff. 1991. *Of Revelation and Revolution: Christianity, Colonialism, and Consciousness in South Africa*. Vol. 1. Chicago: University of Chicago Press.

Connor, Walker. 1984. *The National Question in Marxist-Leninist Theory and Strategy.* Princeton, N.J.: Princeton University Press.

Conquergood, Dwight. 1991. "Rethinking Ethnography: Towards a Critical Cultural Politics." *Communication Monographs* 58 (2):179–94.

Cooper, Robert. 1984. *Resource Scarcity and the Hmong Response: Patterns of Settlement and Economy in Transition.* Singapore: Singapore University Press.

Crisler, Clarence C. 1937. *China's Borderlands and Beyond.* Takoma Park, D.C.: Review and Herald.

Croll, Elisabeth. 1984. "Marriage Choice and Status Groups in Contemporary China." In *Class and Social Stratification in Post-Revolutionary China.* James L. Watson, ed. Pp. 175–97. Cambridge: Cambridge University Press.

Crossley, Pamela K. "Thinking about Ethnicity in Early Modern China." *Late Imperial China* 11 (1):1–34.

Das, Veena. 1995. "On Soap Opera: What Kind of Anthropological Object is It?" In *Worlds Apart: Modernity Through the Prism of the Local.* Daniel Miller, ed. Pp. 169–89. London: Routledge.

Davies, H. R. 1909. *Yunnan: The Link Between India and the Yang-tze.* Cambridge: Cambridge University Press.

Deal, David M. 1979. "Policy Toward Ethnic Minorities in Southwest China, 1927–1965." In *Nationalism and the Crises of Ethnic Minorities in Asia.* Tai S. Kang, ed. Pp. 33–40. Westport, Conn.: Greenwood Press.

———, ed. and trans. n.d. "Guizhou Miao Album." Manuscript.

de Bary, Wm. Theodore, Wing-tsit Chan, and Burton Watson, compilers. 1960. *Sources of Chinese Tradition.* Vol. 1. New York: Columbia University Press.

deBeauclair, Inez. 1960. "A Miao Tribe of Southeast Kweichow and Its Cultural Configuration." *Bulletin of the Institute of Ethnology, Academia Sinica* (Taipei) 10:127–99.

———. 1970. *Tribal Cultures of Southwest China.* Taibei: Orient Cultural Service.

de Certeau, Michel. 1984. *The Practice of Everyday Life.* Berkeley: University of California Press.

Derrida, Jacques. 1988. "Signature Event Context." In *Limited Inc.* Gerald Graff, ed. Samuel Weber and Jeffrey Mehlman, trans. Evanston, Ill.: Northwestern University Press.

Diamond, Elin. 1996. "Introduction." In *Performance and Cultural Politics.* Pp. 1–12. London: Routledge.

Diamond, Elin, ed. 1996. *Performance and Cultural Politics.* London: Routledge.

Diamond, Jared. 1997. *Guns, Germs, and Steel: The Fates of Human Societies.* New York: W. W. Norton.

Diamond, Norma. 1988. "The Miao and Poison: Interactions on China's Southwest Frontier." *Ethnology* 27 (1):1-25.

———. 1995. "Defining the Miao: Ming, Qing, and Contemporary Views." In *Cultural Encounters on China's Ethnic Frontiers.* Steven Harrell, ed. Pp. 92-116. Seattle: University of Washington Press.

Dikötter, Frank. 1992. *The Discourse of Race in Modern China.* Stanford, Calif.: Stanford University Press.

Dirks, Nicholas B. 1990. "History as a Sign of the Modern." *Public Culture* 2 (2):25-32.

D'Orleans, Henri. 1894. *Around Tonkin and Siam.* London: Chapman & Hall.

Dreyer, June Teufel. 1976. *China's Forty Millions: Minority Nationalities and National Integration in the People's Republic of China.* Cambridge, Mass.: Harvard University Press.

Duara, Prasenjit. 1995. *Rescuing History from the Nation.* Chicago: University of Chicago Press.

Eberhard, Wolfram. 1982. *China's Minorities: Yesterday and Today.* Belmont, Calif.: Wadsworth.

Edelstein, Alex S. 1997. *Total Propaganda: From Mass Culture to Popular Culture.* Mahwah, N.J.: Lawrence Erlbaum Associates.

Edkins, J. 1870. "The Miau Tsi Tribes: Their History." *Chinese Recorder* 3:33-36, July; 3:74-76, August.

Eitzen, Hilda. 1988. "Miao Costume: A Minority Art in Chinese Culture." *Central and Inner Asian Studies* 2:86-121.

Eley, Geoff, and Ronald Grigor Suny. 1996. "Introduction: From the Moment of History to the Work of Cultural Representation." In *Becoming National: A Reader.* Pp. 3-37. New York: Oxford University Press.

Eminov, Sandra. 1975. "Folklore and Nationalism in Modern China." *Journal of the Folklore Institute* 12 (2/3):257-77.

Engels, Friedrich. 1972 [1884]. *Origin of the Family, Private Property, and the State.* New York: International Publishers.

Enloe, Cynthia. 1989. *Bananas, Beaches, and Bases: Making Feminist Sense of International Politics.* Berkeley: University of California Press.

———. 1993. *The Morning After: Sexual Politics at the End of the Cold War.* Berkeley: University of California Press.

Enwall, Joakim. 1992. "Miao or Hmong?" *Australian National University Thai-Yunnan Project Newsletter* 17:25-26.

Eoyang, Eugene. 1993. *The Transparent Eye: Reflections on Translation, Chinese Literature, and Comparative Poetics.* Honolulu: University of Hawaii Press.

Evans, Grant. 1983. *The Yellow Rainmakers: Are Chemical Weapons Being Used in Southeast Asia?* London: Verso.

Fabian, Johannes. 1983. *Time and the Other: How Anthropology Makes Its Object.* New York: Columbia University Press.

Fadiman, Anne. 1997. *The Spirit Catches You and You Fall Down: A Hmong Child, Her American Doctors, and the Collision of Two Cultures.* New York: Farrar, Straus and Giroux.

Farquhar, Judith. 1996. "Market Magic: Getting Rich and Getting Personal in Medicine After Mao." *American Ethnologist* 23 (2):239–57.

Farquhar, Judith B., and James L. Hevia. 1993. "Culture and Postwar American Historiography of China." *positions* 1 (2):486–525.

Farquhar, Judith, Tomoko Masuzawa, and Carol Mavor. 1998. "A Note from the Editors." *Cultural Studies* 12 (1):1–2.

Fei Hsiao-t'ung. 1951–52. "The Minority People of Kweichow, I & II." *China Monthly Review* 121:289–94, December; 122:54–63, January.

———. 1979. *Modernization and National Minorities in China.* Montreal: Centre for East Asian Studies, McGill University, OPS 6.

———. 1980. "Ethnic Identification in China." *Social Sciences in China* 1:94–107.

———. 1981. *Toward a People's Anthropology.* Beijing: New World Press.

———. 1988 [1951]. "Qinlao de Miaozu, Youjiu de Lishi (The Hardworking Miao, A Long History)." In *Miaozu Yanjiu Luncong (Collected Essays in Miao Research).* Hu Qiwang and Li Tinggui, eds. Pp. 17–36. Guiyang: Guizhou Nationalities Press.

Feingold, David. 1970. "Opium and Politics in Laos." In *Laos: War and Revolution.* Nina S. Adams and Alfred W. McCoy, eds. Pp. 322–39. New York: Harper and Row.

Feng, H. Y., and J. K. Shryock. 1935. "The Black Magic in China Known as Ku." *Journal of the American Oriental Society* 55 (1):1–30.

Ferdinand, Peter. 1989. "The Economic and Financial Dimension." In *China's Regional Development.* David S. G. Goodman, ed. Pp. 38–56. London: Routledge.

Fiske, John. 1989a. *Understanding Popular Culture.* Boston: Unwin Hyman.

———. 1989b. *Reading the Popular.* Boston: Unwin Hyman.

———. 1989c. *Television Culture.* London: Routledge.

Ford, Clellan S. 1970. *Human Relations Area Files: 1949–1969: A Twenty-Year Report.* New Haven, Conn.: Human Relations Area Files.

Foucault, Michel. 1979a. "Governmentality." *Ideology and Consciousness* 6:5–21.

———. 1979b. *Discipline and Punish: The Birth of the Prison.* New York: Vintage Books.

———. 1980a. *Power/Knowledge: Selected Interviews and Other Writings.* Colin Gordon, ed. New York: Pantheon Books.

———. 1980b. *The History of Sexuality,* Vol. 1: *An Introduction.* New York: Vintage Books.

———. 1983. "The Subject and Power." In *Michel Foucault: Beyond Struc-*

turalism and Hermeneutics. Hubert L. Dreyfus and Paul Rabinow, eds. Pp. 208-26. Chicago: University of Chicago Press.

Fox, Richard G., ed. 1990. *Nationalist Ideologies and the Production of National Cultures.* Washington, D.C.: American Ethnological Society Monograph Series No. 2.

Fraser, Nancy. 1997. *Justice Interruptus: Critical Reflections on the "Poststructuralist" Condition.* New York: Routledge.

Fried, Morton H. 1952. "Land Tenure, Geography, and Ecology in the Contact of Cultures." *American Journal of Economics and Sociology* 11 (4):391-412.

Friedman, Jonathan. 1990. "Being in the World: Globalization and Localization." In *Global Culture: Nationalism, Globalization and Modernity.* Michael Featherstone, ed. Pp. 311-28. London: Sage.

Fritz, Chester. 1981 [1917]. *China Journey.* Seattle: University of Washington Press.

Fu Mao-chi. 1957. "Written Languages for China's Minorities." *People's China* 3:25-31.

Gamewell, Mary Ninde. 1919. "Memorable Visits to Some Tribespeople of Yunnan." *Chinese Recorder* 50:803-15, December.

Garnham, Nicholas. 1992. "The Media and the Public Sphere." In *Habermas and the Public Sphere.* Craig Calhoun, ed. Pp. 359-76. Cambridge, Mass.: MIT Press.

Garrett, W. E. 1974. "No Place to Run: The Hmong of Laos." *National Geographic* 145 (1):78-111.

Gasster, Michael. 1969. *Chinese Intellectuals and the Revolution of 1911.* Seattle: University of Washington Press.

Geddes, W. R. 1970. "Opium and the Miao: A Study in Ecological Adjustment." *Oceania* 41 (1):1-11.

————. 1976. *Migrants of the Mountains: The Cultural Ecology of the Blue Miao (Hmong Njua) of Thailand.* Oxford: Clarendon Press.

Gellner, Ernest. 1983. *Nations and Nationalism.* Ithaca, N.Y.: Cornell University Press.

Gilroy, Paul. 1987. *"There Ain't No Black in the Union Jack": The Cultural Politics of Race and Nation.* Chicago: University of Chicago Press.

————. 1993. *The Black Atlantic: Modernity and Double Consciousness.* Cambridge, Mass.: Harvard University Press.

Ginsburg, Faye. 1991. "Indigenous Media: Faustian Contract or Global Village?" *Cultural Anthropology* 6 (1):92-112.

Gladney, Dru C. 1990. "The Peoples of the People's Republic: Finally in the Vanguard?" *Fletcher Forum of World Affairs* 12 (1):62-76.

————. 1991. *Muslim Chinese: Ethnic Nationalism in the People's Republic.* Cambridge: Harvard University Press.

————. 1994a. "Salman Rushdie in China: Religion, Ethnicity, and State

Definition in the People's Republic." In *Asian Visions of Authority: Religion and the Modern States of East and Southeast Asia*. Charles F. Keyes, Laurel Kendall, and Helen Hardacre, eds. Pp. 255–78. Honolulu: University of Hawaii Press.

———. 1994b. "Representing Nationality in China: Refiguring Majority/Minority Identities." *Journal of Asian Studies* 53 (1):92–123.

———. 1995. "Tian Zhuangzhuang, the Fifth Generation, and Minorities Film in China." *Public Culture* 8 (1):161–75.

Goffman, Erving. 1959. *The Presentation of Self in Everyday Life*. Garden City, N.Y.: Doubleday.

Gold, Thomas B. 1990. "The Resurgence of Civil Society in China." *Journal of Democracy* 1 (1):18–31.

Goodman, David S. G. 1983. "Guizhou and the PRC: The Development of an Internal Colony." In *Internal Colonialism: Essays Around a Theme*. D. Drakakis-Smith, ed. Pp. 107–24. Institute of British Geographers, Developing Areas Research Monograph No. 3.

———. 1999. "State-Society Relations in Reform Shanxi: Elite Interdependence and Accommodation." *Provincial China* 6 (April): 37–65.

Gouldner, Alvin W. 1977–78. "Stalinism: A Study of Internal Colonialism." *Telos* 34:5–48.

Gourdon, Henri. 1931. *L'Indochine*. Paris: Librairie Larousse.

Graham, David Crockett. 1937. "The Ceremonies of the Ch'uan Miao." *Journal of the West China Border Research Society* 9:71–119.

———. 1954. *Songs and Stories of the Ch'uan Miao*. Washington, D.C.: Smithsonian Institution.

———. 1978. *Tribal Songs and Tales of the Ch'uan Miao*. Lou Tsu-k'uang, ed. Taibei: Orient Cultural Service.

Gramsci, Antonio. 1971. *Selections from the Prison Notebooks*. Quentin Hoare and Geoffrey N. Smith, eds. New York: International Publishers.

Grandstaff, Terry B. 1979. "The Hmong, Opium, and the Haw: Speculations on the Origin of Their Association." *Journal of the Siam Society* 67 (2):70–79.

Grant, Bruce. 1995. *In the Soviet House of Culture: A Century of Perestroikas*. Princeton: Princeton University Press.

Grieder, Jerome B. 1981. *Intellectuals and the State in Modern China*. New York: Free Press.

Gu Xuejin. 1984. "*Minzu Xinli Suzhi zai Minzu Shibie Zhong de Zuoyong* (The Use of National Psychological Qualities for Distinguishing Nationalities." *Journal of the South Central Nationalities Institute* 1.

Gu Yongchang. 1980. "Gudai Miaozu Qianxi Wenti Chutan (A Preliminary Inquiry into Some Issues in the Migration of the Ancient Miao)." *Guizhou Minzu Yanjiu (Guizhou Research on Nationalities)* 1.

Guha, Ranajit, and Gayatri Chakravorty Spivak, eds. 1988. *Selected Subaltern Studies*. New York: Oxford University Press.

Guillory, John. 1997. "Bourdieu's Refusal." *Modern Language Quarterly* 58 (4): 367–98.

Guizhou Nationalities Affairs Commission et al., eds. 1987. *Ethnic Costume from Guizhou: Clothing Decorations and Designs from Minority Ethnic Groups in Southwest China*. Beijing: Foreign Languages Press.

Guizhou Nianjian Bianji Bu (Guizhou Yearbook Editorial Department). 1988. *Guizhou Nianjian (Guizhou Yearbook)*. Guiyang: Guizhou People's Press.

Guizhou Sheng Bianjizu (Guizhou Provincial Editing Group). 1986. *Miaozu Shehui Lishi Diaocha (Investigations of Miao Social History)*. Vol. 1. Guiyang: Guizhou Nationalities Press.

———. 1987. *Miaozu Shehui Lishi Diaocha (Investigations of Miao Social History)*. Vols. 2 and 3. Guiyang: Guizhou Nationalities Press.

Guizhou Sheng Di Er Qing Gongye Ju Gongyi Meishu Yanjiu Shi, Guiyang Shi Gongyi Meishu Yanjiu Shi (Arts and Crafts Research Office of the Guizhou Number Two Light Industry Bureau and the Guiyang Arts and Crafts Research Office). 1976. "Xiongdi Minzu Xingxiang Fushi Ziliao (Material on Images and Clothing of the Fraternal Nationalities)." Manuscript.

Guizhou Sheng Shaoshu Minzu Guji Zhengli Chuban Guihua Xiaozu Bangongshi (The Guizhou Provincial Office of the Program for Ordering and Publishing Minority Nationalities Ancient Books Group). 1991. *Kaiqin Ge (Songs of Marriage)*. Guiyang: Guizhou Nationalities Press.

Guizhou Sheng Wenhua Ju (Guizhou Province Cultural Bureau). 1956. *Guizhou Shaoshu Minzu Laran Tu'an (Patterns of Guizhou Minorities Batik)*. Beijing: People's Fine Arts Press.

Guldin, Gregory Eliyu. 1987. "Anthropology in the People's Republic of China: The Winds of Change." *Social Research* 54 (4):757–78.

———. 1988. "Chinese Anthropologies." *Chinese Sociology and Anthropology* 20 (4):3–32.

———. 1991. "Chinese Anthropologies." In *Anthropology in China*. Gregory Eliyu Guldin, ed. Pp. 3–29. Armonk, N.Y.: M. E. Sharpe.

———. 1992. "Anthropology by Other Names: The Impact of Sino-Soviet Friendship on the Anthropological Sciences." *Australian Journal of Chinese Affairs* 27:133–49, January.

———. 1994. *The Saga of Anthropology in China: From Malinowski to Moscow to Mao*. Armonk, N.Y.: M. E. Sharpe.

Gupta, Akhil. 1995. "Blurred Boundaries: The Discourse of Corruption, the Culture of Politics, and the Imagined State." *American Ethnologist* 22 (2): 375–402.

Gupta, Akhil, and James Ferguson. 1997. "Discipline and Practice: 'The Field' as Site, Method, and Location in Anthropology." In *Anthropological Locations: Boundaries and Grounds of a Field Science.* Pp. 1–46. Berkeley: University of California Press.

Habermas, Jürgen. 1987. *The Philosophical Discourse of Modernity.* Cambridge: Polity Press.

———. 1989 [1962]. *The Structural Transformation of the Public Sphere.* Cambridge, Mass.: MIT Press.

———. 1992. "Further Reflections on the Public Sphere." In *Habermas and the Public Sphere.* Craig Calhoun, ed. Pp. 421–61. Cambridge, Mass.: MIT Press.

Hall, Stuart. 1985. "Signification, Representation, Ideology: Althusser and the Post-Structuralist Debates." *Critical Studies in Mass Communication* 2 (2):91–114.

———. 1992. "Cultural Studies and Its Theoretical Legacies." In *Cultural Studies.* Lawrence Grossberg, Cary Nelson, and Paula Treichler, eds. Pp. 277–94. New York: Routledge.

———. 1994. "Cultural Studies: Two Paradigms." In *Contemporary Literary Criticism: Literary and Cultural Studies.* 3rd Ed. Robert Con Davis and Ronald Schleifer, eds. Pp. 610–25. New York: Longman.

———. 1995. "Fantasy, Identity, Politics." In *Cultural Remix: Theories and Politics of the Popular.* Erica Carter, James Donald, and Judith Squires, eds. Pp. 63–69. London: Lawrence & Wishart.

———. 1996a. "Introduction: Who Needs Identity?" In *Questions of Cultural Identity.* Stuart Hall and Paul du Gay, eds. Pp. 1–17. London: Sage.

———. 1996b. "Gramsci's Relevance for the Study of Race and Ethnicity." In *Stuart Hall: Critical Dialogues in Cultural Studies.* David Morley and Kuan-Hsing Chen, eds. Pp. 411–40. London: Routledge.

Hamilton-Merritt, Jane. 1980. "Poison-Gas War in Laos." *Reader's Digest,* October.

———. 1993. *Tragic Mountains: The Hmong, the Americans, and the Secret Wars for Laos, 1942–1992.* Bloomington: Indiana University Press.

Handler, Richard. 1988. *Nationalism and the Politics of Culture in Quebec.* Madison: University of Wisconsin Press.

Hang, Doua. 1986. "Tam Tuab Neeg: Connecting the Generations." In *The Hmong World 1.* Brenda Johns and David Strecker, eds. Pp. 33–41. New Haven, Conn.: Yale Southeast Asia Studies.

Harrell, Stevan. 1990. "Ethnicity, Local Interests, and the State: Yi Communities in Southwest China." *Comparative Studies in Society and History* 32 (3):515–48.

———. 1991. "Anthropology and Ethnology in the PRC: The Intersection of Discourses." *China Exchange News* 19 (2):3–6.

———. 1995a. "Introduction: Civilizing Projects and the Reaction to Them."

In *Cultural Encounters on China's Ethnic Frontiers.* Stevan Harrell, ed. Pp. 3–36. Seattle: University of Washington Press.

———. 1995b. "The History of the History of the Yi." In *Cultural Encounters on China's Ethnic Frontiers.* Stevan Harrell, ed. Pp. 63–91. Seattle: University of Washington Press.

———. 1996. "The Nationalities Question and the Prmi Problem." In *Negotiating Ethnicities in China and Taiwan.* Melissa J. Brown, ed. Pp. 274–96. Berkeley: Institute for East Asian Studies, University of California.

Hartsock, Nancy. 1990. "Foucault on Power: A Theory for Women." In *Feminism/Postmodernism.* Linda J. Nicholson, ed. Pp. 157–75. New York: Routledge.

Harvey, David. 1989. *The Condition of Postmodernity: An Enquiry into the Origins of Cultural Change.* Cambridge, Mass.: Blackwell Publishers.

Havel, Václav. 1991. *Open Letters: Selected Writings, 1965–1990.* New York: Alfred A. Knopf.

He Baogang. 1995. "The Ideas of Civil Society in Mainland China and Taiwan, 1986–92." *Issues and Studies* 31 (6):24–64.

He Guojian. 1991. "Guanyu 'Miaozu Jianshi' Zuyuan Wenti de Zhenglun — Jian Da Zhang Yongguo Xiansheng de Shangque (The Debate Over Problems of Ethnic Origins in the 'Brief History of the Miao' — And a Reply to Mr. Zhang Yongguo's Discussion)." In *Miaoxue Yanjiu (Research in Miao Studies).* Vol. 2. Li Tinggui, ed. Pp. 229–41. Guiyang: Guizhou Nationalities Press.

Hebdige, Dick. 1979. *Subculture: The Meaning of Style.* New York: Routledge.

Heberer, Thomas. 1989. *China and Its National Minorities: Autonomy or Assimilation?* Armonk, N.Y.: M. E. Sharpe.

Hechter, Michael. 1975. *Internal Colonialism: The Celtic Fringe in British National Development, 1536–1966.* Berkeley: University of California Press.

Heng, Geraldine, and Janadas Devan. 1992. "State Fatherhood: The Politics of Nationalism, Sexuality, and Race in Singapore." In *Nationalisms and Sexualities.* Andrew Parker, Mary Russo, Doris Summer, and Patricia Yaeger, eds. Pp. 343–64. New York: Routledge, Chapman and Hall.

Hershatter, Gail. 1993. "The Subaltern Talks Back: Reflections on Subaltern Theory and Chinese History." *positions* 1 (1):103–30.

Hevia, James L. 1995. *Cherising Men from Afar: Qing Guest Ritual and the McCartney Embassy of 1793.* Durham, N.C.: Duke University Press.

Hind, Robert J. 1984. "The Internal Colonial Concept." *Comparative Studies in Society and History.* 26 (3):543–68.

Hobsbawm, Eric, and Terence Ranger, eds. 1983. *The Invention of Tradition.* Cambridge: Cambridge University Press.

Holm, David L. 1984. "Folk Art as Propaganda: The *Yangge* Movement in Yan'an." In *Popular Chinese Literature and Performing Arts in the People's Re-*

public of China, 1949–1979. Bonnie S. McDougall, ed. Pp. 3–35. Berkeley: University of California Press.

Horkheimer, Max, and Theodor W. Adorno. 1944. "The Culture Industry: Enlightenment as Mass Deception." In *The Dialectic of Enlightenment.* English translation, 1972. New York: Continuum.

Hosie, Alexander. 1890. *Three Years in Western China.* London: George Philip.

Hostetler, Laura. 1995. "Chinese Ethnography in the Eighteenth Century: Miao Albums of Guizhou Province." Ph.D. diss., University of Pennsylvania.

Huang, Philip. 1991. "The Paradigmatic Crisis in Chinese Studies: Paradoxes in Social and Economic History." *Modern China* 17 (3):299–341.

Hudspeth, W. H. 1922. "Work Amongst the Miao in Southwest China." *Chinese Recorder* 53:702–5.

———. 1931. "Hwa Miao of Yunnan and Kweichou." *Chinese Recorder* 62: 224–29.

Hung, Chang-tai. 1985. *Going to the People: Chinese Intellectuals and Folk Literature, 1918–1937.* Cambridge, Mass.: Harvard University Press.

Hyde, Sandra. 2000. "Sex Tourism Practices on the Periphery: Eroticizing Ethnicity on the Lancang." In *Ethnographies of the Urban: China in the 1990s.* Nancy Chen, Connie Clark, Suzanne Gottschang, and Lyn Jeffrey, eds. Durham, N.C.: Duke University Press.

Hymes, Dell. 1981. *In Vain I Tried to Tell You.* Philadelphia: University of Pennsylvania Press.

Ivy, Marilyn. 1995. *Discourses of the Vanishing: Modernity, Phantasm, Japan.* Chicago: University of Chicago Press.

Jamieson, C. E. 1923. "The Aborigines of West China." *China Journal of Science and Arts* 1 (4):376–83.

Jenks, Robert D. 1994. *Insurgency and Social Disorder in Guizhou: The "Miao" Rebellion, 1854–1873.* Honolulu: University of Hawaii Press.

Jensen, Lionel M. 1997. *Manufacturing Confucianism: Chinese Traditions and Universal Civilization.* Durham, N.C.: Duke University Press.

Jin Zhou. 1981. *Tibet: No Longer Mediaeval.* Beijing: Foreign Languages Press.

Johnston, R. F. 1908. *From Peking to Mandalay.* London: John Murray.

Keane, John, ed. 1988. *Civil Society and the State.* London: Verso.

Kemp, Emily G. 1921. "The Highways and Byways of Kweichow." *Journal of the North China Branch of the Royal Asiatic Society* 52:158–85.

Kinkley, Jeffrey C. 1985. "Shen Congwen and the Uses of Regionalism in Modern Chinese Literature." *Modern Chinese Literature* 1 (2):157–83.

———. 1987. *The Odyssey of Shen Congwen.* Stanford, Calif.: Stanford University Press.

Kirkby, Richard, and Terry Cannon. 1989. "Introduction." In *China's Regional Development.* David. S. G. Goodman, ed. Pp. 1–19. London: Routledge.

Kligman, Gail. 1988. *The Wedding of the Dead: Ritual, Poetics, and Popular Culture in Transylvania.* Berkeley: University of California Press.

Kuhn, Philip A. 1984. "Chinese Views of Social Classification." In *Class and Social Stratification in Post-Revolution China.* James L. Watson, ed. Pp. 16-28. Cambridge: Cambridge University Press.

Lam Ping-fai, Robert. 1985. *Ethnic Costumes of the Miao People in China.* Hong Kong: Hong Kong Museum of History.

Lancaster, Roger. 1992. *Life Is Hard: Machismo, Danger, and the Intimacy of Power in Nicaragua.* Berkeley: University of California Press.

————. 1997. "Guto's Performance: Notes on the Transvestism of Everyday Life." In *The Gender/Sexuality Reader.* Roger Lancaster and Micaela di Leonardo, eds. Pp. 567-73. New York: Routledge.

Landes, Joan B. 1995. "The Public and the Private Sphere: A Feminist Reconsideration." In *Feminists Read Habermas: Gendering the Subject of Discourse.* Johanna Meehan, ed. Pp. 91-116. New York: Routledge.

Larteguy, Jean, with Yang Dao. 1979. *La Fabuleuse Aventure du Peuple de L'Opium.* Paris: Presses de la Cité.

Latour, Bruno. 1993. *We Have Never Been Modern.* Catherine Porter, trans. Cambridge, Mass.: Harvard University Press.

Lavely, William. 1991. "Marriage and Mobility Under Rural Collectivism." In *Marriage and Inequality in Chinese Society.* Rubie S. Watson and Patricia Buckley Ebrey, eds. Pp. 286-312. Berkeley: University of California Press.

Lavie, Smadar, and Ted Swedenburg. 1996. "Between and Among the Boundaries of Culture: Bridging Text and Lived Experience in the Third Timespace." *Cultural Studies* 10 (1):154-79.

Leach, Edmund R. 1954. *Political Systems of Highland Burma: A Study of Kachin Social Structure.* Boston: Beacon Press.

Lebar, Frank M., Gerald C. Hickey, and John K. Musgrave. 1964. *Ethnic Groups of Mainland Southeast Asia.* New Haven, Conn.: Human Relations Area Files.

Lee, Gar Yia. 1981. "The Effects of Development Measures on the Socio-Economy of the White Hmong." Ph.D. diss., University of Sydney.

Lee, James. 1982. "Food Supply and Population Growth in Southwest China, 1250-1600." *Journal of Asian Studies* 41 (4):711-46.

Leepreecha, Prasit. 1998. "*Ntoo Xeeb*: Cultural Revival on Forest Conservation of the Hmong in Thailand." Paper presented at the First International Workshop of the Hmong/Miao in Asia. Aix-en-Provence, September 11-13.

Lemoine, Jacques. 1972. *Un Village Hmong Vert du Haut Laos: Milieu Technique et Organisation Sociale.*

Leong, Wai-Teng. 1989. "The Culture of the State: National Tourism and the State Manufacture of Cultures." In *Communication for and Against Democ-*

racy. Marc Raboy and Peter A. Bruck, eds. Pp. 75–93. Montreal: Black Rose Books.

Leung, Edwin Pak-wah Leung. 1981–82. "Ethnic Compartmentalization and Regional Autonomy in the People's Republic of China." *Chinese Law and Government* 14 (4):4–108.

Levenson, Joseph R. 1958. *Confucian China and Its Modern Fate: A Trilogy.* Berkeley: University of California Press.

————. 1967. "The Province, the Nation, and the World: The Problem of Chinese Identity." In *Approaches to Modern Chinese History.* Albert Feuerwerker et al., eds. Pp. 268–88. Berkeley: University of California Press.

Lewis, Paul, and Elaine Lewis. 1984. *Peoples of the Golden Triangle.* London: Thames and Hudson.

Li Qianbing et al. 1987. *Guizhou Minzu Jieri (Guizhou National Festivals).* Chinese-English publication. Guiyang: Guizhou Fine Arts Press.

Li Tinggui. 1991. *Leigongshan shang de Miaozu (The Miao on Leigong Mountain).* Guiyang: Guizhou Nationalities Press.

Li Tinggui and Guo Jiusu. 1983. "Miaozu Gushe Yanjiu (Research on the Miao Drum Society)." In *Minzuxue Yanjiu (Researches in Ethnology)* No. 5. Beijing: Nationalities Press.

Li Yuguang and Huang Jike. 1982. "Qing Xiantong Nianjian Zhang Xiumei Lingdao de Miaozu Nongmin Qiyi (The Miao Peasant Uprising led by Zhang Xiumei in the Xiantong Period of the Qing Dynasty)." *Qiandongnan Shehui Kexue* (Social Sciences in Southeast Guizhou) 1.

Lin Yaohua. 1988. "New China's Ethnology: Research and Prospects." *Chinese Sociology and Anthropology* 21 (1):34–55.

Lin Yueh-Hwa (former spelling of Lin Yaohua). 1940. "The Miao-Man Peoples of Kweichow." *Harvard Journal of Asiatic Studies* 5 (3–4):261–345.

————. 1993. "Some Approaches to the Classification of Small Ethnic Groups in South China." *Thai-Yunnan Project Newsletter* 20:12–16.

Litzinger, Ralph A. 1994. "Crafting the Modern Ethnic: Yao Representation and Identity in Post-Mao China." Ph.D. diss., University of Washington.

————. 1995. "Making Histories: Contending Conceptions of the Yao Past." In *Cultural Encounters on China's Ethnic Frontiers.* Stevan Harrell, ed. Pp. 117–39. Seattle: University of Washington Press.

————. 1998. "Memory Work: Reconstituting the Ethnic in Post-Mao China." *Cultural Anthropology* 13 (2):224–56.

————. 1999. "The Politics of the Margin: Reimagining the State in Post-Mao China." In *Cultures of Insecurity: States, Communities, and the Production of Danger.* Jutta Weldes, Mark Laffey, Hugh Gusterson, and Raymond Duvall, eds. Pp. 293–318. Minneapolis: University of Minnesota Press.

————. 2000. *Writing the Margins: Minority Politics in Post-Mao China.* Durham, N.C.: Duke University Press.

Liu Chun. 1954. "National Minorities Enjoy Regional Autonomy." *People's China* 1 (1):9-14.

———. 1966. *The National Question and Class Struggle.* Beijing: Foreign Languages Press.

Liu Dechang. 1989. "Dui Xijiang Miaozu Wenhua Xianxiang de Sikao (Reflections on the Phenomenon of Xijiang Miao Culture)." In *Miaoxue Yanjiu (Research in Miao Studies)*. Vol. 1. Li Tinggui, ed. Guiyang: Guizhou Nationalities Press.

Liu Derong, ed. 1988. *Miaozu Minjian Gushi (Miao Folk Tales).* Kunming: Yunnan People's Press.

Liu, Lydia H. 1991. "The Female Tradition in Modern Chinese Literature: Negotiating Feminisms Across East/West Boundaries." *Genders* 12:22-44.

———. 1995. *Translingual Practice: Literature, National Culture, and Translated Modernity—China, 1900–1937.* Stanford, Calif.: Stanford University Press.

Liu Xian et al. 1981. *La Hua Duo Duo (Flowers of Wax).* Guiyang: Guizhou People's Press.

Liu Yuping. 1992. "Collecting Craze." *China Today* 41 (7):51-55.

Long Boya. 1991. "Miaozu (The Miao Nationality)." In *Guizhou Shaoshu Minzu (Guizhou's Minority Nationalities)*. Zhang Minzhu, ed. Pp. 1-51. Guiyang: Guizhou Nationalities Press.

Lowenthal, David. 1985. *The Past Is a Foreign Country.* Cambridge: Cambridge University Press.

Lu Pu. 1981. *Designs of Chinese Indigo Batik.* Beijing: New World Press.

Lu Simian. 1987. *Zhongguo Minzu Shi (History of China's Ethnic Groups).*

Lufkin, Felicity. 1990. "Images of Minorities in the Art of the People's Republic of China." M.A. thesis, University of California, Berkeley.

Ma Shaoqiao. 1988. " 'Cuan San Miao Yu San Wei' Xin Shi (A New Explanation of 'The Exile of the San Miao to San Wei')." In *Miaozu Yanjiu Luncong (Collected Essays in Miao Research)*. Hu Qiwang and Li Tinggui, eds. Pp. 60-67. Guiyang: Guizhou Nationalities Press.

Ma Xueliang. 1983. *Miaozu Shishi (Miao Epic Poems).* Beijing: China Folk Art and Literature Press.

Ma Yin, ed. 1985. *Questions and Answers About China's Minority Nationalities.* Beijing: New World Press.

———, ed. 1989. *China's Minority Nationalities.* Beijing: Foreign Languages Press.

Ma Zhengrong. 1981. "Guizhou Miaozu Cixiu Yishu (The Embroidery Arts of the Guizhou Miao)." *Zhongguo Meishu (Fine Arts of China)* 1 (5):64-67.

———. 1986. *Guizhou Minzu Minjian Meishu Zhan (Minority and Folk Crafts of Guizhou).* Hong Kong: Hong Kong Arts Centre and Guiyang: Guizhou Branch of the Chinese Artists Association.

MacCannell, Dean. 1973. "Staged Authenticity: Arrangements of Social Space in Tourist Settings." *American Journal of Sociology* 79 (3):589–603.

MacGowan, D. J. 1869-70. "Note on the Chihkiang Miautsz'." *Journal of the North China Branch of the Royal Asiatic Society*, n.s. 6:123–27.

Mackerras, Colin. 1973. *Amateur Theater in China, 1949–1966*. Canberra: Australian National University Press.

———. 1995. *China's Minority Cultures: Identities and Integration Since 1912*. New York: St. Martin's Press.

Mai Ding, ed. 1987. *Folksongs of China's 56 Nationalities*. Beijing: New World Press.

Manganaro, Marc. *Culture, 1922 and After: Conversations in Anthropology and Literary Study*. Princeton, N.J.: Princeton University Press. Forthcoming.

Mani, Lata. 1987. "Contentious Traditions: The Debate on Sati in Colonial India." *Cultural Critique* 7:119–56.

Mankekar, Purnima. 1993a. "National Texts and Gendered Lives: An Ethnography of Television Viewers in a North Indian City." *American Ethnologist* 20 (3):543–63.

———. 1993b. "Television Tales and a Woman's Rage: A Nationalist Recasting of Draupadi's 'Disrobing.'" *Public Culture* 5 (3):469–92.

Mao Zedong. 1967. "Talks at the Yenan Forum on Literature and Art." In *Selected Works of Mao Tse-tung*. Vol. 3, pp. 69–98. Beijing: Foreign Languages Press.

———. 1977 [1957]. "On the Correct Handling of Contradictions Among the People." In *Selected Works of Mao Tse-tung*. Vol. 5, pp. 384–421. Beijing: Foreign Languages Press.

———. 1977. "Criticize Han Chauvinism." In *Selected Works of Mao Tse-tung*. Vol. 5, pp. 87–88. Beijing: Foreign Languages Press.

Marcus, George E. 1995. "Ethnography In/Of the World System: The Emergence of Multi-Sited Ethnography." *Annual Review of Anthropology* 24:95–140.

Marcus, George E., and Fred R. Myers. 1995. "The Traffic in Art and Culture: An Introduction." In *The Traffic in Culture: Refiguring Art and Anthropology*. Berkeley: University of California Press.

Marcuse, Herbert. 1964. *One-Dimensional Man*. Boston: Beacon Press.

Matisoff, James. 1983. "Linguistic Diversity and Language Contact." In *Highlanders of Thailand*. John McKinnon and Wanat Bhruksasri, eds. Kuala Lumpur: Oxford University Press.

McClintock, Anne. 1995. *Imperial Leather: Race, Gender, and Sexuality in the Colonial Contest*. New York: Routledge.

McDougall, Bonnie S. 1980. *Mao Zedong's "Talks at the Yan'an Conference on Literature and Art: A Translation of the 1943 Text with Commentary."* Ann Arbor: University of Michigan Center for Chinese Studies.

McGough, James P. 1979. *Fei Hsiao-t'ung: The Dilemma of a Chinese Intellectual.* White Plains, N.Y.: M. E. Sharpe.

McGrane, Bernard. 1989. *Beyond Anthropology: Society and the Other.* New York: Columbia University Press.

McKhann, Charles F. 1995. "The Naxi and the Nationalities Question." In *Cultural Encounters on China's Ethnic Frontiers.* Stevan Harrell, ed. Pp. 39–62. Seattle: University of Washington Press.

McRobbie, Angela. 1991. *Feminism and Youth Culture: From Jackie to Just Seventeen.* Boston: Unwin Hyman.

Meijer, Irene Costa, and Baukje Prins. 1998. "How Bodies Come to Matter: An Interview with Judith Butler." *Signs* 23 (2):275–86.

Mesny, William. 1905. *Mesny's Chinese Miscellany.* Vol. 4. Shanghai: China Gazette Office.

Miao Ling Feng Lei Chuangzuo Zu (Miaoling Feng Lei Writing Team). 1976. *Miaoling Feng Lei (Wind and Thunder in the Miao Mountains).* Beijing: People's Literature Press.

Miaozu Jianshi Editing Group. 1985. *Miaozu Jianshi (Brief History of the Miao).* Guiyang: Guizhou Nationalities Press.

Michaud, Jean. 1997. "From Southwest China into Upper Indochina: An Overview of Hmong (Miao) Migrations." *Asia Pacific Viewpoint* 38 (2):119–30.

Mickey, Margaret Portia. 1944. "The Hai P'a Miao of Kweichow." *Journal of the West China Border Research Society* 15 (A):57–78.

———. 1947. "The Cowrie Shell Miao of Kweichow." *Papers of the Peabody Museum of American Archaeology and Ethnology* 32 (1):1–80.

Miller, Daniel. 1992. "The Young and the Restless in Trinidad: A Case of the Local and the Global in Mass Consumption." In *Consuming Technologies: Media Information in Domestic Spaces.* Roger Silverstone and Eric Hirsch, eds. Pp. 163–82. London: Routledge.

Millward, James A. 1996. "New Perspectives on the Qing Frontier." In *Remapping China: Fissures in Historical Terrain.* Gail Hershatter, Emily Honig, Jonathan Lipman, and Randall Stross, eds. Pp. 113–29. Stanford, Calif.: Stanford University Press.

Mills, Mary Beth. 1997. "Contesting the Margins of Modernity: Women, Migration, and Consumption in Thailand." *American Ethnologist* 24 (1):37–61.

Minzu Yanjiu Bianji Bu (Research on Nationalities Editorial Board). 1984. "Quanguo Ge Sheng, Shi, Zizhiqu Ge Minzu Renkou (Populations of Each Nationality in All the Provinces, Cities, and Autonomous Regions of the Country)." *Minzu Yanjiu (Research on Nationalities)* 6:70-77.

Mitchell, Timothy. 1988. *Colonising Egypt.* Cambridge: Cambridge University Press.

Modleski, Tania. 1991. "Some Functions of Feminist Criticism: Or, the Scandal of the Mute Body." In *Feminism Without Women: Culture and Criticism in a "Postfeminist" Age*. Pp. 35–58. New York: Routledge.

Moore, W. Robert, et al. 1951. "Portrait of Indochina." *National Geographic* 99(4):461–90.

Morgan, Lewis Henry. 1877. *Ancient Society*. New York: Holt.

Morley, David. 1980. *The "Nationwide" Audience*. London: British Film Institute.

———. 1986. *Family Television: Cultural Power and Domestic Leisure*. London: Comedia.

———. 1991. "Where the Global Meets the Local: Notes from the Sitting Room." *Screen* 32:1–15.

Moseley, George. 1966. *The Party and the National Question in China*. Cambridge, Mass.: MIT Press.

———. 1973. *The Consolidation of the South China Frontier*. Berkeley: University of California Press.

Moser, Leo J. 1985. *The Chinese Mosaic: The Peoples and Provinces of China*. Boulder, Colo.: Westview Press.

Mosse, George L. 1985. *Nationalism and Sexuality: Middle-Class Morality and Sexual Norms in Modern Europe*. Madison: University of Wisconsin Press.

Mottin, Jean. 1980. *The History of the Hmong (Meo)*. Bangkok: Odeon Store.

Mullaney, Steven. 1983. "Strange Things, Gross Terms, Curious Customs: The Rehearsal of Cultures in the Late Renaissance." *Representations* 3:40–67.

Murray, David. 1996. "Homosexuality, Society, and the State: An Ethnography of Sublime Resistance in Martinique." *Identities* 2 (3):249–72.

Nader, Laura. 1989. "Orientalism, Occidentalism, and the Control of Women." *Cultural Dynamics* 2 (3):323–55.

Naquin, Susan, and Evelyn S. Rawski. 1987. *Chinese Society in the Eighteenth Century*. New Haven: Yale University Press.

National Population Census Office of the State Council. 1991. *Major Figures of the Fourth National Population Census of China*. Beijing: China Statistical Publishing House.

National Tourism Administration of the People's Republic of China. 1989. *The Yearbook of China Tourism Statistics*. Beijing: Tourism Press of China.

———. 1990. *The Yearbook of China Tourism Statistics*. Beijing: Tourism Press of China.

New China News Photos Company, ed. 1982. China Official Annual Report 1982/3. Hong Kong: Hong Kong Kingsway International.

Notar, Beth. 1994. "Of Labor and Liberation: Images of Women in Current Chinese Television Advertising." *Visual Anthropology Review* 10 (2):29–44.

Oakes, Timothy S. 1992. "Identity and Poverty in Guizhou: A Cultural-Historical Geography." Unpublished.

————. 1993. "The Cultural Space of Modernity: Ethnic Tourism and Place Identity in China." *Environment and Planning D — Society and Space* 11 (1):47–66.

————. 1995a. "Tourism in Guizhou: Place and the Paradox of Modernity." Ph.D. diss., University of Washington.

————. 1995b. "Shen Congwen's Literary Regionalism and the Gendered Landscape of Chinese Modernity." *Geografiska Annaler* 77B (2):93–107.

————. 1998. *Tourism and Modernity in China.* London: Routledge.

————. 1999. "Selling Guizhou: Cultural Development in an Era of Marketisation." In *The Political Economy of China's Provinces.* Hans Hendrischke and Chong Y. Feng, eds. Pp. 27–67. London: Routledge.

Ong, Aihwa. 1990. "State Versus Islam: Malay Families, Women's Bodies, and the Body Politic in Malaysia." *American Ethnologist* 17 (2):258–76.

————. 1993. "On the Edge of Empires: Flexible Citizenship Among Chinese in Diaspora." *positions* 1 (3):745–78.

————. 1996. "Anthropology, China, and Modernities: The Geopolitics of Cultural Knowledge." In *The Future of Anthropological Knowledge.* Henrietta Moore, ed. Pp. 60–92. London: Routledge.

————. 1997. "Chinese Modernities: Narratives of Nation and Capitalism." In *Ungrounded Empires: The Cultural Politics of Modern Chinese Transnationalism.* Aihwa Ong and Donald Nonini, eds. Pp. 171–202. New York: Routledge.

Ortner, Sherry B. 1998. "Generation X: Anthropology in a Media-Saturated World." *Cultural Anthropology* 13 (3):414–40.

Ou Chaoquan. 1984. "Lun Minzuxue zhi Fazhan wei Kexue—Jinian Engesi 'Jiating, Siyou he Guojia de Qiyuan' Yi Shu Fabiao Yibai Zhounian (On the Development of Ethnology as a Science—In Commemoration of the Centenary of the Publication of Engels' 'The Origin of the Family, Private Property and the State')." *Zhongguo Shehui Kexue* (*Social Sciences in China*) 4:91–108.

Pan Dingzhi. 1989. "Miaozu Chuantong Wenhua de Jidian Sikao (A Reflection on Several Points About Miao Traditional Culture)." In *Miaoxue Yanjiu* (*Research in Miao Studies*). Vol. 1. Li Tinggui, ed. Guiyang: Guizhou Nationalities Press.

Pan Guanghua, ed. 1990. *Zhongguo Miaozu Fengqing* (*The Customs of China's Miao*). Guiyang: Guizhou Nationalities Press.

Parker, Andrew, Mary Russo, Doris Sommer, Patricia Yaeger, eds. 1992. "Introduction." In *Nationalisms and Sexualities.* Pp. 1–18. New York: Routledge.

Parry, Benita. 1987. "Problems of Current Theories of Colonial Discourse." *Oxford Literary Review* 9 (1–2):27–58.

Peng Jianqun. 1983. "A Miao Nationality Village." *China Reconstructs* 32 (3):57–63.

Perry, Elizabeth J. 1994. "State of the Field: Trends in the Study of Chinese Politics—State-Society Relations." *China Quarterly* 139:704-13.

———. 1996. "Introduction: Putting Class in Its Place: Bases of Worker Identity in East Asia." In *Putting Class in Its Place: Worker Identities in East Asia*. Elizabeth J. Perry, ed. Pp. 1-10. Berkeley, Calif.: Institute of East Asian Studies China Research Monograph 48.

Phillips, David R., and Anthony G. O. Yeh. 1989. "Special Economic Zones." In *China's Regional Development*. David S. G. Goodman, ed. Pp. 112-34. London: Routledge.

Pigg, Stacy Leigh. 1996. "The Credible and the Credulous: The Question of 'Villagers' Beliefs' in Nepal." *Cultural Anthropology* 11 (2):160-201.

Pollard, Samuel. 1921. *In Unknown China*. Philadelphia: J. B. Lippincott.

Pollock, Griselda. 1987. "What's Wrong with Images of Women?" In Rosemary Betterton, ed. *Looking On: Images of Femininity in the Visual Arts and Media*. New York: Pandora.

Potter, Sulamith Heins, and Jack M. Potter. 1990. *China's Peasants: The Anthropology of a Revolution*. Cambridge: Cambridge University Press.

Potter, Sulamith Heins. 1983. "The Position of Peasants in Modern China's Social Order." *Modern China* 9 (4):465-99.

Prakash, Gyan. 1992a. "Science 'Gone Native' in Colonial India." *Representations* 40:153-78.

———. 1992b. "Postcolonial Criticism and Indian Historiography." *Social Text* 31/32:8-19.

Price, David H. 1998. "Cold War Anthropology: Collaborators and Victims of the National Security State." *Identities* 4 (3-4):389-430.

Price, Sally. 1989. *Primitive Art in Civilized Places*. Chicago: University of Chicago Press.

Purnell, Herbert C., Jr. 1972. *Miao and Yao Linguistic Studies*. Ithaca, N.Y.: Cornell University Southeast Asia Program Data Paper No. 88.

Qiandongnan Miaozu Dongzu Zizhizhou Gaikuang Editing Group. 1986. *Qiandongnan Miaozu Dongzu Zizhizhou Gaikuang* (*A General Survey of the Southeast Guizhou Miao and Dong Autonomous Prefecture*). Guiyang: Guizhou People's Publishing House.

Quincy, Keith. 1988. *Hmong: History of a People*. Cheney: Eastern Washington University Press.

Radway, Janice A. 1984. *Reading the Romance: Women, Patriarchy, and Popular Literature*. Chapel Hill: University of North Carolina Press.

———. 1988. "Reception Study: Ethnography and the Problems of Dispersed Audiences and Nomadic Subjects." *Cultural Studies* 2 (3):359-67.

Rankin, Mary B. 1986. *Elite Activism and Political Transformation in China: Zhejiang Province, 1865-1911*. Stanford, Calif.: Stanford University Press.

———. 1990. "The Origins of a Chinese Public Sphere: Local Elites and

Community Affairs in the Late Imperial Period." *Etudes Chinoises* 9 (2):12–60.

Ratliff, Martha. n.d. "Vocabulary of Environment and Subsistence in the Hmong-Mien Protolanguage." In Proceedings of the First International Symposium on the Hmong/Miao in Asia. Jean Michaud and Christian Culas, eds. Manuscript.

Reilly, Theresa. 1987. *Richly Woven Traditions: Costumes of the Miao of Southwest China and Beyond.* New York: China Institute in America.

Robbins, Bruce. 1993. "Introduction: The Public as Phantom." In *The Phantom Public Sphere.* Bruce Robbins, ed. Pp. vii–xxvi. Minneapolis: University of Minnesota Press.

Robertson, Jennifer. 1995. "Mon Japon: The Revue Theater as a Technology of Japanese Imperialism." *American Ethnologist* 22 (4):970–96.

Robinson, Julian, Jeanne Guillemin, and Matthew Meselson. 1987. "Yellow Rain: The Story Collapses." *Foreign Policy* 68:100–117.

Rofel, Lisa. 1992. "Rethinking Modernity: Space and Factory Discipline in China." *Cultural Anthropology* 7 (1):93–114, February.

———. 1994. "*Yearnings:* Televisual Love and Melodramatic Politics in Contemporary China." *American Ethnologist* 21 (4):700–722.

———. 1999. *Other Modernities: Gendered Yearnings in China After Socialism.* Berkeley: University of California Press.

Rosaldo, Renato. 1989. *Culture and Truth: The Remaking of Social Analysis.* Boston: Beacon Press.

Rossi, Gail. 1986. "Guizhou Textiles." *Shuttle, Spindle, and Dyepot* 69:39–43.

———. 1987. "A Flourishing Art: China—Guizhou Women Continue to Embroider Their Legends." *Threads* February/March:30–32.

———. 1988. "Enduring Dress of the Miao, Guizhou Province, People's Republic of China." *Ornament* 11 (3):26–31.

Rostow, W. W. 1960. *The Stages of Economic Growth: A Non-Communist Manifesto.* Cambridge: Cambridge University Press.

Rouse, Roger. 1995. "Questions of Identity: Personhood and Collectivity in Transnational Migration to the United States." *Critique of Anthropology* 15 (4):351–80.

Rowe, William. 1989. *Hankow: Conflict and Community in a Chinese City, 1796–1895.* Stanford, Calif.: Stanford University Press.

———. 1990. "The Public Sphere in Modern China." *Modern China* 16 (3):309–29.

Rudelson, Justin Jon. 1997. *Oasis Identities: Uyghur Nationalism Along China's Silk Road.* New York: Columbia University Press.

Ruey Yih-fu. 1960. "The Magpie Miao of South Szechuan." In *Social Structure in Southeast Asia.* G. P. Murdock, ed. Pp. 143–55. New York: Wenner-Gren

Foundation for Anthropological Research, Viking Fund Publications in Anthropology No. 29.

———. 1962. "The Miao: Their Origin and Southward Migration." In *Proceedings of the International Association of Historians of Asia, Second Biennial Conference*. Taipei, Taiwan.

———. 1967. "A Study of the Miao People." In *Historical, Archaeological, and Linguistic Studies on Southern China, South-East Asia, and the Hong Kong Region*. F. S. Drake, ed. Hong Kong: Hong Kong University Press.

Ruey Yih-fu, ed. 1973a. *Eighty-Two Aboriginal Peoples of Kweichow Province in Pictures*. Taipei: Academia Sinica.

———. 1973b. *Sixteen Aboriginal Peoples of Kweichow Province in Pictures*. Taipei: Academia Sinica.

Said, Edward. 1978. *Orientalism*. New York: Vintage Books.

———. 1983. "Traveling Theory." In *The World, the Text, and the Critic*. Pp. 226–47. Cambridge, Mass.: Harvard University Press.

———. 1985. "Orientalism Reconsidered." *Race and Class* 27 (2):1–15.

Saich, Tony. 1994. "The Search for Civil Society and Democracy in China." *Current History* 93 (584):260–64.

Salisbury, Harrison E. 1985. *The Long March: The Untold Story*. New York: Harper and Row.

Sangren, P. Steven. 1995. "'Power' against Ideology: A Critique of Foucaultian Usage." *Cultural Anthropology* 10 (1):3–40.

Savina, F. M. 1924. *Histoire des Miaos*. Hong Kong. Imprimerie de la Société des Missions-Étrangeres.

Schafer, Edward H. 1967. *The Vermilion Bird: T'ang Images of the South*. Berkeley: University of California Press.

Schechner, Richard. 1985. *Between Theater and Anthropology*. Philadelphia: University of Pennsylvania Press.

Schein, Louisa. 1985. "Miao/Hmong Textile Arts: Costume and Commerce." *Focus on Asian Studies* 4 (3):4–13.

———. 1989. "The Dynamics of Cultural Revival Among the Miao in Guizhou." In *Ethnicity and Ethnic Groups in China*. Chien Chiao and Nicholas Tapp, eds. Pp. 199–212. Hong Kong: New Asia Academic Bulletin, Chinese University of Hong Kong.

———. 1993. "Popular Culture and the Production of Difference: The Miao and China." Ph.D. diss., University of California, Berkeley.

———. 1994. "The Consumption of Color and the Politics of White Skin in Post-Mao China." *Social Text* 41:141–64.

———. 1996a. "The Other Goes to Market: The State, the Nation, and Unruliness in Contemporary China." *Identities* 2 (3):197–222.

———. 1996b. "Multiple Alterities: The Contouring of Gender in Miao and

Chinese Nationalisms." In *Women Out of Place: The Gender of Agency and the Race of Nationality*. Brackette F. Williams, ed. Pp. 79-102. New York: Routledge.

————. 1996c. "White Anomalies: Race, Gender, and Notions of Modernity in China." Paper presented at the Association for Asian Studies Meetings, Honolulu, April 13.

————. 1998a. "Importing Miao Brethren to Hmong America: A Not So Stateless Transnationalism." In *Cosmopolitics: Thinking and Feeling Beyond the Nation*. Pheng Cheah and Bruce Robbins, eds. Pp. 163-91. Minneapolis: University of Minnesota Press.

————. 1998b. "Forged Transnationality and Oppositional Cosmopolitanism." *Comparative Urban and Community Research* 6:291-313.

————. 1999. "Of Cargo and Satellites: Imagined Cosmopolitanism." *Postcolonial Studies* 2 (3).

Schell, Orville. 1994. "To Get Rich Is Glorious." *New Yorker* 70 (22): 26-35.

Schneider, Laurence A. 1971. *Ku Chieh-kang and China's New History: Nationalism and the Quest for Alternative Traditions*. Berkeley: University of California Press.

Schotter, P. Aloys. 1908-9. "Notes Ethnographiques sur les Tribus du Kouytcheou (Chine)." *Anthropos* 3:397-425; 4:318-53.

Schwarcz, Vera. 1991. "No Solace from Lethe: History, Memory, and Cultural Identity in Twentieth Century China." *Daedalus* 120 (2):85-112.

Schwartz, Benjamin. 1964. *In Search of Wealth and Power: Yen Fu and the West*. New York: Harper and Row.

Searle, John R. 1969. *Speech Acts: An Essay in the Philosophy of Language*. Cambridge: Cambridge University Press.

Seeley, Thomas D., et al. 1985. "Yellow Rain." *Scientific American* 253 (3):128-37.

Shanghai Museum. 1999. *Chinese Minority Nationalities' Art Gallery*. Exhibition Catalogue. Shanghai: Shanghai Museum.

Sherman, Spencer. 1988. "The Hmong in America. Laotian Refugees in the 'Land of the Giants.'" *National Geographic* 174 (4):586-610.

Shi Xiaojiang, trans. 1985. "The Ribbon Maiden." In *The Slave and the Dragon Maid—Folk Tales from China*. Beijing: Foreign Languages Press.

Shils, Edward. 1991. "The Virtue of Civil Society." *Government and Opposition* 26 (1):3-20.

Siu, Helen F. 1989. "Recycling Rituals: Politics and Popular Culture in Contemporary Rural China." In *Unofficial China: Popular Culture and Thought in the People's Republic of China*. Perry Link, Richard Madsen, and Paul Pickowicz, eds. Pp. 121-37. Boulder: Westview Press.

Skinner, G. William 1964-65. "Marketing and Social Structure in Rural China." *Journal of Asian Studies* 24 (1):3-44; 24 (2):195-228; 24 (3):363-99.

———. 1985. "Presidential Address: The Structure of Chinese History." *Journal of Asian Studies* 44 (2):271–92.

Smalley, William A., Chia Koua Vang, and Gnia Yee Yang. 1990. *Mother of Writing: The Origin and Development of a Hmong Messianic Script*. Chicago: University of Chicago Press.

Snow, Edgar. 1978 [1938]. *Red Star Over China*. 1st revised and enlarged ed. New York: Bantam.

Song Shuhua. 1984. *China's Ethnological Composition and Its Historical Perspective*. Tokyo: Social Sciences and Asia, Institute of Oriental Culture, University of Tokyo.

Spence, Jonathan D. 1981. *The Gate of Heavenly Peace: The Chinese and Their Revolution, 1895–1980*. New York: Penguin Books.

Spencer, J. E. 1940. "Kueichou: An Internal Chinese Colony." *Pacific Affairs* 13 (2):162–72, June.

Spivak, Gayatri Chakravorty. 1988a. "Can the Subaltern Speak?" In *Marxism and the Interpretation of Culture*. Lawrence Grossberg and Cary Nelson, eds. Pp. 271–313. Urbana: University of Illinois Press.

———. 1988b. "Subaltern Studies: Deconstructing Historiography." In *Selected Subaltern Studies*. Ranajit Guha and Gayatri Chakravorty Spivak, eds. Pp. 3–32. Oxford: Oxford University Press.

———. 1990. "Gayatri Spivak on the Politics of the Postcolonial Subject: An Interview with Howard Winant." *Socialist Review* 90 (3):81–97.

Stalin, Joseph. 1975. "Marxism and the National Question." In *Marxism and the National-Colonial Question*. San Francisco: Proletarian Publishers. (In 1913 originally titled *The National Question and Social-Democracy*.)

Stallybrass, Peter, and Allon White. 1986. *The Poetics and Politics of Transgression*. Ithaca, N.Y.: Cornell University Press.

Stocking, George W. 1983. *Observers Observed: Essays on Ethnographic Fieldwork*. Madison: University of Wisconsin Press.

———. 1987. *Victorian Anthropology*. New York: Free Press.

Strand, David. 1989. *Rickshaw Beijing: City People and Politics in 1920s China*. Berkeley: University of California Press.

Strecker, David. 1987. "The Hmong-Mien Languages." *Linguistics of the Tibeto-Burman Area* 10 (2):1–11.

Sun Yat-sen. 1975 [1927]. *San Min Chu I: The Three Principles of the People*. Frank W. Price, trans. New York: Da Capo Press.

Sutton, Donald S. n.d. "Ethnicity and the Miao Frontier in the Eighteenth Century." In Empire and Ethnicity on China's Frontiers during the Ming and Qing. Pamela K. Crossley, Helen F. Siu, and Donald S. Sutton, eds. Manuscript.

Swain, Margaret Byrne. 1990. "Commoditizing Ethnicity in Southwest China." *Cultural Survival* 14 (1):26–32.

Tambiah, Stanley J. 1985. *Culture, Thought, and Social Action: An Anthropological Perspective.* Cambridge, Mass.: Harvard University Press.

Tang Xiaobing. 1993. "Orientalism and the Question of Universality: The Language of Contemporary Chinese Literary Theory." *positions* 1 (2):389–413.

———. 1998. "Decorating Culture: Notes on Interior Design, Interiority, and Interiorization." *Public Culture* 10 (3): 530–48.

Tapp, Nicholas. 1982. "The Relevance of Telephone Directories to a Lineage-Based Society: A Consideration of Some Messianic Myths Among the Hmong." *Journal of the Siam Society* 70:114–27.

———. 1986. *The Hmong in Thailand: Opium People of the Golden Triangle.* London: Anti-Slavery Society.

———. 1989. *Sovereignty and Rebellion: The White Hmong of Northern Thailand.* Singapore: Oxford University Press.

Taussig, Michael. 1993. *Mimesis and Alterity: A Particular History of the Senses.* New York: Routledge.

Taylor, Charles. 1990. "Modes of Civil Society." *Public Culture* 3 (1):95–118.

Thierry, François. 1989. "Empire and Minority in China." In *Minority Peoples in the Age of Nation-States.* Gerard Chaliand, ed. London: Pluto Press.

Thompson, John B. 1995. *The Media and Modernity: A Social Theory of the Media.* Stanford, Calif.: Stanford University Press.

Tian Bing et al. 1981. *Miaozu Wenxue Shi (A History of Miao Literature).* Guiyang: Guizhou People's Press.

Tilley, Christopher. 1997. "Performing Culture in the Global Village." *Critique of Anthropology* 17 (1):67–89.

Tillman, Hoyt Cleveland. 1979. "Proto-Nationalism in Twelfth-Century China? The Case of Ch'en Liang." *Harvard Journal of Asiatic Studies* 39 (2):403–27.

Tölölyan, Khachig. 1991. "The Nation-State and Its Others: In Lieu of a Preface." *Diaspora* 1 (1):3–7.

Torgovnick, Marianna. 1990. *Gone Primitive: Savage Intellects, Modern Lives.* Chicago: University of Chicago Press.

Townsend, James. 1992. "Chinese Nationalism." *Australian Journal of Chinese Affairs* 27:97–130.

Trauzettel, Rolf. 1975. "Sung Patriotism as a First Step Toward Chinese Nationalism." In *Crisis and Prosperity in Sung China.* John Winthrop Haeger, ed. Tucson: University of Arizona Press.

Tsing, Anna Lowenhaupt. 1993. *In the Realm of the Diamond Queen: Marginality in an Out-of-the-Way Place.* Princeton: Princeton University Press.

Turner, Victor. 1986. *The Anthropology of Performance.* New York: Performing Arts Journal Publications.

Tylor, Edward B. 1871. *Primitive Culture.* London: J. Murray.

Unger, Jonathan, and Jean Xiong. 1990. "Life in the Chinese Hinterlands Under the Rural Economic Reforms." *Bulletin of Concerned Asian Scholars* 22 (2):4–17.

Veblen, Thorstein. 1899/1953. *The Theory of the Leisure Class: An Economic Study of Institutions*. New York: Mentor Books.

Wakeman, Frederic Jr. 1975. *The Fall of Imperial China*. New York: Free Press.

———. 1991. *In Search of National Character*. Berkeley: University of California Center for Chinese Studies Pre-Prints No. 1.

———. 1993. "The Civil Society and Public Sphere Debate: Western Reflections on Chinese Political Culture." *Modern China* 19 (2):108–38.

Wan Bixuan. 1991. "Miaozu 'Yin Long' Xisu Chutan (A Preliminary Exploration of the Miao Custom of 'Leading Back the Dragons')." In *Miaoxue Yanjiu (Research in Miao Studies)*. Vol. 2. Li Tinggui, ed. Pp. 86–90. Guiyang: Guizhou Nationalities Press.

Wang Bingyuan and Chen Fengrong. 1984. "Makesizhuyi Minzu Dingyi de Chansheng, Fazhan he Shixian (The Emergence, Development, and Implementation of a Marxist Definition of Nationality)." *Minzu Yanjiu (Research on Nationalities)* 3:1–8.

Wang Fushi. 1985. *Miaoyu Jianzhi (A Brief Account of the Miao Language)*. Beijing: Nationalities Press.

Wang He. 1986. "Traditional Culture and Modernization—A Review of the General Situation of Cultural Studies in China in Recent Years." *Social Sciences in China* 7 (4):9–30.

Wang Huiqin. 1979. "Qing Dai Qianlong Jiaqing Nianjian Miaozu Nongmin Da Qiyi (The Great Miao Peasant Uprising in the Qianlong Jiaqing Period of the Qing Dynasty)." *Guizhou Minzu Yanjiu* 1.

Wang Jing. 1996. *High Culture Fever: Politics, Aesthetics, and Ideology in Deng's China*. Berkeley: University of California Press.

Wang Yongyao. 1989. "Ethnic Costumes Inspire New Fashions." *China Reconstructs*. June: 34–39.

Warner, Michael. 1993. "The Mass Public and the Mass Subject." In *The Phantom Public Sphere*. Bruce Robbins, ed. Pp. 234–56. Minneapolis: University of Minnesota Press.

Watson, James L., ed. 1984. *Class and Social Stratification in Post-Revolution China*. Cambridge: Cambridge University Press.

Weber, Max. 1958. "Class Status, Party." In *Max Weber: Essays in Sociology*. H. H. Gerth and C. Wright Mills, eds. Pp. 180–95. New York: Oxford University Press.

Weng Dujian. 1984. "Lun Zhongguo Minzu Shi (On the History of China's Nationalities)." *Minzu Yanjiu (Research on Nationalities)* 4:1–8.

Westermeyer, Joseph. 1982. *Poppies, Pipes, and People: Opium and Its Use in Laos*. Berkeley: University of California Press.

Weston, Kath. 1993. "Do Clothes Make the Woman? Gender, Performance Theory, and Lesbian Eroticism." *Genders* 17:1–21.

White, Peter T. 1971. "The Lands and Peoples of Southeast Asia: Mosaic of Cultures." *National Geographic* 139 (3):296–329.

Whyte, Martin K. 1992. "Urban China: A Civil Society in the Making?" In *State and Society in China: The Consequences of Reform*. Arthur Lewis Rosenbaum, ed. Pp. 77–102. Boulder, Colo.: Westview Press.

Wiens, Herold J. 1954. *China's March Toward the Tropics*. Hamden, Conn.: Shoestring Press.

Wiens, Mi Chu. 1969. *Anti-Manchu Thought During the Early Ch'ing*. Cambridge: Harvard East Asian Research Center Papers on China 22A.

Williams, Brackette F. 1989. "A Class Act: Anthropology and the Race to Nation Across Ethnic Terrain." *Annual Review of Anthropology* 18:401–44.

——. 1990. "Nationalism, Traditionalism and the Problem of Cultural Inauthenticity." In *Nationalist Ideologies and the Production of National Cultures*. Richard Fox ed. Pp. 112–29. Washington, D.C.: American Ethnological Society Monographs Series No. 2.

——. 1991, *Stains on My Name, War in My Veins: Guyana and the Politics of Cultural Struggle*. Durham, N.C.: Duke University Press.

——. 1996. "Introduction: Mannish Women and Gender After the Act." In *Women Out of Place: The Gender of Agency and the Race of Nationality*. Pp. 1–33. New York: Routledge.

Williams, Maynard Owen. 1935. "By Motor Trail Across French Indochina." *National Geographic* 68:487–534.

Williams, Raymond. 1977. *Marxism and Literature*. Oxford: Oxford University Press.

Willis, Paul. 1977. *Learning to Labor: How Working Class Kids Get Working Class Jobs*. New York: Columbia University Press.

——. 1990. *Common Culture: Symbolic Work at Play in the Everyday Cultures of the Young*. Boulder, Colo.: Westview Press.

Wittfogel, Karl A. 1981 [1957]. *Oriental Despotism: A Comparative Study of Total Power*. New York: Vintage Books.

Wolf, Eric R. 1982. *Europe and the People Without History*. Berkeley: University of California Press.

Wong, How-Man. 1984. "Peoples of China's Far Provinces." *National Geographic* 165 (3):283–333.

Wong Siu-lun. 1979. *Sociology and Socialism in Contemporary China*. London: Routledge & Kegan Paul.

Wu, David Y. H. 1990. "Chinese Minority Policy and the Meaning of Minority Cultures: The Example of the Bai in Yunnan, China." *Human Organization* 49 (1):1–13.

——. 1993. "Chinese Dance and the Invented Subjects of Shaoshu Minzu."

Paper presented at the Subject of China Conference, University of California at Santa Cruz, January 21-23, 1993.

Wu Xinfu. 1989. "Luelun Miaozu Zhixi (A Brief Discussion of the Branches of the Miao Nationality)." In *Miaoxue Yanjiu (Research in Miao Studies)*. Vol. 1. Li Tinggui, ed. Guiyang: Guizhou Nationalities Press.

Wu Xuechou. 1982. "Miaozu Gushi Chuyi (My Humble Opinion on Miao Ancient History)." *Minzu Yanjiu (Research on Nationalities)* 6.

Wu Zelin. 1982. "Minzuxue Tianye Diaocha Fangfa (Ethnological Field Investigation Methods)." *Minzu Tuanjie (Nationalities Unite)* 6.

Xin Jiguang, ed. 1987. *Minority Peoples in China*. Beijing: China Pictorial Publications.

Xiong Yu. 1993. "Analysis of the Changes in Fertility Culture of the Minority Nationalities in Beijing." In *Urban Anthropology in China*. Greg Guldin and Aidan Southall, eds. Pp. 256-67. Leiden: E. J. Brill.

Xu Hualong and Wu Jufen. 1985. *Zhongguo Minjian Fengsu Chuanshuo (Legends About China's Folk Customs)*. Kunming: Yunnan People's Press.

Yang Dali. 1990. "Patterns of China's Regional Development Strategy." *China Quarterly* 122:230-57.

Yang Dao. 1982. "Why Did the Hmong Leave Laos?" In *The Hmong in the West: Observations and Reports*. Bruce T. Downing and Douglas P. Olney, eds. Pp. 3-18. Minneapolis: Center for Urban and Regional Affairs, University of Minnesota.

———. 1993. *Hmong at the Turning Point*. Minneapolis: WorldBridge Associates.

Yang Kaiyi. 1996. "Hmong-Mongolian?" *Hmong Forum* January: 48-62.

Yang Maorui. 1989. "Miaozu Gongtong Xinli Suzhi Chutan (A Preliminary Exploration of the Common Psychological Qualities of the Miao)." In *Miaoxue Yanjiu (Research in Miao Studies)*. Vol. 1. Li Tinggui, ed. Guiyang: Guizhou Nationalities Press.

Yang, Mayfair Meihui, ed. 1999. *Spaces of Their Own: Women's Public Sphere in Transnational China*. Minneapolis: University of Minnesota Press.

———. 1997. "Mass Media and Transnational Subjectivity in Shanghai: Notes on (Re)Cosmopolitanism in a Chinese Metropolis." In *Ungrounded Empires: The Cultural Politics of Modern Chinese Transnationalism*. Aihwa Ong and Donald Nonini, eds. Pp. 287-319. New York: Routledge.

Yang Quan et al. 1982. *Costumes of the Minority Peoples of China*. Kyoto: Binobi.

Yang Tongru. 1985. "Jiefang Qian Miaozu de Minjian Zongjiao (The Folk Religion of the Miao before Liberation)." In *Zhongguo Shaoshu Minzu Zongjiao (The Religion of China's Minority Nationalities)*. Song Enchang, ed. Pp. 367-79. Kunming: Yunnan People's Press.

———. 1989. "Miaozu de 'Miao' Zi Laiyuan ji qi Xuduo Zicheng de Hanyi (The Origin of the 'Miao' Character of the Miao Nationality and the Meanings of Several of their Self-Appellations." In *Miaoxue Yanjiu* (*Research in Miao Studies*). Vol. 1. Li Tinggui, ed. Guiyang: Guizhou Nationalities Press.

Yang Xingju et al., eds. 1991. *Miaozu Sangji* (Miao Funeral Ceremonials). Guiyang: Guizhou Nationalities Press.

Yau, Esther. 1989. "Is China the End of Hermeneutics? Or, Political and Cultural Usage of Non-Han Women in Mainland Chinese Films." *Discourse* 11 (2):115–36.

Yeh Lin. 1965. *A Hundred Flowers Bloom: Amateur Song and Dance Festival of China's National Minorities*. Beijing: China Reconstructs.

Yin Ming. 1977. *United and Equal: The Progress of China's Minority Nationalities*. Beijing: Foreign Languages Press.

Yunnan Sheng Bianjizu (Yunnan Province Editorial Group). 1986. *Zhongyang Fangwentuan Di Er Fentuan: Yunnan Minzu Qingkuang Huiji* (*The Second Team of the Central Interview Team: A Collection on the Situation of the Yunnan Nationalities*). Vol. 2. Kunming: Yunnan Nationalities Press. (Original material from the 1950s.)

Yuval-Davis, Nira, and Flora Anthias. 1989. *Woman–Nation–State*. London: Macmillan.

Zha Jianying. 1994. "Beijing Subnotebooks." *Public Culture* 6 (2):397–406.

———. 1995. *China Pop: How Soap Operas, Tabloids, and Bestsellers Are Transforming a Culture*. New York: W. W. Norton.

Zhang Min, ed. 1991. *Guizhou Shaoshu Minzu* (*Guizhou's Minority Nationalities*). Guiyang: Guizhou Nationalities Press.

Zhang Renwei and Shi Kaizhong. 1992. *Guizhou Minzu Renkou* (*The Population of Guizhou's Nationalites*). Guiyang: Guizhou Nationalities Press.

Zhang Xudong. 1997. *Chinese Modernism in the Era of Reforms*. Durham, N.C.: Duke University Press.

Zhang Yueqi. 1984. " 'Chiyou' Nengfou Yinzuo Miaozu Zuyuan (Can 'Chiyou' Be Cited As the Originator of the Miao People?)." *Minzu Yanjiu* (*Research on Nationalities*) 4:51–52.

Zhang Yongguo. 1989. " 'San Miao Shuo' Zhiyi (Some Doubts About the 'San Miao Theory')." In *Miaoxue Yanjiu* (*Research in Miao Studies*). Vol. 1. Li Tinggui, ed. Guiyang: Guizhou Nationalities Press.

Zhang Yongxiang and Cao Cuiyun. 1984. "Cong Yufa Kan Miaoyu he Hanyu de Miqie Guanxi (How Grammar Reveals the Intimate Relation Between the Miao and Han Languages)." *Zhongyang Minzu Xueyuan Xuebao* (*Journal of the Central Nationalities Institute*) 1.

Zhang Younong et al., eds. 1987. *Guizhou Minzu Jieri* (*Guizhou Nationalities' Festivals*). Guiyang: Guizhou Fine Arts Press.

Zhao Yuchi et al., eds. 1985. *Clothings and Ornaments of China's Miao People*. Beijing: Nationalities Press.

Zheng Lan. 1981. *Travels Through Xishuangbanna: China's Subtropical Home of Many Nationalities*. Beijing: Foreign Languages Press.

Zhi Exiang. 1980. "The Jinuos: China's Newest Nationality." *China Reconstructs* 29 (2):55–61, February.

Zhong Xiu. 1983. *Yunnan Travelogue—100 Days in Southwest China*. Beijing: New World Press.

————. 1984. *Emerging from Primitivity—Travels in the Liangshan Mountains*. Beijing: New World Press.

Zhongguo Shaoshu Minzu Editing Group. 1981. *Zhongguo Shaoshu Minzu (China's Minority Nationalities)*. Beijing: People's Press.

Zhongguo Shehui Kexue Yuan Renkou Yanjiu Suo (Population Research Institute of the Chinese Academy of Social Sciences). 1991. *Zhongguo Renkou Nianjian (Almanac of China's Population)*. Beijing: Economics and Management Press.

Zhongyang Minzu Xueyuan Miaoyao Yanjiu Shi. 1985. *Miaoyaoyu Fangyan Cihui Ji (Collected Vocabularies of the Dialects of the Miao and Yao Languages)*. Beijing: Central Nationalities Press.

Zito, Angela. 1997. *Of Body and Brush: Grand Sacrifice as Text/Performance in Eighteenth-Century China*. Chicago: University of Chicago Press.

Index

Havel, Václav, 141
He Baogang, 142–143
Hebdige, Dick, 291 n.20
Hechter, Michael, 301 n.4
Hegel, G. W. F., 258, 308 n.5, 308 n.6
Hegemony, 13–14, 104, 164, 259, 283, 318 n.7; and culture, 13–14, 259, 283, 318 n.7; and difference, 284; and gender norms, 259
Hei (Black) Miao, 46, 295 n.4
Heng, Geraldine, 302 n.6, 310 n.14
Hershatter, Gail, 233–235, 316 n.6
Hevia, James L., 20, 138, 290 n.13, 303 n.11, 309 n.12, 311 n.1
Hind, Robert J., 301 n.4
Historical recovery, 49
Hmong, xi–xiv, 4, 37, 45–46, 48–50, 57, 66, 169, 281, 295 n.7, 296 n.8, 296 n.10, 296 n.11, 297 n.16, 311 n.5, 315 n.13, 315 n.2 (ch. 8); ethnonym, xi, xiii–xiv, 4, 37; language, xii–xiv, 4; in Southeast Asia, 50, 66; in the West, xi, 45–46, 48–49
Hmu, 40, 62, 299 n.14
Hobsbawm, Eric, 23–24
Holm, David L., 170, 176–177
Homogeneity, 106, 108, 293 n.31
Homogenization, cultural, 86–88
Hong, Wu (emperor), 47
Horkheimer, Max, 15
Hostetler, Laura, 9, 296 n.12, 311 n.1
HRAF. See Human Relations Area Files
Hu Shi, 111
Hua Guofeng (chairman), 180
Huang, Philip, 140, 309 n.11
Hudspeth, W. H., 41–42
Human Relations Area Files (HRAF), 12, 298 n.21
Hybridity, 209–214, 227, 237–238, 273, 314 n.8
Hypergamy, 240, 317 n.9

Identity, 3, 21, 50–67, 95–97, 106–108, 153, 244, 276, 281, 287, 288,

293 n.28, 293 n.30; China's, 3, 153; and commodity, 189; cultural, 200; formation, 62; and the market, 244; Miao, 276; as modern, 253, 276; national, 106–108, 128–129, 286, 318 n.4; and power, 21; production of, 29, 287, 302 n.6; valorization of, 97
Images, 9, 60–62, 87, 90, 105, 135, 143
Imperialist nostalgia, 120
Infantilization, 121, 123, 131, 145, 253
Interior design: as consumption practice, 318 n.9; as status marker, 262–267
Internal colonialism, 5, 10, 74–76, 100–106, 283, 286, 301 n.4; and development in PRC, 74–76
Internal frontier, 301 n.4
Internal orientalism, 30–31, 100–131, 286, 298 n.2, 302 n.6; and gender, 101, 119–123
Interpellation, 1, 21, 73–74, 79, 95, 160, 174, 298 n.1; and ethnic tourism, 73, 79; state, 73, 79, 95
Ivy, Marilyn, 36, 119, 288

Jade Emperor, 56
Jamieson, C. E., 46, 295 n.7
Jenks, Robert, 59–60, 297 n.18
Jensen, Lionel M., 36–37, 294 n.1
Jiang Yingliang, 47
Jiang Zemin, 231
Jin Ou, 186–189, 199, 200
Jing Qiao (Offerings to the Bridge), 214, 313 n.5
Jiuli, 35, 41, 42, 295 n.3
Johnston, R. F., 46

Kaili, 100–101, 184–186, 191
Karaoke, 268, 319 n.10
Keane, John, 308 n.6
Kemp, Emily G., 289 n.5
Kinkley, Jeffrey C., 43, 295 n.6
Kuhn, Philip A., 18

Miao (*continued*)
60-62; handicraft, 1, 44, 51, 61,
191-193; history, 35-67, 283-284;
hospitality rituals, 29, 63-65, 100-
101, 125, 180-181, 190, 194, 230,
255-256, 314 n.8; language, 52;
marriage rite of subservience,
255; marriage strategizing, 239-
241; mountain dwellers, 55-56;
as nomadic, 48-49, 52, 55-56;
political organization, 295 n.7;
prestige, symbols of, 7, 210, 235-
239, 262-267; production and
marketing of handicrafts, 191-
193; rebels, 7, 49, 50, 58-60, 61,
68, 190, 283, 295 n.7; relations to
other ethnic groups, 41-44, 180-
181, 209-210, 289 n.4; religious
practices, 53-54, 60-62, 214-216,
219-221, 291 n.16; rice harvest,
160-163; ritual calendar, 214-216;
script, 312 n.3; sociality, 255-257,
269; social organization, 52-53;
song, 51, 65, 269; subsistence
practices, 52, 56; and swidden
agriculture, 56, 291 n.16; as threat
to moral order, 61; weddings,
254-258, 262-267, 277; women,
53, 60-62, 209
Miao albums, 7-9, 51, 66, 296 n.12
Miao origins: ethnonymic, 36-
41; geographic, 44-50; historic,
48-49
Miao rebellions. *See* Rebellions
Miao Studies Association, 315 n.1
*Miaozu Jianshi. See Brief History of
the Miao*
Michaud, Jean, 289 n.3
Mickey, Margaret Portia, 47
Mills, Mary Beth, 293 n.32
Millward, James A., 5, 289 n.4, 301
n.4
Mineral resources, 6
Ministry of Culture, 306 n.22
Minoritization, 2, 4, 66, 96

Minority cultural producers, 132,
169-202
Minority cultural production, 155-
159, 235-239, 267-271, 311 n.2;
and authenticity, 156-159; and
tourism, 155-159
Minority Nationality Historical
Survey, 299 n.10
Minority policy, 10, 35-67, 80-91,
170-179, 286-288; birth planning,
96, 300 n.22
Minzu gongzuo. See Nationalities
work
Minzu shibie (ethnic classification),
14, 51, 66, 73, 82-86, 91, 95-98,
114, 294 n.2, 295 n.3; language,
52, 84-85, 299 n.12, 299 n.13,
299 n.14; religious, 221; self-
classification, xiii-xiv, 69, 85-86,
97-99; *sheng/shu*, 7, 56-57, 289
n.6, 290 n.7; stage, 83-84, 299 n.11
Miscegenation, 108
Missionaries, 114, 297 n.20, 298 n.6
Mitchell, Timothy, 104, 302 n.7
Modernity, 2, 4, 17, 19-20, 22-25,
59, 104, 115, 120, 164, 183, 199-202,
209-210, 213, 227, 233, 238-239,
245, 247, 254-267, 273, 276-279,
288, 293 n.32, 307 n.2, 318 n.4;
alternative, 293 n.32; autonomy
of art, 199-200; Chinese, 134,
232, 239, 253, 283-285, 307 n.2;
colonial, 104; and consumption,
265-267; as cultural production,
22-25; and *duige*, 251-252; and
gender distinctions, 276; as hegemonic, 284; and Maoist minority
policy, 59; and nostalgia, 227; as
performance, 258-262, 278; as
self-conscious awareness, 258; as
structure of feeling, 25; and subjecthood, 233; as urban fashion,
248; and youth, 263
Modernization, 22-23, 77-79, 128-
129, 163, 181, 185, 257, 276-279,

Population: Hmong/Miao world-
wide, 297 n.16; Miao, 69; mi-
nority, 3, 70–71, 97; Xijiang, 294
n.34
Positional superiority, 128
Post-Maoism. *See* Reform era
Postsocialism. *See* Reform era
Potter, Jack, 313 n.6
Potter, Sulamith, 301 n.4, 313 n.6
Poverty, 5, 59, 74, 76, 78, 164, 166,
170, 172, 262
Power, 3, 104, 293 n.27
Prakash, Gyan, 239
Price, David, 298 n.21
Production, tributary mode of, 308
n.4
Production brigade (*dadui*), 269, 315
n.10
Progress, 276–278, 296 n.15
Propaganda (*xuanchuan*), 170, 176–
179, 189, 199, 201, 311 n.3
Public culture, 151, 154–155
Public sphere, 139–142, 165, 308 n.7,
307 n.8, 309 n.11, 309 n.12, 310 n.21
Publishing, 312 n.1, 312 n.2, 312 n.3

Qiandongnan. *See* Southeast Gui-
zhou
Queer studies, 259
Quincy, Keith, 35, 296 n.8

Radway, Janice, 291 n.19, 292 n.21
Rankin, Mary B., 309 n.11
Rape, 107
Ratliff, Martha, 46
Rebels, Miao as, 7, 49, 50, 58–60, 61,
68, 190, 283, 295 n.7
Reception theory, 291 n.19
Red Army, 290 n.10
Red Guards, 175
Reform (post-Mao) era, 88–91, 96,
113–114, 119, 137–150, 183, 226, 238,
239–241, 263, 278, 286–288, 292
n.22, 293 n.32; birth-planning
policy, 96, 300 n.22, 302 n.7; body
culture, 310 n.15; Chinese intellec-

tuals in, 233; ethnic currency in,
147–150; household responsibility,
226; nationality cultural policy,
88–91, 286–88; (re)production
of difference, 88, 119, 144–150;
revival, 31, 88–91, 93, 98, 114, 187,
204–207, 209–228, 313 n.6; state
representations, 143; status distinctions, 137; urbanization, 183.
See also Economic reforms
"Remoteness" (*pianpi*), 4–5
Representation: and authenticity,
205; colonial, 296 n.15; of gender
and sexual mores, 7–9; as globalized Western regime, 103; and
identity, 29–30; Miao Albums,
7–9, 51, 66, 296 n.12; of Miao as
rebellious, 58–60; in Western
media, 50; of minorities, 87–88,
132; of national character, 58–60;
of non-Han, 120–123; of peasants,
132; power of, 104; production of,
105; of White Western woman,
307 n.28; of women, 132
Republican period, 72, 91, 297 n.20
Revival. *See* Reform era
Revolutionary Alliance, 304 n.15
Revolutionary Arts, 170
Ribbon Maiden legend, 44
Ritual(s), 184–187, 214–216, 220–
228, 255–257, 313 n.6, 314 n.8, 315
n.12, 315 n.13; Bao Tong Shou Ri
(Day of Protecting the Lives of
Children), 313 n.5; Cai Huashan
(Stepping on Flower Mountain),
220; calendar (Xijiang), 214–216;
Chiguzhang, 185, 215; and Chi-
nese state, 216, 220, 257, 313 n.6;
Chixinjie (Festival of Eating the
New), 214; Chunjie (Spring Fes-
tival), 214; displacement, 313 n.6;
drinking, 255–257; and ethnic
identification, 257; Jing Qiao
(Offerings to the Bridge), 214, 313
n.5; Miaonian (Miao New Year),
215, 221; popular, 187; Poshui-

jie (Water-splashing Festival), 243, 307 n.1; Qingming, 214; revivals, 89, 216, 313 n.6; Saozhai (Sweeping the Village), 215; shamanic, 187–189; Siyueba (Fourth Moon Eighth Day Festival), 181, 235–239, 253, 271–277, 280; as spectacle, 89, 222; as transaction, 258; tree-conserving ritual, 315 n.13; Zhao Long (Calling the Dragons), 214, 222–227

Robbins, Bruce, 308 n.7, 308 n.8
Robertson, Jennifer, 103–104
Rofel, Lisa, 25, 293 n.32
Rong Mu, 189
Rosaldo, Renato, 120, 291 n.15
Rostow, W. W., 23
Rouse, Roger, 293 n.28
Rowe, William, 309 n.11
Rudelson, Justin, 298 n.2, 300 n.20, 313 n.6
Ruey Yih-fu, 37–38, 295 n.3, 296 n.12, 298 n.6
Rushdie, Salman, 154

Said, Edward, 30, 101–105, 128, 130, 303 n.8
San Miao, 35–39, 42, 47, 48, 295 n.3
Savina, F. M., 44–46, 55, 296 n.8
Schafer, Edward H., 9
Schein, Louisa, 293 n.29, 294 n.33, 310 n.3, 312 n.7, 312 n.9, 315 n.9, 319 n.1
Schell, Orville, 310 n.15
Schwarcz, Vera, 305 n.17
Schwartz, Benjamin, 111
Seventh Five Year Plan, 298 n.4
Sex tourism, 9, 310 n.17
Sexuality, 9, 62–63, 107–108, 123, 125–127, 151–155, 300 n.18, 303 n.9; and cultural production on minorities, 112, 151–155; displaced, 300 n.18; and national identity, 107–108; and state cultural authority, 303 n.9; as transgressive, 9, 62

Shamanism, 53, 87, 187–189, 214–216
Shang Langde Village, 190, 311 n.5
Shen Congwen, 113, 295 n.6
Shenzhen, 133
Shils, Edward, 308 n.6
Shujing (Book of Documents), 37–38
Sino-Japanese War, 110–111, 113
Siu, Helen, 313 n.6
Siyueba (Fourth Moon Eighth Day Festival), 181, 235–239, 253, 271–277, 280
Skinner, G. William, 244, 317 n.12
Snow, Edgar, 290 n.10
Socialist era. *See* Maoist era
Southeast Guizhou (Qiandongnan), 7, 28, 47, 52, 62, 65, 85, 100, 116, 163, 185–186, 189, 226, 236, 281, 290 n.7, 297 n.18, 301 n.1, 305 n.20
Southwest China, 5, 74–79, 92
Spatial hierarchy, 244–245
"Speaking bitterness," 316 n.6
Special Economic Zones, 77, 133
Spectatorship, 198, 228, 238–239, 260–261; as modern, 252–253, 280–281
Spencer, J. E., 301 n.4
Spivak, Gayatri, 234, 316 n.5
Stalin, Josef, 316 n.3
Stallybrass, Peter, 244
State, 14, 68, 72, 90, 91, 138–143, 154–155, 163–164, 216, 221, 288, 292 n.26; as benefactor, 139, 221; discourse, 164; and the Han majority, 139; images, 143; as multinational, 72; power and autonomous spaces, 139; and society, 138–143, 154–155, 163; and subject formation, 69, 95, 292 n.26
State, the Chinese, 139, 216–220, 227–228, 257, 276–277; birth-planning policy, 227; and Miao ritual funding, 221; and modernization, 257; and the production of ritual meaning, 220; and ritual revivals, 216, 220, 227–228

Louisa Schein is Assistant Professor of Anthropology at Rutgers University.

Library of Congress Cataloging-in-Publication Data

Schein, Louisa
Minority rules : the Miao and the feminine in China's cultural politics /
Louisa Schein.
p.   cm. — (Body, commodity, text)
Includes bibliographical references and index.
ISBN 0-8223-2408-3 (alk. paper). — ISBN 0-8223-2444-X (pbk. : alk. paper)
1. Hmong (Asian people) — China.   2. Hmong (Asian people) — China —
Social life and customs.   3. Ethnic relations — Political aspects.   I. Title.
II. Series.
DS731.M5S3   2000
305.895'942 — dc21   99-36861